MEMOIR
ON THE
SAWUNT WAREE STATE
W. COURTNEY & J.W. AULD

TO WHICH ARE APPENDED
A CENSUS OF THE SAWUNT WAREE DISTRICTS
FOR THE YEAR 1851
H.L. ANDERSON
COPIES OF TREATIES, AGREEMENTS, & C.

OBSERVATIONS ON ANCIENT COPPER TABLETS
EXCAVATED IN THE SAWUNT WAREE DISTRICTS

STATISTICAL REPORT
ON THE
PORTUGUESE SETTLEMENTS IN INDIA

SELECTIONS FROM THE RECORDS OF THE BOMBAY GOVERNMENT

MEMOIR

ON THE

SAWUNT WAREE STATE

W. COURTNEY & J. W. AULD

TO WHICH ARE APPENDED
A CENSUS OF THE SAWUNT WAREE DISTRICTS
FOR THE YEAR 1851
H.L. ANDERSON
COPIES OF TREATIES, AGREEMENTS, & C.

OBSERVATIONS ON ANCIENT COPPER TABLETS
EXCAVATED IN THE SAWUNT WAREE DISTRICTS

STATISTICAL REPORT

ON THE

PORTUGUESE SETTLEMENTS IN INDIA

CAPTAIN KOL

ISBN : 978-93-5324-583-2 (HB)

First Published, Bombay, 1855

Published, 2020

Published by

Facsimile Publisher
12 Pragati Market
Ashok Vihar, Ph-2
Delhi-110052
E-mail: books@facsimilepublisher.com

Printed at: G. Print Process, Delhi.

Godavari District Gazetteer

Author: F. R. HEMINGWAY

SELECTIONS FROM THE RECORDS OF THE BOMBAY GOVERNMENT.

No. X.—New Series.

MEMOIR ON THE SAWUNT WAREE STATE.

BY

Mr. W. COURTNEY and Major J. W. AULD,

POLITICAL SUPERINTENDENTS.

WITH BRIEF NOTES RELATIVE TO THE STATE BY THE LATTER OFFICER.

TO WHICH ARE APPENDED,

A CENSUS OF THE SAWUNT WAREE DISTRICTS

FOR THE YEAR 1851;

Prepared by Mr. H. L. ANDERSON, Political Superintendent.

A PAPER CONTAINING INFORMATION RELATIVE TO THE SAWUNT WAREE STATE;

Prepared in the Year 1818,

By Captain GIDEON HUTCHINSON.

COPIES OF TREATIES, AGREEMENTS, &c.,

CONCLUDED BY THE HON. EAST INDIA COMPANY WITH THE SAWUNT WAREE STATE,

Between the Years 1730 *and* 1843.

OBSERVATIONS ON ANCIENT COPPER TABLETS, EXCAVATED IN THE SAWUNT WAREE DISTRICTS,

Accompanied by Fac-similes and Translations of the Inscriptions thereon;

By Major G. LeGRAND JACOB, Political Superintendent.

STATISTICAL REPORT ON THE PORTUGUESE SETTLEMENTS IN INDIA.

EXTRACTED, IN THE YEAR 1850, FROM OFFICIAL DOCUMENTS,

By Captain KOL,

CHIEF SECRETARY TO THE GOVERNMENT OF PORTUGUESE INDIA.

TO WHICH ARE ADDED,

COPIES OF TREATIES, &c.,

CONCLUDED BETWEEN GREAT BRITAIN AND PORTUGAL,

Between the Years 1661 *and* 1850.

EDITED BY R. HUGHES THOMAS, ASSISTANT SECRETARY, POLITICAL DEPARTMENT.

Bombay:

PRINTED FOR GOVERNMENT

AT THE

BOMBAY EDUCATION SOCIETY'S PRESS.

1855.

CONTENTS.

LIST OF PLATES, &c.

MEMOIR

ON THE

SAWUNT WAREE STATE.

SUBMITTED TO GOVERNMENT ON NOVEMBER 30TH, 1843,

BY MR. W. COURTNEY,

POLITICAL SUPERINTENDENT;

WITH CONTINUATION TO THE CLOSE OF THE YEAR 1853,

BY MAJOR J. W. AULD,

POLITICAL SUPERINTENDENT.

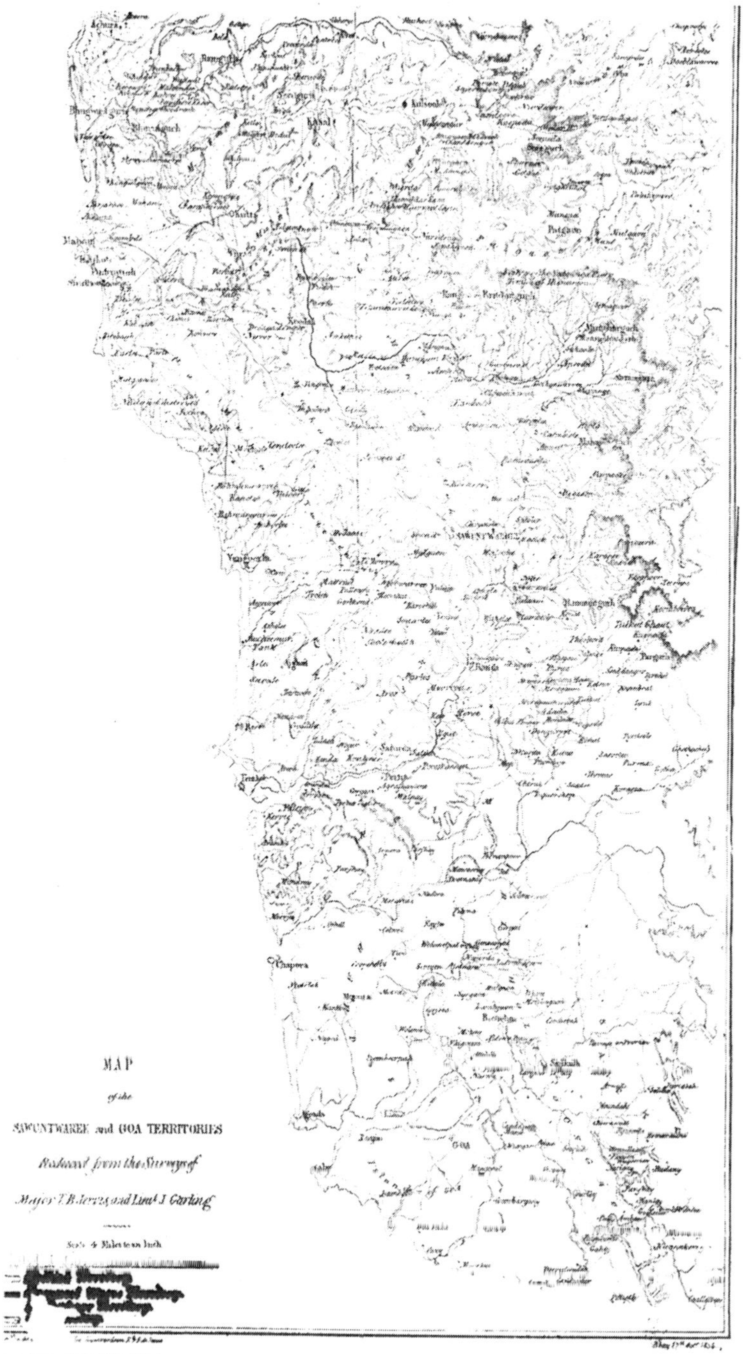
MAP
of the
SAWUNTWAREE and GOA TERRITORIES
Major T. B. Jervis and Lieut. J. Garling
Chapora
GOA
SAWUNTWAREE

MEMOIR ON THE SAWUNT WAREE STATE.

The Waree State forms the southern part of what was formerly known by the name of the "Konkun-Putee," or the territory lying between the Sahyadree range of Ghauts and the sea. It is comprised between parallels 15° and 17° of N. lat., and 73° and 75° of E. long.

It is not known with any accuracy who was the founder of the present reigning family of Bhonslay, but it is believed that the Waree State formed a province of the territories under the Beejapoor Kings, and that it was held by feudal tenure from that dynasty, by the ancestors of the present family, long before it became an independent princedom.

Some 300 years since an ancestor of the present family, by name Mang Sawunt, is supposed to have rebelled against the Mahomedan power, established himself at the village of Horowde, in this principality, and carried on constant war with the troops of Delhi and Beejapoor. There is no proof extant to show that he established his independence, but he would seem to have succeeded in repulsing the troops sent to subjugate him. On his death he was deified, and his Muth or shrine is still to be seen at the village of Horowde, which he made his capital.

There are no records to show who succeeded this Mang Sawunt; but it is believed that his successors, wanting the prowess and courage which he displayed, were soon subjugated to the Mahomedan yoke, and became again feudatories of the empire.

About the year A. D. 1627 Khem Sawunt ascended the throne,* and was succeeded in 1640 by his son Som Sawunt, who died after a short reign of eighteen months, and was succeeded by his brother Lukum Sawunt, who died in 1665, without issue. His brother Phond Sawunt then reigned for ten years, and on his death in 1675 his second son, Khem Sawunt, ascended the throne.

This chieftain appears to have succeeded in establishing his independence of the Musulman power; he afterwards assisted them in their wars with Shivajee, the founder of the Maratha empire, at that time beginning to be formidable; and carried on constant wars with the neighbouring Portuguese State of Goa; and during his reign the boundaries of the State were considerably extended.

* A genealogical table of the Bhonslay family from this date is annexed.

2

In the year 1707 Khem Sawunt concluded a Treaty with Shao Raja, the successor of Shivajee, as he found himself unable alone to cope with his extending influence and authority; and the Beejapoor dynasty, owing to their declining power, could render him no assistance. By this Treaty Shao Raja gave to the Bhonslay family of Sawunt Waree an Inam-putru (deed of gift), confirming them in their possessions, with full sovereignty, and assigning to them, conjointly with Angria, half the revenues of the Salsee Mahal.

In the year 1709 Khem Sawunt was succeeded by his nephew Phond Sawunt. This chieftain cultivated the arts of peace, and turned his attention to settling and increasing his revenues. During his reign the present Jumabundee settlement was carried into operation, through a Karkoon under his authority, named Gunoo Ram. No regular survey or measurement of lands was made; but the produce was assessed by what is termed a Nuzur-mangna, or rough estimate by inspection. He also imposed a number of extra cesses, receivable in kind from the Ryuts, for the current expenditure of himself and his household; and carried this system so far, that even the minutest item was provided for, without the outlay of money.

The Kolhapoor forces at this time invaded the Waree State, under Ramchundru Punt Bowrékur, the Amatyu, but were repulsed, and obliged to retire; and constant skirmishes took place with the Portuguese and Angria.

In this chieftain's reign the first Treaty was concluded with the English East India Company. It seems to have been occasioned by the piracies on British commerce committed by Kanojee Angria and his successors on the Colaba Gadee, and bears date the 12th January 1729-30.* It consists of VII. Articles; and after stipulating for perpetual peace and friendship between Phond Sawunt Bhonslay, the Sir Desaee, and the Honorable Company, and providing for their mutually assisting one another's ships at sea, and affording help in case of wreck, goes on to conclude an offensive and defensive alliance against the son of Kanojee Angria, who is characterized as the mutual enemy of both powers.

At about this period Nag Sawunt, the second son of Phond Sawunt, overran and subjugated the Heri and Chundrugur Mahals, above the Ghauts; He established a Thana in the latter, and built the fort of Gundhurwugur. The Chundrugur Mahal was afterwards taken from him, but the Heri Talooka is still in the possession of Myna Baee, his son's widow.

Towards the close of Phond Sawunt's reign, his eldest son Nar Sawunt rebelled against him, and on his father's attempting to reduce him he threw himself into a fort near the town of Waree, and while looking out of a window was shot dead by the troops sent against him. His widow brought her son Ramchundru Sawunt, and having delivered him up to Phond Sawunt, performed Sutee on the funeral pile of her husband.

* This Treaty was ratified by the Government of Bombay on the 17th April 1730.

Phond Sawunt was so deeply affected by these tragical events that he resigned the Gadee in favour of his grandson Ramchundru Sawunt, and retired into private life. This occurred about the year 1738.

When Ramchundru Sawunt came to the throne he was assisted in the management of affairs by Jyram Sawunt, his uncle, who continued to share the chief power with him till about 1752.

This Jyram Sawunt is represented to have been a man not only of great personal courage, but also of immense bodily strength. He carried on extensive wars, and overran, and for a time retained possession, of the Bardese Mahal of the Goa territories. During his reign Toolajee Angria made an inroad into the Waree territory with a strong force, but was defeated at Koodal with great loss, and compelled to retreat; and Jyram Sawunt followed him as far as Sanja, near Rutnageeree, ravaging the country with fire and sword.

Towards the close of his reign, Jyram Sawunt quarrelled with his nephew Ramchundru Sawunt, and retired to Koodal in disgust, where he shortly after died, and Ramchundru Sawunt did not survive him for more than two years.

Ramchundru Sawunt left one son, Khem Sawunt, known by the name of Khem Sawunt the Great. He ascended the throne on his father's death about 1755, and reigned for forty-eight years. In 1763 he married Luxoomee Baee, the daughter of Juyajee Sindia, and a half-sister of the celebrated Mahadajee Sindia, through whose influence with the Court of Delhi, the Emperor conferred on Khem Sawunt the title of Rajey Bahadoor, and some other privileges of royalty.

In consequence of the Chieftain of Waree still continuing his piratical attacks on British commerce, about the beginning of the year 1765, an expedition was sent against these corsairs, under the command of Major Gordon and Captain Watson, of the Bombay Marine. They took the fort of Eshwuntgur, or Réree, and changed its name to Fort Augustus, intending to have kept possession of it.

On the 7th April 1765, however, a Treaty of XIX. Articles was concluded with Khem Sawunt, by which, the British Government agreed to restore Réree to the Sir Desaee, on his renouncing all pretensions to the territory situated between the Karlee and Salsee rivers, from the sea shore to the foot of the Ghauts; agreeing to indemnify the Honorable Company for the expenses of the war, to the amount of Rs. 1,00,000; permitting a factory to be built by them in any part of his dominions adjacent to the sea shore; promising not to molest their ships or commerce, or keep any vessels equipped for war; and surrendering the fort of Musooree within eight days.

This Treaty was not observed by the Sir Desaee; and, in consequence, in the following year Mr. Mostyn was deputed, with full powers, by the Government of Bombay, to effect some further settlement: and on the 24th October 1766 another Treaty of XV. Articles was concluded with the Bhonslay.

By this agreement the Sir Desaee promised to send two hostages to

Bombay; to pay Rs. 2,00,000 for the expenses of the war, of which Rs. 80,000 should be paid in three months, before the fort of Réree was given up to him, and the remaining Rs. 1,20,000 in two years, by two equal instalments; and find good security for its payment. He further promised to mortgage the fort of Vingorla, with all its revenues, for thirteen years, or till such time as the money was paid up; and to allow the Company to establish a factory there under their own flag. This arrangement being concluded, Réree was restored.

In a short time, however, the hostages made their escape, and the agents of the mortgagee were prevented from collecting the revenues. On the expiration of the thirteen years, the Waree Government demanded the restoration of Vingorla, and on its being refused, in consequence of the mortgagee not having been permitted to realize the revenues, it was attacked and taken by the Sir Desaee in 1780.

In 1778, the Kolhapoor Raja, envious of the distinctions which had been conferred on the Waree Chief by the Emperor of Delhi, attacked the Her Talooka, captured the forts of Gundhurwugur, Nursingur, and Bhurutgur, and overran a great part of the Waree territory. In 1793, however, these forts were restored to Waree through Sindia's influence; and the Raja of Kolhapoor was again confined to his own proper dominions.

With a few intermissions, however, and with various successes, Khem Sawunt continued at war with Kolhapoor for the greater part of his reign; he was also almost constantly engaged in hostilities with the Portuguese, who succeeded shortly before his death in wresting from him the provinces of Deehoolee, Sanklee, and Pedna, and annexing them to the Goa territories: he had before lost in the early part of his reign the half share of the Salsee Mahal, which was taken possession of by the Peshwa on the defeat and capture of Toolajee Angria.

Khem Sawunt died in A. D. 1803, and great disturbances took place soon after his death, in consequence of his having no heirs male in the direct line, and the intrigues and plots to which this circumstance gave rise among the other male descendants of his grandfather, Phond Sawunt, to secure the vacant throne. Two of these in particular, named Jyram Sawunt, called also Bawa Saheb, aided by his father Som Sawunt, and Shreeram Sawunt or Rao Saheb, carried their intrigues so far as to engage in open hostility against each other; till at length Som Sawunt and his son were shut up in the fort at Waree by the troops of Shreeram Sawunt, and on the palace being attacked, Som Sawunt fired a train of powder, and perished with all his family (excepting his son Phond Sawunt, who was at the time shut up in the fort of Réree) in the flames.

Shreeram Sawunt, having thus got rid of his rival, soon compelled Luxoomee Baee, the widow of Khem Sawunt, who was endeavouring to carry on affairs as regent, to adopt his son Ramchundru Sawunt or Bhow Saheb. This adoption took place in 1805, and Luxoomee Baee continued to manage affairs as regent during his minority.

In the meantime, constant warfare was carried on by Kolhapoor, with varied success, till, in 1807, the Raja of Kolhapoor took the field in person; and having defeated the Waree army at Chowkoolee with great loss, descended by the Munohur and Hunmunt Ghauts into the Konkun, and blockaded the capital. He was, however, unsuccessful in his attempts to take the fort. In this desperate state of affairs, the Waree Government called in the aid of Appa Desaee Nepaneekur, who sent a large force to raise the siege of Waree, and also invaded the Kolhapoor territories; and thus compelled the Raja to return with his troops to defend his own capital.

No sooner was the Kolhapoor force withdrawn, than Appajee Soobrao, the Nepanee general, made himself master of the whole Waree territory; he placed Luxoomee Baee the regent, and her adopted son Bhow Saheb, under a strict surveillance, and endeavoured to establish the authority of his master over the State. Bhow Saheb, the heir to the Gadee, was found strangled in his bed, and it is believed the act was perpetrated by order of Appajee Soobrao; and not without the concurrence of Phond Sawunt, the next heir to the Gadee, who hoped to profit by his removal. Shortly after, Luxoomee Baee also fell a victim to the hardships and ill-treatment she had undergone: she died in 1808.

On her death, Doorga Baee, the second widow of Khem Sawunt, became regent; though affairs were nominally carried on in the name of Phond Sawunt, the son of Som Sawunt, who had escaped the general destruction of his family at Waree, as above related.

In 1809, Phond Sawunt took advantage of the weak state of the Nepaneekur's army, the greater part of which had been withdrawn to maintain the war above the Ghauts, to expel his forces from the country, and re-establish the authority of the Bhonslay family. The Sirdars, however, through whose instrumentality these successes were gained, soon became too powerful to be controlled: they established themselves in the different forts in the Waree State, and became perfectly independent of the Government, plundering not only the inhabitants, but attacking foreign powers, and pillaging their commerce.

These depredations continued till A. D. 1812, when, in consequence of repeated acts of piracy having been perpetrated on British commerce, a Treaty was negotiated, through Captain Schuyler, the envoy at Goa, with Phond Sawunt, on the 3rd October, by which, in order to the effectual suppression of these evils, the chieftain agreed to cede in full sovereignty to the British Government the fort of Vingorla, and the battery of Gunaram Tembé, with the port and proper limits thereof; to deliver up all vessels found equipped in a warlike manner; to allow no vessel to leave the port of Newtee without being searched by the British authorities, who were to be allowed to station a guard of troops there for the purpose; and promised that if hereafter any Waree subjects were guilty of piracy, the forts of Rérec and Newtee should also be given up to the Honorable Company.

Shortly after the conclusion of this Treaty, Phond Sawunt died, and Doorga

Baee, who still continued to manage affairs, sent for his son, Khem Sawunt, —the present chieftain, who had been taken by Soobrao Ghatgay, his maternal grandfather, to Toregul above the Ghauts,—and set him up as heir to the throne; though, in consequence of his tender age, for he was then only eight years old, she managed to keep the chief power in her own hands as regent.

In 1812 the Waree troops captured the fort of Bhurutgur from Kolhapoor, but were obliged immediately afterwards to surrender it to a British force under Colonel Dowse, and it was by them again restored to Kolhapoor.

In 1815 the Turufs of Wurad and Malund, together with all the villages to the north of the Karlee river, were taken possession of by the British Government, in exchange for the Sindhoodoorg Tunkha* in the Turufs of Páth and Huwélee, which were given up to Waree.

The Portuguese troops in 1817 made an inroad into the Oosup Turuf of the Waree State, and plundered and burnt the house of the Oosupkur Desaee. To avenge this aggression Sumbhoo Govind Sir Soobhedar, who commanded at Réree, plundered the fort of Tirakole, belonging to the Portuguese. This led to the fort of Réree being besieged by the Goa troops: they sat down before the place with twenty-five pieces of cannon, and carried on active operations against it for twenty-seven days, but were unable to effect its reduction, and were finally obliged to raise the siege.

At this time the Government of Waree appears to have been completely unable to control the power of its own Sirdars: Sumbhajee Sawunt held the fort of Réree, Babnoo Gopal occupied Newtee, and Chundroba Soobhedar maintained himself at Banda. These powerful chiefs plundered in all directions with perfect impunity, setting the authority of the Sir Desaee completely at defiance. During these troubles, Doorga Baee died, and the two remaining widows of Khem Sawunt, Savitree Baee and Nurmuda Baee, became regents.

Early in 1819, in consequence of repeated acts of depredation having been committed in British territory, by subjects of the State of Sawunt Waree, a force, under the command of Sir W. Grant Keir, moved to the frontier of this State, to obtain redress, and enforce the following demands:—

1st.—The surrender of certain offenders.

2nd.—The repayment of property plundered.

3rd.—The removal of Sumbhajee Sawunt and Babnoo Gopal from authority.

4th.—The surrender of the forts of Réree and Newtee for three years.

These demands were not conceded, and hostilities commenced. Waree soon surrendered, but the fort of Réree held out against the British force, and was regularly invested.

The British batteries opened on the 13th of February, and in the evening of the same day the outworks were carried by assault. The principal portion of the garrison evacuated the place during the night, and the fort surrendered the following morning.

* Assignments upon revenue for the support of the fort of Malwan.

A Treaty was concluded with the regency of Waree on behalf of Khem Sawunt, under date 17th February 1819, by which they agreed not again to employ Sumbhajee Sawunt and Babnoo Gopal; to deliver up to the British Government such of the perpetrators of the late depredations as they might be able to apprehend, as well as to surrender in future all subjects of the Waree State who might be guilty of plundering British territories, or that of its allies; to cede to the Honorable Company in perpetuity the forts of Réree and Newtee, together with the Turufs of Páth and Azgaum, and the whole line of sea coast from the Karlee river to the Portuguese possessions; and to admit any British detachment into the Sawunt Waree territories, and afford it every assistance in seizing plunderers and freebooters.

Captain Hutchinson was sent as Political Agent to Waree, and through him, another Treaty was concluded with the regency, under date the 17th February 1820, by which the British Government, to evince that it demanded the cession of the Páth and Azgaum districts, given up by the foregoing Treaty for the sole purpose of putting an effectual stop to the depredations committed in its own territories by Waree subjects, restored the whole of the above districts, with the exception of the forts of Réree and Newtee, and the villages forming the line of sea coast.

In 1820, a settlement was concluded, through Captain Hutchinson, of a dispute with the Kolhapoor Government relative to the Tunkha, or assignment on the revenues, of the Munohur Turuf, for the support of His Highness' fort of Munohur. By this agreement the rights of Kolhapoor in that district, and the amount of revenue to which it was entitled, were defined, and the sovereignty was declared to belong to Waree.

In the latter part of the year 1820, Captain Hutchinson's appointment at Waree was abolished; and the future political relations with this State were confided to the Judge of Rutnageeree, from whom they were afterwards, in 1822, transferred to the Collector.

In 1822, some disputes of long standing between the Waree and Kolhapoor Durbars, relative to the Tunkhas or assignment of revenues for the support of the forts of Prusidgur and Nursingur, were finally adjusted. It was settled, that in lieu of making collections from the five Turufs of Kulsoolee, Naroor, Boorduvee, Huwélee, and Mangaum, the Kolhapoor State should receive, annually, a money payment of Rs. 7,834-6-8 from the Waree Government, and be debarred from all interference with those districts.

For the annual payment of this sum during ten years, and for the liquidation of the balance due to Kolhapoor on account of the three years during which the collections had been suspended, a security was brought forward by the Waree regency. Previously, however, to the first payment, a tract of country above the Ghauts, to the above annual amount, was made over from the British territories, in the Southern Muratha Country, to Kolhapoor, in 1826, under the condition that the above sum should be paid annually by Waree to the Company.

The affairs of the Waree State, which had continued till this time to be managed by the regency, were in A. D. 1822 entrusted to the present chieftain, Khem Sawunt, or, as he was more commonly called, Bapoo Saheb, then in his nineteenth year; and he was formally invested with the chief authority through the intervention of the British Government, much against the wishes of the Baees, who were very desirous of keeping the administration of affairs in their own hands.

Bapoo Saheb soon showed himself to be a weak and incompetent chief, destitute of the firmness necessary to keep his disorderly Sirdars in check, or maintain any regularity in his financial affairs. By his extravagance and dissipation the revenues, which ought to have been applied to the liquidation of his pecuniary engagements, were squandered in other ways, and no arrangements were made for the payment of the amount on account of the exchange of territory with Kolhapoor above adverted to, and the allowance guaranteed by the British Government to a Sirdar named Chundroba Soobhedar.

By 1830 these payments had fallen so greatly into arrears, that it was found necessary, after repeated remonstrances made to the chieftain had failed, to induce him to adopt any measures for their liquidation, to sequestrate a part of the Turufs of Pâth, Azgaum, Huwélee, and Boorduvee, with the view of compelling the Sir Desaee to fulfil his engagements.

This measure at length opened the eyes of the Waree Government to the necessity of making immediate arrangements for the liquidation of the arrears, and future payment of these sums; and in the following year the attachment was again removed.

In 1828 Phond Sawunt, an influential Sirdar, went out into open rebellion against his sovereign, in consequence of the oppression and injustice to which he had been subjected. He seized the hill fort of Mahadeogur, of which he had formerly been Killedar; and successfully resisted all the efforts of the Waree Government to reduce him. The Sir Desaee solicited and obtained the assistance of the Bombay Government in his difficulties, and in 1830 a British detachment was sent against the fort, which was immediately evacuated by the rebels, who fled into the adjoining territories of the Inchulkurunjeekur.

In 1832, Phond Sawunt again succeeded in making himself master of Mahadeogur, and in the same year other influential persons raised the standard of rebellion also; and the country soon became one scene of anarchy and confusion. The weakness and disorganization of the Waree Government soon compelled the British Government to an armed interference in its internal affairs: a force was sent into the country; the fort of Mahadeogur was taken and dismantled, and terms of accommodation were arranged with the other insurgents; but Phond Sawunt and his sons again absconded, and continued in rebellion till 1838, when an amnesty was granted to them by the British Government.

On the restoration of tranquillity in 1832, the Sir Desaee was compelled to enter into an Agreement of IV. Articles, under date 25th December 1832, by which he bound himself not to remove his minister without the consent of the British Government, and to afford him every support in effecting a retrenchment in the expenditure.

This agreement the Sir Desaee never entered into with sincerity; and no sooner was order in a measure restored, and his immediate fears removed, than this weak and vacillating chief relaxed into his former state; and instead of supporting, thwarted, and did all in his power to get his minister removed; another formidable rebellion shortly broke out, and British troops were again sent to assist in putting it down.

In 1836, the customs leviable on the military road passing through this State from the port of Vingorla to the Ram Ghaut were transferred to the British Government, and in 1838 an Agreement of VI. Articles was concluded with the chieftain, under date the 15th September, by which the whole of the customs of the Waree State became the property of the Honorable Company, and the levy of transit duties was abolished.

The state of affairs at Waree under so weak and dissipated a chief did not, as might be supposed, improve; the pay of the Sirdars, and others in the employ of the State, remained long overdue; acts of the most flagrant injustice were perpetrated to oblige favourites, and tyranny and oppression soon again raged throughout the country. The aggrieved subjects of this injustice sought redress in the only way in which they believed it could be obtained, and endeavoured by an appeal to arms to wring from their imbecile sovereign's fears, what they were unable to obtain from his justice.

Rebellion, violence, bloodshed, and all the concomitant evils of a weak and vicious administration were the consequence; and instead of learning wisdom by the past, and introducing a better state of things, no sooner was the danger averted—no sooner had the rebellious been overawed, and reduced to obedience by the armed intervention of the British Government, than the same system was again followed, to be again consummated by the same results.

This state of things could at length no longer be borne; and on the breaking out of another formidable rebellion in 1838, it was considered inexpedient to employ British troops any more in merely suppressing resistance to a chief to whom already three or four times a like aid had been afforded in a similar way, and who had proved himself utterly unfit to rule. The removal of the Sir Desaee from all authority was therefore considered to be an indispensable part of the new arrangement rendered necessary. The country was temporarily placed under British management, to be hereafter restored to the Sir Desaee, or his family, when there should appear a sufficient prospect of their governing it well.

A Political Superintendent was appointed under this arrangement to manage the country; but his exertions to reform the administration of this

3

long misgoverned State were for a considerable time impeded by the disturbances occasioned by malcontent individuals, who were, or expected to be, losers by the indispensable reductions effected in the public expenditure.

Owing to the shelter which these parties received in the Goa territories, they were enabled to organize two serious invasions of the Waree territory : on the first occasion, they got temporary possession of the fort of Waree, and of the person of the chieftain, his family, and the minister ; on the second they captured the fort of Hunmuntgur, blockaded the passes, and committed great atrocities.

On both occasions, the insurrections were with little difficulty put down ; the principal leaders were apprehended and punished, and tranquillity was again restored.

In order to diminish the expense, as well as increase the efficiency of the Waree military force, a local corps was raised, and placed under the command of European officers, the expense of which forms a debit on the revenues of the State.

As soon as this corps was organized, the large regular force, which it had been previously found necessary to keep up at Waree, was gradually diminished; and in a little more than a year from its first formation the state of affairs had so much improved as to admit of the entire withdrawal of the British troops from the territory. On the restoration of tranquillity, measures were adopted to afford to all classes of the community efficient protection from oppression, and the ready redress of every grievance.

The financial affairs of the State, which, under the Native administration, were in a state of absolute bankruptcy, have since been greatly improved : by strict economy in the public expenditure the large debt due to the British Government has been considerably reduced, and arrangements are in progress to relieve the public finances, as far as possible, from future embarrassment.

Khem Sawunt, or Bapoo Saheb, the present Sir Desaee, was born in A. D. 1804. He has four sons, the eldest of whom, Phond Sawunt, or, as he is more commonly called, Anna Saheb, was born in the year 1828.

The Waree State, as it exists at present, is bounded on the North by the Karlee river, and the Salsee Mahal of the Malwan Talooka in the Rutnageeree Collectorate ; on the East by the line of Ghauts ; on the South by the Tirakole creek and the Portuguese possessions ; and on the West by the Vingorla Mahal of the Rutnageeree Zillah. Its greatest length from north to south is nearly fifty miles, and its greatest breadth rather more than thirty ; and it may contain an area of perhaps 1,200 square miles.

This principality presents the same general features as are to be found in the greater part of the Southern Konkun, except that the jungle is more dense, and the country more difficult, in the vicinity of the Ghauts. The climate, considering the rankness of the vegetation, is much better than might be expected: the principal diseases are low fever, dysentery, and inflammatory complaints; but cholera, and some of the more virulent and fatal epidemics of India, are by no means common.

The staple produce of the State is rice; the inferior grains, such as Nachnee, Hurik, Moong, &c. are cultivated in the high lands and amongst the hills in considerable quantity. The soil is principally a light sand, full of stones and gravel, and incapable of yielding the superior kinds of produce, such as cotton, tobacco, sugar-cane, &c. Cocoanuts and Sooparee are exported, but excepting in these two products, the country does not yield sufficient for its own consumption; and grain of all kinds is annually imported from the Deccan in large quantities.

The principal manufactures of the Waree State are gold and silver embroidery work on saddle-cloths and horse-appointments, and scabbards of swords; Native guns, swords, daggers, spear-heads, &c. Punkhas, painted toys, sealing-wax, and fire-works; but it exports scarcely any of these, and consequently they are, generally speaking, only manufactured in small quantities, sufficient to meet the local demand.

The imports are metals, Europe piece goods, paper, &c. from Bombay; sugar, dates, spices of all kinds, salt fish, cocoanut oil, &c. from the coast; rice, gram, Dhal, and other grains, onions, garlic, pepper, tobacco, snuff, Ganja, opium, cotton, and indigo, and all kinds of Native cloths, from the Deccan; and fruits, paper, poultry, candles, &c. from Goa.

But little trade is, however, carried on: the merchants are devoid of enterprise, and possess little or no capital; and, owing to a great part of the necessaries of life being imported from foreign countries, and this State producing scarcely anything which can be exchanged for these, a constant drain of the precions metals is going on, which cannot but have a bad effect on its financial prosperity.

The inhabitants are chiefly cultivators. They are a warlike race, accustomed to the use of arms from their childhood, and our Native army is largely recruited from among the Muratha Sawunts of this principality. They are an extremely poor, ignorant, and superstitious race, easily led, and ready at any time to follow any leader who will give them a seer of rice a day. They are almost all provided with arms; it is not therefore to be wondered at that insurrectionary movements have at all times been so easily got up in this State; particularly when the country presents such remarkable facilities for irregular warfare, being covered with a dense, almost impenetrable jungle, and abounding in wild and inaccessible fastnesses.

The principal road through this State is the great military road, made by the British Government, from Belgaum down the Ram Ghaut to the port of Vingorla; besides this there are Native roads from the Deccan, by the Tulkut Ghaut, to Banda and the Goa territory; down the Parpolee Ghaut to Waree and Vingorla, with a branch road through Bowlát and Banda, into the Portuguese possessions; down the Hunmunt Ghaut, by Neroor, Waroos, and Mangaum, to Vingorla and Páth; and by the Ghotgha Ghaut through this State to the port of Malwan: there are also cross-roads leading into the Goa territory on one side, and the Company's on the other, and numerous small passes in the line of Ghauts, from the upper to the lower country.

The chief rivers are the Gudnudee, which rises near the Ghotgha Ghaut, separates the Salsee Mahal from the Kulsoolee and Boorduvee Turufs of this State, and empties itself into the sea north of Malwan. The Karlee river takes its rise in the Hunmunt Ghaut, passes by the villages of Nanelee, Mangaum, Koodal, Bambolee, Bhao, Surumbul, Neroor, and Chendwun; and falls into the sea to the south of Malwan, forming for a considerable distance the boundary between the Company's territories and the Waree State. The Banda river rises in the Ghauts near the fort of Munohur, flows past the villages of Sangélee, Wotownee, Insoolee, Banda, Kas, Satosee, Kowtench, and Arownda, and empties itself into the sea to the south of the fort of Tirakole. From Banda towards the sea this river divides Waree from the Portuguese territories. The Tulowra river rises at Wazrat, passes Hodowla, Tulowra, Toolsee, and Matond, into the sea at Mochee-Mar, a hamlet of Vingorla. The Tilaree, called also Koodasee river, rises at the Ram Ghaut, crosses the great military road twice, and enters the Goa territory at Munéree. The Kulna river takes its rise at the Tulkut Ghaut, crosses the road at Kulna, and passes into the Goa State. There are also a number of small streams besides the above, which in the rainy season, owing to the proximity of the Ghauts, soon swell into considerable rivers.

The revenues of the Waree State amount at present to about Rs. 2,25,000, and the expenditure is fixed at considerably under Rs. 2,00,000; leaving a surplus revenue for the liquidation of its debts. The Waree State is not tributary to the British Government, or to any foreign power: its customs, as already stated, have been transferred to the Honorable Company.

A corps was raised in 1839 by the orders of the British Government for service within the limits of this principality. It received the name of the Sawunt Waree Local Corps, and is officered from the line. It is paid from the revenues of the State, and is not bound to serve in foreign territory.

This levy consists of 426 rank and file, 18 Havildars, 6 Jemadars, and 2 Commissioned European Officers, with 6 Buglers; it is disciplined, armed, and clothed in the same way as the Company's irregular corps, and is maintained at an annual cost of about Rs. 45,620.*

There is no other military force kept up in the Waree State, though there

* Since the date of this Memoir, the Sawunt Waree Local Corps has been increased to 520 rank and file, 8 Jemadars, 32 Havildars, 8 Buglers, &c. with 3 European Commissioned Officers. The present total annual cost of this corps may be estimated at about Rs. 50,000.

is still a large number of what are termed Sunudkuree sepoys (from their receiving their pay by a Sunud, or grant on the revenues of the land in their occupancy), who are liable to serve one month in the year as a sort of militia: they are a mixed rabble, and of little use in maintaining the public tranquillity.

The maintenance of the general police of the country is borne by its own finances. The system has great undergone great improvements: the State has been sub-divided into three parts, each division being placed under a distinct district police officer, with a number of peons at his disposal. Foujdars have been appointed in every village, and instructed in their duties. These become the heads of the rural police in their own villages, having under them the Mahars or village watchmen. They report all occurrences of importance to the district officer, who communicates the information to head quarters. From the Foujdars and the rural police being unpaid, however, but little energy is evinced in the discharge of their duties.

Posts are also established at suitable distances, where parties of the local corps are stationed, for the preservation of the public peace, and security to life and property; and, generally, the system of police followed in the Company's districts has been introduced in Waree.

Owing to the wretched police of the contiguous State of Goa, and the shelter which criminals absconding from this territory find there, the arrangements adopted in this State for the apprehension of offenders, and prevention of crime, are in many cases to a considerable extent rendered inoperative: little cordial assistance or co-operation is rendered by the Portuguese authorities; and, in general, offenders from this State find shelter the moment they cross the frontier.

CONTINUATION OF THE FOREGOING MEMOIR, BY MAJOR J. W. AULD.

Nothing worthy of record occurred in the early part of 1844. The monsoon of this year had not, however, closed, when the Political Superintendent received information from the Political Agent at Belgaum of the existence of serious disturbances in the Kolhapoor territory, more particularly in the neighbourhood of the fort of Bhoodurgur, and it became necessary to adopt precautionary measures throughout this State to prevent the Kolhapoor rebels above the Ghauts tampering with any discontented or evil-disposed subjects of this State.

Major Benbow, the Acting Commandant of the Sawunt Waree Local Corps, was therefore requested to station a detachment of his corps at the village of Neroor, immediately at the foot of the Hunmunt Ghaut, being on the direct road from Waree to the disturbed quarter of the Kolhapoor country, with the view of protecting, if possible, this principality from aggression, as well as of preventing the insurgents as far as practicable from deriving any aid from this State; and at the same time watching the proceedings of the two forts of Prusidgur (also called Rangna) and Munohur, supposed to be secretly well-affected towards the cause of the insurgents.

But notwithstanding these precautionary measures, the Gurkurees of the fort of Munohur descended from that fortress during the night of the 10th October 1844 in force, and entered the village of Gotus, in this State, where they attacked the house of Ghunusham Krishn Gotuskur, the Subnis of the fort of Munohur, and also the Koolkurnee of Gotus, carrying off his two brothers, and burning all the public and private papers in their possession.

This aggression and act of violence on a subject of this State was perpetrated within two or three miles of the detachment of the local corps, and showed but too plainly that the Gurkurees of Munohur had joined the cause of the insurgents above the Ghauts,—a fact which was before suspected, though extremely doubtful.

Mr. Courtney, at the time Political Superintendent of Waree, seeing the turn affairs had taken, consulted Major Benbow as to the best course to be pursued for due protection of the Waree State from aggression; and both these gentlemen were of opinion that no further detachments could be spared from head quarters, but other arrangements were made, to admit of reinforcing the Parpolee detachment, at the foot of a Ghaut of the same name, a little to the south of Munohur, and leading from the Kolhapoor country into the Waree territory.

Again on the night of the 11th October, the Gurkurees of Munohur came down in force, about 200 strong, and attacked a detachment of the Sawunt Waree Local Corps under a Jemadar stationed at Dookanwaree, and after some desultory fighting, were repulsed by the Jemadar, with a loss on our side of two wounded. Reinforcements were immediately sent to the Jemadar.

The Political Superintendent in the mean time adopted such measures as the small force at his disposal would admit of, for the protection of life and property throughout the State, and against the inroads of the insurgents. The Sunudkurees, and all other armed retainers, were summoned, with the view to defensive measures, but this was not a duty they had much heart for, and very few of them attended to the call.

On the 13th of October 1844 Major Benbow marched against the Gurkurees of Munohur and Rangna, forts belonging to the Kolhapoor State, but adjoining the frontier of this principality. The former fortress was reported to be occupied by between four and five hundred men, and the latter, it was said, held 700 Gurkurees. Though they had not then openly committed any aggressive act on this State, still it was well enough known that they were secretly aiding and assisting those of Munohur; and when Major Benbow marched out, the Rangna Gurkurees at once joined those of Munohur, and he was threatened on all sides by large bodies of insurgents. Matters now daily assumed a more serious aspect, and it became necessary to reinforce Major Benbow's detachment by a party of 50 men from Waree, under the Soobedar of the local corps; and Lieutenant Colonel Wyllie, the officer commanding at Vingorla, was at the same time warned to hold a detachment in readiness to march on Waree, if found necessary, at a moment's notice.

Outrages now became general, and almost of every day occurrence, throughout the State. On the 30th of October 1844 a gang of armed men attacked some carts at the village of Sasolee on the Ram Ghaut road, murdered two cartmen, and broke open some casks of liquor, under the impression that they contained gunpowder, and other military stores. The Gurkurees, too, again attacked the village of Dookanwaree, from which the detachment of the Sawunt Waree Local Corps had been withdrawn. On this occasion they carried off a quantity of grain, and threatened the inhabitants with violence.

Similar outrages were perpetrated in all quarters throughout the State during the month of November 1844, and Lieutenant Price, the Adjutant of the Sawunt Waree Local Corps, was ordered to join a detachment of his men at Waroos, and take it on with the least possible delay to the village of Dookanwaree, near the foot of the Hunmunt Ghaut, and not far distant from Munohur, with the view to the protection of that part of the country. All these numerous acts of aggression just referred to were duly reported to the Political Agent at Belgaum, for the information of Lieutenant Colonel Outram, at this time on special duty at Kolhapoor.

Phond Sawunt, a Sirdar of some note belonging to Waree, though he had not up to this date (November 1844) been suspected of disaffection, and his eight sons, now openly espoused the cause of the insurgents, and Anna Saheb, the eldest son of the Sir Desaee, left Waree on the night of the 16th November 1844, and joined Baba Desaee, a son of Phond Sawunt, who was waiting with some followers near at hand, and went off with them towards Munohur.

Anna Saheb was at this time but a mere lad, not more than sixteen years of age, and had been seduced away from the palace by some of Phond Sawunt's family, who had, as already observed, one and all gone into open rebellion, and they knew full well that nothing but desperate measures afforded them a chance of security from the punishment their crimes deserved, and hence their persuading this foolish young man to join and make common cause with them, trusting to the immunity they hoped to enjoy themselves by doing everything in his name.

Rumours had, previous to Anna Saheb's flight, reached the Political Superintendent, that the Gurkurees intended to make an attempt to carry off some one from Waree, but no one had the most distant idea that Anna Saheb had been so far talked over by the Phond Sawunts and their emissaries as voluntarily to join their party; and this unlooked for event could only be accounted for on the supposition that they must have made large promises as to the power and grandeur he could at once gain by espousing their cause.

When the late events were duly considered, it became very apparent that the Phond Sawunts had been all along playing a deep game, and their influence and power, more particularly after they had secured the person of the heir apparent, were very considerable, and the whole country, as was fully expected, was thrown into confusion.

Nor were these anticipations of approaching evil without just grounds; and it became necessary to have recourse to the most active measures, for the country was now in a complete state of rebellion, and the officer commanding at Vingorla was in consequence requested to send every available man he could spare to Waree.

Major Benbow, the officer commanding the Sawunt Waree Local Corps, at the time on duty in the districts, was also communicated with, and warned as to the existence of numerous plots, as well as of the circumstance of Anna Saheb's flight; on learning which, and that the capital was threatened, he fell back with his detachment on Waree, which place he reached on the evening of the 17th November 1844.

The same night a company of the 10th Regt. N. I., under the command of Captain Hume, arrived at Waree from Vingorla, and as Major Benbow had been previously reinforced by the arrival of a detachment of 60 rank and file of the 16th Regt. Madras N. I. from Sasolee, he was enabled to make sufficient arrangements for the protection of the capital.

Nothing, however, was attempted by the insurgents, who were in all probability too busily engaged in securing the person of Anna Saheb, and placing him beyond the reach of pursuit, which they did by taking him up into the fort of Munohur, and delivering him over to the Gurkurees, who, in honour of his arrival in the fortress, fired a salute on the occasion, which was distinctly heard at Waree.

It was now reported (19th November 1844) that the Phond Sawunts had entrenched themselves in the strong and difficult country under the Ghauts, and had stockaded the passes leading to their villages. It was also said, and proved to be true, that about 200 men who escaped from the fort of Bhoodurgur (in the Kolhapoor territory) had joined them, as well as a number of disaffected characters from the Goa frontier, so that, with the Gurkurees of Munohur, the rebel force amounted to nearly 1,000 strong, and Major Benbow was in consequence cautioned to act on the defensive, until sufficiently reinforced to assume an offensive attitude.

The insurrection now (towards the end of November 1844) began daily to assume a more formidable aspect, and orders for the payment of the revenue due to the State were issued by the insurgents in the name of the Government, and under the signature of the Sir Desaee's son; and in all the villages of the Munohur and Mangaum Turufs, payments were enforced, notwithstanding that the Political Superintendent issued proclamations, prohibiting any one from paying revenue to the insurgents, or aiding them in any way whatever; and strictly forbidding all subjects of the State from joining the insurrection.

On the night of the 19th November 1844, a large party of the insurgents came down almost to the gates of Waree, firing their matchlocks and blowing horns; but on the officer commanding turning out with a party of the local corps, they decamped with all practicable speed in the direction of their strongholds in the hills. They, however, perhaps effected as much as was intended—annoyance to the troops engaged in the protection of the capital; for with all their numbers no one feared that the insurgents would in reality attack Waree in earnest.

The conduct of Phond Sawunt and his sons was most deceitful and ungrateful, for not only had a free pardon been granted them by Government for all their past misdeeds (neither few nor trifling), but, it would appear, they had ever received at the hands of the Political Superintendent the greatest consideration and personal kindness. Nor had they any possible cause for complaint: at a time when the Nemnook of almost every other Sirdar of this State was unavoidably reduced, a very handsome allowance was granted to them, and which was afterwards increased one-third; besides the villages they had previously held were restored to them. A large house was expressly set aside for their residence when they visited Waree; no interference with their retainers, no mistrust of their armed followers, no suspicion of their own fidelity, had ever been exhibited; in fact they were treated in all respects and on all occasions with marked distinction and honour, and the most ready and open confidence in their good faith ever displayed before the eyes of the community; but perhaps this very honour and distinction were the cause of their treachery and ultimate ruin.

About this time (November 22nd, 1844) a detachment of the 7th Regt. N. I., consisting of 200 rank and file, under command of Captain Skipper, proceeding under instructions from Major Benbow to take the post at the village of Sangélee, three or four miles east of Kulumbeest, Phond Sawunt's village, was attacked by large bodies of insurgents, led by the sons of Phond Sawunt in person, and after some skirmishing and fighting, compelled to retire, with a loss of 3 killed and 22 wounded, including, amongst the latter, Ensign Collier, who is represented to have been wounded twice in the gallant and zealous performance of his duty. On this occasion it was afterwards ascertained that the insurgents had 4 killed and about 30 wounded, and that they had four small field-pieces with them.

On learning of this disaster, Captain Hume, the officer then commanding at Waree, dispatched 200 men under the command of Lieutenant Bate, of the 7th Regt. N. I., to reinforce Captain Skipper; but notwithstanding this addition to his force, he was obliged to fall back on Mandkhol, half way between Sangélee and Waree.

Shortly after this unfortunate mishap, the insurgents made an attempt to tamper with the Soobedar and five Jemadars of the Sawunt Waree Local

4

Corps, and did all in their power to induce these officers, with the men under them, to join the rebel cause. The letter on this subject from Tan Sawunt, *alias* Baba Desaee, one of the sons of Phond Sawunt, to the address of the Soobedar, was handed over by this officer to his own immediate commanding officer, Major Benbow; and as a token of approbation for their fidelity and attachment to the State, Government directed that a present of Rs. 300 should be given to the Soobedar, and Rs. 150 to each of the Jemadars; and the corps was at the same time augmented by the addition of two companies, both with the view of rewarding the most deserving men of this fine corps, and of giving employment to some more of the young men in the State, who might otherwise join in the disturbances. A second in command was also appointed to the corps.

Early in January 1845 the insurrection had spread throughout the length and breadth of the State, and the greatest insecurity prevailed to life and property, even in the immediate vicinity of the military posts, and it was unsafe to move in any direction without a strong escort, and not always even then. As an instance, may be noticed the case of two young officers proceeding down the road from Belgaum to Vingorla, with a cavalry escort, who were fired upon by some miscreants concealed in the jungle about a coss only from Banda, and one of them, Ensign Faure, of the 2nd Eur. Regt. L. I., was mortally wounded, and he died the same evening.

The nature of the country, covered for miles on every side with densely thick jungle, rendered it next to impossible to check with anything like effect the perpetration of such outrages; and barbarous acts of cruelty, and even murders, were of too frequent occurrence, and that too in the near neighbourhood of the military outposts, and where they were indefatigable in patroling in every direction.

In short, every endeavour was made to arrest the further progress of the rebellion. Orders were issued to assemble the Gaonkurs, Koolkurnees, and Foujdars, with the view of trying to make them in some way responsible for their villagers, to account for those who might be absent, to produce all the arms in the village, and to cut down as far as practicable the jungle in their immediate vicinity.

In the early stage of the insurrection, an attempt was also made to intimidate others from joining by threats of punishment in case of assistance or shelter; and on the other hand, by rewards for any information given of the insurgents; but little or nothing was effected: the rebels were either too powerful, and their vengeance too certain to be incurred by compliance, or the spirit of disaffection was very prevalent all over the country.

And yet it was not possible to suppose that the great mass of the people could at heart have been favourable to the rebels. They were well aware of the great advantages they had enjoyed under British rule, as well of the tyranny and oppression they had to expect from the insurgent chiefs. But the lower orders generally seem to have been too long accustomed to follow their lawless leaders, and obey their behests in former times of commotion, to care what happened, or how long the existing state of affairs continued.

For the purpose of capturing and subduing the armed marauders who were infesting the State, two faithful Sirdars, one of the Banda Soobhedars and the other Baboo Rao Rana, were authorised (January 1845) to entertain 50 men each, on a salary of Rs. 4 per mensem, and the services of the former of these Sirdars were placed under the Banda Kumavisdar, and those of the latter under the Koodal Kumavisdar, as a temporary measure. Martial law was proclaimed under the authority of Government on the 14th of this month.

Another proclamation under the orders of Government was issued immediately afterwards, inviting all those who would without delay separate themselves from the insurgents, excepting the members of the Phond Sawunt's family, and sundry others who had made themselves conspicuous as leaders in the rebellion, as well as some of those who had personally participated in the atrocities which were committed, to return to their homes and occupations, under a promise of pardon for the past. Such a measure was conceived at that time, when martial law had been proclaimed, and troops were about to attack the enemy from all sides, as calculated to produce good results.

Lieutenant Colonel Outram, who had been deputed by Government to put down the insurrection, marched on the 16th of January 1845 on Kulumbeest with the whole of his available force. General Delamotte was encamped with the head quarters of his force at the top of the Hunmunt Ghaut, and field detachments under Lieutenant Colonel Carruthers, C.B., and Colonel Wallace, were likewise encamped, the former at the foot of the Hunmunt Ghaut, and the latter on the crest of a hill overlooking the Seevapoor valley, between the Ghaut and a hill called Susedoorg. Though no regular attack was for some time made on the enemy, yet Colonel Wallace occasionally threw shot and shell into Seevapoor* from the hill where he was encamped, and thus rendered the rebel position as unpleasant as it was unsafe.

About the middle of this month (January) a new difficulty arose in the appearance of Soobhana Nikum, a notorious leader, who had made his escape from Belgaum, and had been dispatched by the insurgents to the neighbourhood of Malwan, there to endeavour to raise the standard of rebellion among the Honorable Company's subjects, and cause, if possible, a diversion in favour of the insurgents in this territory. He issued some proclamations in the name of the Kolhapoor Government, to which power Malwan and its dependencies formerly belonged, inviting all good Hindoos to join him immediately, under threats of incurring the heaviest penalties; and he succeeded in attaching some few discontented spirits for a time to his cause.

About the same date, in the northern part of this principality, a person named Dajee Luxoomon Kala, who was formerly a personal servant of Anna Saheb (the heir apparent), also made himself conspicuous, by heading a party

* Seevapoor is immediately under the fortress of Munohur.

of insurgents, and not only collecting the revenues of the State, but likewise sending his emissaries into the neighbouring Turufs of Wurad and Pendoor, which formerly belonged to this principality, to realize the revenues of the Honorable Company's villages there.

On the Ram Ghaut road, another leader, named Hir Sawunt Dingnekur, a Sirdar of this State, assembled (January 1845) a number of followers, and threatened the Baitsee outpost, and Major Lucas, of the 8th Regt. Madras N. I., marched with his detachment in that direction to relieve this party, and endeavour again to open the communication by that line of road, which had been for a length of time almost entirely suspended.

Owing to the near proximity of the Goa frontier, and the great facilities enjoyed by the insurgents for doing so undetected, in consequence of the high road being closed, considerable quantities of ammunition found their way across the border, and the Desaees in that neighbourhood had numerous opportunities of assisting the insurgents in this territory; and though, at the commencement of the rebellion, means were taken to prevent the manufacture of gunpowder within this territory, this proved of little avail, for the rebels obtained large supplies of the materials for making it from the Deccan, and set up a manufactory of their own in the jungles of Seevapoor and Sursingé.

It has been observed that Colonel Wallace, from his elevated position, annoyed the rebels by firing and shelling into Seevapoor, the village immediately under the stronghold of Munohur, at this time in the possession of the rebels, who had, in consequence, removed their families and effects into the neighbouring jungles of Parpolee, Verlé, and Sursingé, where the Phond Sawunts had also conveyed their wives, children, and property, and, it was said, had stored large quantities of grain, &c. with the view of seeking shelter in these dense jungles when driven from the fortress of Munohur.

Seeing such formidable preparations going on all round for their circumvention, the spirit of the insurgents now (towards the end of January 1845) appeared to be considerably broken: numerous desertions from their cause daily took place, and a change for the better was perceptible in the public feeling respecting their ultimate success; the collection of the public revenues, which had been suspended for a length of time, again commenced, and the inhabitants of many of the villages began to return to their homes and occupations.

To the great energy and spirit displayed by Lieutenant Colonel Outram, and the salutary dread inspired by the promulgation of martial law, while room was permitted by the offer of pardon to the less guilty for large numbers to abandon the rebel cause, was this satisfactory and so much desired change to be attributed.

The Huwélkur and Oosupkur Desaees joined Hir Sawunt Dingnekur, who, as stated, had assembled a number of followers in the neighbourhood of the Ram Ghaut, and raised the standard of revolt against the Waree Government, while the Purmekur Desaee, one of the brothers of the Oosupkur Desaee, whose villages are close to the town of Baitsee, behaved remarkably well, and showed no disposition whatever to countenance the disaffection of the other Desaees; but, on the contrary, evinced his attachment to our cause, by performing services calculated to bring on him the enmity and vengeance of the rebels.

These insurgents, it may be observed, had no connection with the Phond Sawunts, further than that they had been encouraged to throw off their allegiance by the impunity so long enjoyed by the rebels in other parts of the principality. The Desaees pleaded as their grievance, that they had been deprived of their Huks on the customs by the British Government, and that their right to nominate the Foujdars of their villages had been infringed; but the truth was, so many robberies had taken place on the roads leading to their villages, both in the neighbourhood of the Ram Ghaut and towards the Goa frontier, and so many complaints were made of the insecurity for travellers in passing through them, that it became absolutely necessary to improve, if possible, the rural police in these districts.

With this view Mr. Courtney, at the time Political Superintendent, requested the Desaees to nominate the Foujdars to the different villages, and to inform him of their names, in order that they might have the usual Sunuds given them. The Desaees objected to this measure, on the ground that they were themselves at the head of the police in their districts. It was then intimated to them, that if that were the case, it was their duty to prevent such complaints of insecurity to life and property, and that as they had not done so, it was incumbent that some responsible person should be nominated to each village as the Foujdar, in the same way as had been done in other parts of the principality with good results; and that if they did not select fit and proper persons for Foujdars, Mr. Courtney informed them that he would be compelled to do so for the safety of the traffic on the road. Three years, however, elapsed, and the evil was in no way abated; and Mr. Courtney was at last compelled to appoint a Foujdar to each village. But it was not until a year and a half afterwards that the Desaees went into rebellion, and made this one subject of complaint.

It may be here noticed that the inheritance of the Desaee of Purma was a half share of the Oosup estates and rights, held in joint tenure with the Oosup Desaees: the latter were declared to have forfeited all the possessions they held in the Waree territory, in consequence of their connection with the rebellion, and Government took the opportunity thus offered to reward the Purma Desaee, who, as already observed, remained faithful to his allegiance, by conferring upon him the forfeited rights of the Oosup branch on tenure of service. The Purma Desaee being at that time childless, Government directed, as another mode of testifying how highly his services were appreciated, that permission should be given him to adopt a son.

Nothing could be worse than the confusion and discontent that now (January 1845) prevailed throughout the State; and although large bodies of regular troops occupied the country in every direction, little could be done against an enemy concealed in a densely thick jungle.

On the morning of the 27th of January 1845, the force under Major General Delamotte took possession of the forts of Munohur and Munsuntosh, which it was found the enemy had evacuated during the night, and had made their escape towards the Goa frontier, closely followed by the force under Colonel Outram. The rebels obtained a temporary shelter with the Oosup and Huwélee Desaees, also in the rebellion, as just noticed, and whose villages border on the Goa settlement. They were attacked and routed with considerable loss, and compelled to seek shelter in the southern boundary of this State, and in the neighbouring Portuguese possessions.

Under the authority of Government, a proclamation was issued on the 13th February 1845, offering a reward of Rs. 3,000 for the apprehension of Phond Sawunt's three elder sons, viz. Bheem Sawunt *alias* Nana Desaee, Tan Sawunt *alias* Baba Desaee, and Hunmunt Sawunt. A further sum of Rs. 1,000 each was offered for Appoo Desaee and Phond Sawunt himself, the latter an old man upwards of eighty years of age, yet strong and hale; Appoo Desaee being a drunken, dissipated character. No one, however, succeeded in capturing any of these rebels, who were shortly afterwards driven to seek shelter in the Goa territory.

The insurgents, on leaving the fort of Munohur, created disturbances in the villages on the Ram Ghaut road, plundered travellers, and surrounded Baitsee, where there was a small military post. With these marauders the Oosupkur and Huwélkur Desaees, and some of the inhabitants in the neighbourhood of Baitsee, together with the Sunudkuree sepoys of the fort of Awara, joined and threatened to attack the detachment at Baitsee, but no attack took place, and the insurgents sought safety in flight, knowing that Colonel Outram's force was in pursuit.

The Huwelkur Desaee had established a Chowkee at Moolus, at the foot of the Ram Ghaut, and, with the view to obstruct in some degree the passage of troops from Belgaum, had dug deep trenches across the road; and the Oosupkur had done the same at the Mangelee Ghaut; and to add to the confusion this state of affairs created, the insurgents who had obtained shelter at the hands of the Portuguese authorities on the Goa frontier used to cross into this territory at night, and commit all kinds of outrage and depredation.

Phond Sawunt, his sons, and Anna Saheb, the chieftain's eldest son, after leaving the fort of Munohur, sought refuge in the Kolbag jungle, between Neturdé and Mope; from thence they were conveyed to the dense jungles of Jogsawuntachiwaree, and they were concealed (February 1845) in the neighbourhood of the village of Wuraodé, in the province of Pedna, in the Goa country, where they remained for some days awaiting the orders of the Goa Government as to whether shelter would be afforded in the Portuguese possessions or not.

Troops were now stationed and actively engaged in all quarters of the State. Colonel Outram took up a position in the neighbourhood of the Goa frontier, east of Banda, and detachments of British troops were placed on the Waree side, both to prevent communication being carried on between the insurgents who had fled for safety into the Goa country, and their families in this State, and also to act as a check on the proceedings of the Goa authorities.

The Oosupkur and Huwélkur Desaees had made themselves conspicuous as leaders in the insurrection in the neighbourhood of Baitsee, and at the foot of the Ram Ghaut, from whence they were driven,after considerable difficulty and opposition, by the force under Colonel Outram, when they concealed themselves in the thick jungles which surround all their villages, and thus active operations in a manner ceased for a time.

When the insurgents were fairly driven across the border into the Goa country, and thus beyond our reach, it became necessary to ascertain the intentions of the Government of that State in respect to them. Captain Arthur, Military Secretary to the Honorable the Governor, was therefore deputed in February 1845 to Goa, for the purpose of conferring with the Governor General of that settlement in regard to the best means to be adopted for preventing the insurgents from Waree finding an asylum in the Goa territory, and for apprehending those who had already sought shelter within the limits of that State.

But the Goa Government did not afford any satisfactory information relative to the actual proceedings and measures which it purposed to adopt, consequent on the repeated requisitions which had been made for the surrender of all the offenders against the British Government, who had sought refuge in the country under the Goa jurisdiction.

Neither could it be ascertained what course the Goa Government intended to adopt towards Portuguese subjects who had aided in the disturbances in the Waree districts; and it became necessary to depute Captain Arthur a second time to Goa, for the purpose of ascertaining, if possible, the final determination of the Governor General upon the points at issue; but with no better success.

This mission having failed, the British Government, in the latter end of the year 1845, directed Major Jacob, then Political Superintendent of Waree, to place himself in communication with the Governor General of Goa, in the hope of obtaining, for the information of Government, a decided answer as to what were the intentions of His Excellency in regard to the surrender of the offenders who had taken refuge within the Goa territory.

The result of Major Jacob's inquiries on the subject, however, were equally unsatisfactory, and were reported to Government on the 16th of January 1846, when, in a reply dated 16th April of the same year, Major Jacob was informed that Government had resolved not further to agitate with the Goa authorities, the question of surrendering the Waree offenders, amongst whom were the Phond Sawunts, together with the chieftain's eldest son Anna Saheb, and many other rebel chiefs, all of whom sought and found an asylum in the

Portuguese territory. The total number of Waree fugitives reported and acknowledged to have been in custody of the Goa authorities was 161, of which some 15 or 20 were men of influence.

Their quarters and treatment at Goa, whether good or bad, did not, however, long please the fugitives, for in May 1847 they began to adopt measures for procuring pardon, and returning, if possible, to their homes in the Waree country, and transmitted a packet through the late minister Moro Krishn Lelé to the address of Major Jacob. This packet was found to contain letters to Major Jacob, and the late minister, from certain of the Waree offenders at Goa named in the margin; it also contained petitions to the Bombay Government, praying for pardon and restoration to their former state for the parties named therein, to the number of 92.

Huwélkur Desaee, Oosup ditto, Tamboolkur ditto, Hoomruskur, Bapoo Ghatgay, and others.

The first named petitioners, the Oosup and Huwélee Desaees, were in arms, and had set the authority of the British Government, as well as that of the Waree State, at open defiance, before the chieftain's son, Anna Saheb, joined the other rebels: it has also been alleged that these Sirdars were in a manner unconnected with the Phond Sawunt leaders, though they latterly made common cause with them.

The Tamboolkur's petition was from the younger sons of Phond Sawunt's second wife, half brothers to the other sons Nana, Baba, Appoo, and Hunmunt Desaees, the leaders, and most conspicuous men in the rebellion. These latter, it would seem, did not concur in the prayer of the petitions from the other Waree fugitives, either supposing it hopeless to expect pardon, or continuing to retain their enmity to British rule.

Anna Saheb had likewise addressed his uncle Aba Saheb Patunkur (the present Khasgee Karbharee), praying him to exert himself, and intercede in his behalf for pardon, and permission to return to Waree. This paper was duly laid before the Political Superintendent.

It ultimately ended in Major Jacob transmitting (May 1847) the petitions above referred to for the information and instructions of Government. Major Jacob intimated in his letter on the occasion, that the cause of public order had nothing to fear from any exercise of clemency that might be shown to the humbler followers, who had not personally committed any atrocity; and further remarked, in regard to the nominal head of the rebellion, the young prince, that he was doubtless made a mere tool of by the intriguing and dangerous family of Kulumbeest, from whose grasp, after the one fatal step, he was never able to extricate himself.

But Government deemed it inexpedient to negotiate with these rebels for their release, so long as they were detained by the Goa authorities, though it was intimated that very probably clemency might be extended to the greater number of them were they surrendered to the British Government; and Major Jacob was directed to intimate (October 1847), on a suitable opportunity, to the Goa authorities, that he would be happy to recommend to the clemency of the Bombay Government, and with a view to their release on security, those humbler followers of the leaders in the Waree disturbances who might not personally have committed any heinous offence.

About this time, the Government of Portugal recommended to Her Britannic Majesty's Government the grant of a general pardon to the Sawunt Waree rebels who were refugees in Goa, and Major Jacob was accordingly, in November 1847, called upon by the Bombay Government for his opinion as to the advisability, or otherwise, of the clemency applied for in their behalf, being wholly, or in part, extended to the refugee insurgents. Major Jacob, after giving the subject his attentive consideration, submitted his opinion on the inexpediency of extending clemency to Baba Desaee, Phond Sawunt's second son, who was the real head of the rebellion below the Ghauts, cordially supported by the whole Tamboolkur family; neither did Major Jacob deem it at all advisable to pardon Phond Sawunt and his other two elder sons, Nana and Hunmunt Desaees. He further doubted the propriety of pardoning the Oosup and Huwélee Desaees and Bhonslay Sirdars for some time, though he thought mercy might eventually be extended even to them; and, moreover, he considered it would be positively unsafe to forgive some men of less rank, such as Hir Sawunt Dingnekur, Baba Bhogta, Yesoo Koobul, Phutum Bhut, Nana Tulgaonkur, and sundry others. He, however, recommended, that after a time the younger sons of Phond Sawunt might perhaps be pardoned, and his opinion was also in favour of Anna Saheb, the eldest son of the Sir Desaee, having clemency extended to him, subject to certain conditions.

In accordance with the instructions he had received in December 1847, Major Jacob deputed Lieutenant Schneider, the adjutant of the local corps, to communicate in a friendly way with Mr. Gomes, the Secretary to the Goa Government, about the prisoners in custody at Goa, and a list was jointly made out by those gentlemen of 64 persons, supposed to be of the humblest classes. On examining the Political Superintendent's records, however, it was found that some of this number stood charged as murderers, gang robbers, and leaders of bands of marauders, so that the list was reduced to 45, and then submitted to the Bombay Government, with a recommendation for clemency being extended towards them. The result was a grant in May 1848 of authority to the Political Superintendent to make a communication to the Goa Government, proposing to permit all minor participators in the insurrection under surveillance at Goa to return to the Waree territory under a promise of free pardon being extended to them for their past offences, on their furnishing security for their future good conduct.

These refugees, including the Oosup and Huwélkur Desaees, and the four sons of Phond Sawunt by his youngest wife, as well as his grandson, accordingly returned to the Waree State. Four of the refugees, who were known to have committed atrocious crimes, were, on conviction, sentenced

5

according to the merits of their deeds, and all the others were granted a free pardon on the terms above recorded.

Anna Saheb arrived at Waree from Goa on the 21st of August 1849, having accepted the conditions on which pardon was granted to him; but in consideration of the loss of life, and other evil consequences which ensued from Anna Saheb's joining the insurgents under the Phond Sawunts, thereby extending and protracting the rebellion, Government felt itself precluded from granting him any more favourable terms than those already authorised, viz. his being permitted to return and reside at Waree on a pension of Rs. 100 per mensem, but with a forfeiture of all rights he would have possessed, present and prospective, on the Sawunt Waree State, had he not personally joined the insurgents, and thereby given them the weight and influence of his name, when he had not a shadow of a pretext for participating in the rebellion.

Matters having been thus arranged for the pardon and return to their homes of these Desaees (March 1850), it became requisite to settle the question of a provision for their maintenance. The younger sons and the grandson of Phond Sawunt, named in the margin, were entirely destitute on their arrival at Waree, possessing actually nothing but the clothes on their backs; and after Major Jacob had made himself acquainted with their characters, and had ascertained that they had nothing to do with the insurrection, beyond following the elders of their family, suggested to Government that some trifling allowance should be made for their support. This was the more necessary, since the Tamboolkur patrimony had dwindled down amongst many descendants to little or nothing. Phond Sawunt, as Killedar of Mahadeogur, it is true, had nevertheless always a considerable following, and a power over the country far beyond his mere rank as a local Desaee and Sirdar of the State.

Sabajee, Tatoba, Laroba, and Bhoj Desaees; and Atmaram Desaee, the grandson.

The provision originally allotted to him, through the interference of Government, on the appointment of the first Political Superintendent (Mr. Spooner) in 1838, consisted of the revenues of the villages noted in the margin, and entered in the accounts at Peerkhanee Rs. 1,580-13-9 per annum, but producing much more to one all powerful over the villagers.

This provision of course ceased with the rebellion, and the patrimony only, a (Nufa) profit of Company's Rs. 2-9-2 per annum, remained, which was also confiscated at its close. The younger sons, and the grandson, above named, had therefore absolutely nothing, and their relations by marriage were also in poverty; and Major Jacob, in consequence, sought and obtained the sanction of Government (April 1850) for a pittance of Rs. 5 per mensem being allowed to each under the head of Siledars.

Kulumbeest, Parpolee, Ambolee, with Gela, Werlé, Bowlat; as also the Waree Tunkha on Azra, villages of Guwsé, Murewar, Keetowré, Parpolee, Kandgaum, Dabheel, Khurpuré, Soolgaum, Hulolee, Shelup, and Dewardé.

The pardoned Oosup and Huwélkur Desaees have also been provided for from the proceeds of their confiscated estates, but their present incomes are no more than subsistence money, yet quite as much as they had any just reason to expect, after their long continued participation in the disturbances.

The British force engaged in quelling the insurrection below the Ghauts consisted of the left wing 2nd Queen's royals; one company of H. M.'s 17th foot; the 7th Regt. Bombay N. I.; detachments of the 10th, 21st, and 23rd Regts. Bombay N. I.; the 3rd Regt. Madras N. I.; detachments of the 8th and 16th Regts. Madras N. I.; detachments of Madras L. C.; a detachment of Poona Auxiliary Horse; and one company of Sappers and Miners, besides a very considerable force above, in the Belgaum and Kolhapoor country, under the immediate command of Major General Delamotte.

The troops had most harassing duties to perform during the rebellion, and the wonder was it was put down so soon, for the country presented so many remarkable facilities for irregular warfare, that it often happened that the result of the best laid plans proved most unsatisfactory. There was no want of secret enemies to the introduction of British rule at Waree, but where an open foe could seldom be met with, the troops employed in quelling the disturbances were rarely engaged in fair fight. The system that had to be pursued was one of hunting the rebels out of their strongholds and dense jungles, and this duty, the most unpleasant that troops can be employed on, was performed with unwearied zeal and cheerfulness by all engaged on the occasion.

The Sawunt Waree Local Corps is now the only force retained for the preservation of peace, and for the general security of life and property throughout the State. The present strength of the corps is adequate to the various duties required of it, the best possible arrangements being made with the men available; and outposts are established throughout the districts. The southern frontier is well guarded against inroads from the Goa territory, where anarchy and confusion have long unhappily prevailed.

Several of the Waree fugitives of note are still under the protection of the Goa Government, and though it was implicitly guaranteed that these dangerous characters should be kept in safe custody, it is a notorious fact that certain of them have been employed, and furnished with arms and armed followers, under the delusion that such wicked and faithless men will aid the Goa Government in the suppression of the long existing unhappy confusion that prevails in the Satary Mahal of that settlement. The Waree fugitives may for a time consider it expedient to conduct themselves honestly and properly, but if most stringent arrangements are not made for their security and more strict custody, the chances are, such turbulent spirits will sooner or later give the Goa Government cause to repent the indulgence and confidence that have been reposed in them.

After the insurrection had been put down, and tranquillity had been restored, it was decided by the Court of Directors and the Government of India, that the position which Sawunt Waree was henceforth to occupy amongst the Southern Muratha States in relation to the British Government, in consequence of the uniform disaffection and faithlessness of its engagements which had marked the history of this State from its first connection with us, added to the fact of our having been obliged to set aside the present titular chief on account of his incapacity and misconduct, and of the heir apparent having joined and taken an active portion in the rebellion, would have warranted the British Government in declaring the State confiscated, and its territories annexed to the British possessions; but the Governor General in Council, in consideration that the disturbances had not taken place while the State was under the government of its own chief, but were committed while the principality was under our management, and that the widely spread feelings of disaffection and rebellion were in a great measure, if not entirely, caused by the dislike to British rule, determined that no change should be made in the chief's position. British administration was, however, to be carried on during his life in the same manner as heretofore, and he and his family supported, as hitherto, by a fixed allowance.

Peace and tranquillity now reign where, previously to Government having taken the Sawunt Waree State under its management in the year 1838, all was turmoil and confusion; and though discontent, as may be naturally expected, still prevails in many quarters, in consequence of the altered state of affairs, the great mass of the people is undoubtedly happier and more secure than when under the Native dynasty.

The Sir Desaee's character has been often described, and it does not appear that any material change has taken place in his disposition of late years. He is a soft, good-natured, and, if left alone, an inoffensive man; he is said to have a certain degree of intelligence—low cunning is perhaps a better term for it; he is decidedly weak, fickle, and easily played on by any designing party. He associates chiefly with Khuwases and other menials, and is at a loss to sustain the most commonplace conversation with more suitable companions. His time is chiefly engrossed by superstitious observances and ceremonies, &c. &c.; and, so far as these keep him from brooding over the degradation consequent on loss of political power, they are doubtless very useful.

In all the little petty intrigues that go on in the palace, and amongst people connected with the different parties and interests, the Sir Desaee is seldom mixed up: in truth he has neither head nor inclination to meddle much in such affairs, though some of those about him do, and at times succeed, in interesting him in their own squabbles, that have sprung, perhaps, from finding themselves outwitted by greater adepts at intrigue.

The Sir Desaee's eldest son, Phond Sawunt, better known as Anna Saheb, was, as has been noticed, seduced away from his father's roof by Baba Desaee in the latter part of the year 1844, and joined in the rebellion. The rebel leaders made a mere tool of him, carrying on all their unlawful acts in his name; for when the lad took this fatal step of joining the rebel cause, he was only between sixteen and seventeen years of age, and was neither a restless, ambitious, nor intelligent youth.

It was said, and in all probability with some truth, that Jankee Baee, the Sir Desaee's youngest wife, was the secret cause of Anna Saheb's joining the rebels. She had gained ascendancy over him, and it was ascertained that interviews with her and the Tamboolkur Desaees had been frequent previous to the insurrection. Her object, of course, was to get Anna Saheb to commit himself, and thus to a certain extent clear the way for her own son's succession to the Gadee. Jankee Baee is fond of intrigue, and she has many friends able and willing to assist her, none more so than her uncle Narayen Rao Khanvilkur, a deep, cunning, and intriguing man, hostile to our interference with this State: his character has long been known, and on a late occasion it was found necessary to caution him against mixing himself up in matters that did not concern him.

The Sir Desaee has had three wives. The first, Luxoomee Baee (the sister of Aba Saheb Patunkur, the present Khasgee Karbharee), died on the 25th April 1832. She left three children—Sahebjee a daughter, born 16th May 1824, married the 7th April 1835 to Bhowanjee Rajey Jhoonjur Rao Ghatgay of Bood, in the Satara country; Anna Saheb, the eldest son above alluded to, who was born on the 23rd March 1828; and Bayama, born on the 18th April 1831, married 27th April 1844 to Nagojee Rao, eldest son of Pownojee Rao, Sir Desaee of Jamboot, a petty chiefship just above the Ghauts.

The second wife, Savitree Baee, whose family live in retired obscurity at the neighbouring village of Mazgaum, and possess neither influence nor wealth. She has one child, a son, Ramchundru Sawunt *alias* Bhow Saheb, who was born on the 9th of August 1838. He is a dull, and not very intelligent youth. Savitree Baee is of quiet disposition. She never had much influence over her husband, and they have been estranged for some time past, in consequence of petty squabbles in the palace. She has long been on bad terms with the youngest wife, Jankee Baee, and naturally enough suspects her of a desire to supplant her and her son; and there can be no doubt her suspicions are well grounded.

Jankee Baee, the youngest wife of the Sir Desaee, has two children, the elder Som Sawunt *alias* Aba Saheb, who was born 4th May 1842. He is a sharp, intelligent boy, and fond of his studies, though as yet not very far advanced with them. Her second son, Bawa Saheb, was born on the 19th March 1848, and is therefore still a mere child, but is an interesting boy, and promises to be an intelligent youth.

Anna Saheb had, previous to his quitting his father's roof and joining in the insurrection, received the first rudiments of his education, that is, could read, write, and cypher a little; but an effectual stop was put to his studies by the unhappy step he took, and for some time after his return to Waree, on being admitted to clemency after his past offences, it was found necessary to place him under restraint, being at times quite out of his mind, caused by the evil course and dissipated life he had been living, so that his studies were never resumed, and much of the little learning he ever had, was lost.

For the last two years or so he has been sane enough, and lately, to give him something to do, his uncle (Aba Saheb) was recommended to induce him to read for an hour or two daily with the Pundit who teaches his younger brothers, by way of amusement, and affording some food for his mind; and he has kept to his reading longer than was expected he would, considering that he is now up in years, and, it may be inferred, less inclined to renew his studies than if they had never been so long and so unhappily interrupted.

The education of the two other sons, Bhow Saheb and Aba Saheb, has been regularly and carefully attended to for some years past; and though their progress has not been so great as we had a right to expect, they are far from ignorant Native youths, and perhaps the want of a more able teacher had something to do with their backwardness; but steps have lately been taken to remedy this evil. The younger son, Bawa Saheb, is just about to enter on his studies, and, as has already been observed, he is a promising and intelligent child, and having the advantage of an early beginning, we may hope the more from him.

Several of the old Sirdars and Native gentry of the State, both male and female, have died within the last ten years. Amongst the departed may be mentioned Dhar Rao Khanvilkur, first cousin to the Sir Desaee, who died in the month of March 1844. He was in the receipt of an allowance of Peerkhanee Rs. 360 per annum. After his death an allowance of Peerkhanee Rs. 120 per annum was continued to his widow.

Madhow Rao Patunkur, father-in-law of the Sir Desaee, died on the 10th July 1844. He received Peerkhanee Rs. 360 per annum. Peerkhanee Rs. 120 were continued to his widow, Bala Baee.

Yemoona Baee *alias* Dadee Baee, widow of Shreeram Sawunt, died on the 20th September 1845. She was the widow of the first cousin of the present chief, and mother of Ramchundru Sawunt, who reigned from A. D. 1803 to 1808. This lady was in the receipt of a stipend from the State of Rs. 3,300 per annum. She left issue one daughter, now a widow, named Shaba Baee, who had been for twenty years residing under her mother's roof, and two grand-daughters, one married to Venkut Rao Patunkur, the maternal uncle of Anna Saheb, and the other to Bhowanjee Rao Rajey Ghatgay, a Sirdar of Kolhapoor.

The Dowager Ranee Nurmuda Baee expired on the night of the 6th June 1849, aged seventy-six, of gradual decay of nature. This lady was one of the four widows of Khem Sawunt (here commonly called the great), who died in 1803, after reigning forty-eight years, and succeeded jointly with Savitree Baee to the regency, on the death of Doorga Baee,* the second widow, that is from

* Doorga Baee died 17th January 1819.

the 28th December 1818 to the 11th February 1823. Nurmuda Baee was much respected by the community, and possessed more influence over the Sirdars than any other person of her time at Waree. She was at the time of her death in the receipt of an annual allowance of Rs. 2,964.

Pokhrojee Rao Dhar Rao *alias* Bapoo Saheb Nimbalkur, grandson of the Sir Desaee Khem Sawunt, by Luxoomee Baee, of the house of His Highness Sindia, died here on the 26th November 1850. He was in the receipt of a reduced stipend of Rs. 360. He left a son seven years old, and two widows. An allowance of Rs. 350 is now continued to the family.

Yeshwunt Rao Dhar Rao *alias* Bala Saheb Nimbalkur died on the 15th October 1853. He was a brother of Pokhrojee Rao Nimbalkur. He has left a son, aged about fifteen years, and two widows. A reduced allowance of Rs. 340 per annum is now continued to the family.

Babnee *alias* Aka Baee Patunkur, sister to the present Sir Desaee's father, also his mother-in-law, her daughter being given in marriage to him, by whom the eldest son Anna Saheb was born, died 15th December 1853.

The late minister Moro Krishn Lelé died on the morning of 29th June 1847. He had been unable to attend the Kucheree for some days, but no alarm was felt until the day preceding his death, when he rapidly sunk under his disease, the force of which he had till then so successfully struggled against as to have concealed his danger even from his friends.

In reporting the death of the minister, the Political Superintendent spoke favourably of his character, and observed that he did not believe he had the slightest participation in the rebellion; and accounted for his enjoying so little general influence, however much his character was otherwise calculated to ensure it, from the fact that we had deprived him of all power, and that he (the minister) was kept in place by us without reference to Durbar wishes; but that a more upright, firm, yet conciliatory person, and of unpretending manners, it would be difficult to find.

Moro Punt was a devout Bramin, and of rare integrity of character. He had many enemies, for all who thought him the obstacle to their own chance of being ministers, or to their requests of divers sorts being complied with, or who feared his bringing their misdeeds to light, were disposed to look on him with feelings of jealous dislike; yet by none such, whatever evil they might impute to him, was it ever whispered of his being accessible to a bribe; a circumstance redounding to his honour in a community such as this, the more especially as he was of a generous disposition, and daily fed and lodged numbers who were in distress; thus he died leaving no wealth.

Moro Punt was a great upholder of all the old customs of the State, a stickler for every Braminical form and institution, and opposed to alterations: he was slow in responding to references made requiring his opinion, and rendered very little assistance in enforcing measures of economy. On the other hand, his advice was useful in checking undue haste in matters connected with the entangled system of revenue here in force; his experience and opinions were valuable, and his just and well expressed sentiments as an assessor of the criminal court materially contributed to fulfil the ends for which this mixed system was established. In all Durbar matters and caste disputes his loss was seriously felt.

Little now remains to be noticed save the lines of communication for general traffic.

The only road of importance at present running through this State is the one from Belgaum by way of the Ram Ghaut to Vingorla; other two Ghauts are now in course of construction, both leading into the Waree country, the first the Tulkut Ghaut, and the other the Parpolee Ghaut: these roads, when finished, will be of great advantage, not merely to this district, but to the country both above and below the Ghauts. The lines through the hills have been selected with great skill and attention, and by officers thoroughly understanding their work, and so gradual and easy is the ascent that loaded carts will pass up or down with perfect facility

The Tulkut Ghaut road will join the Vingorla road near Banda, and the Parpolee Ghaut road also joins the Vingorla road three miles from Waree. At present this road from the foot of the Ghaut is but an indifferent line, and only as yet a cleared way, but when the Ghaut is completed, it is in contemplation to improve and repair the whole road.

The Malwan road has also for some years been slowly progressing, and has lately been much improved, and finished to the village of Pingoolee, about ten or eleven miles distant. There are numbers of Native roads intersecting the country in all directions, but they are of the very worst description. With the two Ghaut lines, however, above referred to, in addition to the Ram Ghaut road, and the Malwan one, the State will soon be tolerably well off in respect to internal communication.

It has been generally admitted that the Parpolee and Tulkut lines of Ghaut, though neither is yet finished, display considerable science in the selection of the lines.

Venkut Rao *alias* Aba Saheb Patunkur, the present Khasgee Karbharee, is a Native gentleman of high and honorable character, and has always used his best endeavours to promote the good government and best interests of the State. From our first connection with Waree in 1838, four Political Superintendents have borne testimony to the high sense entertained of his services, as well as to his intelligence, conciliatory disposition, and general upright behaviour in all matters relating to the welfare of the people and country. He is a person in whom every confidence may be placed; he rendered good and faithful service to Government during the rebellion in 1844 and 1845; and it is recorded that he made himself equally useful during the earlier disturbances in 1838-39. In a word, his conduct has been honest and straightforward from first to last in his relations with us, and he is entitled to all credit and consideration, which he has fairly and justly earned by a long course of faithful services.

Atmaram Sheoram, the chief hereditary Chitnees of the State, who is associated with Aba Saheb in his various duties, is a most intelligent and valuable officer, and he is generally respected by the community at large. He is a sensible, well-behaved person, and justly enjoys the esteem of all who know him, both as regards his public and private character.

Descriptions of the Munohur, Waree, Koodal, Banda, and Awara Forts, are annexed, marked A to E. A rough map of Munohur Fort is also appended, marked F.

A short memorandum of the expenses incurred in quelling the insurrection forms Appendix G.

Ditto ditto of the date on which the mint of the Peerkhanee coinage at Sawunt Waree was suppressed, and Company's currency introduced (H), which is followed by a genealogical table of the Sir Desaee's family.

The respective ages of the four sons of the Sir Desaee are—

1st, Phond Sawunt *alias* Anna Saheb, aged 26 years.
2nd, Ramchundru Sawunt *alias* Bhow Saheb, aged 15 years.
3rd, Som Sawunt *alias* Aba Saheb, aged 12 years.
4th, Naroba Desaee *alias* Bawa Saheb, aged 6 years.

A.

MUNOHUR FORT.

The hill fort of Munohur lies NNE. from Waree. It is a solid mass of rock, and is perhaps one of the strongest forts in India. It constitutes an outwork of the Konkun against the Deccan, to which, however, it is connected by a narrow ridge about two miles long. It is of an angular shape. Its height is about 2,500 feet. Its greatest length is 440 yards, and its breadth 350 yards. It has two strong gates to a single entrance, which is approached by a flight of steps cut through the solid rock, and is a stronghold that may certainly be pronounced in good hands impregnable.

The fortress, previous to 1845, belonged to Kolhapoor, but after the rebellion was quelled, the place and its revenues were entirely disconnected from Kolhapoor, and transferred to the Waree State. The Gurkurees were permitted to retain their lands on certain conditions, but were declared to have forfeited all their money claims; and those of them who inhabited the Kolhapoor territory were directed to quit Waree and reside above the Ghauts.

B.

WAREE FORT.

This fort is situated in the Sawunt Waree territory, and is the residence of the Sir Desaee and of the Political Superintendent. It lies about 13 miles ENE. of Vingorla, and 7 miles NNW. from Banda. The walls are built of loose stone and mud, and are in a dilapidated state.

The fort is of an irregular shape, and is constructed of towers and curtains, loop-holed. The bastions are not capable of holding ordnance from their dilapidated state, and there are no embrasures. The towers are roofed over. There are three entrances to this fort. The principal, or north entrance is flanked by two towers, but the gate is of no strength. A ditch runs round the fort on the north-east and south sides (dry in the fair season, but filled during the monsoon). On the west side is a large tank 280 yards wide, by 650 yards in length, which comes close up to the fort wall. The fort is enclosed on three sides by buildings and trees, within 25 yards of the fort walls. There are several pieces of ordnance of different calibre, all unserviceable ; only two (brass) are mounted on carriages. There are several wells of good water in the fort. All the buildings are tiled, and the Peta contains about 10,000 inhabitants. The local corps lines are situated outside the fort, on the north side, and about 280 yards from the north entrance.

This fort is of no strength, and could make little or no resistance against regular troops. A few pieces of ordnance placed on the northern side of the tank would bring the walls down in a few hours. The walls being roofed over, afford plenty of accommodation for troops inside the fort. There are also Sudurs which are at present used as jail, treasury, and other Native offices.

C.

KOODAL FORT.

This fort is situated in the Waree territory, 13 miles NW. of Waree, and 12 miles NNE. of Vingorla. It is of an irregular shape, erected upon a rising ground about 160 yards long, by the same in breadth (in the broadest part), having a dry ditch all round, but is a place of no strength. The Kumavisdar of the district resides in the fort, which is built of loose stone and mud, and consists of bastions, with connecting curtains, but in a very dilapidated condition. The parapet wall inside varies about 2½ to 3 feet in height, and the towers are in a very crumbling state. The only building in the fort is the Kumavisdar's Kucheree, within which the detachment of sepoys is accommodated. There is also a stone Musjid, which might be converted into a store-room by adding a roof and doors. There are 12 pieces of ordnance of different calibre in this fort, all unserviceable. There is only one well in the fort, but the water is not good, and seldom used for drinking purposes. The entrance to this fort is in the south-eastern angle, having three gateways to it, neither of which is of any strength. There is a sally-port on the western side, the gateway of which is very narrow, and in a very dilapidated state. The village contains about 250 good tiled houses, with several wells of good water. There is good encamping ground on the north-east, near the river.

This fort could offer but little resistance against regular troops, as the walls can with the greatest ease be entered in every direction without even scaling ladders, and there is good cover for troops in the Peta, within 100 yards of the south-east entrance.

D.

BANDA FORT.

Situated in the Waree territory, on the Vingorla road, about 18 miles ESE. of Vingorla, and 7 miles nearly south from Sawunt Waree. It is erected on a rising ground, on the left bank of the Tirakole river. The fort is built partly of good masonry, and partly of loose stones and mud, but in a state of dilapidation. It is irregularly shaped, lying nearly due east and west, being about 100 yards in length, by about 50 yards in breadth. It is constructed of towers connected by curtains, and both are loop-holed. The towers are in too dilapidated a state to admit of ordnance being used on them. The towers are roofed over, as also are the walls, affording good cover for troops. The Sudur or Kucheree is well calculated for stores, as is also another building. The entrance to this fort is on the south-eastern angle: the gateway is of no strength, and is exposed to view, and the ascent to it is very gradual. There is a sally-port on the western side, leading down to the river by a flight of narrow steps. There are a few pieces of ordnance of different calibre, but all are unserviceable. There is no tank or well in the fort. It is of no strength, and could make little or no resistance against troops. The gateway is partially exposed, and the only water to be had is from the river, and a well which is about 60 yards outside the entrance gate. The Peta is within musket-range of the gateway, and would afford good cover to an attacking party unprovided with guns. There is excellent encamping ground on the right bank of the river, and also on the left bank north of the fort.

E.

AWARA FORT.

Situated in the Waree territory, about 300 yards on the north side of the Vingorla road, and being at a distance from the village of Baitsee of about one mile and a half in a NNE. direction. The fort was surrounded by a dry ditch, covered with thick brushwood, and bamboo jungle, almost concealing it on the southern and western sides. The village is entirely destroyed. The little strength this fort could boast of was its gateway, but it was completely exposed to view, and could have offered very little resistance. The walls were built of stones and mud. There was an outwork on the north side, which was connected with the fort by a very thick bamboo hedge on the eastern side, and on the western by a low wall. But, as already observed, it was dismantled in May 1845.

G.

The charge on the Waree State for the extraordinary expenses incurred in quelling the insurrection, including interest, amounted in all to Rs. 4,89,067-12-8. Of this sum Rs. 2,35,572-7-0 had been liquidated up to the month of April 1854. A balance of Rs. 2,53,495-5-8 now remains due, which is being gradually though slowly reduced, at the rate of about Rs. 40,000 per annum.

H.

The mint of the Peerkhanee coinage at Sawunt Waree was suppressed in the year 1845, under the authority of Government, and Company's currency was introduced throughout the Waree territory instead. The value of the Peerkhanee rupee was fixed by Government at the average rate recommended by the Mint Committee, namely 87.175 per cent.; and according to this rate the whole revenues were converted into Company's rupees. (May 1848.)

GENEALOGICAL TABLE OF THE BHONSLAY FAMILY OF SAWUNT WAREE.

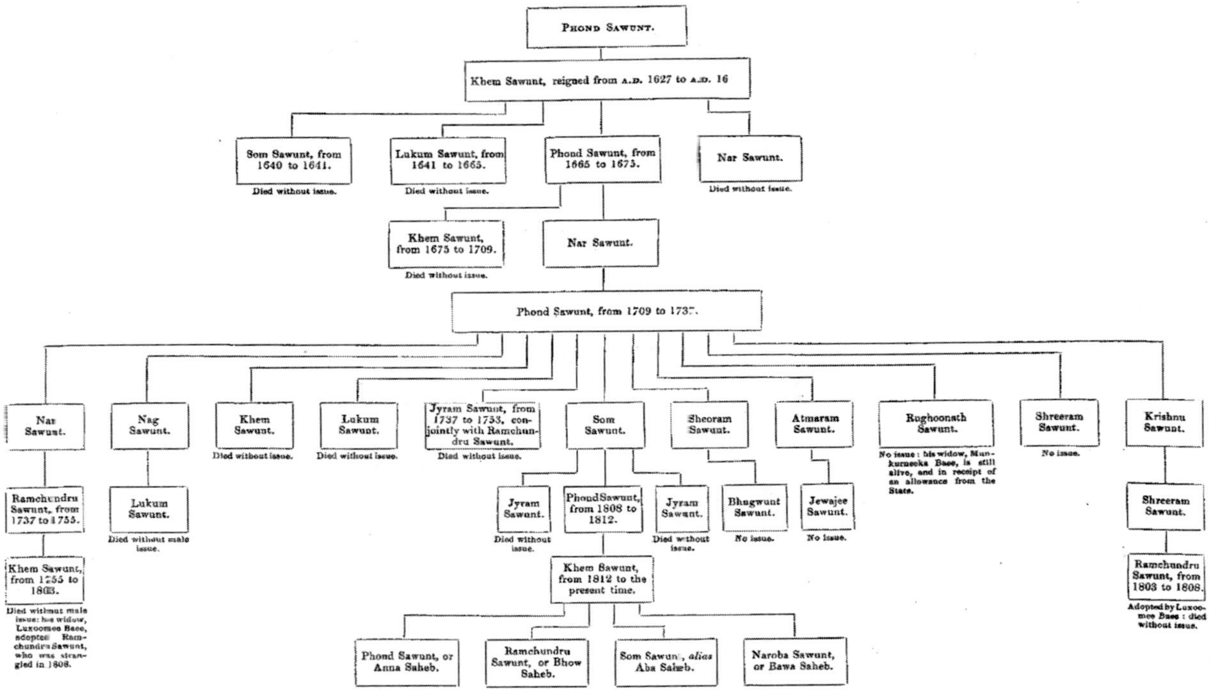

F.

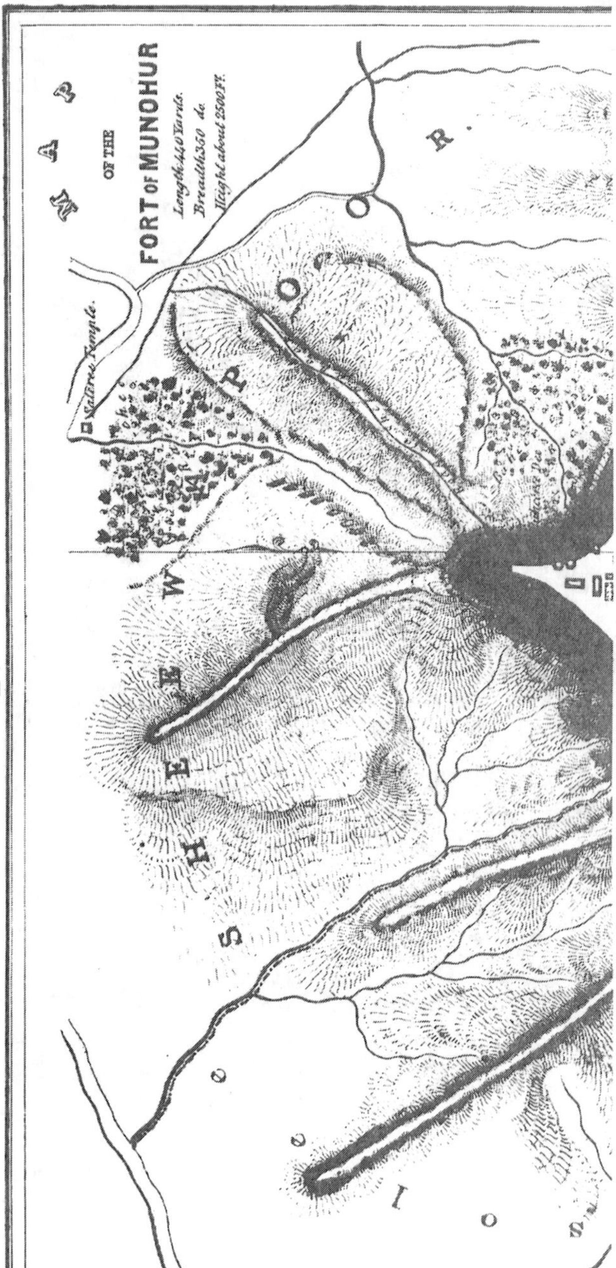
MAP
OF THE
FORT OF MUNOHUR
Length 440 Yards.
Breadth 350 do.
Height about 2500 Ft.
Sal Tree Temple.

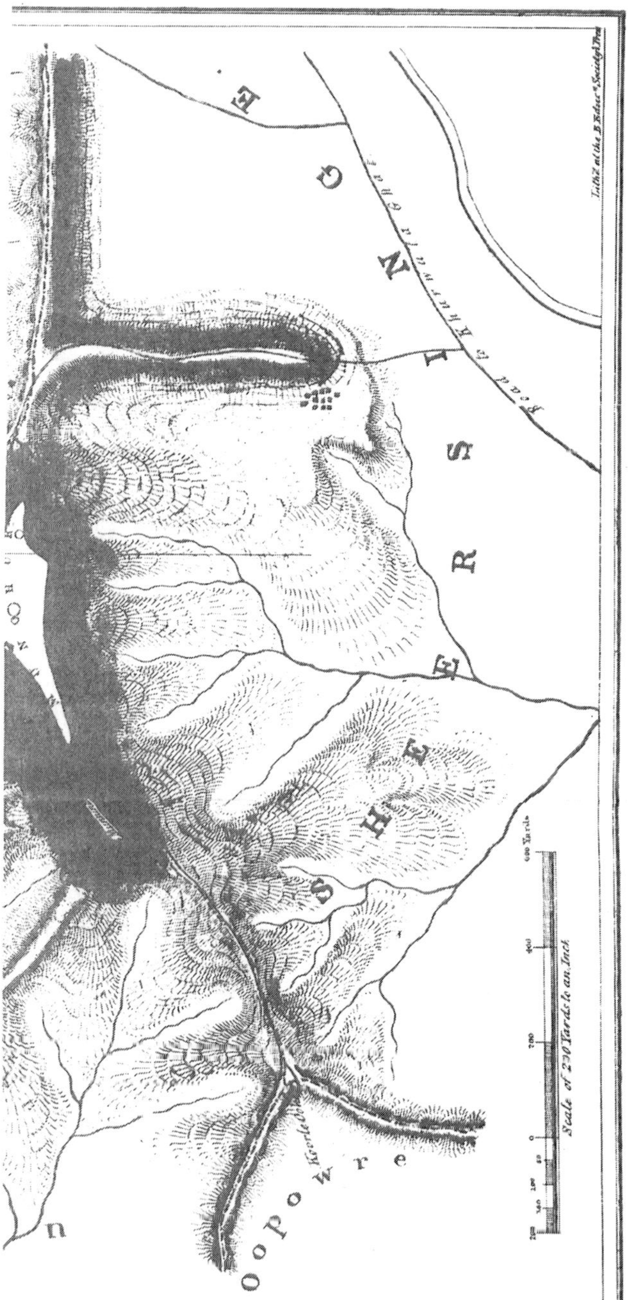
Oopowre
Scale of 230 Yards to an Inch
600 Yards
400
200
0

Statement showing the Number of Schools at the different Villages under the Sawunt Waree State, as also the Number of Students attending them.

No.	Names of Villages.	Number of Schools in each Village.	Number of Students.
	PRIVATE SCHOOLS.		
	Waree Division.		
1	Mangaum	1	9
2	Akeree	2	16
3	Kolgaum	2	32
4	Ghaonulé	1	4
5	Mazgaum	1	13
6	Churate	1	5
7	Adelee	1	11
8	Toolus	1	5
9	Horowdé	1	17
10	Mulgaum	3	33
11	Newjé	1	10
12	Naroor	1	9
	Banda Division.		
13	Saturdé	2	13
14	Podlos	1	13
15	Insoolee	1	11
16	Azgaum	2	30
17	Teerowdé	1	2
18	Aronda	1	9
19	Banda	2	15
20	Kusnee	1	10
	Koodal Division.		
21	Koodal	1	25
22	Walawul	1	10
23	Pawus	1	20
24	Anow	1	20
25	Neroor	3	27
26	Hoomur Mula	1	15
27	Pingoolee	1	15
28	Chendwun	1	20
29	Pot	2	22
30	Kuwutee	1	10
31	Ambrud.	1	15
32	Bordawé	1	5
33	Pokhrun	1	10
34	Waree	4	108
	Total	47	589

8

No.	Names of Villages.	Number of Schools in each Village.	Number of Students.
	GOVERNMENT SCHOOLS.		
1	Waree	1	175
2	Banda	1	53
	Total..	2	228
	Grand Total..	49	817

BRIEF NOTES

RELATIVE TO

THE SAWUNT WAREE STATE.

BY

MAJOR J. W. AULD,

POLITICAL SUPERINTENDENT AT SAWUNT WAREE.

Submitted to Government on the 1*st July* 1854.

EDITED BY R. HUGHES THOMAS, ASSISTANT SECRETARY, POLITICAL DEPARTMENT.

Brief Notes by Major J. W. Auld, *Political Superintendent at Sawunt Waree, containing information on the following points connected with that State*:—

I. Name, title, and age of chief.
II. Usual place of residence.
III. Names and ages of legitimate male issue, and of the principal persons of the Court.
IV. Whether tributary or not; if so, to whom, and annual amount of tribute.
V. Estimated gross annual revenue.
VI. Boundaries of territory, and estimated area in square miles.
VII. Prevailing nature of the soil, usual means of irrigation, and general features of the country.
VIII. Natural and industrial resources.
IX. Routes, approaches, and means of communication by land and water.
X. Climate, and average range of thermometer.
XI. Average annual fall of rain.
XII. Estimated population.
XIII. Religion, language, tribes, and castes.
XIV. Brief notice of the mode in which civil and criminal justice are administered.
XV. Nature of punishments awarded for criminal offences.
XVI. Educational measures.
XVII. Progress of vaccination.
XVIII. Prevalent diseases.

SAWUNT WAREE.

Name, Title, and Age of Chief.

I. Khem Sawunt Bhonslay Rajey Bahadoor, Sir Desaee of the province of Koodal and its dependencies, aged fifty years.

Usual Place of Residence.

II. The fort of Soondur Waree, or Sawunt Waree.

III. The following are the four legitimate sons of the Sir Desaee :—

Names and Ages of legitimate Male Issue, and of the principal persons of the Court.

1, Phond Sawunt *alias* Anna Saheb, aged twenty-six years.

2, Ramchundru Sawunt *alias* Bhow Saheb, aged fifteen years.

3, Som Sawunt *alias* Aba Saheb, aged twelve years.

4, Naroba Desaee *alias* Bawa Saheb, aged six years.

The principal persons of the Court are—

1, Venkut Rao Aba Saheb Patunkur.
2, Jan Rao Dhar Rao Nimbalkur.
3, Buheerjee Rao Appa Saheb Patunkur.
4, Man Dhaté Soorvé.
5, Soobrao Nimbalkur.
6, Jotyajee Rao Patunkur.
7, Dowlut Dulvee Bhonslay.
8, Atmaram Sheoram Chitnis.
9, Gunesh Roodru Chitnis.
10, Antajee Gopal Subnis.
11, Luxoomon Dhondeo Lelé.
12, Sid Sawunt Bhonslay.
13, Jeewun Rao, Desaee of Purma.
14, Sooban Rao Bajee Ghatgay.
15, Kasee Rao Sirké.
16, Khundé Rao Mohité.
17, Narayen Rao Khanvilkur.
18, Kool Sawunt Bhonslay.
19, Jeewajee Atmaram Pagnees.
20, Balkrishna Ramchundru Rangnekur.
21, Shamjee Ramchundru Furnis.
22, Narayen Mahadajee Potnis.
23, Dhondoo Sumbhoo Sir Soobhedar.
24, Esso Babno Soobhedar.
25, Sukharam } Soobhedars of Danda.
26, Sudoba }

Whether Tributary or not; if so, to whom, and Annual Amount of Tribute.

IV. Not tributary to any power; but the country is at present under the superintendence of the British Government.

Estimated gross Annual Revenue.

V. The average annual gross revenues of the Waree State may be reckoned at a little more than Rs. 2,00,000.

Boundaries of Territory, and estimated Area in Square Miles.

VI. The Sawunt Waree territory is bounded on the North by the Karlee river, and the Salsee Mahal of the Malwan Talooka of the Rutnageeree Zilla; on the East by the line of Ghauts; on the South by the Tirakole creek and the Portuguese possessions; and on the West by the Vingorla Mahal of the Rutnageeree Collectorate. It contains an estimated area of about 900 square miles.

Prevailing Nature of the Soil, usual Means of Irrigation, and General Features of the Country.

VII. The nature of the soil is principally a light sand, full of stones and gravel, incapable of yielding the superior kinds of produce, such as cotton, tobacco, gram, wheat, Jowaree, and Bajree.

The means of irrigation in the Sawunt Waree territory are the rains for the monsoon crops. During the dry season, the land is irrigated by means of water raised from the Nulas, wells, and tanks, and thus rendered capable of yielding a dry season crop. The water from the Nulas is conducted into and through the fields and gardens by means of narrow water-courses. The water of the wells and tanks is generally drawn by a Lat, which is a long beam or spar supported by a perpendicular forked post, with a bucket attached to one end by means of a long bamboo, and a weight at the other sufficient to raise the bucket when full of water. These Lats are worked by a single man, and the water thus drawn emptied into a water-course at the mouth of the well, and conducted to all parts of the fields.

This principality presents the same general features as are to be found in the greater part of the Southern Konkun. The jungles are dense, and the hills are generally very steep and inaccessible, particularly as they approach the Ghauts, and abound with many wild beasts of prey. The temperature in the winter months, though not cold, is pleasant and agreeable. The heat during the months of April and May is excessive, and in the monsoon months the rain is very heavy.

Natural and Industrial Resources.

VIII. The natural resources of this small State are very limited indeed. It possesses few if any advantages of position; it is cut off from the sea coast, and the only two navigable rivers, or rather creeks, scarcely deserving notice, are the Karlee and Tirakole, of which mention will be subsequently made. Markets there are none, nor can Waree boast of any marts of consequence in its neighbourhood. The only mineral product is iron ore, which is found in each of the three divisions of the State, though not in any very great abundance: it is worked in a few villages of the Waree, Banda, and Koodal divisions, and the iron is pronounced to be of good, if not of superior quality. The country yields a little salt, but it is of a most inferior kind. The muddy nature of the soil where it is produced imparts to it a colour that gives it the appearance of very dirty-looking earth, and it is difficult for a person who may not before have seen the salt to recognize it as such when exposed in the bazar for sale; and yet, with all its impurity, it is very generally used by the Natives of the State.

The teak forests are of no great extent, and the trees as yet of but moderate size; they are, however, progressing towards perfection, and every care and attention is paid to the protection of the young trees. The fisheries, though small, might be turned to some account, if there were markets to receive the supply that might be furnished.

The natural products are rice; the inferior grains, such as Nachnee, Wuree, Hurik, Til, Moong, &c. are cultivated in the high lands and amongst the hills in considerable quantities. Cocoanuts and Sooparee are produced, but excepting in these two last mentioned products, the country does not yield sufficient for its own consumption, and grain of all kinds is annually imported from the Deccan in large quantities.

With regard to industrial resources, the chief, and indeed only manufactures are gold and silver embroidery work on saddle-cloths, and horse-appointments, and scabbards of swords, Native guns, swords, daggers, spear-heads, &c.; Punkhas, painted toys, sealing-wax, and fire-works; but it exports scarcely any of these, and consequently they are, generally speaking, only manufactured in small quantities sufficient to meet the local demand.

Routes, Approaches, and Means of Communication by Land and Water.

IX. The principal roads throughout this State are from Belgaum down the Ram Ghaut to the port of Vingorla; from the Deccan by the Tulkut Ghaut to Banda and the Goa territory; down the Parpolee Ghaut to Waree and Vingorla, with a branch-road through Bowlut and Banda into the Portuguese possessions; down the Hunmunt Ghaut by Naroor, Waroos, and Mangaum to Vingorla and Páth; down the Rangna Ghaut by Naroor, Hateree, and Anow to Malwan, with a branch-road through Toolsoolee and Pingoolee to Vingorla; and by the Ghotgha Ghaut through this State to the port of Malwan.

There are also numerous cross-roads leading into the Goa territory on one side, and the Company's on the other, and various small passes in the line of Ghauts from the upper to the lower country.

The chief means of communication by land are two lines of road, one from Malwan to Waree, and the other from Belgaum to Vingorla, the latter meeting the Waree line at Banda.

The only water communication is by the Tirakole creek on the south, inland as far as Banda, where, however, small boats only can be used at any distance from the mouth of the creek, and on the north by the Karlee creek as far as Sonowra, near Koodal.

Climate, and average Range of Thermometer.

X. Sawunt Waree is situated in lat. 15° 56′ N., long. 74° E., altitude 355 feet. The general aspect of the country is hilly, and covered with dense jungle. The climate partakes somewhat of that of Malwan or Vingorla proper, but is modified by being more elevated above the sea, and in a higher latitude. Taking the year throughout, it may be a little cooler. The cold season begins about the middle of November, and the sudden transition from the moist warm month of October to the cold dry air of November is very disagreeable. There are violent northwesters from February to the middle of May, the wind strong, and blowing in gusts. There are generally a few showers of rain in April, and sometimes in May, accompanied with thunder and lightning, which invariably come from about north-east, and they are preceded by mists and fogs, coming from the same direction. The regular hot months are March, April, and May. The hot dry winds prevail occasionally in March from 1 to 3 P. M., which are unpleasant, and even hurtful to those whose constitutions are not acclimated. The sky is generally overcast during this season with clouds. The rainy season commences early in June, and ends about the middle of October. The average range of thermometer is, of the maximum 79°44, and minimum 75°89.

Average Annual Fall of Rain.

XI. The annual fall of rain is very unequal—it may be considered to range from 110 to 150 inches. The average annual fall during three years has been registered at 134.45, the greatest monthly fall at 65.8, and the extreme daily fall at 7.67.

Estimated Population.

XII. The estimated population of the Waree State, according to the census for the year 1852, is as follows :—

Males	78,398
Females..	73,808
Total.. ..	152,206

Religion, Language, Tribes, and Castes.

XIII. The predominant religions in the Waree State are Hindoo, Mahomedan, and Christian : the followers of the last-mentioned are Roman Catholic. The languages in use are generally the Murathee and Urdu. The latter is spoken by the Mahomedan population. The original language used throughout the State by Hindoos, excepting the higher classes, is impure Murathee, and was termed Koodalee, from its being peculiar to the district of that name, and to the southern Talooka of the Rutnageeree Collectorate; but this dialect is now gradually being superseded by a purer Murathee. Most of the Native Christians speak a mixture of Murathee and Portuguese, neither language very perfectly spoken, but nevertheless such as is in general use among the people of a great part of the Goa territory.

The Hindoos of the Waree State may be divided into the following classes :—

The Bramins; the Murathas, with the Sir Desaee at their head; the Wanees, and the Shoodras. The first of these act chiefly as priests and Karkoons, scarcely any of them following any other occupation; the second are soldiers, servants of the State, and cultivators of the soil; the third are engaged in trade; and the last form the labouring class. These, again, may be subdivided into numerous and various sects.

The Mahomedan population chiefly consists of four sects, viz. Shaik, Syud, Puthan, and Mogul, in all numbering about 3,000. The Native Christians number about 2,000 souls.

Brief Notice of the Mode in which Civil and Criminal Justice are administered.

XIV. As respects civil justice, there is but one court of first resort, under an officer styled the Nayadhish. All suits are first brought before the Political Superintendent in the shape of petitions, which are referred to the Nayadhish for investigation. In doing this, this officer follows a similar process of summoning the defendants, witnesses, &c. to that prescribed in the Regulations—in short, the procedure of the Honorable Company's Courts. This being done, and the case being ready for hearing, the Nayadhish has then to hear the pleadings of the parties if themselves in attendance, or their Vukeels or accredited agents, after which he passes his decision. His decree is binding, whatever the amount, unless appealed against within thirty days from the date thereof. The Political Superintendent himself sits as a court of appeal, and he receives, if necessary, any further proofs the parties may have to produce, and passes his decision, from which a further appeal only lies to Government, the time for the presentation of this appeal being ninety days from the date of the decision. The limits of appeal from the Political Superintendent's decision to Government are respectively above Rs. 500 and 1000, according as he may reverse or confirm the decree of the lower court. A fee is levied according to the following scale, as sanctioned by Government on the 14th February 1843, from the losing party :—

If the sum sued for, or decreed, as the case may be, do not exceed one rupee, the amount of the fee is four annas.

If it be above	but do not exceed	the amount of the fee is		
Rs. 1	Rs. 2	0	8	0
2	5	1	0	0
5	10	2	0	0
10	20	3	8	0
20	40	5	0	0
40	65	7	0	0
65	100	10	0	0
100	200	15	0	0
200	500	22	0	0
500	1,000	30	0	0
1,000	2,000	50	0	0
2,000	5,000	100	0	0
5,000	10,000	200	0	0
10,000	20,000	350	0	0
20,000	50,000	500	0	0
50,000	1,00,000	800	0	0
1,00,000 to whatever amount..	..	.. 1,200	0	0

When the fee is payable by plaintiff it is levied in proportion to the amount claimed, and when by the defendant to the amount decreed. On suits withdrawn during process, half the amount of the fixed fee is levied; and on suits struck off the file, from one-half to two-thirds of the stated amount.

As to criminal justice, the State is divided into three Kumavisdarees, and each Kumavisdar has magisterial powers of simple imprisonment up to twenty days, and of fine up to Rs. 15. The Kotwal of the town of Waree has like powers within its limits. All cases requiring more serious treatment are referred, together with the documents of the case, to the Political Superintendent. There is only one criminal court, namely the Superintendent's, but as he is vested with the powers of a Session Judge, he may up to that limit sit by himself, or, if more serious cases are to be disposed of, he selects, from amongst the officers of the State and Sirdars, three assessors, whose opinions he records. A sentence is then passed by the Political Superintendent, which is submitted for the confirmation of Government, pending the receipt of which the prisoner is kept in custody.

Nature of Punishments awarded for Criminal Offences.

XV. All punishments laid down in the Criminal Code are awarded, as the nature of the crimes demand.

Educational Measures.

XVI. There are two Government vernacular schools, one at the town of Waree, and the other at Banda. The former is paid by the Waree State, and the latter partly by the Waree Government, and partly by the inhabitants of that village. Besides this, there are 47 indigenous schools throughout the villages, the expenses of which are defrayed by the inhabitants of those villages, but they are not regularly kept up, as their existence depends on the circumstances and pleasure of the inhabitants.

Progress of Vaccination.

XVII. Vaccination is progressing favourably in the Waree districts. It was established here in the year 1844, and for nearly two years the Natives appeared sceptical as to the benefits to be derived; but this doubt has entirely been removed since the numerous proofs they have observed in its favour, and now they have great confidence in the operation as a preventive against that disease. During the past eight years and six months 37,743 persons have been vaccinated, and of these 34,802 have been successful, and 2,941 unsuccessful.

Prevalent Diseases.

XVIII. The diseases that have been most prevalent in this country for the last fourteen years have been fevers of the intermitting and remitting types, acute dysentery, affections of the stomach, lungs, pleura, bowels, and urinary organs, and rheumatism. The latter disease prevails pretty extensively at all seasons of the year, the most acute from November to April, but the most frequent in the cold weather of December and January, during which period swellings of the large joints and acute pyrexia are frequent. In the latter, pains about the shoulders, elbows, wrists, knees, and ankles, with more or less loss of power, are the symptoms chiefly complained of.

CENSUS

OF THE

SAWUNT WAREE STATE,

For the Year 1851.

PREPARED BY MR. H. L. ANDERSON, POLITICAL SUPERINTENDENT.

Castes.	Names of Villages.	No. of Houses.	Males according to Age. Birth to 10 Years.	11 to 20 Years.	21 to 30 Years.	31 to 40 Years.	41 to 50 Years.	51 to 60 Years.	61 to 70 Years.	71 to 80 Years.	81 to 90 Years.	91 to 100 Years and upwards.
	1	2	3	4	5	6	7	8	9	10	11	12
	Turuf Mangaum.											
Bramins	1. Mangaum.	35	43	20	14	13	18	11	..	..	..	..
Hindoos of other castes		566	590	349	295	222	175	121	26	2	..	..
Musulmans		10	14	6	3	..	3	5	..	..	..	..
Native Christians		9	11	1	6	6	2	..	..	..	..	..
Seedees		..	..	..	..	..	..	..	..	..	..	..
		620	658	376	318	241	198	137	26	2	..	..
Bramins	2. Kolgaum.	17	12	16	9	7	6	9	1	1	..	..
Hindoos of other castes		354	245	238	232	131	107	47	20	5	..	..
Musulmans		120	97	79	71	49	39	12	3	1	1	..
Native Christians		7	3	5	3	1	..	1	..	..	..	..
Seedees		..	..	..	..	..	..	..	..	..	..	..
		498	357	338	315	188	152	69	24	7	1	..
Bramins	3. Akeree.	19	18	10	14	11	9	5	3	1	2	..
Hindoos of other castes		376	295	238	194	158	104	31	9	4	3	..
Musulmans		..	..	..	..	..	..	..	..	..	..	..
Native Christians		5	4	1	2	1	..	..	..	..	..	..
Seedees		..	..	..	..	..	..	..	..	..	..	..
		400	317	249	210	170	113	36	12	5	5	..
Bramins	4. Koonkeree.	..	..	..	..	..	..	..	..	..	..	..
Hindoos of other castes		180	206	132	105	71	37	26	26	3	..	..
Musulmans		3	2	1	1	1	1	..	1	..	..	..
Native Christians		..	..	..	..	..	..	..	..	..	..	..
Seedees		..	..	..	..	..	..	..	..	..	..	..
		183	208	133	106	72	38	26	27	3	..	..
Bramins	5. Majgaum.	33	21	22	20	9	9	5	1	2	1	1
Hindoos of other castes		224	230	167	134	80	41	27	10	10	7	7
Musulmans		29	23	27	20	9	8	4	1	..	..	..
Native Christians		9	6	4	3	3	1	..	..	..	..	..
Seedees		4	..	1	1	2	1	..	..	..	..	..
		299	280	221	178	103	63	36	12	12	8	8

Division for the Year 1851.

Females according to Age.												
Birth to 10 Years.	11 to 20 Years.	21 to 30 Years.	31 to 40 Years.	41 to 50 Years.	51 to 60 Years.	61 to 70 Years.	71 to 80 Years.	81 to 90 Years.	91 to 100 Years and upwards.	Total of each Caste. *	Grand Total.	Remarks.
13	14	15	16	17	18	19	20	21	22	23	24	
28	33	14	17	15	7	4	1	..	..	238		
575	294	240	213	215	187	69	18	2	..	3,593		
13	2	2	5	6	2	2	1	..	..	64		
10	5	4	4	1	2	..	..	..	..	52		
..	..	..	..	..	..	..	..	..	..	..		
626	334	260	239	237	198	76	20	2	..	3,947	3,947	
6	11	13	12	3	6	6	1	..	..	119		
223	209	211	166	123	71	27	5	3	..	2,063		
67	44	83	50	27	15	2	..	..	..	640		
4	6	3	1	3	1	..	..	..	..	31		
..	..	..	..	..	..	..	..	..	..	..		
300	270	310	229	156	93	35	6	3	..	2,853	2,853	
18	11	18	12	6	6	2	1	..	..	147		
273	169	211	155	102	37	35	12	4	3	2,037		
..	..	..	..	..	..	..	..	..	..	..		
4	1	1	1	..	2	2	..	1	..	20		
..	..	..	..	..	..	..	..	..	..	..		
295	181	230	168	108	45	39	13	5	3	2,204	2,204	
..	..	..	..	..	..	..	..	..	..	..		
226	149	84	49	59	38	25	12	3	2	1,253		
2	3	1	2	..	..	..	1	..	..	16		
..	..	..	..	..	..	..	..	..	..	..		
..	..	..	..	..	..	..	..	..	..	..		
228	152	85	51	59	38	25	13	3	2	1,269	1,269	
19	19	21	14	9	4	..	2	3	2	184		
117	136	120	82	68	32	9	8	7	7	1,302		
11	16	13	8	8	2	..	..	..	..	150		
4	5	6	2	1	1	..	..	..	..	36		
1	1	3	..	..	..	..	..	..	..	10		
152	177	163	106	86	39	9	10	10	9	1,682	1,682	

CASTES.	Names of Villages.	No. of Houses.	MALES according to Age.									
			Birth to 10 Years.	11 to 20 Years.	21 to 30 Years.	31 to 40 Years.	41 to 50 Years.	51 to 60 Years.	61 to 70 Years.	71 to 80 Years.	81 to 90 Years.	91 to 100 Years and upwards.
	1	2	3	4	5	6	7	8	9	10	11	12
	Turuf MANGAUM.											
Bramins	6. JHARAP.	31	33	16	11	9	5	6	1	1	..	1
Hindoos of other castes		77	80	30	38	30	21	12	2	2	..	..
Musulmans		47	50	20	11	21	11	5	4	..	..	..
Native Christians		..	..	..	..	..	..	..	..	..	..	..
Seedees		..	..	..	..	..	..	..	..	..	..	..
		155	163	66	60	60	37	23	7	3	..	1
Bramins	7. NANELEE.	3	5	2	2	1	..	..	..	..	..	..
Hindoos of other castes		110	106	53	58	25	25	10	1	..	..	..
Musulmans		11	2	8	3	4	3	..	3	..	..	..
Native Christians		1	..	..	..	..	..	..	..	..	..	..
Seedees		..	..	..	..	..	..	..	..	..	..	..
		125	113	63	63	30	28	10	4	..	..	..
Bramins	8. BAMURDE.	27	26	12	16	10	4	6	2	..	..	..
Hindoos of other castes		117	122	63	53	40	30	15	2	3	..	..
Musulmans		..	..	..	..	..	..	..	..	..	..	..
Native Christians		..	..	..	..	..	..	..	..	..	..	..
Seedees		..	..	..	..	..	..	..	..	..	..	..
		144	148	75	69	50	34	21	4	3	..	..
Bramins	9. SALGAUM.	41	50	16	21	15	9	9	4	1	..	..
Hindoos of other castes		271	309	162	148	113	27	58	12	8	1	..
Musulmans		..	..	..	..	..	..	..	..	..	..	..
Native Christians		..	..	..	..	..	..	..	..	..	..	..
Seedees		..	..	..	..	..	..	..	..	..	..	..
		312	359	178	169	128	36	67	16	9	1	..
Bramins	10. CHURATE.	3	3	1	1	3	2	1	..	..	..	..
Hindoos of other castes		53	42	39	37	19	11	3	1	2	4	4
Musulmans		..	..	..	..	..	..	..	..	..	..	..
Native Christians		23	31	12	16	9	12	4	..	1	1	1
Seedees		..	..	..	..	..	..	..	..	..	..	..
		79	76	52	54	31	25	8	1	3	5	5

Females according to Age.												
Birth to 10 Years.	11 to 20 Years.	21 to 30 Years.	31 to 40 Years.	41 to 50 Years.	51 to 60 Years.	61 to 70 Years.	71 to 80 Years.	81 to 90 Years.	91 to 100 Years and upwards.	Total of each Caste.	Grand Total.	Remarks.
13	14	15	16	17	18	19	20	21	22	23	24	
32	12	9	7	15	3	3	..	1	..	165		
72	32	40	30	22	19	5	2	..	..	437		
48	25	15	18	12	7	1	2	..	..	250		
..	..	..	..	..	..	..	..	..	..	..		
..	..	..	..	..	..	..	..	..	..	..		
152	69	64	55	49	29	9	4	1	..	852	852	
3	1	2	..	2	..	..	..	..	..	18		
101	39	50	26	29	14	2	1	..	..	540		
8	4	3	3	4	1	1	..	..	..	47		
..	2	..	..	..	..	1	..	..	..	3		
..	..	..	..	..	..	..	..	..	..	..		
112	46	55	29	35	15	4	1	..	..	608	608	
25	8	10	12	5	4	2	..	..	..	142		
123	60	56	46	27	18	18	2	..	..	678		
..	..	..	..	..	..	..	..	..	..	..		
..	..	..	..	..	..	..	..	..	..	..		
..	..	..	..	..	..	..	..	..	..	..		
148	68	66	58	32	22	20	2	..	..	820	820	
41	13	20	14	11	7	7	4	1	..	243		
292	162	147	86	51	52	34	9	4	..	1,675		
..	..	..	..	..	..	..	..	..	..	..		
..	..	..	..	..	..	..	..	..	..	..		
..	..	..	..	..	..	..	..	..	..	..		
333	175	167	100	62	59	41	13	5	..	1,918	1,918	
2	2	1	2	3	..	..	..	..	..	21		
43	33	33	30	18	9	1	2	4	4	339		
..	..	..	..	..	..	..	..	..	..	..		
21	23	14	11	3	1	1	1	1	1	164		
..	..	..	..	..	..	..	..	..	..	..		
66	58	48	43	24	10	2	3	5	5	524	524	

11

Castes.	Names of Villages.	No. of Houses.	Males according to Age. Birth to 10 Years.	11 to 20 Years.	21 to 30 Years.	31 to 40 Years.	41 to 50 Years.	51 to 60 Years.	61 to 70 Years.	71 to 80 Years.	81 to 90 Years.	91 to 100 Years and upwards.
	1	2	3	4	5	6	7	8	9	10	11	12
	Turuf Mangaum.											
Bramins	11. Otowne.	21	19	15	12	6	9	2	..	..	..	..
Hindoos of other castes		150	97	75	69	46	31	21	3	2	1	..
Musulmans		..	..	..	..	..	..	..	..	..	..	..
Native Christians		2	1	..	1	1	..	..	..	..	..	..
Seedees		..	..	..	..	..	..	..	..	..	..	..
		173	117	90	82	53	40	23	3	2	1	..
Bramins	12. Ghaonule.	11	8	5	6	3	4	4	1	1	..	..
Hindoos of other castes		274	255	197	136	103	79	58	23	3	..	..
Musulmans		..	..	..	..	..	..	..	..	..	..	..
Native Christians		2	1	..	1	1	..	..	..	..	..	..
Seedees		..	..	..	..	..	..	..	..	..	..	..
		287	264	202	143	107	83	62	24	4	..	..
Bramins	13. Karewde.	5	5	6	3	..	..	4	..	..	..	..
Hindoos of other castes		80	90	57	48	26	26	17	5	4	..	..
Musulmans		..	..	..	..	..	..	..	..	..	..	..
Native Christians		..	..	..	..	..	..	..	..	..	..	..
Seedees		..	..	..	..	..	..	..	..	..	..	..
		85	95	63	51	26	26	21	5	4	..	..
Bramins	14. Mandkoolee.	21	27	12	7	13	8	9	4	..	..	..
Hindoos of other castes		64	57	41	25	25	18	10	5	..	..	..
Musulmans		..	..	..	..	..	..	..	..	..	..	..
Native Christians		..	..	..	..	..	..	..	..	..	..	..
Seedees		..	..	..	..	..	..	..	..	..	..	..
		85	84	53	32	38	26	19	9	..	..	..
Bramins	15. Toolsoolee.	16	13	7	8	9	9	4	6	1	1	..
Hindoos of other castes		155	99	82	53	70	50	34	21	8	2	..
Musulmans		..	..	..	..	..	..	..	..	..	..	..
Native Christians		..	..	..	..	..	..	..	..	..	..	..
Seedees		..	..	..	..	..	..	..	..	..	..	..
		171	112	89	61	79	59	38	27	9	3	..

Females according to Age.												
Birth to 10 Years.	11 to 20 Years.	21 to 30 Years.	31 to 40 Years.	41 to 50 Years.	51 to 60 Years.	61 to 70 Years.	71 to 80 Years.	81 to 90 Years.	91 to 100 Years and upwards.	Total of each Caste.	Grand Total.	Remarks.
13	14	15	16	17	18	19	20	21	22	23	24	
11	11	11	6	2	5	..	..	..	1	110		
95	74	53	50	46	26	9	1	..	..	699		
..	..	..	..	..	..	..	..	..	..	..		
..	1	..	2	..	..	..	..	..	..	6		
..	..	..	..	..	..	..	..	..	..	..		
106	86	64	58	48	31	9	1	..	1	815	815	
4	4	10	3	2	1	1	2	..	..	59		
185	165	140	113	68	85	34	9	1	..	1,654		
..	..	..	..	..	..	..	..	..	..	..		
..	1	..	..	1	1	..	..	..	..	6		
..	..	..	..	..	..	..	..	..	..	..		
189	170	150	116	71	87	35	11	1	..	1,719	1,719	
2	4	..	2	2	2	..	..	..	..	30		
90	57	44	34	21	16	8	8	..	..	551		
..	..	..	..	..	..	..	..	..	..	..		
..	..	..	..	..	..	..	..	..	..	..		
..	..	..	..	..	..	..	..	..	..	..		
92	61	44	36	23	18	8	8	..	..	581	581	
22	5	9	16	7	6	3	3	..	..	151		
57	29	29	21	23	12	8	2	..	..	362		
..	..	..	..	..	..	..	..	..	..	..		
..	..	..	..	..	..	..	..	..	..	..		
..	..	..	..	..	..	..	..	..	..	..		
79	34	38	37	30	18	11	5	..	..	513	513	
14	9	11	5	7	5	3	1	2	1	116		
112	91	59	60	40	34	18	2	3	1	839		
..	..	..	..	..	..	..	..	..	..	..		
..	..	..	..	..	..	..	..	..	..	..		
..	..	..	..	..	..	..	..	..	..	..		
126	100	70	65	47	39	21	3	5	2	955	955	

Castes.	Names of Villages.	No. of Houses.	Males according to Age.									
			Birth to 10 Years.	11 to 20 Years.	21 to 30 Years.	31 to 40 Years.	41 to 50 Years.	51 to 60 Years.	61 to 70 Years.	71 to 80 Years.	81 to 90 Years.	91 to 100 Years and upwards.
	1	2	3	4	5	6	7	8	9	10	11	12
	Turuf Tulowre.											
Bramins	16. Tulowre.	18	11	9	6	11	4	4	1	..	..	..
Hindoos of other castes		291	226	149	118	156	129	57	33	9	5	2
Musulmans		..	..	..	..	..	..	..	..	..	..	..
Native Christians		2	..	..	1	1	..	..	..	..	..	..
Seedees		..	..	..	..	..	..	..	..	..	..	..
		311	237	158	125	168	133	61	34	9	5	2
Bramins	17. Wazrat.	2	..	..	1	..	..	..	..	..	..	..
Hindoos of other castes		77	53	44	39	44	16	10	4	4	1	1
Musulmans		..	..	..	..	..	..	..	..	..	..	..
Native Christians		..	..	..	..	..	..	..	..	..	..	..
Seedees		..	..	..	..	..	..	..	..	..	..	..
		79	53	44	40	44	16	10	4	4	1	1
Bramins	18. Mulgaum.	37	44	27	28	14	8	3	1	1	..	..
Hindoos of other castes		208	230	127	110	84	59	31	16	2	..	..
Musulmans		..	..	..	..	..	..	..	..	..	..	..
Native Christians		2	4	3	3	1	1	..	1	..	..	..
Seedees		..	..	..	..	..	..	..	..	..	..	..
		247	278	157	141	99	68	34	18	3	..	..
Bramins	19. Toolus.	28	21	17	7	16	9	7	2	3	1	..
Hindoos of other castes		322	228	164	121	165	121	69	23	13	3	3
Musulmans		..	..	..	..	..	..	..	..	..	..	..
Native Christians		2	2	1	1	2	1	..	..	..	..	..
Seedees		..	..	..	..	..	..	..	..	..	..	..
		352	251	182	129	183	131	76	25	16	4	3
Bramins	20. Horowde.	14	10	7	4	6	4	4	3	..	..	..
Hindoos of other castes		193	95	77	70	73	66	47	32	16	5	2
Musulmans		..	..	..	..	..	..	..	..	..	..	..
Native Christians		3	2	4	2	1	3	..	1	1	1	..
Seedees		..	..	..	..	..	..	..	..	..	..	..
		210	107	88	76	80	73	51	36	17	6	2

Females according to Age.										Total of each Caste	Grand Total.	Remarks.
Birth to 10 Years.	11 to 20 Years.	21 to 30 Years.	31 to 40 Years.	41 to 50 Years.	51 to 60 Years.	61 to 70 Years.	71 to 80 Years.	81 to 90 Years.	91 to 100 Years and upwards.			
13	14	15	16	17	18	19	20	21	22	23	24	
13	12	3	10	5	3	..	..	..	..	92		
230	128	87	135	123	58	29	14	3	5	1,696		
..	..	..	..	..	..	..	..	..	..	..		
2	2	..	1	1	..	..	..	..	..	8		
..	..	..	..	..	..	..	..	..	..	..		
245	142	90	146	129	61	29	14	3	5	1,796	1,796	
..	..	1	..	..	..	..	..	..	..	2		
59	40	39	38	26	8	4	1	1	..	432		
..	..	..	..	..	..	..	..	..	..	..		
..	..	..	..	..	..	..	..	..	..	..		
..	..	..	..	..	..	..	..	..	..	..		
59	40	40	38	26	8	4	1	1	..	434	434	
31	24	19	14	12	13	3	3	..	..	245		
185	92	130	93	55	27	12	7	..	..	1,260		
..	..	..	..	..	..	..	..	..	..	..		
2	1	3	..	..	1	..	..	..	..	20		
..	..	..	..	..	..	..	..	..	..	..		
218	117	152	107	67	41	15	10	..	..	1,525	1,525	
..	26	11	10	16	11	5	2	..	2	160		
188	162	94	145	117	67	21	12	3	2	1,721		
..	..	..	..	..	..	..	..	..	..	..		
2	1	1	1	..	..	..	..	..	..	12		
..	..	..	..	..	..	..	..	..	..	..		
190	189	106	156	127	78	26	14	3	4	1,893	1,893	
10	9	..	6	5	5	1	1	..	..	75		
106	90	63	67	64	57	25	14	8	2	979		
..	..	..	..	..	..	..	..	..	..	..		
3	3	1	1	1	1	1	1	1	..	28		
..	..	..	..	..	..	..	..	..	..	..		
119	102	64	74	70	63	27	16	9	2	1,082	1,082	

12

Castes.	Names of Villages.	No. of Houses.	Males according to Age. Birth to 10 Years.	11 to 20 Years.	21 to 30 Years.	31 to 40 Years.	41 to 50 Years.	51 to 60 Years.	61 to 70 Years.	71 to 80 Years.	81 to 90 Years.	91 to 100 Years and upwards.
	1	2	3	4	5	6	7	8	9	10	11	12
	Turuf Mangaum.											
Bramins	21. Nimle.	6	5	3	3	2	2	2	1	..	..	..
Hindoos of other castes		162	113	80	73	67	62	35	34	13	12	6
Musulmans		3	..	..	..	1	1	..	1	..	..	..
Native Christians		..	..	..	..	..	..	..	..	..	..	..
Seedees		.	..	..	..	..	..	..	..	..	..	..
		171	118	83	76	70	65	37	36	13	12	6
Bramins	22. Nerowdee.	4	3	2	2	..	2	1	1	..	1	..
Hindoos of other castes		120	53	60	42	46	44	35	27	14	7	3
Musulmans		..	..	..	..	..	..	..	..	..	..	..
Native Christians		..	..	..	..	..	..	..	..	..	..	..
Seedees		..	..	..	..	..	..	..	..	..	..	..
		124	56	62	44	46	46	36	28	14	8	3
Bramins	23. Muth.	8	5	4	4	2	3	3		1	1	1
Hindoos of other castes		143	100	64	52	57	55	45	28	20	11	5
Musulmans		..	..	..	..	..	..	..	..	..	..	..
Native Christians		..	..	..	..	..	..	..	..	..	..	..
Seedees		..	..	..	..	..	..	..	..	..	..	..
		151	105	68	56	59	58	48	28	21	12	6
Bramins	24. Adelee.	14	8	8	3	7	5	3	3	1	..	..
Hindoos of other castes		135	81	77	50	60	42	45	30	8	5	4
Musulmans		..	..	..	..	..	..	..	..	..	..	..
Native Christians		..	..	..	..	..	..	..	..	..	..	..
Seedees		..	..	..	..	..	..	..	..	..	..	..
		149	89	85	53	67	47	48	33	9	5	4
Bramins	25. Nhawelee.	5	2	4	3	3	3	5	..	2	..	..
Hindoos of other castes		63	49	19	20	23	24	18	5	1	2	..
Musulmans		..	..	..	..	..	..	..	..	..	..	..
Native Christians		..	..	..	..	..	..	..	..	..	..	..
Seedees		..	..	..	..	..	..	..	..	..	..	..
		68	51	23	23	26	27	23	5	3	2	..

Females according to Age.												
Birth to 10 Years.	11 to 20 Years.	21 to 30 Years.	31 to 40 Years.	41 to 50 Years.	51 to 60 Years.	61 to 70 Years.	71 to 80 Years.	81 to 90 Years.	91 to 100 Years and upwards.	Total of each Caste.	Grand Total.	Remarks.
13	14	15	16	17	18	19	20	21	22	23	24	
4	4	1	3	4	2	1	1	1	..	39		
119	101	51	72	56	46	41	14	9	4	1,008		
1	1	1	..	2	1	1	..	..	..	10		
..	..	..	..	..	..	..	..	..	..	..		
..	..	..	..	..	..	..	..	..	..	..		
124	106	53	75	62	49	43	15	10	4	1,057	1,057	
4	..	2	2	..	2	2	..	..	..	24		
48	49	40	44	31	36	19	9	7	2	616		
..	..	..	..	..	..	..	..	..	..	..		
..	..	..	..	..	..	..	..	..	..	..		
..	..	..	..	..	..	..	..	..	..	..		
52	49	42	46	31	38	21	9	7	2	640	640	
3	5	2	3	1	3	1	1	..	..	43		
97	91	48	61	40	38	26	14	5	4	861		
..	..	..	..	..	..	..	..	..	..	..		
..	..	..	..	..	..	..	..	..	..	..		
..	..	..	..	..	..	..	..	..	..	..		
100	96	50	64	41	41	27	15	5	4	904	904	
7	7	3	5	3	3	..	..	..	..	66		
83	79	43	53	41	33	23	6	6	2	771		
..	..	..	..	..	..	..	..	..	..	..		
..	..	..	..	..	..	..	..	..	..	..		
..	..	..	..	..	..	..	..	..	..	..		
90	86	46	58	44	36	23	6	6	2	837	837	
3	3	1	3	2	2	1		..	..	37		
38	20	20	20	22	11	11	3	3	2	311		
..	..	..	..	..	..	..	..	..	..	..		
..	..	..	..	..	..	..	..	..	..	..		
..	..	..	..	..	..	..	..	..	..	..		
41	23	21	23	24	13	12	3	3	2	348	348	

Castes.	Names of Villages.	No. of Houses.	Males according to Age. Birth to 10 Years.	11 to 20 Years.	21 to 30 Years.	31 to 40 Years.	41 to 50 Years.	51 to 60 Years.	61 to 70 Years.	71 to 80 Years.	81 to 90 Years.	91 to 100 Years and upwards.
	1	2	3	4	5	6	7	8	9	10	11	12
	Turuf MANGAUM.											
Bramins	26. WETORE.	35	22	21	24	9	11	5	..	1	..	..
Hindoos of other castes		109	116	57	78	47	11	5	1	..	..	..
Musulmans		..	..	..	..	..	..	..	..	..	..	..
Native Christians		..	..	..	..	..	..	..	..	..	..	..
Seedees		..	..	..	..	..	..	..	..	..	..	..
		144	138	78	102	56	22	10	1	1	..	..
Bramins	27. MATOND.	21	19	10	10	11	10	6	6	1	2	..
Hindoos of other castes		266	189	121	112	128	123	82	27	14	5	3
Musulmans		..	..	..	..	..	..	..	..	..	..	..
Native Christians		1	..	1	..	..	1	..	..	..	..	..
Seedees		..	..	..	..	..	..	..	..	..	..	..
		288	208	132	122	139	134	88	33	15	7	3
	Kureat NAROOR.											
Bramins	28. NAROOR.	11	15	5	7	3	2	..	..	..	..	..
Hindoos of other castes		204	206	133	103	79	40	24	6	4	3	..
Musulmans		..	..	..	..	..	..	..	..	..	..	..
Native Christians		1	2	3	..	2	..	..	..	..	..	..
Seedees		..	..	..	..	..	..	..	..	..	..	..
		216	223	141	110	84	42	24	6	4	3	..
Bramins	29. WAROOS.	..	..	..	..	..	..	..	..	..	..	..
Hindoos of other castes		60	54	58	31	23	5	4	1	1	2	2
Musulmans		..	..	..	..	..	..	..	..	..	..	..
Native Christians		2	1	2	2	..	..	..	..	..	..	..
Seedees		..	..	..	..	..	..	..	..	..	..	..
		62	55	60	33	23	5	4	1	1	2	2
Bramins	30. GOTUS.	13	18	12	1	7	8	3	1	..	..	..
Hindoos of other castes		248	194	155	104	87	84	49	21	8	4	4
Musulmans		..	..	..	..	..	..	..	..	..	..	..
Native Christians		1	..	..	1	..	..	1	..	..	..	..
Seedees		..	..	..	..	..	..	..	..	..	..	..
		262	212	167	106	94	92	53	22	8	4	4

FEMALES according to Age.										Total of each Caste.	Grand Total.	REMARKS.
Birth to 10 Years.	11 to 20 Years.	21 to 30 Years.	31 to 40 Years.	41 to 50 Years.	51 to 60 Years.	61 to 70 Years.	71 to 80 Years.	81 to 90 Years.	91 to 100 Years and upwards.			
13	14	15	16	17	18	19	20	21	22	23	24	
16	24	20	11	15	10	..	..	..	..	189		
99	61	61	44	24	16	6	1	1	..	628		
..	..	..	..	..	..	..	..	..	..	..		
..	..	..	..	..	..	..	..	..	..	..		
..	..	..	..	..	..	..	..	..	..	..		
115	85	81	55	39	26	6	1	1	..	817	817	
19	6	8	10	8	5	1	..	..	..	132		
183	128	78	123	115	81	27	13	7	2	1,561		
..	..	..	..	..	..	..	..	..	..	..		
..	1	..	..	1	..	..	..	..	..	4		
..	..	..	..	..	..	..	..	..	..	..		
202	135	86	133	124	86	28	13	7	2	1,697	1,697	
8	10	3	6	5	..	1	..	..	..	65		
195	116	113	71	42	15	9	4	2	..	1,165		
..	..	..	..	..	..	..	..	..	..	..		
2	2	1	..	..	..	..	..	..	..	12		
..	..	..	..	..	..	..	..	..	..	..		
205	128	117	77	47	15	10	4	2	..	1,242	1,242	
..	..	..	..	..	..	..	..	..	..	..		
58	37	29	24	8	8	3	2	2	2	354		
..	..	..	..	..	..	..	..	..	..	..		
3	2	..	1	..	..	..	..	..	..	11		
..	..	..	..	..	..	..	..	..	..	..		
61	39	29	25	8	8	3	2	2	2	365	365	
14	4	5	5	10	6	3	1	..	..	98		
209	126	113	90	83	50	23	15	8	4	1,431		
..	..	..	..	..	..	..	..	..	..	..		
1	..	..	..	1	..	..	..	..	..	4		
..	..	..	..	..	..	..	..	..	..	..		
224	130	118	95	94	56	26	16	8	4	1,533	1,533	

13

Castes.	Names of Villages.	No. of Houses.	Males according to Age. Birth to 10 Years.	11 to 20 Years.	21 to 30 Years.	31 to 40 Years.	41 to 50 Years.	51 to 60 Years.	61 to 70 Years.	71 to 80 Years.	81 to 90 Years.	91 to 100 Years and upwards.
	1	2	3	4	5	6	7	8	9	10	11	12
	Kureat Naroor.											
Bramins	31. Amberee.	..	..	..	..	..	..	..	..	..	..	..
Hindoos of other castes		60	60	27	28	17	12	11	4	2	2	1
Musulmans		..	..	..	..	..	..	..	..	..	..	..
Native Christians......		..	..	..	..	..	..	..	..	..	..	..
Seedees................		..	..	..	..	..	..	..	..	..	..	..
		60	60	27	28	17	12	11	4	2	2	1
Bramins	32. Chaphelee.	1	2	..	..	..	..	1	..	..	..	..
Hindoos of other castes		62	36	27	39	29	26	12	7	3	..	..
Musulmans		..	..	..	..	..	..	..	..	..	..	..
Native Christians......		1	1	1	1	..	..	..	..	..	..	..
Seedees................		..	..	..	..	..	..	..	..	..	..	..
		64	39	28	40	29	26	13	7	3	..	..
Bramins	33. Kerewde.	1	..	..	..	..	1	..	..	..	..	..
Hindoos of other castes		125	85	84	62	44	30	22	16	2	..	..
Musulmans		..	..	..	..	..	..	..	..	..	..	..
Native Christians......		3	2	3	1	2	1	..	..	..	..	..
Seedees................		..	..	..	..	..	..	..	..	..	..	..
		129	87	87	63	46	32	22	16	2	..	..
Bramins	34. Neelelee.	1	..	..	..	..	1	..	..	..	..	..
Hindoos of other castes		64	78	49	39	25	11	12	1	3	2	1
Musulmans		..	..	..	..	..	..	..	..	..	..	..
Native Christians......		1	..	1	..	..	..	..	..	..	..	..
Seedees................		..	..	..	..	..	..	..	..	..	..	..
		66	78	50	39	25	12	12	1	3	2	1
Bramins	35. Toolsoolee.	..	..	..	..	..	..	..	..	..	..	..
Hindoos of other castes		130	114	74	59	36	32	20	13	4	1	..
Musulmans		..	..	..	..	..	..	..	..	..	..	..
Native Christians......		2	2	..	..	1	..	..	..	..	..	..
Seedees................		..	..	..	..	..	..	..	..	..	..	..
		132	116	74	59	37	32	20	13	4	1	..

Females according to Age.										Total of each Caste.	Grand Total.	Remarks.
Birth to 10 Years.	11 to 20 Years.	21 to 30 Years.	31 to 40 Years.	41 to 50 Years.	51 to 60 Years.	61 to 70 Years.	71 to 80 Years.	81 to 90 Years.	91 to 100 Years and upwards.			
13	14	15	16	17	18	19	20	21	22	23	24	
..	..	..	..	..	..	..	..	..	..	..		
51	30	26	29	8	6	2	3	3	1	323		
..	..	..	..	..	..	..	..	..	..	..		
..	..	..	..	..	..	..	..	..	..	..		
..	..	..	..	..	..	..	..	..	..	..		
51	30	26	29	8	6	2	3	3	1	323	323	
..	..	2	..	..	..	..	..	..	..	5		
27	34	24	23	26	14	4	..	..	..	331		
..	..	..	..	..	..	..	..	..	..	..		
..	1	1	..	..	..	..	..	..	..	5		
..	..	..	..	..	..	..	..	..	..	..		
27	35	27	23	26	14	4	..	..	..	341	341	
..	..	1	..	..	..	..	1	..	..	3		
73	55	42	34	46	26	7	4	..	..	632		
..	..	..	..	..	..	..	..	..	..	..		
3	1	..	2	2	1	..	..	..	..	18		
..	..	..	..	..	..	..	..	..	..	..		
76	56	43	36	48	27	7	5	..	..	653	653	
..	..	..	1	..	..	..	..	..	..	2		
30	28	26	21	12	1	..	..	1	2	342		
..	..	..	..	..	..	..	..	..	..	..		
..	..	1	..	..	..	..	..	..	..	2		
..	..	..	..	..	..	..	..	..	..	..		
30	28	27	22	12	1	..	..	1	2	346	346	
..	..	..	..	..	..	..	..	..	..	..		
121	33	90	43	22	20	24	2	..	..	708		
..	..	..	..	..	..	..	..	..	..	..		
4	1	2	..	..	1	..	..	..	..	11		
..	..	..	..	..	..	..	..	..	..	..		
125	34	92	43	22	21	24	2	..	..	710	719	

Castes.	Names of Villages.	No. of Houses.	Males according to Age. Birth to 10 Years.	11 to 20 Years.	21 to 30 Years.	31 to 40 Years.	41 to 50 Years.	51 to 60 Years.	61 to 70 Years.	71 to 80 Years.	81 to 90 Years.	91 to 100 Years and upwards.
	1	2	3	4	5	6	7	8	9	10	11	12
	Kureat Naroor.											
Bramins	36. Newje.	4	2	5	2	..	1	1	..	..	..	..
Hindoos of other castes		131	143	86	82	53	23	15	16	..	2	..
Musulmans		..	..	..	..	..	..	..	..	..	..	..
Native Christians		..	..	..	..	..	..	..	..	..	..	..
Seedees		..	..	..	..	..	..	..	..	..	..	..
		135	145	91	84	53	24	16	16	..	2	..
Bramins	37. Wasolee.	..	..	..	..	..	..	..	..	..	..	..
Hindoos of other castes		26	17	10	13	11	5	3	1	..	..	..
Musulmans		..	..	..	..	..	..	..	..	..	..	..
Native Christians		..	..	..	..	..	..	..	..	..	..	..
Seedees		..	..	..	..	..	..	..	..	..	..	..
		26	17	10	13	11	5	3	1	..	..	..
Bramins	38. Neroor.	5	3	2	5	1	1	2	1	..	..	..
Hindoos of other castes		267	174	151	123	117	61	26	14	4	2	1
Musulmans		..	..	..	..	..	..	..	..	..	..	..
Native Christians		2	..	1	..	..	..	2	..	..	..	..
Seedees		..	..	..	..	..	..	..	..	..	..	..
		274	177	154	128	118	62	30	15	4	2	1
	Turuf Munohur.											
Bramins	39. Kalelee.	14	13	3	13	8	4	4	..	1	..	..
Hindoos of other castes		168	187	101	88	67	23	29	7	1	..	..
Musulmans		2	2	..	1	1	..	1	..	..	..	..
Native Christians		2	1	..	..	1	1	..	..	..	..	..
Seedees		..	..	..	..	..	..	..	..	..	..	..
		186	203	104	102	77	28	34	7	2	..	..
Bramins	40. Sangelee.	7	6	..	4	2	3	1	2	1	..	..
Hindoos of other castes		230	219	140	116	114	97	48	34	18	10	4
Musulmans		..	..	..	..	..	..	..	..	..	..	..
Native Christians		..	..	..	..	..	..	..	..	..	..	..
Seedees		..	..	..	..	..	..	..	..	..	..	..
		237	225	140	120	116	100	49	36	19	10	4

Females according to Age.										Total of each Caste.	Grand Total.	Remarks.
Birth to 10 Years.	11 to 20 Years.	21 to 30 Years.	31 to 40 Years.	41 to 50 Years.	51 to 60 Years.	61 to 70 Years.	71 to 80 Years.	81 to 90 Years.	91 to 100 Years and upwards.			
13	14	15	16	17	18	19	20	21	22	23	24	
5	2	2	1	1	..	2	..	..	..	24		
138	68	85	29	32	37	15	2	2	..	828		
..	..	..	..	..	..	..	..	..	..	..		
..	..	..	..	..	..	..	..	..	..	..		
..	..	..	..	..	..	..	..	..	..	..		
143	70	87	30	33	37	17	2	2	..	852	852	
..	..	..	..	..	..	..	..	..	..	..		
13	8	10	6	3	6	..	..	..	..	106		
..	..	..	..	..	..	..	..	..	..	..		
..	..	..	..	..	..	..	..	..	..	..		
..	..	..	..	..	..	..	..	..	..	..		
13	8	10	6	3	6	..	..	..	..	106	106	
2	3	3	1	4	..	..	..	..	..	28		
170	143	110	75	54	30	7	8	3	2	1,275		
..	..	..	..	..	..	..	..	..	..	..		
2	1	..	..	..	1	..	..	..	..	7		
..	..	..	..	..	..	..	..	..	..	..		
174	147	113	76	58	31	7	8	3	2	1,310	1,310	
18	6	9	2	5	1	5	1	..	..	93		
205	89	98	53	48	44	7	2	..	..	1,049		
3	..	1	..	1	..	..	..	..	..	10		
4	1	2	..	..	..	..	..	..	..	10		
..	..	..	..	..	..	..	..	..	..	..		
230	96	110	55	54	45	12	3	..	..	1,162	1,162	
2	3	2	3	3	2	..	..	..	..	34		
201	141	64	112	95	70	30	21	9	7	1,550		
..	..	..	..	..	..	..	..	..	..	..		
..	..	..	..	..	..	..	..	..	..	..		
..	..	..	..	..	..	..	..	..	..	..		
203	144	66	115	98	72	30	21	9	7	1,584	1,584	

14

Castes.	Names of Villages.	No. of Houses.	Males according to Age. Birth to 10 Years.	11 to 20 Years.	21 to 30 Years.	31 to 40 Years.	41 to 50 Years.	51 to 60 Years.	61 to 70 Years.	71 to 80 Years.	81 to 90 Years.	91 to 100 Years and upwards.
	1	2	3	4	5	6	7	8	9	10	11	12
	Turuf Munohur.											
Bramins	41. Kesree.	1	2	..	..	1	..	..	..	..	..	..
Hindoos of other castes		49	43	13	17	16	18	8	5	3	..	1
Musulmans		..	..	..	..	..	..	..	..	..	..	..
Native Christians		..	..	..	..	..	..	..	..	..	..	..
Seedees		..	..	..	..	..	..	..	..	..	..	..
		50	45	13	17	17	18	8	5	3	..	1
Bramins	42. Parpolee.	..	..	..	..	..	..	..	..	..	..	..
Hindoos of other castes		29	6	15	7	14	11	6	5	2	..	..
Musulmans		..	..	..	..	..	..	..	..	..	..	..
Native Christians		..	..	..	..	..	..	..	..	..	..	..
Seedees		..	..	..	..	..	..	..	..	..	..	..
		29	6	15	7	14	11	6	5	2	..	..
Bramins	43. Sursinge.	..	..	..	..	..	..	..	..	..	..	..
Hindoos of other castes		87	61	29	28	31	34	24	14	5	3	1
Musulmans		..	..	..	..	..	..	..	..	..	..	..
Native Christians		..	..	..	..	..	..	..	..	..	..	..
Seedees		..	..	..	..	..	..	..	..	..	..	..
		87	61	29	28	31	34	24	14	5	3	1
Bramins	44. Kandoolee.	..	..	..	..	..	..	..	..	..	..	..
Hindoos of other castes		60	51	33	28	27	21	17	7	3	2	..
Musulmans		..	..	..	..	..	..	..	..	..	..	..
Native Christians		..	..	..	..	..	..	..	..	..	..	..
Seedees		..	..	..	..	..	..	..	..	..	..	..
		60	51	33	28	27	21	17	7	3	2	..
Bramins	45. Ambergaum.	..	..	..	..	..	..	..	..	..	..	..
Hindoos of other castes		178	113	84	71	79	65	44	25	14	8	6
Musulmans		..	..	..	..	..	..	..	..	..	..	..
Native Christians		1	..	1	..	1	..	1	..	..	..	..
Seedees		..	..	..	..	..	..	..	..	..	..	..
		179	113	85	71	80	65	45	25	14	8	6

Females according to Age.												
Birth to 10 Years.	11 to 20 Years.	21 to 30 Years.	31 to 40 Years.	41 to 50 Years.	51 to 60 Years.	61 to 70 Years.	71 to 80 Years.	81 to 90 Years.	91 to 100 Years and upwards.	Total of each Caste.	Grand Total.	Remarks.
13	14	15	16	17	18	19	20	21	22	23	24	
..	..	1	..	1	..	..	..	..	..	5		
35	13	17	15	14	14	11	5	2	1	251		
..	..	..	..	..	..	..	..	..	..	..		
..	..	..	..	..	..	..	..	..	..	..		
..	..	..	..	..	..	..	..	..	..	..		
35	13	18	15	15	14	11	5	2	1	256	256	
..	..	..	..	..	..	..	..	..	..	..		
12	7	11	14	12	8	6	2	1	..	139		
..	..	..	..	..	..	..	..	..	..	..		
..	..	..	..	..	..	..	..	..	..	..		
..	..	..	..	..	..	..	..	..	..	..		
12	7	11	14	12	8	6	2	1	..	139	139	
..	..	..	..	..	..	..	..	..	..	..		
53	34	19	25	29	27	5	9	1	..	432		
..	..	..	..	..	..	..	..	..	..	..		
..	..	..	..	..	..	..	..	..	..	..		
..	..	..	..	..	..	..	..	..	..	..		
53	34	19	25	29	27	5	9	1	..	432	432	
..	..	..	..	..	..	..	..	..	..	..		
48	35	23	28	21	14	6	6	3	2	375		
..	..	..	..	..	..	..	..	..	..	..		
..	..	..	..	..	..	..	..	..	..	..		
..	..	..	..	..	..	..	..	..	..	..		
48	35	23	28	21	14	6	6	3	2	375	375	
..	..	..	..	..	..	..	..	..	..	..		
128	90	63	67	65	49	24	16	9	5	1,025		
..	..	..	..	..	..	..	..	..	..	..		
2	1	..	1	..	1	..	..	..	..	8		
..	..	..	..	..	..	..	..	..	..	..		
130	91	63	68	65	50	24	16	9	5	1,033	1,033	

Castes.	Names of Villages.	No. of Houses.	Males according to Age. Birth to 10 Years.	11 to 20 Years.	21 to 30 Years.	31 to 40 Years.	41 to 50 Years.	51 to 60 Years.	61 to 70 Years.	71 to 80 Years.	81 to 90 Years.	91 to 100 Years and upwards.
	1	2	3	4	5	6	7	8	9	10	11	12
	Turuf Munohur.											
Bramins	46. Werle.	..	..	..	..	..	..	..	..	..	..	..
Hindoos of other castes		99	77	50	35	34	15	12	4	..	..	1
Musulmans		..	..	..	..	..	..	..	..	..	..	..
Native Christians......		2	2	3	..	..	2	..	..	..	..	..
Seedees................		..	..	..	..	..	..	..	..	..	..	..
		101	79	53	35	34	17	12	4	..	..	1
Bramins	47. Poolas.	1	1	1	..	..	3	..	..	..	..	..
Hindoos of other castes		150	102	76	59	66	58	41	18	12	5	7
Musulmans		..	..	..	..	..	..	..	..	..	..	..
Native Christians......		2	..	2	..	2	..	..	..	..	..	..
Seedees................		..	..	..	..	..	..	..	..	..	..	..
		153	103	79	59	68	61	41	18	12	5	7
Bramins	48. Kulumbeest.	..	..	..	..	..	..	..	..	..	..	..
Hindoos of other castes		123	72	55	49	53	41	41	24	11	3	3
Musulmans		..	..	..	..	..	..	..	..	..	..	..
Native Christians.....		1	1	1	2	1	..	..	..	..	..	..
Seedees................		..	..	..	..	..	..	..	..	..	..	..
		124	73	56	51	54	41	41	24	11	3	3
Bramins	49. Satoolee.	..	..	..	..	..	..	..	..	..	..	..
Hindoos of other castes		11	5	9	5	6	3	1	2	1	1	2
Musulmans		..	..	..	..	..	..	..	..	..	..	..
Native Christians......		..	..	..	..	..	..	..	..	..	..	..
Seedees................		..	..	..	..	..	..	..	..	..	..	..
		11	5	9	5	6	3	1	2	1	1	2
Bramins	50. Bowlat.	..	..	..	..	..	..	..	..	..	..	..
Hindoos of other castes		12	4	6	5	6	7	5	1	..	..	..
Musulmans		..	..	..	..	..	..	..	..	..	..	..
Native Christians......		..	..	..	..	..	..	..	..	..	..	..
Seedees................		..	..	..	..	..	..	..	..	..	..	..
		12	4	6	5	6	7	5	1	..	..	..

Females according to Age.										Total of each Caste.	Grand Total.	Remarks.
Birth to 10 Years.	11 to 20 Years.	21 to 30 Years.	31 to 40 Years.	41 to 50 Years.	51 to 60 Years.	61 to 70 Years.	71 to 80 Years.	81 to 90 Years.	91 to 100 Years and upwards.			
13	14	15	16	17	18	19	20	21	22	23	24	
..	..	..	..	..	..	..	..	..	..	..		
77	46	37	29	26	14	8	3	..	..	468		
..	..	..	..	..	..	..	..	..	..	..		
6	1	1	1	1	..	..	..	..	..	17		
..	..	..	..	..	..	..	..	..	..	..		
83	47	38	30	27	14	8	3	..	..	485	485	
..	..	..	1	..	..	..	..	..	..	6		
108	70	51	59	46	33	9	11	1	2	834		
..	..	..	..	..	..	..	..	..	..	..		
..	1	..	..	1	1	..	..	..	..	7		
..	..	..	..	..	..	..	..	..	..	..		
108	71	51	60	47	34	9	11	1	2	847	847	
..	..	..	..	..	..	..	..	..	..	..		
73	42	52	47	41	37	17	13	4	2	680		
..	..	..	..	..	..	..	..	..	..	..		
..	..	1	..	..	1	..	..	..	..	7		
..	..	..	..	..	..	..	..	..	..	..		
73	42	53	47	41	38	17	13	4	2	687	687	
..	..	..	..	..	..	..	..	..	..	..		
6	3	5	3	3	4	1	1	1	..	62		
..	..	..	..	..	..	..	..	..	..	..		
..	..	..	..	..	..	..	..	..	..	..		
..	..	..	..	..	..	..	..	..	..	..		
6	3	5	3	3	4	1	1	1	..	62	62	
..	..	..	..	..	..	..	..	..	..	..		
3	5	5	5	4	7	3	1	..	..	67		
..	..	..	..	..	..	..	..	..	..	..		
..	..	..	..	..	..	..	..	..	..	..		
..	..	..	..	..	..	..	..	..	..	..		
3	5	5	5	4	7	3	1	..	..	67	67	

15

Castes.	Names of Villages.	No. of Houses.	Males according to Age.									
			Birth to 10 Years.	11 to 20 Years.	21 to 30 Years.	31 to 40 Years.	41 to 50 Years.	51 to 60 Years.	61 to 70 Years.	71 to 80 Years.	81 to 90 Years.	91 to 100 Years and upwards.
	1	2	3	4	5	6	7	8	9	10	11	12
	Turuf MUNOHUR.											
Bramins	51. DEOSOO.	..	..	..	..	..	..	..	..	..	..	..
Hindoos of other castes		39	11	23	17	22	15	9	2	..	..	..
Musulmans		..	..	..	..	..	..	..	..	..	..	..
Native Christians......		..	..	..	..	..	..	..	..	..	..	..
Seedees................		..	..	..	..	..	..	..	..	..	..	..
		39	11	23	17	22	15	9	2	..	..	..
Bramins	52. OOPOWRE.	..	..	..	..	..	..	..	..	..	..	..
Hindoos of other castes		69	47	11	24	25	27	17	5	4	..	..
Musulmans		..	..	..	..	..	..	..	..	..	..	..
Native Christians......		1	..	..	..	1	..	..	..	..	..	..
Seedees................		..	..	..	..	..	..	..	..	..	..	..
		70	47	11	24	26	27	17	5	4	..	..
Bramins	53. DANOLEE.	..	..	..	..	..	..	..	..	..	..	..
Hindoos of other castes		16	6	8	7	6	5	3	1	1	1	1
Musulmans		..	..	..	..	..	..	..	..	..	..	..
Native Christians......		..	..	..	..	..	..	..	..	..	..	..
Seedees................		..	..	..	..	..	..	..	..	..	..	..
		16	6	8	7	6	5	3	1	1	1	1
Bramins	54. MORE.	..	..	..	..	..	..	..	..	..	..	..
Hindoos of other castes		70	82	33	39	32	26	14	11	3	2	..
Musulmans		..	..	..	..	..	..	..	..	..	..	..
Native Christians......		1	2	..	1	..	1	..	..	..	..	..
Seedees................		..	..	..	..	..	..	..	..	..	..	..
		71	84	33	40	32	27	14	11	3	2	..
Bramins	55. MANDKHOLE.	2	1	..	1	1	..	1	..	..	..	..
Hindoos of other castes		144	91	45	55	54	48	27	20	11	5	3
Musulmans		..	..	..	..	..	..	..	..	..	..	..
Native Christians......		..	..	..	..	..	..	..	..	..	..	..
Seedees................		..	..	..	..	..	..	..	..	..	..	..
		146	92	45	56	55	48	28	20	11	5	3

Females according to Age.										Total of each Caste.	Grand Total.	Remarks.
Birth to 10 Years.	11 to 20 Years.	21 to 30 Years.	31 to 40 Years.	41 to 50 Years.	51 to 60 Years.	61 to 70 Years.	71 to 80 Years.	81 to 90 Years.	91 to 100 Years and upwards.			
13	14	15	16	17	18	19	20	21	22	23	24	
..	..	..	..	..	..	..	..	..	..	..		
11	19	17	13	14	8	3	1	..	..	185		
..	..	..	..	..	..	..	..	..	..	..		
..	..	..	..	..	..	..	..	..	..	..		
..	..	..	..	..	..	..	..	..	..	..		
11	19	17	13	14	8	3	1	..	..	185	185	
..	..	..	..	..	..	..	..	..	..	..		
45	16	25	27	18	11	5	..	..	1	308		
..	..	..	..	..	..	..	..	..	..	..		
..	1	..	..	1	..	..	..	..	..	3		
..	..	..	..	..	..	..	..	..	..	..		
45	17	25	27	19	11	5	..	..	1	311	311	
..	..	..	..	..	..	..	..	..	..	..		
8	8	5	4	5	5	2	4	..	1	81		
..	..	..	..	..	..	..	..	..	..	..		
..	..	..	..	..	..	..	..	..	..	..		
..	..	..	..	..	..	..	..	..	..	..		
8	8	5	4	5	5	2	4	..	1	81	81	
..	..	..	..	..	..	..	..	..	..	..		
69	36	38	27	23	11	7	3	1	..	457		
2	..	1	..	..	..	..	..	..	..	7		
..	..	..	..	..	..	..	..	..	..	..		
71	36	39	27	23	11	7	3	1	..	464	464	
1	..	..	1	..	..	..	..	..	..	6		
86	47	65	53	45	25	11	10	7	4	712		
..	..	..	..	..	..	..	..	..	..	..		
..	..	..	..	..	..	..	..	..	..	..		
..	..	..	..	..	..	..	..	..	..	..		
87	47	65	54	45	25	11	10	7	4	718	718	

Castes.	Names of Villages.	No. of Houses.	Males according to Age.									
			Birth to 10 Years.	11 to 20 Years.	21 to 30 Years.	31 to 40 Years.	41 to 50 Years.	51 to 60 Years.	61 to 70 Years.	71 to 80 Years.	81 to 90 Years.	91 to 100 Years and upwards.
	1	2	3	4	5	6	7	8	9	10	11	12
	Turuf Munohur.											
Bramins	56. Kerewde.	2	4	2	2	..	2	..	..	..	..	..
Hindoos of other castes		139	89	58	49	57	43	45	25	17	7	2
Musulmans		..	..	..	..	..	..	..	..	..	..	..
Native Christians		1	2	..	1	..	1	2	1	1	..	..
Seedees		..	..	..	..	..	..	..	..	..	..	..
		142	95	60	52	57	46	47	26	18	7	2
Bramins	57. Wowleeye.	..	..	..	..	..	..	..	..	..	..	..
Hindoos of other castes		33	12	24	11	17	7	6	1	2	..	..
Musulmans		..	..	..	..	..	..	..	..	..	..	..
Native Christians		..	..	..	..	..	..	..	..	..	..	..
Seedees		..	..	..	..	..	..	..	..	..	..	..
		33	12	24	11	17	7	6	1	2	..	..
Bramins	58. Ambolee.	..	..	..	..	..	..	..	..	..	..	..
Hindoos of other castes		123	67	69	47	66	42	25	15	13	4	3
Musulmans		..	..	..	..	..	..	..	..	..	..	..
Native Christians		1	..	..	1	1	1	..	..	..	..	..
Seedees		..	..	..	..	..	..	..	..	..	..	..
		124	67	69	48	67	43	25	15	13	4	3
Bramins	......	538	500	302	274	213	179	131	45	20	9	3
Hindoos of other castes	......	8,346	6,862	4,698	3,950	3,422	2,472	1,589	752	322	143	83
Musulmans	......	225	190	141	110	86	66	27	13	1	1	..
Native Christians	......	93	81	50	49	39	28	11	3	3	2	1
Seedees	......	4	..	1	1	2	1	..	..	..	..	..
	Grand Total Waree Division....	9,206	7,633	5,192	4,384	3,762	2,746	1,758	813	346	155	87

Sawunt Waree, Political Superintendent's Office, Camp Belgaum, 30th October 1852.

Females according to Age.										Total of each Caste.	Grand Total.	Remarks.
Birth to 10 Years.	11 to 20 Years.	21 to 30 Years.	31 to 40 Years.	41 to 50 Years.	51 to 60 Years.	61 to 70 Years.	71 to 80 Years.	81 to 90 Years.	91 to 100 Years and upwards.			
13	14	15	16	17	18	19	20	21	22	23	24	
3	1	2	1	1	..	1	..	..	..	19		* Grand Total .. .. 52,658 { Males .. .. 26,876; Females 25,782
96	48	60	56	47	32	29	13	7	2	782		
..	..	..	..	..	..	..	..	..	..	..		
2	1	..	1	..	1	..	..	..	..	13		
..	..	..	..	..	..	..	..	..	..	..		
101	50	62	58	48	33	30	13	7	2	814	814	
..	..	..	..	..	..	..	..	..	..	..		
13	15	9	14	9	11	5	2	1	..	159		
..	..	..	..	..	..	..	..	..	..	..		
..	..	..	..	..	..	..	..	..	..	..		
..	..	..	..	..	..	..	..	..	..	..		
13	15	9	14	9	11	5	2	1	..	159	159	
..	..	..	..	..	..	..	..	..	..	..		
80	54	58	52	53	29	19	5	6	3	710		
..	..	..	..	..	..	..	..	..	..	..		
..	..	1	2	1	..	..	..	..	..	7		
..	..	..	..	..	..	..	..	..	..	..		
80	54	59	54	54	29	19	5	6	3	717	717	
390	292	250	221	184	124	58	26	8	6	3,235		
6,461	4,236	3,661	3,204	2,580	1,794	848	369	158	83	47,687		
153	95	119	86	60	28	7	4	..	..	1,187		
83	66	44	32	19	17	5	2	3	1	539		
1	1	3	..	..	..	..	..	..	..	10		
7,088	4,690	4,077	3,543	2,843	1,963	918	401	169	90	52,658	*52,658	

(Signed) H. L. ANDERSON,
Political Superintendent.

Castes.	Names of Villages.	No. of Houses.	Males according to Age. Birth to 10 Years.	11 to 20 Years.	21 to 30 Years.	31 to 40 Years.	41 to 50 Years.	51 to 60 Years.	61 to 70 Years.	71 to 80 Years.	81 to 90 Years.	91 to 100 Years and upwards.
	1	2	3	4	5	6	7	8	9	10	11	12
Bramins	1. Banda.	27	23	24	15	11	9	6	..	..	1	..
Hindoos of other castes		239	186	93	116	88	67	40	18	14	1	..
Musulmans		43	42	25	15	23	10	6	5	..	..	..
Native Christians.....		1	2	..	1	1	2	..	..	..	..	..
Seedees................		3	1	2	2	1	..	..	..	..	..	..
		313	254	144	149	124	88	52	23	14	2	..
Bramins	2. Dabheel.	..	..	..	..	..	..	..	..	..	..	..
Hindoos of other castes		6	4	..	4	1	2	1	..	..	..	..
Musulmans		..	..	..	..	..	..	..	..	..	..	..
Native Christians.....		..	..	..	..	..	..	..	..	..	..	..
Seedees.................		..	..	..	..	..	..	..	..	..	..	..
		6	4	..	4	1	2	1	..	..	..	..
Bramins	3. Asneeye.	10	2	4	6	4	1	3	2	..	..	..
Hindoos of other castes		48	30	13	9	10	12	21	7	4	3	..
Musulmans		..	..	..	..	..	..	..	..	..	..	..
Native Christians		..	..	..	..	..	..	..	..	..	..	..
Seedees............ ..		..	..	..	..	..	..	..	..	..	..	..
		58	32	17	15	14	13	24	9	4	3	..
Bramins	4. Bhalawul.	..	..	..	..	..	..	..	..	..	..	..
Hindoos of other castes		22	19	5	15	11	1	4	..	..	..	..
Musulmans		..	..	..	..	..	..	..	..	..	..	..
Native Christians.....		1	1	..	1	..	..	..	..	..	..	..
Seedees................		..	..	..	..	..	..	..	..	..	..	..
		23	20	5	16	11	1	4	..	..	..	..
Bramins	5. Dingne.	1	1	1	1	..	1	..	..	..	..	..
Hindoos of other castes		46	48	19	12	24	13	8	1	..	..	..
Musulmans		2	..	1	2	2	..	..	..	..	..	..
Native Christians......		2	1	..	2	..	..	..	..	..	..	..
Seedees................		..	..	..	..	..	..	..	..	..	..	..
		51	50	21	17	26	14	8	1	..	..	..

Division, for the Year 1851.

Females according to Age.										Total of each Caste.	Grand Total.	Remarks.
Birth to 10 Years.	11 to 20 Years.	21 to 30 Years.	31 to 40 Years.	41 to 50 Years.	51 to 60 Years.	61 to 70 Years.	71 to 80 Years.	81 to 90 Years.	91 to 100 Years and upwards.			
13	14	15	16	17	18	19	20	21	22	23	24	
22	14	23	7	4	4	2	..	..	..	165		
176	63	110	84	63	54	27	34	5	..	1,239		
28	5	16	21	10	6	7	9	..	..	228		
2	..	2	..	..	2	..	..	1	..	13		
3	..	2	1	..	..	..	..	..	1	13		
231	82	153	113	77	66	36	43	6	1	1,658	1,658	
..	..	..	..	..	..	..	..	..	..	..		
3	..	2	2	1	2	..	..	..	..	22		
..	..	..	..	..	..	..	..	..	..	..		
..	..	..	..	..	..	..	..	..	..	..		
..	..	..	..	..	..	..	..	..	..	..		
3	..	2	2	1	2	..	..	..	..	22	22	
6	1	3	1	2	2	3	1	..	..	41		
22	12	16	11	19	15	10	4	1	..	219		
..	..	..	..	..	..	..	..	..	..	..		
..	..	..	..	..	..	..	..	..	..	..		
..	..	..	..	..	..	..	..	..	..	..		
28	13	19	12	21	17	13	5	1	..	260	260	
..	..	..	..	..	..	..	..	..	..	..		
13	12	6	6	1	8	1	..	..	..	102		
..	..	..	..	..	..	..	..	..	..	..		
2	..	1	..	..	..	..	..	..	..	5		
..	..	..	..	..	..	..	..	..	..	..		
15	12	7	6	1	8	1	..	..	..	107	107	
1	1	..	1	2	..	..	..	..	..	9		
41	25	28	14	8	6	..	..	..	..	247		
..	2	..	..	1	..	..	..	..	..	8		
2	..	2	..	..	..	..	..	..	..	7		
..	..	..	..	..	..	..	..	..	..	..		
44	28	30	15	11	6	..	..	..	..	271	271	

Castes.	Names of Villages.	No. of Houses.	Males according to Age. Birth to 10 Years.	11 to 20 Years.	21 to 30 Years.	31 to 40 Years.	41 to 50 Years.	51 to 60 Years.	61 to 70 Years.	71 to 80 Years.	81 to 90 Years.	91 to 100 Years and upwards.
	1	2	3	4	5	6	7	8	9	10	11	12
Bramins	6. Wapholee.	2	1	5	..	1	1	1	..	..	..	..
Hindoos of other castes		102	86	65	40	23	24	16	5	..	..	..
Musulmans		7	6	3	5	3	1	3	..	..	..	..
Native Christians		..	..	..	..	..	..	..	..	..	..	..
Seedees		..	..	..	..	..	..	..	..	..	..	..
		111	93	73	45	27	26	20	5	..	..	..
Bramins	7. Koombhowre.	..	..	..	..	..	..	..	..	..	..	..
Hindoos of other castes		23	9	10	14	3	3	3	..	..	..	..
Musulmans		..	..	..	..	..	..	..	..	..	..	..
Native Christians		..	..	..	..	..	..	..	..	..	..	..
Seedees		..	..	..	..	..	..	..	..	..	..	..
		23	9	10	14	3	3	3	..	..	..	..
Bramins	8. Phondeeye.	1	1	1	..	..	..	..	..	..	..	..
Hindoos of other castes		9	12	2	2	4	2	1	..	..	..	..
Musulmans		..	..	..	..	..	..	..	..	..	..	..
Native Christians		1	1	1	..	..	..	..	..	..	..	..
Seedees		..	..	..	..	..	..	..	..	..	..	..
		11	14	4	2	4	2	1	..	..	..	..
Bramins	9. Dongurpal.	..	..	..	..	..	..	..	..	..	..	..
Hindoos of other castes		15	17	12	5	4	6	1	..	..	..	..
Musulmans		..	..	..	..	..	..	..	..	..	..	..
Native Christians		..	..	..	..	..	..	..	..	..	..	..
Seedees		..	..	..	..	..	..	..	..	..	..	..
		15	17	12	5	4	6	1	..	..	..	..
Bramins	10. Tulkut.	3	1	2	1	2	1	..	..	..	..	..
Hindoos of other castes		35	29	11	10	18	2	1	1	..	..	..
Musulmans		..	..	..	..	..	..	..	..	..	..	..
Native Christians		..	..	..	..	..	..	..	..	..	..	..
Seedees		..	..	..	..	..	..	..	..	..	..	..
		38	30	13	11	20	3	1	1	..	..	..

Females according to Age.										Total of each Caste.	Grand Total.	Remarks.
Birth to 10 Years.	11 to 20 Years.	21 to 30 Years.	31 to 40 Years.	41 to 50 Years.	51 to 60 Years.	61 to 70 Years.	71 to 80 Years.	81 to 90 Years.	91 to 100 Years and upwards.			
13	14	15	16	17	18	19	20	21	22	23	24	
1	2	2	..	1	1	1	..	..	..	17		
83	49	47	35	39	10	7	2	..	..	531		
10	5	4	3	2	..	..	..	..	..	45		
..	..	..	..	..	..	..	..	..	..	..		
..	..	..	..	..	..	..	..	..	..	..		
94	56	53	38	42	11	8	2	..	..	593	593	
..	..	..	..	..	..	..	..	..	..	..		
18	8	7	7	8	3	..	..	..	..	93		
..	..	..	..	..	..	..	..	..	..	..		
..	..	..	..	..	..	..	..	..	..	..		
..	..	..	..	..	..	..	..	..	..	..		
18	8	7	7	8	3	..	..	..	..	93	93	
2	..	..	1	..	..	..	..	..	..	5		
6	4	5	1	1	..	..	..	..	..	40		
..	..	..	..	..	..	..	..	..	..	..		
1	..	1	1	..	..	..	..	..	..	5		
..	..	..	..	..	..	..	..	..	..	..		
9	4	6	3	1	..	..	..	..	..	50	50	
..	..	..	..	..	..	..	..	..	..	..		
11	5	7	3	5	..	1	..	..	..	77		
..	..	..	..	..	..	..	..	..	..	..		
..	..	..	..	..	..	..	..	..	..	..		
..	..	..	..	..	..	..	..	..	..	..		
11	5	7	3	5	..	1	..	..	..	77	77	
3	1	1	1	..	..	..	..	..	..	13		
28	10	20	4	5	8	2	..	..	..	149		
..	..	..	..	..	..	..	..	..	..	..		
..	..	..	..	..	..	..	..	..	..	..		
..	..	..	..	..	..	..	..	..	..	..		
31	11	21	5	5	8	2	..	..	..	162	162	

17

Castes.	Names of Villages.	No. of Houses.	Males according to Age. Birth to 10 Years.	11 to 20 Years.	21 to 30 Years.	31 to 40 Years.	41 to 50 Years.	51 to 60 Years.	61 to 70 Years.	71 to 80 Years.	81 to 90 Years.	91 to 100 Years and upwards.
	1	2	3	4	5	6	7	8	9	10	11	12
Bramins	11. Koljhur.	..	..	..	..	..	..	..	..	..	..	..
Hindoos of other castes		59	61	39	35	18	14	8	4	3	..	..
Musulmans		..	..	..	..	..	..	..	..	..	..	..
Native Christians		..	..	..	..	..	..	..	..	..	..	..
Seedees		..	..	..	..	..	..	..	..	..	..	..
		59	61	39	35	18	14	8	4	3	..	..
Bramins	12. Konas.	8	3	1	2	2	3	1	..	..	..	..
Hindoos of other castes		32	17	15	18	19	5	5	2	..	..	..
Musulmans		..	..	..	..	..	..	..	..	..	..	..
Native Christians		..	..	..	..	..	..	..	..	..	..	..
Seedees		..	..	..	..	..	..	..	..	..	..	..
		40	20	16	20	21	8	6	2	..	..	..
Bramins	13. Khudpude.	..	..	..	..	..	..	..	..	..	..	..
Hindoos of other castes		1	..	..	1	..	..	..	..	..	..	..
Musulmans		..	..	..	..	..	..	..	..	..	..	..
Native Christians		..	..	..	..	..	..	..	..	..	..	..
Seedees		..	..	..	..	..	..	..	..	..	..	..
		1	..	..	1	..	..	..	..	..	..	..
Bramins	14. Tamboolee.	..	..	..	..	..	..	..	..	..	..	..
Hindoos of other castes		51	40	19	21	15	19	5	2	1	..	..
Musulmans		..	..	..	..	..	..	..	..	..	..	..
Native Christians		..	..	..	..	..	..	..	..	..	..	..
Seedees		..	..	..	..	..	..	..	..	..	..	..
		51	40	19	21	15	19	5	2	1	..	..
Bramins	15. Sassolee.	..	..	..	..	..	..	..	..	..	..	..
Hindoos of other castes		74	83	38	30	33	12	1	..	..	..	..
Musulmans		..	..	..	..	..	..	..	..	..	..	..
Native Christians		1	..	..	..	1	..	..	..	..	..	..
Seedees		..	..	..	..	..	..	..	..	..	..	..
		75	83	38	30	34	12	1	..	..	..	..

Females according to Age.										Total of each Caste.	Grand Total.	Remarks.
Birth to 10 Years.	11 to 20 Years.	21 to 30 Years.	31 to 40 Years.	41 to 50 Years.	51 to 60 Years.	61 to 70 Years.	71 to 80 Years.	81 to 90 Years.	91 to 100 Years and upwards.			
13	14	15	16	17	18	19	20	21	22	23	24	
..	..	..	..	..	..	..	..	..	..	..		
67	21	30	28	9	5	10	1	..	..	353		
..	..	..	..	..	..	..	..	..	..	..		
..	..	..	..	..	..	..	..	..	..	..		
..	..	..	..	..	..	..	..	..	..	..		
67	21	30	28	9	5	10	1	..	..	353	353	
2	1	5	1	..	..	..	..	..	..	21		
9	17	27	15	5	1	..	..	..	..	155		
..	..	..	..	..	..	..	..	..	..	..		
..	..	..	..	..	..	..	..	..	..	..		
..	..	..	..	..	..	..	..	..	..	..		
11	18	32	16	5	1	..	..	..	..	176	176	
..	..	..	..	..	..	..	..	..	..	..		
..	1	..	..	1	..	..	..	..	..	3		
..	..	..	..	..	..	..	..	..	..	..		
..	..	..	..	..	..	..	..	..	..	..		
..	..	..	..	..	..	..	..	..	..	..		
..	1	..	..	1	..	..	..	..	..	3	3	
..	..	..	..	..	..	..	..	..	..	..		
48	20	25	12	8	6	1	1	..	..	243		
..	..	..	..	..	..	..	..	..	..	..		
..	..	..	..	..	..	..	..	..	..	..		
..	..	..	..	..	..	..	..	..	..	..		
48	20	25	12	8	6	1	1	..	..	243	243	
..	..	..	..	..	..	..	..	..	..	..		
37	44	36	31	6	3	..	..	..	..	354		
..	..	..	..	..	..	..	..	..	..	..		
1	..	1	..	..	..	..	..	..	..	3		
..	..	..	..	..	..	..	..	..	..	..		
38	44	37	31	6	3	..	..	..	..	357	357	

Castes.	Names of Villages.	No. of Houses.	Males according to Age.									
			Birth to 10 Years.	11 to 20 Years.	21 to 30 Years.	31 to 40 Years.	41 to 50 Years.	51 to 60 Years.	61 to 70 Years.	71 to 80 Years.	81 to 90 Years.	91 to 100 Years and upwards.
	1	2	3	4	5	6	7	8	9	10	11	12
Bramins	16. PHOOKEREE.	..	..	..	..	..	..	..	..	..	..	..
Hindoos of other castes		45	9	24	18	11	4	4	1	2	..	..
Musulmans		..	..	..	..	..	..	..	..	..	..	..
Native Christians......		..	..	..	..	..	..	..	..	..	..	..
Seedees..................		..	..	..	..	..	..	..	..	..	..	..
		45	9	24	18	11	4	4	1	2	...	..
Bramins	17. DEGWE.	1	2	1	1	..	1	..	..	..	..	..
Hindoos of other castes		73	82	45	35	32	16	4	..	..	..	..
Musulmans		1	..	..	..	..	1	..	..	..	..	..
Native Christians......		2	..	1	1	..	..	..	..	..	..	..
Seedees..................		..	..	..	..	..	..	..	..	..	..	..
		77	84	47	37	32	18	4	..	..	..	..
Bramins	18. VELOWDE.	..	..	..	..	..	..	..	..	..	..	..
Hindoos of other castes		82	74	45	34	19	25	9	9	1	..	..
Musulmans		..	..	..	..	..	..	..	..	..	..	..
Native Christians......		6	6	..	..	6	1	1	..	..	..	..
Seedees..................		..	..	..	..	..	..	..	..	..	..	..
		88	80	45	34	25	26	10	9	1	..	..
Bramins	19. GALEL.	3	..	..	3	1	1	1	..	..	..	..
Hindoos of other castes		17	15	6	6	8	3	..	..	..	..	..
Musulmans		..	..	..	..	..	..	..	..	..	..	..
Native Christians......		..	..	..	..	..	..	..	..	..	..	..
Seedees..................		..	..	..	..	..	..	..	..	..	..	..
		20	15	6	9	9	4	1	...	..	..	..
Bramins	20. NETURDE.	..	..	..	..	..	..	..	..	..	..	..
Hindoos of other castes		48	57	27	27	13	8	5	2	1	..	..
Musulmans		..	..	..	..	..	..	..	..	..	..	..
Native Christians......		..	..	..	..	..	..	..	..	..	..	..
Seedees.....		..	..	..	..	..	..	..	..	..	..	..
		48	57	27	27	13	8	5	2	1	..	..

Females according to Age.										Total of each Caste.	Grand Total.	Remarks.
Birth to 10 Years.	11 to 20 Years.	21 to 30 Years.	31 to 40 Years.	41 to 50 Years.	51 to 60 Years.	61 to 70 Years.	71 to 80 Years.	81 to 90 Years.	91 to 100 Years and upwards.			
13	14	15	16	17	18	19	20	21	22	23	24	
..	..	..	..	..	..	..	..	..	..	..		
18	21	21	10	6	2	2	1	..	..	154		
..	..	..	..	..	..	..	..	..	..	..		
..	..	..	..	..	..	..	..	..	..	..		
..	..	..	..	..	..	..	..	..	..	..		
18	21	21	10	6	2	2	1	..	..	154	154	
1	1	..	1	..	..	..	..	..	..	8		
71	46	46	22	7	3	..	..	..	..	409		
..	..	..	..	1	..	..	..	..	..	2		
..	1	..	1	..	..	..	1	..	..	5		
..	..	..	..	..	..	..	..	..	..	..		
72	48	46	24	8	3	..	1	..	..	424	424	
..	..	..	..	..	..	..	..	..	..	..		
71	32	39	34	21	16	13	4	..	..	446		
..	..	..	..	..	..	..	..	..	..	..		
6	2	2	..	4	..	2	..	..	..	30		
..	..	..	..	..	..	..	..	..	..	..		
77	34	41	34	25	16	15	4	..	..	476	476	
..	1	3	1	..	..	..	..	..	..	11		
7	6	8	7	3	4	..	1	..	..	74		
..	..	..	..	..	..	..	..	..	..	..		
..	..	..	..	..	..	..	..	..	..	..		
..	..	..	..	..	..	..	..	..	..	..		
7	7	11	8	3	4	..	1	..	..	85	85	
..	..	..	..	..	..	..	..	..	..	..		
41	25	24	18	13	1	5	1	..	1	269		
..	..	..	..	..	..	..	..	..	..	..		
..	..	..	..	..	..	..	..	..	..	..		
..	..	..	..	..	..	..	..	..	..	..		
41	25	24	18	13	1	5	1	..	1	269	269	

18

Castes.	Names of Villages.	No. of Houses.	Males according to Age.									
			Birth to 10 Years.	11 to 20 Years.	21 to 30 Years.	31 to 40 Years.	41 to 50 Years.	51 to 60 Years.	61 to 70 Years.	71 to 80 Years.	81 to 90 Years.	91 to 100 Years and upwards.
	1	2	3	4	5	6	7	8	9	10	11	12
Bramins	21. Phunsowde.	..	..	..	..	..	..	..	..	..	..	..
Hindoos of other castes		11	9	5	3	6	4	1	..	..	..	..
Musulmans		..	..	..	..	..	..	..	..	..	..	..
Native Christians		..	..	..	..	..	..	..	..	..	..	..
Seedees		..	..	..	..	..	..	..	..	..	..	..
		11	9	5	3	6	4	1	..	..	..	..
Bramins	22. Surbule.	..	..	..	..	..	..	..	..	..	..	..
Hindoos of other castes		45	51	25	27	19	10	10	1	..	..	..
Musulmans		..	..	..	..	..	..	..	..	..	..	..
Native Christians		..	..	..	..	..	..	..	..	..	..	..
Seedees		..	..	..	..	..	..	..	..	..	..	..
		45	51	25	27	19	10	10	1	..	..	..
Bramins	23. Gharap.	..	..	..	..	..	..	..	..	..	..	..
Hindoos of other castes		20	15	7	10	9	1	..	..	..	..	..
Musulmans		..	..	..	..	..	..	..	..	..	..	..
Native Christians		..	..	..	..	..	..	..	..	..	..	..
Seedees		..	..	..	..	..	..	..	..	..	..	..
		20	15	7	10	9	1	..	..	..	..	..
Bramins	24. Oodelee.	..	..	..	..	..	..	..	..	..	..	..
Hindoos of other castes		..	..	..	..	..	..	..	..	..	..	..
Musulmans		..	..	..	..	..	..	..	..	..	..	..
Native Christians		..	..	..	..	..	..	..	..	..	..	..
Seedees		..	..	..	..	..	..	..	..	..	..	..
		..	..	..	..	..	..	..	..	..	..	..
Bramins	25. Newlee.	..	..	..	..	..	..	..	..	..	..	..
Hindoos of other castes		..	..	..	..	..	..	..	..	..	..	..
Musulmans		..	..	..	..	..	..	..	..	..	..	..
Native Christians		..	..	..	..	..	..	..	..	..	..	..
Seedees		..	..	..	..	..	..	..	..	..	..	..
		..	..	..	..	..	..	..	..	..	..	..

Females according to Age.												
Birth to 10 Years.	11 to 20 Years.	21 to 30 Years.	31 to 40 Years.	41 to 50 Years.	51 to 60 Years.	61 to 70 Years.	71 to 80 Years.	81 to 90 Years.	91 to 100 Years and upwards.	Total of each Caste.	Grand Total.	Remarks.
13	14	15	16	17	18	19	20	21	22	23	24	
..	..	..	..	..	..	..	..	..	..	..		
14	2	5	4	..	..	..	..	..	..	53		
..	..	..	..	..	..	..	..	..	..	..		
..	..	..	..	..	..	..	..	..	..	..		
..	..	..	..	..	..	..	..	..	..	..		
14	2	5	4	..	..	..	..	..	..	53	53	
..	..	..	..	..	..	..	..	..	..	..		
60	24	26	11	7	6	2	..	..	..	279		
..	..	..	..	..	..	..	..	..	..	..		
..	..	..	..	..	..	..	..	..	..	..		
..	..	..	..	..	..	..	..	..	..	..		
60	24	26	11	7	6	2	..	..	..	279	279	
..	..	..	..	..	..	..	..	..	..	..		
12	13	8	7	2	2	..	..	..	..	86		
..	..	..	..	..	..	..	..	..	..	..		
..	..	..	..	..	..	..	..	..	..	..		
..	..	..	..	..	..	..	..	..	..	..		
12	13	8	7	2	2	..	..	..	..	86	86	
..	..	..	..	..	..	..	..	..	..	..		
..	..	..	..	..	..	..	..	..	..	..		
..	..	..	..	..	..	..	..	..	..	..		
..	..	..	..	..	..	..	..	..	..	..		
..	..	..	..	..	..	..	..	..	..	..		
..	..	..	..	..	..	..	..	..	..	..		
..	..	..	..	..	..	..	..	..	..	..		
..	..	..	..	..	..	..	..	..	..	..		
..	..	..	..	..	..	..	..	..	..	..		
..	..	..	..	..	..	..	..	..	..	..		
..	..	..	..	..	..	..	..	..	..	..		
..	..	..	..	..	..	..	..	..	..	..	..	

Castes.	Names of Villages.	No. of Houses.	Males according to Age.									
			Birth to 10 Years.	11 to 20 Years.	21 to 30 Years.	31 to 40 Years.	41 to 50 Years.	51 to 60 Years.	61 to 70 Years.	71 to 80 Years.	81 to 90 Years.	91 to 100 Years and upwards.
	1	2	3	4	5	6	7	8	9	10	11	12
Bramins	26. Kulue.	..	..	..	..	..	..	..	..	..	..	..
Hindoos of other castes		24	19	14	15	8	5	4	..	..	..	..
Musulmans		..	..	..	..	..	..	..	..	..	..	..
Native Christians		1	2	..	..	1	..	..	..	..	..	..
Seedees		..	..	..	..	..	..	..	..	..	..	..
		25	21	14	15	9	5	4	..	..	..	..
Bramins	27. Koombrul.	..	..	..	..	..	..	..	..	..	..	..
Hindoos of other castes		56	48	23	21	18	21	12	6	2	..	..
Musulmans		..	..	..	..	..	..	..	..	..	..	..
Native Christians		..	..	..	..	..	..	..	..	..	..	..
Seedees		..	..	..	..	..	..	..	..	..	..	..
		56	48	23	21	18	21	12	6	2	..	..
Bramins	28. Jholumbe.	..	..	..	..	..	..	..	..	..	..	..
Hindoos of other castes		38	36	15	8	6	10	3	1	..	..	..
Musulmans		..	..	..	..	..	..	..	..	..	..	..
Native Christians		..	..	..	..	..	..	..	..	..	..	..
Seedees		..	..	..	..	..	..	..	..	..	..	..
		38	36	15	8	6	10	3	1	..	..	..
Bramins	29. Oogare.	..	..	..	..	..	..	..	..	..	..	..
Hindoos of other castes		23	20	12	8	4	8	3	1	2	..	..
Musulmans		..	..	..	..	..	..	..	..	..	..	..
Native Christians		..	..	..	..	..	..	..	..	..	..	..
Seedees		..	..	..	..	..	..	..	..	..	..	..
		23	20	12	8	4	8	3	1	2	..	..
Bramins	30. Morgam.	..	..	..	..	..	..	..	..	..	..	..
Hindoos of other castes		76	69	43	31	32	7	3	..	..	..	..
Musulmans		..	..	..	..	..	..	..	..	..	..	..
Native Christians		1	..	..	..	..	..	..	..	..	..	..
Seedees		..	..	..	..	..	..	..	..	..	..	..
		77	69	43	31	32	7	3	..	..	..	..

Females according to Age.										Total of each Caste.	Grand Total.	Remarks.
Birth to 10 Years.	11 to 20 Years.	21 to 30 Years.	31 to 40 Years.	41 to 50 Years.	51 to 60 Years.	61 to 70 Years.	71 to 80 Years.	81 to 90 Years.	91 to 100 Years and upwards.			
13	14	15	16	17	18	19	20	21	22	23	24	
..	..	..	..	..	..	..	..	..	..	..		
20	5	17	10	3	1	..	..	..	..	121		
..	..	..	..	..	..	..	..	..	..	..		
..	..	1	1	..	..	..	..	..	..	5		
..	..	..	..	..	..	..	..	..	..	..		
20	5	18	11	3	1	..	..	..	..	126	126	
..	..	..	..	..	..	..	..	..	..	..		
33	15	24	22	20	12	9	1	..	..	287		
..	..	..	..	..	..	..	..	..	..	..		
..	..	..	..	..	..	..	..	..	..	..		
..	..	..	..	..	..	..	..	..	..	..		
33	15	24	22	20	12	9	1	..	..	287	287	
..	..	..	..	..	..	..	..	..	..	..		
28	10	16	11	6	2	3	..	..	..	155		
..	..	..	..	..	..	..	..	..	..	..		
..	..	..	..	..	..	..	..	..	..	..		
..	..	..	..	..	..	..	..	..	..	..		
28	10	16	11	6	2	3	..	..	..	155	155	
..	..	..	..	..	..	..	..	..	..	..		
16	11	5	8	5	5	2	3	1	..	114		
..	..	..	..	..	..	..	..	..	..	..		
..	..	..	..	..	..	..	..	..	..	..		
..	..	..	..	..	..	..	..	..	..	..		
16	11	5	8	5	5	2	3	1	..	114	114	
..	..	..	..	..	..	..	..	..	..	..		
53	31	41	28	4	4	1	..	..	..	347		
..	..	..	..	..	..	..	..	..	..	..		
..	..	1	..	1	..	..	..	..	..	2		
..	..	..	..	..	..	..	..	..	..	..		
53	31	42	28	5	4	1	..	..	..	349	349	

19

Castes.	Names of Villages.	No. of Houses.	Males according to Age. Birth to 10 Years.	11 to 20 Years.	21 to 30 Years.	31 to 40 Years.	41 to 50 Years.	51 to 60 Years.	61 to 70 Years.	71 to 80 Years.	81 to 90 Years.	91 to 100 Years and upwards.
	1	2	3	4	5	6	7	8	9	10	11	12
Bramins	31. Adalee.	..	..	..	..	..	..	..	..	..	..	..
Hindoos of other castes		56	36	31	24	13	16	5	2	..	..	..
Musulmans		..	..	..	..	..	..	..	..	..	..	..
Native Christians		1	..	2	1	..	..	..	..	..	..	..
Seedees		..	..	..	..	..	..	..	..	..	..	..
		57	36	33	25	13	16	5	2	..	..	..
Bramins	32. Padwe.	..	..	..	..	..	..	..	..	..	..	..
Hindoos of other castes		..	..	..	..	..	..	..	..	..	..	..
Musulmans		..	..	..	..	..	..	..	..	..	..	..
Native Christians		..	..	..	..	..	..	..	..	..	..	..
Seedees		..	..	..	..	..	..	..	..	..	..	..
		..	..	..	..	..	..	..	..	..	..	..
Bramins	33. Majgaum.	..	..	..	..	..	..	..	..	..	..	..
Hindoos of other castes		13	12	6	3	7	1	..	..	..	..	..
Musulmans		..	..	..	..	..	..	..	..	..	..	..
Native Christians		..	..	..	..	..	..	..	..	..	..	..
Seedees		..	..	..	..	..	..	..	..	..	..	..
		13	12	6	3	7	1	..	..	..	..	..
	Turuf Saturde.											
Bramins	34. Saturde.	25	41	16	12	14	15	6	1	1	..	..
Hindoos of other castes		130	121	41	67	46	35	21	6	2	..	..
Musulmans		1	2	..	..	..	1	..	..	..	..	..
Native Christians		8	3	2	6	1	..	..	..	..	..	..
Seedees		..	..	..	..	..	..	..	..	..	..	..
		164	167	59	85	61	51	27	7	3	..	..
Bramins	35. Padlos.	2	3	2	..	3	..	..	1	..	..	..
Hindoos of other castes		49	36	26	22	17	8	7	4	2	..	..
Musulmans		..	..	..	..	..	..	..	..	..	..	..
Native Christians		..	..	..	..	..	..	..	..	..	..	..
Seedees		..	..	..	..	..	..	..	..	..	..	..
		51	39	28	22	20	8	7	5	2	..	..

Females according to Age.										Total of each Caste.	Grand Total.	Remarks.
Birth to 10 Years.	11 to 20 Years.	21 to 30 Years.	31 to 40 Years.	41 to 50 Years.	51 to 60 Years.	61 to 70 Years.	71 to 80 Years.	81 to 90 Years.	91 to 100 Years and upwards.			
13	14	15	16	17	18	19	20	21	22	23	24	
..	..	..	..	..	..	..	..	..	..	..		
59	20	15	24	9	3	1	..	..	..	258		
..	..	..	..	..	..	..	..	..	..	..		
..	1	..	..	1	..	..	..	..	..	5		
..	..	..	..	..	..	..	..	..	..	..		
59	21	15	24	10	3	1	..	..	..	263	263	
..	..	..	..	..	..	..	..	..	..	..		
..	..	..	..	..	..	..	..	..	..	..		
..	..	..	..	..	..	..	..	..	..	..		
..	..	..	..	..	..	..	..	..	..	..		
..	..	..	..	..	..	..	..	..	..	..		
..	..	..	..	..	..	..	..	..	..	..	..	
..	..	..	..	..	..	..	..	..	..	..		
9	4	7	1	3	..	..	..	..	..	53		
..	..	..	..	..	..	..	..	..	..	..		
..	..	..	..	..	..	..	..	..	..	..		
..	..	..	..	..	..	..	..	..	..	..		
9	4	7	1	3	..	..	..	..	..	53	53	
21	16	19	9	8	9	2	3	..	..	193		
115	34	67	40	37	23	11	1	..	..	667		
1	..	..	1	..	..	..	..	..	..	5		
9	5	3	..	2	1	..	..	..	..	32		
..	..	..	..	..	..	..	..	..	..	..		
146	55	89	50	47	33	13	4	..	..	897	897	
2	..	2	3	1	1	1	..	..	..	19		
21	18	19	20	11	15	4	..	..	..	230		
..	..	..	..	..	..	..	..	..	..	..		
..	..	..	..	..	..	..	..	..	..	..		
..	..	..	..	..	..	..	..	..	..	..		
23	18	21	23	12	16	5	..	..		249	249	

Castes.	Names of Villages.	No. of Houses.	Males according to Age.									
			Birth to 10 Years.	11 to 20 Years.	21 to 30 Years.	31 to 40 Years.	41 to 50 Years.	51 to 60 Years.	61 to 70 Years.	71 to 80 Years.	81 to 90 Years.	91 to 100 Years and upwards.
	1	2	3	4	5	6	7	8	9	10	11	12
	Turuf Saturde.											
Bramins	36. Sherle.	1	..	..	2	..	..	..	..	..	..	..
Hindoos of other castes		99	124	60	43	40	30	12	2	..	..	..
Musulmans		..	..	..	..	..	..	..	..	..	..	..
Native Christians		1	2	..	..	1	..	..	..	..	..	..
Seedees		..	..	..	..	..	..	..	..	..	..	..
		101	126	60	45	41	30	12	2	..	..	..
Bramins	37. Ronapal.	1	..	..	..	..	..	1	..	..	..	..
Hindoos of other castes		50	25	18	18	13	10	5	2	..	..	..
Musulmans		..	..	..	..	..	..	..	..	..	..	..
Native Christians		..	..	..	..	..	..	..	..	..	..	..
Seedees		..	..	..	..	..	..	..	..	..	..	..
		51	25	18	18	13	10	6	2	..	..	..
Bramins	38. Neegode.	..	..	..	..	..	..	..	..	..	..	..
Hindoos of other castes		81	95	75	64	37	16	4	..	..	2	..
Musulmans		..	..	..	..	..	..	..	..	..	..	..
Native Christians		..	..	..	..	..	..	..	..	..	..	..
Seedees		..	..	..	..	..	..	..	..	..	..	..
		81	95	75	64	37	16	4	..	..	2	..
Bramins	39. Jusoolee.	2	..	3	1	1	2	..	..	..	..	..
Hindoos of other castes		236	127	163	119	98	68	36	8	2	..	..
Musulmans		15	13	14	8	2	5	2	1	..	..	..
Native Christians		5	3	5	7	4	1	2	..	..	..	..
Seedees		..	..	..	..	..	..	..	..	..	..	..
		258	143	185	135	105	76	40	9	2	..	..
Bramins	40. Kovetunee.	6	4	2	6	2	2	..	..	..	..	..
Hindoos of other castes		89	69	48	61	44	19	8	1	..	..	..
Musulmans		..	..	..	..	..	..	..	..	..	..	..
Native Christians		8	10	2	2	8	1	1	..	..	..	..
Seedees		..	..	..	..	..	..	..	..	..	..	..
		103	83	52	69	54	22	9	1	..	..	..

Females according to Age.												
Birth to 10 Years.	11 to 20 Years.	21 to 30 Years.	31 to 40 Years.	41 to 50 Years.	51 to 60 Years.	61 to 70 Years.	71 to 80 Years.	81 to 90 Years.	91 to 100 Years and upwards.	Total of each Caste.	Grand Total.	Remarks.
13	14	15	16	17	18	19	20	21	22	23	24	
1	1	..	..	1	1	..	..	..	..	6		
51	49	47	34	28	3	6	..	..	..	529		
..	..	..	..	..	..	..	..	..	..	..		
1	..	..	1	..	..	..	..	..	..	5		
..	..	..	..	..	..	..	..	..	..	..		
53	50	47	35	29	4	6	..	..	..	540	540	
..	..	..	..	..	..	1	..	..	..	2		
21	13	23	19	16	10	2	..	..	..	195		
..	..	..	..	..	..	..	..	..	..	..		
..	..	..	..	..	..	..	..	..	..	..		
..	..	..	..	..	..	..	..	..	..	..		
21	13	23	19	16	10	3	..	..	..	197	197	
..	..	..	..	..	..	..	..	..	..	..		
72	48	41	31	19	5	3	..	1	1	514		
..	..	..	..	..	..	..	..	..	..	..		
..	..	..	..	..	..	..	..	..	..	..		
..	..	..	..	..	..	..	..	..	..	..		
72	48	41	31	19	5	3	..	1	1	514	514	
1	2	..	2	1	..	1	1	..	..	15		
112	87	107	93	80	48	28	10	..	..	1,186		
12	12	5	8	5	3	2	..	..	..	92		
3	6	6	1	1	2	..	1	..	..	42		
..	..	..	..	..	..	..	..	..	..	..		
128	107	118	104	87	53	31	12	..	..	1,335	1,335	
7	2	4	2	..	2	1	..	..	..	34		
78	26	53	44	29	19	4	..	..	..	503		
..	..	..	..	..	..	..	..	..	..	..		
8	3	1	5	2	..	1	2	..	..	46		
..	..	..	..	..	..	..	..	..	..			
93	31	58	51	31	21	6	2	..	..	583	583	

20

Castes.	Names of Villages.	No. of Houses.	Males according to Age. Birth to 10 Years.	11 to 20 Years.	21 to 30 Years.	31 to 40 Years.	41 to 50 Years.	51 to 60 Years.	61 to 70 Years.	71 to 80 Years.	81 to 90 Years.	91 to 100 Years and upwards.
	1	2	3	4	5	6	7	8	9	10	11	12
	Turuf Saturde.											
Bramins	41. Sonoorlee.	1	..	..	1	..	..	..	1	..	..	..
Hindoos of other castes		163	187	87	68	49	44	26	4	1	..	..
Musulmans		..	..	..	..	..	..	..	..	..	..	..
Native Christians		..	..	..	..	..	..	..	..	..	..	..
Seedees		..	..	..	..	..	..	..	..	..	..	..
		164	187	87	69	49	44	26	5	1	..	..
Bramins	42. Mudoore.	17	18	11	7	5	5	4	1	..	..	..
Hindoos of other castes		87	54	62	77	43	30	12	4	1	..	..
Musulmans		1	2	1	..	..	1	..	..	..	..	..
Native Christians		1	3	1	1	1	..	..	..	..	..	..
Seedees		..	..	..	..	..	..	..	..	..	..	..
		106	77	75	85	49	36	16	5	1	..	..
Bramins	43. Waree Phunsowre.	..	..	..	..	..	..	..	..	..	..	..
Hindoos of other castes		..	..	..	..	..	..	..	..	..	..	..
Musulmans		..	..	..	..	..	..	..	..	..	..	..
Native Christians		..	..	..	..	..	..	..	..	..	..	..
Seedees		..	..	..	..	..	..	..	..	..	..	..
		..	..	..	..	..	..	..	..	..	..	..
Bramins	44. Satelee.	1	..	2	..	..	1	..	..	..	..	..
Hindoos of other castes		35	36	13	13	7	10	12	3	1	..	..
Musulmans		..	..	..	..	..	..	..	..	..	..	..
Native Christians		..	..	..	..	..	..	..	..	..	..	..
Seedees		..	..	..	..	..	..	..	..	..	..	..
		36	36	15	13	7	11	12	3	1	..	..
Bramins	45. Aros.	44	34	27	39	18	18	9	2	2	..	1
Hindoos of other castes		161	151	128	107	65	39	28	14	..	..	3
Musulmans		5	4	..	2	3	..	1	1	..	..	.
Native Christians		..	..	..	..	..	..	..	..	..	..	..
Seedees		..	..	..	..	..	..	..	..	..	..	..
		210	189	155	148	86	57	38	17	2	..	4

FEMALES according to Age.										Total of each Caste.	Grand Total.	REMARKS.
Birth to 10 Years.	11 to 20 Years.	21 to 30 Years.	31 to 40 Years.	41 to 50 Years.	51 to 60 Years.	61 to 70 Years.	71 to 80 Years.	81 to 90 Years.	91 to 100 Years and upwards.			
13	14	15	16	17	18	19	20	21	22	23	24	
1	1	..	..	..	1	..	..	..	..	5		
169	81	89	53	43	6	2	1	..	..	910		
..	..	..	..	..	..	..	..	..	..	..		
...	..	..	..	..	..	..	..	..	..	..		
..	..	..	..	..	..	..	..	..	..	..		
170	82	89	53	43	7	2	1	..	..	915	915	
11	10	6	8	6	..	..	..	..	..	92		
48	49	55	34	31	20	7	..	..	..	527		
1	1	..	1	..	..	..	..	..	..	7		
..	1	1	..	..	1	..	..	..	..	9		
..	..	..	..	..	..	..	..	..	..	..		
60	61	62	43	37	21	7	..	..	..	635	635	
..	..	..	..	..	..	..	..	..	..	..		
..	..	..	..	..	..	..	..	..	..	..		
..	..	..	..	..	..	..	..	..	..	..		
..	..	..	..	..	..	..	..	..	..	..		
..	..	..	..	..	..	..	..	..	..	..		
..	..	..	..	..	..	..	..	..	..	..	..	
1	..	1	..	..	..	..	..	..	..	5		
34	3	11	21	9	5	1	2	..	..	181		
..	..	..	..	..	..	..	..	..	..	..		
..	..	..	..	..	..	..	..	..	..	..		
..	..	..	..	..	..	..	..	..	..	..		
35	3	12	21	9	5	1	2	..	..	186	186	
46	27	27	15	11	9	3	..	..	1	289		
139	97	82	56	47	32	16	1	..	..	1,005		
1	..	3	..	..	2	1	..	..	..	18		
..	..	..	..	..	..	..	..	..	..	..		
..	..	..	..	..	..	..	..	..	..	..		
186	124	112	71	58	43	20	1	..	1	1,312	1,312	

Castes.	Names of Villages.	No. of Houses.	Males according to Age. Birth to 10 Years.	11 to 20 Years.	21 to 30 Years.	31 to 40 Years.	41 to 50 Years.	51 to 60 Years.	61 to 70 Years.	71 to 80 Years.	81 to 90 Years.	91 to 100 Years and upwards.
	1	2	3	4	5	6	7	8	9	10	11	12
	Turuf Saturde.											
Bramins	46. Kas.	11	4	2	8	1	3	1	1	..	..	..
Hindoos of other castes		116	110	61	71	56	43	17	5	1	..	..
Musulmans		..	..	..	..	..	..	..	..	..	..	..
Native Christians		..	..	..	..	..	..	..	..	..	..	..
Seedees		..	..	..	..	..	..	..	..	..	..	..
		127	114	63	79	57	46	18	6	1	..	..
Bramins	47. Satose.	3	2	3	4	2	2	..	1	..	..	..
Hindoos of other castes		91	89	29	54	33	32	18	7	3	..	..
Musulmans		..	..	..	..	..	..	..	..	..	..	..
Native Christians		1	1	..	1	..	..	..	..	..	..	..
Seedees		..	..	..	..	..	..	..	..	..	..	..
		95	92	32	59	35	34	18	8	3	..	..
Bramins	48. Wete.	..	..	..	..	..	..	..	..	..	..	..
Hindoos of other castes		36	54	28	26	17	13	1	3	1	..	..
Musulmans		..	..	..	..	..	..	..	..	..	..	..
Native Christians		..	..	..	..	..	..	..	..	..	..	..
Seedees		..	..	..	..	..	..	..	..	..	..	..
		36	54	28	26	17	13	1	3	1	..	..
Bramins	49. Azgaum.	109	85	59	50	43	28	26	8	3	..	1
Hindoos of other castes		345	309	193	154	122	109	51	13	2	..	..
Musulmans		2	2	..	..	1	2	..	..	..	..	..
Native Christians		28	16	20	12	12	7	2	1	..	..	..
Seedees		..	..	..	..	..	..	..	..	..	..	..
		484	412	272	216	178	146	79	22	5	..	1
Bramins	50. Terowde.	5	10	9	4	2	4	1	..	..	..	..
Hindoos of other castes		80	66	31	26	23	30	11	2	..	..	..
Musulmans		..	..	..	..	..	..	..	..	..	..	..
Native Christians		1	1	..	1	..	..	..	..	..	..	..
Seedees		..	..	..	..	..	..	..	..	..	..	..
		86	77	40	31	25	34	12	2	..	..	..

Females according to Age.												
Birth to 10 Years.	11 to 20 Years.	21 to 30 Years.	31 to 40 Years.	41 to 50 Years.	51 to 60 Years.	61 to 70 Years.	71 to 80 Years.	81 to 90 Years.	91 to 100 Years and upwards.	Total of each Caste.	Grand Total.	Remarks.
13	14	15	16	17	18	19	20	21	22	23	24	
4	1	4	1	..	3	1	..	..	..	34		
79	53	63	57	40	18	7	2	..	..	683		
..	..	..	..	..	..	..	..	..	..	..		
..	..	..	..	..	..	..	..	..	..	..		
..	..	..	..	..	..	..	..	..	..	..		
83	54	67	58	40	21	8	2	..	..	717	717	
2	2	5	5	1	1	2	..	..	..	32		
80	38	52	31	24	20	12	..	..	..	522		
..	..	..	..	..	..	..	..	..	..	..		
..	..	1	..	..	..	..	..	..	..	3		
..	..	..	..	..	..	..	..	..	..	..		
82	40	58	36	25	21	14	..	..	..	557	557	
..	..	..	..	..	..	..	..	..	..	..		
47	23	29	7	6	7	2	..	..	..	264		
..	..	..	..	..	..	..	..	..	..	..		
..	..	..	..	..	..	..	..	..	..	..		
..	..	..	..	..	..	..	..	..	..	..		
47	23	29	7	6	7	2	..	..	..	264	264	
85	61	48	45	27	22	10	2	..	..	603		
299	181	149	116	111	82	33	3	..	..	1,927		
1	1	2	..	1	..	..	..	1	..	11		
22	18	9	10	4	4	2	..	1	..	140		
..	..	..	..	..	..	..	..	..	..	..		
407	261	208	171	143	108	45	5	2	..	2,681	2,081	
6	5	5	5	5	1	..	1	..	..	58		
61	30	21	25	33	18	8	2	1	4	392		
..	..	..	..	..	..	..	..	..	..	..		
..	1	1	..	..	1	..	..	..	..	5		
..	..	..	..	..	..	..	..	..	..	..		
67	36	27	30	38	20	8	3	1	4	455	455	

21

Castes.	Names of Villages.	No. of Houses.	Males according to Age. Birth to 10 Years.	11 to 20 Years.	21 to 30 Years.	31 to 40 Years.	41 to 50 Years.	51 to 60 Years.	61 to 70 Years.	71 to 80 Years.	81 to 90 Years.	91 to 100 Years and upwards.
	1	2	3	4	5	6	7	8	9	10	11	12
	Turuf Saturde.											
Bramins	51. Asolee.	28	29	14	16	7	12	9	6	2	..	..
Hindoos of other castes		294	198	134	109	102	92	71	46	20	2	..
Musulmans		9	7	2	3	4	3	..	1	1	..	..
Native Christians		6	3	4	5	2	1	..	1	..	..	..
Seedees		..	..	..	..	..	..	..	..	..	..	..
		337	237	154	133	115	108	80	54	23	2	..
Bramins	52. Aronde.	27	19	16	13	10	14	4	..	..	..	..
Hindoos of other castes		266	240	134	145	87	65	36	22	1	..	..
Musulmans		5	4	3	1	2	1	2	1	..	..	..
Native Christians		16	13	7	3	4	8	1	..	..	..	..
Seedees		..	..	..	..	..	..	..	..	..	..	..
		314	276	160	162	103	88	43	23	1	..	..
Bramins	53. Tulaone.	12	15	7	9	3	6	2	1	1	..	..
Hindoos of other castes		106	102	73	52	33	22	13	..	1	..	..
Musulmans		..	..	..	..	..	..	..	..	..	..	..
Native Christians		12	22	5	4	3	2	..	..	..	..	..
Seedees		..	..	..	..	..	..	..	..	..	..	..
		130	139	85	65	39	30	15	1	2	..	..
Bramins	54. Kinle.	1	2	..	..	1	..	..	..	..	..	..
Hindoos of other castes		25	20	17	6	10	4	4	1	..	..	..
Musulmans		7	16	2	3	6	5	..	..	..	..	..
Native Christians		26	30	7	15	9	3	3	1	..	..	..
Seedees		..	..	..	..	..	..	..	..	..	..	..
		59	68	26	24	26	12	7	2	..	..	..
Bramins	55. Nanos.	..	..	..	..	..	..	..	..	..	..	..
Hindoos of other castes		15	12	8	10	3	7	2	..	..	..	..
Musulmans		..	..	..	..	..	..	..	..	..	..	..
Native Christians		1	..	1	..	..	1	..	..	..	..	..
Seedees		..	..	..	..	..	..	..	..	..	..	..
		16	12	9	10	3	8	2	..	..	..	..

Females according to Age.										Total of each Caste.	Grand Total.	Remarks.
Birth to 10 Years.	11 to 20 Years.	21 to 30 Years.	31 to 40 Years.	41 to 50 Years.	51 to 60 Years.	61 to 70 Years.	71 to 80 Years.	81 to 90 Years.	91 to 100 Years and upwards.			
13	14	15	16	17	18	19	20	21	22	23	24	
24	10	9	11	3	6	5	3	..	..	166		
150	102	98	96	87	69	46	27	1	1	1,451		
2	5	2	2	4	3	1	1	..	..	41		
4	3	1	3	..	3	1	..	..	..	31		
..	..	..	..	..	..	..	..	..	..	..		
180	120	110	112	94	81	53	31	1	1	1,689	1,689	
22	10	19	6	16	9	2	..	..	..	160		
212	110	119	122	71	91	39	..	..	..	1,494		
3	..	..	2	2	4	1	..	..	..	26		
10	2	5	3	9	3	1	..	..	..	69		
..	..	..	..	..	..	..	..	..	..	..		
247	122	143	133	98	107	43	..	..	..	1,749	1,749	
11	4	7	4	3	2	2	..	..	..	77		
82	38	49	33	34	27	4	2	..	..	565		
..	..	..	..	..	..	..	..	..	..	..		
7	3	5	6	3	1	1	..	..	..	62		
..	.	..	..	..	..	..	..	..	..	..		
100	45	61	43	40	30	7	2	..	..	704	704	
1	1	..	..	..	..	..	..	..	..	5		
12	9	4	14	8	4	2	..	..	..	115		
8	..	8	5	5	..	..	..	..	..	58		
27	4	11	13	7	3	2	..	..	..	135		
..	..	..	..	..	..	..	..	..	..	..		
48	14	23	32	20	7	4	..	..	..	313	313	
..	..	..	..	..	..	..	..	..	..	..		
14	10	10	6	1	6	..	..	..	..	89		
..	..	..	..	..	..	..	..	..	..	..		
..	..	..	1	..	..	..	..	..	..	3		
..	..	..	..	..	..	..	..	..	..	..		
14	10	10	7	1	6	..	..	..	..	92	92	

Castes.	Names of Villages.	No. of Houses.	Males according to Age. Birth to 10 Years.	11 to 20 Years.	21 to 30 Years.	31 to 40 Years.	41 to 50 Years.	51 to 60 Years.	61 to 70 Years.	71 to 80 Years.	81 to 90 Years.	91 to 100 Years and upwards.
	1	2	3	4	5	6	7	8	9	10	11	12
	Turuf Saturde.											
Bramins	56. Gooldoove.	1	..	4	..	..	1	..	..	..	..	..
Hindoos of other castes		39	38	29	24	15	11	10	1	..	..	..
Musulmans		..	..	..	..	..	..	..	..	..	..	..
Native Christians		..	..	..	..	..	..	..	..	..	..	..
Seedees		..	..	..	..	..	..	..	..	..	..	..
		40	38	33	24	15	12	10	1	..	..	..
Bramins	57. Muneree.	1	1	..	..	..	1	..	..	..	..	..
Hindoos of other castes		68	38	47	44	39	27	8	7	..	..	..
Musulmans		8	4	5	4	3	3	1	..	..	..	..
Native Christians		..	..	..	..	..	..	..	..	..	..	..
Seedees		..	..	..	..	..	..	..	..	..	..	..
		77	43	52	48	42	31	9	7	..	..	..
Bramins	58. Oosup.	4	9	3	4	..	1	1	1	..	..	..
Hindoos of other castes		107	127	72	28	26	5	6	2	5	..	..
Musulmans		6	6	6	4	2	1	..	..	..	..	..
Native Christians		..	..	..	..	..	..	..	..	..	..	..
Seedees		..	..	..	..	..	..	..	..	..	..	..
		117	142	81	36	28	7	7	3	5	..	..
Bramins	59. Koodase.	1	2	1	1	1	..	..	..	..	..	..
Hindoos of other castes		127	101	48	63	55	26	15	..	..	..	..
Musulmans		1	..	1	..	1	..	1	..	..	..	..
Native Christians		1	..	1	..	..	..	..	..	..	..	..
Seedees		..	..	..	..	..	..	..	..	..	..	..
		130	103	51	64	57	26	16	..	..	..	..
Bramins	60. Jhure.	..	..	..	..	..	..	..	..	..	..	..
Hindoos of other castes		20	15	10	10	8	6	7	4	..	..	..
Musulmans		..	..	..	..	..	..	..	..	..	..	..
Native Christians		..	..	..	..	..	..	..	..	..	..	..
Seedees		..	..	..	..	..	..	..	..	..	..	..
		20	15	10	10	8	6	7	4	..	..	..

Females according to Age.												
Birth to 10 Years.	11 to 20 Years.	21 to 30 Years.	31 to 40 Years.	41 to 50 Years.	51 to 60 Years.	61 to 70 Years.	71 to 80 Years.	81 to 90 Years.	91 to 100 Years and upwards.	Total of each Caste.	Grand Total.	Remarks.
13	14	15	16	17	18	19	20	21	22	23	24	
1	..	..	1	..	..	..	..	..	..	7		
31	34	16	14	10	18	4	1	..	..	256		
..	..	..	..	..	..	..	..	..	..	..		
..	..	..	..	..	..	..	..	..	..	..		
..	..	..	..	..	..	..	..	..	..	..		
32	34	16	15	10	18	4	1	..	..	263	263	
..	..	..	..	..	..	1	..	..	..	3		
39	47	43	29	12	3	1	..	..	..	383		
3	3	4	3	2	..	..	..	..	..	35		
..	..	..	..	..	..	..	..	..	..	..		
..	..	..	..	..	..	..	..	..	..	..		
42	50	47	32	14	3	2	..	..	..	421	421	
8	2	3	4	2	1	..	..	..	..	39		
102	50	38	15	3	..	11	..	..	..	490		
13	5	6	2	1	..	..	..	..	..	46		
..	..	..	..	..	..	..	..	..	..	..		
..	..	..	..	..	..	..	..	..	..	..		
123	57	47	21	6	1	11	..	..	..	575	575	
..	2	..	..	..	..	..	..	..	..	7		
54	38	71	44	12	2	..	..	..	..	529		
..	..	1	..	..	..	..	..	..	..	4		
..	1	..	..	..	..	..	..	..	..	2		
..	..	..	..	..	..	..	..	..	..	..		
54	41	72	44	12	2	..	..	..	..	542	542	
..	..	..	..	..	..	..	..	..	..	..		
13	16	10	7	4	1	..	..	..	..	111		
..	..	..	..	..	..	..	..	..	..	..		
..	..	..	..	..	..	..	..	..	..	..		
..	..	..	..	..	..	..	..	..	..	..		
13	16	10	7	4	1	..	..	..	..	111	111	

22

Castes.	Names of Villages.	No. of Houses.	Males according to Age. Birth to 10 Years.	11 to 20 Years.	21 to 30 Years.	31 to 40 Years.	41 to 50 Years.	51 to 60 Years.	61 to 70 Years.	71 to 80 Years.	81 to 90 Years.	91 to 100 Years and upwards.
	1	2	3	4	5	6	7	8	9	10	11	12
	Turuf Saturde.											
Bramins	61. Wujre.	8	7	2	2	3	2	4	1	..	..	..
Hindoos of other castes		39	17	19	11	16	17	10	19	6	4	..
Musulmans		..	..	..	..	..	..	..	..	..	..	..
Native Christians		..	...	..	..	..	..	..	..	..	..	..
Seedees		..	..	..	..	..	..	..	..	..	..	..
		47	24	21	13	19	19	14	20	6	4	..
Bramins	62. Bodde.	..	..	..	..	..	..	..	..	..	..	..
Hindoos of other castes		13	11	8	10	1	2	2	..	..	..	..
Musulmans		..	..	..	..	..	..	..	..	..	..	..
Native Christians		..	..	..	..	..	..	..	..	..	..	..
Seedees		..	..	..	..	..	..	..	..	..	..	..
		13	11	8	10	1	2	2	..	..	..	..
Bramins	63. Aee.	..	..	..	..	..	..	..	..	..	..	..
Hindoos of other castes		58	33	39	29	15	4	3	10	10	..	..
Musulmans		..	..	..	..	..	..	..	..	..	..	..
Native Christians		..	..	..	..	..	..	..	..	..	..	..
Seedees		..	..	..	..	..	..	..	..	..	..	..
		58	33	39	29	15	4	3	10	10	..	..
Bramins	64. Sonawul.	..	..	..	..	..	..	..	..	..	..	..
Hindoos of other castes		30	3	4	13	12	10	15	6	1	..	..
Musulmans		..	..	..	..	..	..	..	..	..	..	..
Native Christians		..	..	..	..	..	..	..	..	..	..	..
Seedees		..	..	..	..	..	..	..	..	..	..	..
		30	3	4	13	12	10	15	6	1	..	..
Bramins	65. Khanyale.	..	..	..	..	..	..	..	..	..	..	..
Hindoos of other castes		16	11	12	9	3	1	..	..	..	..	..
Musulmans		..	..	..	..	..	..	..	..	..	..	..
Native Christians		..	..	..	..	..	..	..	..	..	..	..
Seedees		..	..	..	..	..	..	..	..	..	..	..
		16	11	12	9	3	1	..	..	..	..	..

FEMALES according to Age.										Total of each Caste.	Grand Total.	REMARKS.
Birth to 10 Years.	11 to 20 Years.	21 to 30 Years.	31 to 40 Years.	41 to 50 Years.	51 to 60 Years.	61 to 70 Years.	71 to 80 Years.	81 to 90 Years.	91 to 100 Years and upwards.			
13	14	15	16	17	18	19	20	21	22	23	24	
8	1	7	..	4	3	1	..	..	..	45		
..	20	23	11	19	15	17	2	1	..	227		
..	..	..	..	..	..	..	..	..	..	..		
..	..	..	..	..	..	..	..	..	..	..		
..	..	..	..	..	..	..	..	..	..	..		
8	21	30	11	23	18	18	2	1	..	272	272	
..	..	..	..	..	..	..	..	..	..	..		
14	8	7	3	..	..	..	..	..	..	66		
..	..	..	..	..	..	..	..	..	..	..		
..	..	..	..	..	..	..	..	..	..	..		
..	..	..	..	..	..	..	..	..	..	..		
14	8	7	3	..	..	..	..	..	..	66	66	
..	..	..	..	..	..	..	..	..	..	..		
47	45	8	8	12	11	..	..	..	..	274		
..	..	..	..	..	..	..	..	..	..	..		
..	..	..	..	..	..	..	..	..	..	..		
..	..	..	..	..	..	..	..	..	..	..		
47	45	8	8	12	11	..	..	..	..	274	274	
..	..	..	..	..	..	..	..	..	..	..		
1	3	11	12	12	10	6	1	..	..	120		
..	..	..	..	..	..	..	..	..	..	..		
..	..	..	..	..	..	..	..	..	..	..		
..	..	..	..	..	..	..	..	..	..	..		
1	3	11	12	12	10	6	1	..	..	120	120	
..	..	..	..	..	..	..	..	..	..	..		
14	6	2	5	5	3	..	..	..	..	71		
..	..	..	..	..	..	..	..	..	..	..		
..	..	..	..	..	..	..	..	..	..	..		
..	..	..	..	..	..	..	..	..	..	..		
14	6	2	5	5	3	..	..	..	..	71	71	

Castes.	Names of Villages.	No. Houses.	Males according to Age. Birth to 10 Years.	11 to 20 Years.	21 to 30 Years.	31 to 40 Years.	41 to 50 Years.	51 to 60 Years.	61 to 70 Years.	71 to 80 Years.	81 to 90 Years.	91 to 100 Years and upwards.
	1	2	3	4	5	6	7	8	9	10	11	12
	Turuf Saturde.											
Bramins	66. Matne.	..	..	..	..	..	..	..	..	..	..	..
Hindoos of other castes		44	34	14	20	11	22	15	8	3	..	..
Musulmans		..	..	..	..	..	..	..	..	..	..	..
Native Christians.....		..	..	..	..	..	..	..	..	..	..	..
Seedees...............		..	..	..	..	..	..	..	..	..	..	..
		44	34	14	20	11	22	15	8	3	..	..
Bramins	67. Virdee.	..	..	..	..	..	..	..	..	..	..	..
Hindoos of other castes		54	39	47	39	19	8	2	1	..	..	..
Musulmans		..	..	..	..	..	..	..	..	..	..	..
Native Christians.....		..	..	..	..	..	..	..	..	..	..	..
Seedees...............		..	..	..	..	..	..	..	..	..	..	..
		54	39	47	39	19	8	2	1	..	..	..
Bramins	68. Tulekhole.	..	..	..	..	..	..	..	..	..	..	..
Hindoos of other castes		54	41	43	36	21	11	5	4	..	..	..
Musulmans		..	..	..	..	..	..	..	..	..	..	..
Native Christians.....		..	..	..	..	..	..	..	..	..	..	..
Seedees...............		..	..	..	..	..	..	..	..	..	..	..
		54	41	43	36	21	11	5	4	..	..	..
Bramins	69. Khokrul.	5	8	3	3	..	2	1	1	..	..	..
Hindoos of other castes		43	39	24	24	23	13	6	3	..	..	..
Musulmans		..	..	..	..	..	..	..	..	..	..	..
Native Christians.....		..	..	..	..	..	..	..	..	..	..	..
Seedees...............		..	..	..	..	..	..	..	..	..	..	..
		48	47	27	27	23	15	7	4	..	..	..
Bramins	70. Geerowre.	..	..	..	..	..	..	..	..	..	..	..
Hindoos of other castes		27	27	13	14	9	9	1	2	..	1	..
Musulmans		..	..	..	..	..	..	..	..	..	..	..
Native Christians.....		..	..	..	..	..	..	..	..	..	..	..
Seedees...............		..	..	..	..	..	..	..	..	..	..	..
		27	27	13	14	9	9	1	2	..	1	..

Females according to Age.										Total of each Caste.	Grand Total.	Remarks.
Birth to 10 Years.	11 to 20 Years.	21 to 30 Years.	31 to 40 Years.	41 to 50 Years.	51 to 60 Years.	61 to 70 Years.	71 to 80 Years.	81 to 90 Years.	91 to 100 Years and upwards.			
13	14	15	16	17	18	19	20	21	22	23	24	
..	..	..	..	..	..	..	..	..	..	..		
31	10	12	14	18	12	1	3	1	..	229		
..	..	..	..	..	..	..	..	..	..	..		
..	..	..	..	..	..	..	..	..	..	..		
..	..	..	..	..	..	..	..	..	..	..		
31	10	12	14	18	12	1	3	1	..	229	229	
..	..	..	..	..	..	..	..	..	..	..		
38	41	29	11	4	3	2	1	1	..	285		
..	..	..	..	..	..	..	..	..	..	..		
..	..	..	..	..	..	..	..	..	..	..		
..	..	..	..	..	..	..	..	..	..	..		
38	41	29	11	4	3	2	1	1	..	285	285	
..	..	..	..	..	..	..	..	..	..	..		
39	44	29	15	7	6	2	..	..	..	303		
..	..	..	..	..	..	..	..	..	..	..		
..	..	..	..	..	..	..	..	..	..	..		
..	..	..	..	..	..	..	..	..	..	..		
39	44	29	15	7	6	2	..	..	..	303	303	
5		1	5	..	2	1	..	..	..	32		
29	17	30	22	15	2	13	..	..	..	260		
..	..	..	..	..	..	..	..	..	..	..		
..	..	..	..	..	..	..	..	..	..	..		
..	..	..	..	..	..	..	..	..	..	..		
34	17	31	27	15	4	14	..	..	..	292	292	
..	..	..	..	..	..	..	..	..	..	..		
21	9	11	11	4	2	3	..	..	..	140		
..	..	..	..	..	..	..	..	..	..	..		
..	..	..	..	..	..	..	..	..	..	..		
..	..	..	..	..	..	..	..	..	..	..		
24	9	11	11	4	2	3	..	..	..	140	140	

23

Castes.	Names of Villages.	No. of Houses.	Males according to Age.									
			Birth to 10 Years.	11 to 20 Years.	21 to 30 Years.	31 to 40 Years.	41 to 50 Years.	51 to 60 Years.	61 to 70 Years.	71 to 80 Years.	81 to 90 Years.	91 to 100 Years and upwards.
	1	2	3	4	5	6	7	8	9	10	11	12
	Turuf Saturde.											
Bramins	71. Satelee.	1	2	2	1	1	1	1	..	..	..	..
Hindoos of other castes		97	43	63	68	58	28	8	..	..	..	..
Musulmans		..	..	..	..	..	..	..	..	..	..	..
Native Christians		1	..	1	..	..	..	..	..	..	..	..
Seedees		..	..	..	..	..	..	..	..	..	..	..
		99	45	66	69	59	29	9	..	..	..	..
Bramins	72. Puntoorlee.	..	..	..	..	..	..	..	..	..	..	..
Hindoos of other castes		28	20	9	15	6	10	8	4	3	..	..
Musulmans		..	..	..	..	..	..	..	..	..	..	..
Native Christians		..	..	..	..	..	..	..	..	..	..	..
Seedees		..	..	..	..	..	..	..	..	..	..	..
		28	20	9	15	6	10	8	4	3	..	..
Bramins	73. Purme.	3	1	1	2	4	..	..	..	..	..	..
Hindoos of other castes		94	67	73	52	41	16	..	..	..	..	..
Musulmans		15	6	13	12	5	1	..	..	..	..	..
Native Christians		..	..	..	..	..	..	..	..	..	..	..
Seedees		..	..	..	..	..	..	..	..	..	..	..
		112	74	87	66	50	17	..	..	..	..	..
Bramins	74. Pikoolee.	..	..	..	..	..	..	..	..	..	..	..
Hindoos of other castes		75	62	43	32	33	25	14	4	1	..	..
Musulmans		..	..	..	..	..	..	..	..	..	..	..
Native Christians		..	..	..	..	..	..	..	..	..	..	..
Seedees		..	..	..	..	..	..	..	..	..	..	..
		75	62	43	32	33	25	14	4	1	..	..
Bramins	75. Kusne.	..	..	..	..	..	..	..	..	..	..	..
Hindoos of other castes		50	48	30	26	29	17	5	3	..	..	..
Musulmans		..	..	..	..	..	..	..	..	..	..	..
Native Christians		..	..	..	..	..	..	..	..	..	..	..
Seedees		..	..	..	..	..	..	..	..	..	..	..
		50	48	30	26	29	17	5	3	..	..	..

Females according to Age.												
Birth to 10 Years.	11 to 20 Years.	21 to 30 Years.	31 to 40 Years.	41 to 50 Years.	51 to 60 Years.	61 to 70 Years.	71 to 80 Years.	81 to 90 Years.	91 to 100 Years and upwards.	Total of each Caste.	Grand Total.	Remarks.
13	14	15	16	17	18	19	20	21	22	23.	24	
1	2	1	1	..	..	..	..	..	..	13		
25	38	64	53	38	19	4	..	..	..	509		
..	..	..	..	..	..	..	..	..	..	..		
1	1	1	..	..	..	..	..	..	..	4		
..	..	..	..	..	..	..	..	..	..	..		
27	41	66	54	38	19	4	..	..	..	526	526	
..	..	..	..	..	..	..	..	..	..	..		
11	11	7	14	6	7	..	..	..	..	131		
..	..	..	..	..	..	..	..	..	..	..		
..	..	..	..	..	..	..	..	..	..	..		
..	..	..	..	..	..	..	..	..	..	..		
11	11	7	14	6	7	..	..	..	..	131	131	
3	2	4	1	..	..	..	..	..	..	18		
90	70	54	35	12	2	..	..	..	..	512		
10	12	10	5	1	..	..	..	..	..	75		
..	..	..	..	..	..	..	..	..	..	..		
..	..	..	..	..	..	..	..	..	..	..		
103	84	68	41	13	2	..	..	..	..	605	605	
..	..	..	..	..	..	..	..	..	..	..		
47	27	40	30	29	12	6	..	..	..	405		
..	..	..	..	..	..	..	..	..	..	..		
..	..	..	..	..	..	..	..	..	..	..		
..	..	..	..	..	..	..	..	..	..	..		
47	27	40	30	29	12	6	..	..	..	405	405	
..	..	..	..	..	..	..	..	..	..	..		
23	29	20	28	15	7	5	1	..	..	286		
..	..	..	..	..	..	..	..	..	..	..		
..	..	..	..	..	..	..	..	..	..	..		
..	..	..	..	..	..	..	..	..	..	..		
23	29	20	28	15	7	5	1	..	..	286	286	

Castes.	Names of Villages.	No. of Houses.	Males according to Age. Birth to 10 Years.	11 to 20 Years.	21 to 30 Years.	31 to 40 Years.	41 to 50 Years.	51 to 60 Years.	61 to 70 Years.	71 to 80 Years.	81 to 90 Years.	91 to 100 Years and upwards.
	1	2	3	4	5	6	7	8	9	10	11	12
	Turuf Saturde.											
Bramins	76. Konal.	..	..	..	..	..	..	..	..	..	..	..
Hindoos of other castes		27	18	13	9	9	11	4	1	..	..	..
Musulmans		..	..	..	..	..	..	..	..	..	..	..
Native Christians		..	..	..	..	..	..	..	..	..	..	..
Seedees		..	..	..	..	..	..	..	..	..	..	..
		27	18	13	9	9	11	4	1	..	..	..
Bramins	77. Palie.	..	..	..	..	..	..	..	..	..	..	..
Hindoos of other castes		18	11	14	12	1	1	..	..	..	..	..
Musulmans		..	..	..	..	..	..	..	..	..	..	..
Native Christians		..	..	..	..	..	..	..	..	..	..	..
Seedees		..	..	..	..	..	..	..	..	..	..	..
		18	11	14	12	1	1	..	..	..	..	..
Bramins	78. Mangelee.	..	..	..	..	..	..	..	..	..	..	..
Hindoos of other castes		111	69	58	71	61	33	14	..	..	..	..
Musulmans		..	..	..	..	..	..	..	..	..	..	..
Native Christians		..	..	..	..	..	..	..	..	..	..	..
Seedees		..	..	..	..	..	..	..	..	..	..	..
		111	69	58	71	61	33	14	..	..	..	..
Bramins	79. Ambudgam.	..	..	..	..	..	..	..	..	..	..	..
Hindoos of other castes		29	19	12	21	8	17	12	6	1	..	..
Musulmans		..	..	..	..	..	..	..	..	..	..	..
Native Christians		..	..	..	..	..	..	..	..	..	..	..
Seedees		..	..	..	..	..	..	..	..	..	..	..
		29	19	12	21	8	17	12	6	1	..	..
Bramins	80. Ambelee.	..	..	..	..	..	..	..	..	..	..	..
Hindoos of other castes		12	14	8	6	4	3	1	..	..	..	..
Musulmans		..	..	..	..	..	..	..	..	..	..	..
Native Christians		..	..	..	..	..	..	..	..	..	..	..
Seedees		..	..	..	..	..	..	..	..	..	..	..
		12	14	8	6	4	3	1	..	..	..	..

Females according to Age.												
Birth to 10 Years.	11 to 20 Years.	21 to 30 Years.	31 to 40 Years.	41 to 50 Years.	51 to 60 Years.	61 to 70 Years.	71 to 80 Years.	81 to 90 Years.	91 to 100 Years and upwards.	Total of each Caste.	Grand Total.	Remarks.
13	14	15	16	17	18	19	20	21	22	23	24	
..	..	..	..	..	..	..	..	..	..	..		
6	12	8	6	10	5	3	..	..	..	115		
..	..	..	..	..	..	..	..	..	..	..		
..	..	..	..	..	..	..	..	..	..	..		
..	..	..	..	..	..	..	..	..	..	..		
6	12	8	6	10	5	3	..	..	..	115	115	
..	..	..	..	..	..	..	..	..	..	..		
15	16	6	2	1	..	..	..	..	..	79		
..	..	..	..	..	..	..	..	..	..	..		
..	..	..	..	..	..	..	..	..	..	..		
..	..	..	..	..	..	..	..	..	..	..		
15	16	6	2	1	..	..	..	..	..	79	79	
..	..	..	..	..	..	..	..	..	..	..		
76	59	64	46	9	4	1	..	..	..	565		
..	..	..	..	..	..	..	..	..	..	..		
..	..	..	..	..	..	..	..	..	..	..		
..	..	..	..	..	..	..	..	..	..	..		
76	59	64	46	9	4	1	..	..	..	565	565	
..	..	..	..	..	..	..	..	..	..	..		
17	10	9	16	14	7	2	3	..	..	174		
..	..	..	..	..	..	..	..	..	..	..		
..	..	..	..	..	..	..	..	..	..	..		
..	..	..	..	..	..	..	..	..	..	..		
17	10	9	16	14	7	2	3	..	..	174	174	
..	..	..	..	..	..	..	..	..	..	..		
9	11	6	1	..	..	..	..	..	..	63		
..	..	..	..	..	..	..	..	..	..	..		
..	..	..	..	..	..	..	..	..	..	..		
..	..	..	..	..	..	..	..	..	..	..		
9	11	6	1	..	..	..	..	..	..	63	63	

24

Castes.	Names of Villages.	No. of Houses.	Males according to Age. Birth to 10 Years.	11 to 20 Years.	21 to 30 Years.	31 to 40 Years.	41 to 50 Years.	51 to 60 Years.	61 to 70 Years.	71 to 80 Years.	81 to 90 Years.	91 to 100 Years and upwards.
	1	2	3	4	5	6	7	8	9	10	11	12
	Turuf SATURDE.											
Bramins	81. KAMTE.	..	..	..	..	..	..	..	..	..	..	..
Hindoos of other castes		..	..	..	..	..	..	..	..	..	..	..
Musulmans		..	..	..	..	..	..	..	..	..	..	..
Native Christians		..	..	..	..	..	..	..	..	..	..	..
Seedees		..	..	..	..	..	..	..	..	..	..	..
		..	..	..	..	..	..	..	..	..	..	..
Bramins	82. HEWALE.	..	..	..	..	..	..	..	..	..	..	..
Hindoos of other castes		36	37	13	18	16	10	4	1	1	..	..
Musulmans		..	..	..	..	..	..	..	..	..	..	..
Native Christians		..	..	..	..	..	..	..	..	..	..	..
Seedees		..	..	..	..	..	..	..	..	..	..	..
		36	37	13	18	16	10	4	1	1	..	..
Bramins	83. PATIE.	..	..	..	..	..	..	..	..	..	..	..
Hindoos of other castes		64	68	39	29	17	15	7	9	1	..	..
Musulmans		..	..	..	..	..	..	..	..	..	..	..
Native Christians		..	..	..	..	..	..	..	..	..	..	..
Seedees		..	..	..	..	..	..	..	..	..	..	..
		64	68	39	29	17	15	7	9	1	..	..
Bramins	84. AEENOWRE.	5	..	5	1	..	..	2	1	..	..	..
Hindoos of other castes		46	52	17	14	14	8	8	2	..	..	..
Musulmans		..	..	..	..	..	..	..	..	..	..	..
Native Christians		..	..	..	..	..	..	..	..	..	..	..
Seedees		..	..	..	..	..	..	..	..	..	..	..
		51	52	22	15	14	8	10	3	..	..	..
Bramins	85. PAL.	..	..	..	..	..	..	..	..	..	..	..
Hindoos of other castes		38	38	22	12	10	8	4	1	..	..	..
Musulmans		..	..	..	..	..	..	..	..	..	..	..
Native Christians		..	..	..	..	..	..	..	..	..	..	..
Seedees		..	..	..	..	..	..	..	..	..	..	..
		38	38	22	12	10	8	4	1	..	..	..

Females according to Age.										Total of each Caste.	Grand Total.	Remarks.
Birth to 10 Years.	11 to 20 Years.	21 to 30 Years.	31 to 40 Years.	41 to 50 Years.	51 to 60 Years.	61 to 70 Years.	71 to 80 Years.	81 to 90 Years.	91 to 100 Years and upwards.			
13	14	15	16	17	18	19	20	21	22	23	24	
..	..	..	..	..	..	..	..	..	..	..		
..	..	..	..	..	..	..	..	..	..	..		
..	..	..	..	..	..	..	..	..	..	..		
..	..	..	..	..	..	..	..	..	..	..		
..	..	..	..	..	..	..	..	..	..	..		
..	..	..	..	..	..	..	..	..	..	..		
..	..	..	..	..	..	..	..	..	..	..		
30	17	16	13	12	7	4	2	1	..	202		
..	..	..	..	..	..	..	..	..	..	..		
..	..	..	..	..	..	..	..	..	..	..		
..	..	..	..	..	..	..	..	..	..	..		
30	17	16	13	12	7	4	2	1	..	202	202	
..	..	..	..	..	..	..	..	..	..	..		
67	24	25	22	19	9	12	1	2	..	366		
..	..	..	..	..	..	..	..	..	..	..		
..	..	..	..	..	..	..	..	..	..	..		
..	..	..	..	..	..	..	..	..	..	..		
67	24	25	22	19	9	12	1	2	..	366	366	
..	2	..	1	3	..	..	..	..	1	16		
39	17	18	16	12	9	4	..	3	..	233		
..	..	..	..	..	..	..	..	..	..	..		
..	..	..	..	..	..	..	..	..	..	..		
..	..	..	..	..	..	..	..	..	..	..		
39	19	18	17	15	9	4	..	3	1	249	240	
..	..	..	..	..	..	..	..	..	..	..		
31	18	16	7	8	11	3	..	..	..	189		
..	..	..	..	..	..	..	..	..	..	..		
..	..	..	..	..	..	..	..	..	..	..		
..	..	..	..	..	..	..	..	..	..	..		
31	18	16	7	8	11	3	..	..	..	189	189	

Castes.	Names of Villages.	No. of Houses.	Males according to Age. Birth to 10 Years.	11 to 20 Years.	21 to 30 Years.	31 to 40 Years.	41 to 50 Years.	51 to 60 Years.	61 to 70 Years.	71 to 80 Years.	81 to 90 Years.	91 to 100 Years and upwards.
	1	2	3	4	5	6	7	8	9	10	11	12
	Turuf Saturde.											
Bramins	86. Surgwe.	..	..	..	..	..	..	..	..	..	..	..
Hindoos of other castes		38	28	16	13	10	6	4	3	..	..	..
Musulmans		..	..	..	..	..	..	..	..	..	..	..
Native Christians		..	..	..	..	..	..	..	..	..	..	..
Seedees		3	6	2	2	..	1	..	1	..	..	..
		41	34	18	15	10	7	4	4	..	..	..
Bramins	87. Kendreboodrook.	..	..	..	..	..	..	..	..	..	..	..
Hindoos of other castes		6	5	2	2	4	1	..	..	..	..	..
Musulmans		..	..	..	..	..	..	..	..	..	..	..
Native Christians		..	..	..	..	..	..	..	..	..	..	..
Seedees		..	..	..	..	..	..	..	..	..	..	..
		6	5	2	2	4	1	..	..	..	..	..
Bramins	88. Kendrekhoord.	..	..	..	..	..	..	..	..	..	..	..
Hindoos of other castes		4	4	2	1	1	2	..	..	..	..	..
Musulmans		..	..	..	..	..	..	..	..	..	..	..
Native Christians		..	..	..	..	..	..	..	..	..	..	..
Seedees		..	..	..	..	..	..	..	..	..	..	..
		4	4	2	1	1	2	..	..	..	..	..
Bramins	89. Bamurde.	..	..	..	..	..	..	..	..	..	..	..
Hindoos of other castes		16	9	4	10	1	4	1	1	..	..	..
Musulmans		..	..	..	..	..	..	..	..	..	..	..
Native Christians		1	3	2	1	1	..	..	..	..	..	..
Seedees		1	1	..	1	1	..	..	..	..	..	..
		18	13	6	12	3	4	1	1	..	..	..
Bramins	90. Ghatewre.	..	..	..	..	..	..	..	..	..	..	..
Hindoos of other castes		..	..	..	..	..	..	..	..	..	..	..
Musulmans		..	..	..	..	..	..	..	..	..	..	..
Native Christians		..	..	..	..	..	..	..	..	..	..	..
Seedees		..	..	..	..	..	..	..	..	..	..	..
		..	..	..	..	..	..	..	..	..	..	..

Females according to Age.										Total of each Caste.	Grand Total	Remarks.
Birth to 10 Years.	11 to 20 Years.	21 to 30 Years.	31 to 40 Years.	41 to 50 Years.	51 to 60 Years.	61 to 70 Years.	71 to 80 Years.	81 to 90 Years.	91 to 100 Years and upwards.			
13	14	15	16	17	18	19	20	21	22	23	24	
..	..	..	..	..	..	..	..	..	..	..		
37	12	18	12	13	7	..	1	..	..	180		
..	..	..	..	..	..	..	..	..	..	..		
..	..	..	..	..	..	..	..	..	..	..		
3	1	4	1	..	1	1	..	..	..	23		
40	13	22	13	13	8	1	1	..	..	203	203	
..	..	..	..	..	..	..	..	..	..	..		
5	3	2	1	..	2	1	..	..	..	28		
..	..	..	..	..	..	..	..	..	..	..		
..	..	..	..	..	..	..	..	..	..	..		
..	..	..	..	..	..	..	..	..	..	..		
5	3	2	1	..	2	1	..	..	..	28	28	
..	..	..	..	..	..	..	..	..	..	..		
4	1	2	..	1	1	..	..	..	..	19		
..	..	..	..	..	..	..	..	..	..	..		
..	..	..	..	..	..	..	..	..	..	..		
..	..	..	..	..	..	..	..	..	..	..		
4	1	2	..	1	1	..	..	..	..	19	19	
..	..	..	..	..	..	..	..	..	..	..		
9	8	7	4	2	1	1	..	1	..	63		
..	..	..	..	..	..	..	..	..	..	..		
2	..	..	..	..	1	..	..	..	..	10		
..	..	1	..	..	..	..	..	..	..	4		
11	8	8	4	2	2	1	..	1	..	77	77	
..	..	..	..	..	..	..	..	..	..	..		
..	..	..	..	..	..	..	..	..	..	..		
..	..	..	..	..	..	..	..	..	..	..		
..	..	..	..	..	..	..	..	..	..	..		
..	..	..	..	..	..	..	..	..	..	..		
..	..	..	..	..	..	..	..	..	..	..	..	

25

Castes.	Names of Villages.	No. of Houses.	Males according to Age. Birth to 10 Years.	11 to 20 Years.	21 to 30 Years.	31 to 40 Years.	41 to 50 Years.	51 to 60 Years.	61 to 70 Years.	71 to 80 Years.	81 to 90 Years.	91 to 100 Years and upwards.
	1	2	3	4	5	6	7	8	9	10	11	12
	Turuf Saturde.											
Bramins	91. Khuradee.	..	..	..	..	..	..	..	..	..	..	..
Hindoos of other castes		..	..	..	..	..	..	..	..	..	..	..
Musulmans		..	..	..	..	..	..	..	..	..	..	..
Native Christians		..	..	..	..	..	..	..	..	..	..	..
Seedees		..	..	..	..	..	..	..	..	..	..	..
		..	..	..	..	..	..	..	..	..	..	..
Bramins	92. Terwunmere.	..	..	..	..	..	..	..	..	..	..	..
Hindoos of other castes		50	35	20	25	29	20	9	1	..	..	..
Musulmans		..	..	..	..	..	..	..	..	..	..	..
Native Christians		5	..	1	4	3	1	..	..	..	..	..
Seedees		..	..	..	..	..	..	..	..	..	..	..
		55	35	21	29	32	21	9	1	..	..	..
Bramins	93. Konal.	..	..	..	..	..	..	..	..	..	..	..
Hindoos of other castes		31	34	18	11	13	9	3	1	..	..	..
Musulmans		..	..	..	..	..	..	..	..	..	..	..
Native Christians		..	..	..	..	..	..	..	..	..	..	..
Seedees		..	..	..	..	..	..	..	..	..	..	..
		31	34	18	11	13	9	3	1	..	..	..
Bramins	94. Ghotge.	..	..	..	..	..	..	..	..	..	..	..
Hindoos of other castes		40	36	14	18	12	5	4	1	..	..	..
Musulmans		..	..	..	..	..	..	..	..	..	..	..
Native Christians		..	..	..	..	..	..	..	..	..	..	..
Seedees		..	..	..	..	..	..	..	..	..	..	..
		40	36	14	18	12	5	4	1	..	..	..
Bramins	95. Seeringe.	..	..	..	..	..	..	..	..	..	..	..
Hindoos of other castes		41	43	16	11	23	9	2	..	1	..	..
Musulmans		..	..	..	..	..	..	..	..	..	..	..
Native Christians		..	..	..	..	..	..	..	..	..	..	..
Seedees		..	..	..	..	..	..	..	..	..	..	..
		41	43	16	11	23	9	2	..	1	..	..

Females according to Age.										Total of each Caste.	Grand Total.	Remarks.
Birth to 10 Years.	11 to 20 Years.	21 to 30 Years.	31 to 40 Years.	41 to 50 Years.	51 to 60 Years.	61 to 70 Years.	71 to 80 Years.	81 to 90 Years.	91 to 100 Years and upwards.			
13	14	15	16	17	18	19	20	21	22	23	24	
..	..	..	..	..	..	..	..	..	..	..		
..	..	..	..	..	..	..	..	..	..	..		
..	..	..	..	..	..	..	..	..	..	..		
..	..	..	..	..	..	..	..	..	..	..		
..	..	..	..	..	..	..	..	..	..	..		
..	..	..	..	..	..	..	..	..	..	..	..	
..	..	..	..	..	..	..	..	..	..	..		
25	19	32	22	16	14	2	..	..	..	269		
..	..	..	..	..	..	..	..	..	..	..		
..	4	3	1	1	..	..	..	..	..	18		
..	..	..	..	..	..	..	..	..	..	..		
25	23	35	23	17	14	2	..	..	..	287	287	
..	..	..	..	..	..	..	..	..	..	..		
16	14	15	14	5	4	..	..	..	..	157		
..	..	..	..	..	..	..	..	..	..	..		
..	..	..	..	..	..	..	..	..	..	..		
..	..	..	..	..	..	..	..	..	..	..		
16	14	15	14	5	4	..	..	..	..	157	157	
..	..	..	..	..	..	..	..	..	..	..		
34	15	19	12	7	4	2	1	..	..	184		
..	..	..	..	..	..	..	..	..	..	..		
..	..	..	..	..	..	..	..	..	..	..		
..	..	..	..	..	..	..	..	..	..	..		
34	15	19	12	7	4	2	1	..	..	184	184	
..	..	..	..	..	..	..	..	..	..	..		
36	7	21	21	3	1	2	1	..	..	197		
..	..	..	..	..	..	..	..	..	..	..		
..	..	..	..	..	..	..	..	..	..	..		
..	..	..	..	..	..	..	..	..	..	..		
36	7	21	21	3	1	2	1	..	..	197	197	

Castes.	Names of Villages.	No. of Houses.	Males according to Age. Birth to 10 Years.	11 to 20 Years.	21 to 30 Years.	31 to 40 Years.	41 to 50 Years.	51 to 60 Years.	61 to 70 Years.	71 to 80 Years.	81 to 90 Years.	91 to 100 Years and upwards.
	1	2	3	4	5	6	7	8	9	10	11	12
	Turuf Saturde.											
Bramins	96. Sirwul.	..	..	..	..	..	..	..	..	..	..	..
Hindoos of other castes		12	9	4	5	3	2	..	2	..	..	..
Musulmans		..	..	..	..	..	..	..	..	..	..	..
Native Christians		..	..	..	..	..	..	..	..	..	..	..
Seedees		..	..	..	..	..	..	..	..	..	..	..
		12	9	4	5	3	2	..	2	..	..	..
Bramins	97. Bhekoolee.	..	..	..	..	..	..	..	..	..	..	..
Hindoos of other castes		23	17	9	9	6	5	1	..	..	..	..
Musulmans		..	..	..	..	..	..	..	..	..	..	..
Native Christians		..	..	..	..	..	..	..	..	..	..	..
Seedees		..	..	..	..	..	..	..	..	..	..	..
		23	17	9	9	6	5	1	..	..	..	..
Bramins	98. Ker.	1	..	..	..	1	..	..	..	..	..	..
Hindoos of other castes		53	53	17	10	13	20	4	1	..	..	..
Musulmans		..	..	..	..	..	..	..	..	..	..	..
Native Christians		..	..	..	..	..	..	..	..	..	..	..
Seedees		..	..	..	..	..	..	..	..	..	..	..
		54	53	17	10	14	20	4	1	..	..	..
Bramins	99. Khudpude.	..	..	..	..	..	..	..	..	..	..	..
Hindoos of other castes		..	..	..	..	..	..	..	..	..	..	..
Musulmans		..	..	..	..	..	..	..	..	..	..	..
Native Christians		..	..	..	..	..	..	..	..	..	..	..
Seedees		..	..	..	..	..	..	..	..	..	..	..
		..	..	..	..	..	..	..	..	..	..	..
Bramins	100. Chowkool.	..	..	..	..	..	..	..	..	..	..	..
Hindoos of other castes		243	248	181	132	90	63	21	14	10	11	..
Musulmans		..	..	..	..	..	..	..	..	..	..	..
Native Christians		1	2	2	..	..	..	..	..	..	..	..
Seedees		..	..	..	..	..	..	..	..	..	..	..
		244	250	183	132	90	63	21	14	10	11	..

Females according to Age.										Total of each Caste.	Grand Total.	Remarks.
Birth to 10 Years.	11 to 20 Years.	21 to 30 Years.	31 to 40 Years.	41 to 50 Years.	51 to 60 Years.	61 to 70 Years.	71 to 80 Years.	81 to 90 Years.	91 to 100 Years and upwards.			
13	14	15	16	17	18	19	20	21	22	23	24	
..	..	..	..	..	..	..	..	..	..	..		
10	2	4	1	1	5	..	..	..	..	48		
..	..	..	..	..	..	..	..	..	..	..		
..	..	..	..	..	..	..	..	..	..	..		
..	..	..	..	..	..	..	..	..	..	..		
10	2	4	1	1	5	..	..	..	..	48	48	
..	..	..	..	..	..	..	..	..	..	..		
24	14	6	6	4	3	1	..	..	..	105		
..	..	..	..	..	..	..	..	..	..	..		
..	..	..	..	..	..	..	..	..	..	..		
..	..	..	..	..	..	..	..	..	..	..		
24	14	6	6	4	3	1	..	..	..	105	105	
1	..	..	..	..	..	..	..	..	..	2		
38	12	17	14	12	6	4	..	..	..	221		
..	..	..	..	..	..	..	..	..	..	..		
..	..	..	..	..	..	..	..	..	..	..		
..	..	..	..	..	..	..	..	..	..	..		
39	12	17	14	12	6	4	..	..	..	223	223	
..	..	..	..	..	..	..	..	..	..	..		
..	..	..	..	..	..	..	..	..	..	..		
..	..	..	..	..	..	..	..	..	..	..		
..	..	..	..	..	..	..	..	..	..	..		
..	..	..	..	..	..	..	..	..	..	..		
..	..	..	..	..	..	..	..	..	..	..	..	
..	..	..	..	..	..	..	..	..	..	..		
224	119	118	66	43	33	32	14	19	3	1,441		
..	..	..	..	..	..	..	..	..	..	..		
..	1	..	1	1	1	..	..	..	..	8		
..	..	..	..	..	..	..	..	..	..	..		
224	120	118	67	44	34	32	14	19	3	1,449	1,449	

26

Castes.	Names of Villages.	No. of Houses.	Males according to Age.									
			Birth to 10 Years.	11 to 20 Years.	21 to 30 Years.	31 to 40 Years.	41 to 50 Years.	51 to 60 Years.	61 to 70 Years.	71 to 80 Years.	81 to 90 Years.	91 to 100 Years and upwards.
	1	2	3	4	5	6	7	8	9	10	11	12
	Turuf Saturde.											
Bramins	101. Awara.	..	..	..	..	..	..	..	..	..	..	..
Hindoos of other castes		28	26	8	17	11	5	3	..	..	..	..
Musulmans		17	12	12	13	5	4	..	2	..	..	..
Native Christians......		..	..	..	..	..	..	..	..	..	..	..
Seedees.................		..	..	..	..	..	..	..	..	..	..	..
		45	38	20	30	16	9	3	2	..	..	..
Bramins	......	382	330	233	215	143	138	84	29	9	1	2
Hindoos of other castes	......	5,992	5,105	3,252	2,937	2,217	1,572	819	332	111	24	3
Musulmans	......	145	126	88	72	62	39	16	11	1	..	..
Native Christians......	......	140	125	65	68	58	28	10	3	..	..	..
Seedees.................	......	7	8	4	5	2	1	..	1	..	..	..
	Grand Total of the Banda Division	6,666	5,694	3,642	3,297	2,482	1,778	929	376	121	25	5

Sawunt Waree, Political Superintendent's Office, Camp Belgaum, 30th October 1852.

Females according to Age.										Total of each Caste.	Grand Total.	Remarks.
Birth to 10 Years.	11 to 20 Years.	21 to 30 Years.	31 to 40 Years.	41 to 50 Years.	51 to 60 Years.	61 to 70 Years.	71 to 80 Years.	81 to 90 Years.	91 to 100 Years and upwards.			
13	14	15	16	17	18	19	20	21	22	23	24	
..	..	..	..	..	..	..	..	..	..	..		* Grand Total.. 35,317 { Males.... 18,349 / Females.. 16,968
22	15	22	6	3	6	1	..	..	..	145		
16	11	9	4	5	1	..	..	..	..	94		
..	..	..	..	..	..	..	..	..	..	..		
..	..	..	..	..	..	..	..	..	..	..		
38	26	31	10	8	7	1	..	..	..	239	239	
311	186	209	143	101	80	40	11	1	1	2,267		
4,416	2,643	2,832	2,111	1,485	984	483	136	39	10	31,511		
109	62	70	57	40	19	12	10	1	..	795		
108	57	59	48	36	23	10	4	2	..	704		
6	1	7	2	..	1	1	..	..	1	40		
4,950	2,949	3,177	2,361	1,662	1,107	546	161	43	12	35,317	*35,317	

(Signed) H. L. ANDERSON,
Political Superintendent.

Census of the Koodal Division,

Castes.	Names of Villages.	No. of Houses.	Males according to Age. Birth to 10 Years.	11 to 20 Years.	21 to 30 Years.	31 to 40 Years.	41 to 50 Years.	51 to 60 Years.	61 to 70 Years.	71 to 80 Years.	81 to 90 Years.	91 to 100 Years and upwards.
	1	2	3	4	5	6	7	8	9	10	11	12
	Turuf Huwelee.											
Bramins	1. Koodal.*	25	40	14	12	16	5	7	1	..	..	..
Hindoos of other castes		188	248	160	84	75	33	23	2	1	1	..
Musulmans		24	36	22	13	12	7	5	2	3	1	..
Native Christians		2	1	2	..	..	1	..	..	..	..	..
Seedees		..	..	..	..	..	..	..	..	..	..	..
		239	325	198	109	103	46	35	5	4	2	..
Bramins	2. Walawul.	90	93	71	41	35	25	20	7	2	..	..
Hindoos of other castes		241	230	170	100	68	65	20	13	2	..	..
Musulmans		3	..	2	2	1	2	..	2	..	..	..
Native Christians		..	..	..	..	..	..	..	..	..	..	..
Seedees		..	..	..	..	..	..	..	..	..	..	..
		334	323	243	143	104	92	40	22	4	..	..
Bramins	3. Naroor.	79	116	62	49	25	27	12	5	2	..	..
Hindoos of other castes		419	480	297	224	139	105	46	2	1	..	..
Musulmans		8	7	5	3	5	1	2	1	..	..	..
Native Christians		1	4	2	1	1	1	2	1	..	..	..
Seedees		..	..	..	..	..	..	..	..	..	..	..
		507	607	366	277	170	134	62	9	3	..	..
Bramins	4. Surumbul.	2	..	3	2	..	..	1	..	..	..	..
Hindoos of other castes		169	225	117	70	75	51	17	12	1	..	1
Musulmans		1	1	1	..	..	..	1	1	..	..	..
Native Christians		..	..	..	..	..	..	..	..	..	..	..
Seedees		..	..	..	..	..	..	..	..	..	..	..
		172	226	121	72	75	51	19	13	1	..	1
Bramins	5. Sonowre.	14	16	7	5	5	3	1	2	..	..	..
Hindoos of other castes		98	95	66	65	19	14	15	10	12	..	..
Musulmans		..	..	..	..	..	..	..	..	..	..	..
Native Christians		..	..	..	..	..	..	..	..	..	..	..
Seedees		..	..	..	..	..	..	..	..	..	..	..
		112	111	73	70	24	17	16	12	12	..	..

for the Year 1851.

Females according to Age.										Total of each Caste.	Grand Total.	Remarks.
Birth to 10 Years.	11 to 20 Years.	21 to 30 Years.	31 to 40 Years.	41 to 50 Years.	51 to 60 Years.	61 to 70 Years.	71 to 80 Years.	81 to 90 Years.	91 to 100 Years and upwards.			
13	14	15	16	17	18	19	20	21	22	23	24	
22	12	10	8	6	7	2	1	1	..	164		
180	129	110	60	30	31	9	1	..	..	1,177		
35	18	15	7	7	3	2	1	..	..	189		
1	1	1	1	1	..	..	..	..	..	9		
..	..	..	..	..	..	..	..	..	..	..		
238	160	136	76	44	41	13	3	1	..	1,539	1,539	
112	58	45	23	31	16	10	1	..	..	590		
255	159	112	71	68	45	28	12	..	..	1,418		
3	1	1	..	..	1	1	..	..	..	16		
..	..	..	..	..	..	..	..	..	..	..		
..	..	..	..	..	..	..	..	..	..	..		
370	218	158	94	99	62	39	13	..	..	2,024	2,024	
90	52	56	33	23	18	8	2	..	..	580		
440	257	223	142	103	53	13	1	..	..	2,526		
9	3	5	2	4	1	..	..	..	..	48		
2	..	1	1	2	1	1	..	..	..	20		
..	..	..	..	..	..	..	..	..	..	..		
541	312	285	178	132	73	22	3	..	..	3,174	3,174	
2	1	1	..	2	1	..	..	..	..	13		
170	112	104	73	47	29	14	2	..	..	1,120		
1	..	..	1	1	..	..	..	..	..	7		
..	..	..	..	..	..	..	..	..	..	..		
..	..	..	..	..	..	..	..	..	..	..		
173	113	105	74	50	30	14	2	..	..	1,140	1,140	
20	7	5	4	4	4	3	1	..	..	87		
82	54	64	18	20	23	8	5	..	..	570		
..	..	..	..	..	..	..	..	..	..	..		
..	..	..	..	..	..	..	..	..	..	..		
..	..	..	..	..	..	..	..	..	..	..		
102	61	69	22	24	27	11	6	..	..	667	667	

27

Castes.	Names of Villages.	No. of Houses.	Males according to Age.									
			Birth to 10 Years.	11 to 20 Years.	21 to 30 Years.	31 to 40 Years.	41 to 50 Years.	51 to 60 Years.	61 to 70 Years.	71 to 80 Years.	81 to 90 Years.	91 to 100 Years and upwards.
	1	2	3	4	5	6	7	8	9	10	11	12
	Turuf Huwelee.											
Bramins	6. Bebownee.	25	21	16	16	6	10	9	2	2	..	..
Hindoos of other castes		74	54	50	41	29	12	7	2	1	..	..
Musulmans		..	..	..	..	..	..	..	..	..	..	..
Native Christians		..	..	..	..	..	..	..	..	..	..	..
Seedees		..	..	..	..	..	..	..	..	..	..	..
		99	75	66	57	35	22	16	4	3	..	..
Bramins	7. Bamboolee.	19	15	9	7	4	4	4	3	1	..	..
Hindoos of other castes		43	70	54	41	30	23	21	8	1	..	..
Musulmans		..	..	..	..	..	..	..	..	..	..	..
Native Christians		..	..	..	..	..	..	..	..	..	..	..
Seedees		..	..	..	..	..	..	..	..	..	..	..
		62	85	63	48	34	27	25	11	2	..	..
Bramins	8. Wader Warowde.	3	4	..	2	1	1	..	..	..	..	..
Hindoos of other castes		61	44	31	35	22	16	4	2	..	..	..
Musulmans		..	..	..	..	..	..	..	..	..	..	..
Native Christians		..	..	..	..	..	..	..	..	..	..	..
Seedees		..	..	..	..	..	..	..	..	..	..	..
		64	48	31	37	23	17	4	2	..	..	..
Bramins	9. Bow.	21	10	11	16	5	3	2	2	..	1	..
Hindoos of other castes		113	86	60	81	29	22	10	11	1	1	..
Musulmans		..	..	..	..	..	..	..	..	..	..	..
Native Christians		..	..	..	..	..	..	..	..	..	..	..
Seedees		..	..	..	..	..	..	..	..	..	..	..
		134	96	71	97	34	25	12	13	1	2	..
Bramins	10. Anow.	5	15	2	5	7	3	2	..	..	..	..
Hindoos of other castes		198	240	141	86	66	32	28	9	3	..	..
Musulmans		..	..	..	..	..	..	..	..	..	..	..
Native Christians		..	..	..	..	..	..	..	..	..	..	..
Seedees		..	..	..	..	..	..	..	..	..	..	..
		203	255	143	91	73	35	30	9	3	..	..

Females according to Age.										Total of each Caste.	Grand Total.	Remarks.
Birth to 10 Years.	11 to 20 Years.	21 to 30 Years.	31 to 40 Years.	41 to 50 Years.	51 to 60 Years.	61 to 70 Years.	71 to 80 Years.	81 to 90 Years.	91 to 100 Years and upwards.			
13	14	15	16	17	18	19	20	21	22	23	24	
24	10	10	11	8	9	5	..	..	..	159		
75	31	25	28	16	21	4	3	..	..	399		
..	..	..	..	..	..	..	..	..	..	..		
..	..	..	..	..	..	..	..	..	..	..		
..	..	..	..	..	..	..	..	..	..	..		
99	41	35	39	24	30	9	3	..	..	558	558	
14	8	10	1	8	5	5	3	..	..	101		
69	36	37	32	20	19	21	1	..	..	483		
..	..	..	..	..	..	..	..	..	..	..		
..	..	..	..	..	..	..	..	..	..	..		
..	..	..	..	..	..	..	..	..	..	..		
83	44	47	33	28	24	26	4	..	..	584	584	
3	1	1	2	1	..	..	..	..	..	16		
48	26	34	22	14	4	1	..	..	..	303		
..	..	..	..	..	..	..	..	..	..	..		
..	..	..	..	..	..	..	..	..	..	..		
..	..	..	..	..	..	..	..	..	..	..		
51	27	35	24	15	4	1	..	..	..	319	319	
14	8	10	7	10	2	1	2	2	..	106		
85	52	64	47	23	15	11	3	1	..	602		
..	..	..	..	..	..	..	..	..	..	..		
..	..	..	..	..	..	..	..	..	..	..		
..	..	..	..	..	..	..	..	..	..	..		
99	60	74	54	33	17	12	5	3	..	708	708	
9	3	4	4	2	2	1	..	..	..	59		
255	138	118	67	43	40	14	..	..	..	1,280		
..	..	..	..	..	..	..	..	..	..	..		
..	..	..	..	..	..	..	..	..	..	..		
..	..	..	..	..	..	..	..	..	..	..		
264	141	122	71	45	42	15	..	..	..	1,339	1,330	

Castes.	Names of Villages.	No. of Houses.	Males according to Age.									
			Birth to 10 Years.	11 to 20 Years.	21 to 30 Years.	31 to 40 Years.	41 to 50 Years.	51 to 60 Years.	61 to 70 Years.	71 to 80 Years.	81 to 90 Years.	91 to 100 Years and upwards.
	1	2	3	4	5	6	7	8	9	10	11	12
	Turuf Huwelee.											
Bramins	11. Moolde.	..	..	..	..	..	..	..	..	..	..	..
Hindoos of other castes		62	72	25	29	21	34	7	7	..	..	..
Musulmans		..	..	..	..	..	..	..	..	..	..	..
Native Christians......		..	..	..	..	..	..	..	..	..	..	..
Seedees................		..	..	..	..	..	..	..	..	..	..	..
		62	72	25	29	21	34	7	7	..	..	..
Bramins	12. Pundoor.	9	6	9	2	..	6	2	..	..	..	..
Hindoos of other castes		77	74	54	27	26	9	14	7	5	..	1
Musulmans		..	..	..	..	..	..	..	..	..	..	..
Native Christians......		..	..	..	..	..	..	..	..	..	..	..
Seedees................		..	..	..	..	.	..	..	..	..	..	..
		86	80	63	29	26	15	16	7	5	..	1
Bramins	13. Wader Hoomurwula.	..	..	..	..	..	..	..	..	..	..	..
Hindoos of other castes		117	140	45	51	26	34	15	13	7	..	..
Musulmans		..	..	..	..	..	..	..	..	..	..	..
Native Christians......		..	..	..	..	..	..	..	..	..	..	..
Seedees................		..	..	..	..	..	..	..	..	..	..	..
		117	140	45	51	26	34	15	13	7	..	..
Bramins	14. Ambudpul.	1	..	..	1	..	..	..	1	..	..	..
Hindoos of other castes		57	72	30	19	14	8	6	..	..	2	..
Musulmans		..	..	..	..	..	..	..	..	..	..	..
Native Christians......		..	..	..	..	..	..	..	..	..	..	..
Seedees................		..	..	..	..	..	..	..	..	..	..	..
		58	72	30	20	14	8	6	1	..	2	..
Bramins	15. Powus.	9	2	4	5	4	2	2	..	..	..	..
Hindoos of other castes		176	90	148	134	84	65	18	19	3	..	..
Musulmans		..	..	..	..	..	..	..	..	..	..	..
Native Christians......		..	..	..	..	..	..	..	..	..	..	..
Seedees................		..	..	..	..	..	..	..	..	..	..	..
		185	92	152	139	88	67	20	19	3	..	..

Females according to Age.										Total of each Caste.	Grand Total.	Remarks.
Birth to 10 Years.	11 to 20 Years.	21 to 30 Years.	31 to 40 Years.	41 to 50 Years.	51 to 60 Years.	61 to 70 Years.	71 to 80 Years.	81 to 90 Years.	91 to 100 Years and upwards.			
13	14	15	16	17	18	19	20	21	22	23	24	
..	..	..	..	..	..	..	..	..	..	..		
60	24	31	29	28	9	..	..	..	..	376		
..	..	..	..	..	..	..	..	..	..	..		
..	..	..	..	..	..	..	..	..	..	..		
..	..	..	..	..	..	..	..	..	..	..		
60	24	31	29	28	9	..	..	..	..	376	376	
10	3	5	3	..	1	..	..	..	..	47		
47	51	28	23	7	19	5	1	1	..	399		
..	..	..	..	..	..	..	..	..	..	..		
..	..	..	..	..	..	..	..	..	..	..		
..	..	..	..	..	..	..	..	..	..	..		
57	54	33	26	7	20	5	1	1	..	446	446	
..	..	..	..	..	..	..	..	..	..	..		
150	67	65	53	27	13	3	4	..	..	713		
..	..	..	..	..	..	..	..	..	..	..		
..	..	..	..	..	..	..	..	..	..	..		
..	..	..	..	..	..	..	..	..	..	..		
150	67	65	53	27	13	3	4	..	..	713	713	
1	..	..	1	..	..	..	..	..	..	4		
56	19	32	16	6	2	1	2	1	..	286		
..	..	..	..	..	..	..	..	..	..	..		
..	..	..	..	..	..	..	..	..	..	..		
..	..	..	..	..	..	..	..	..	..	..		
57	19	32	17	6	2	1	2	1	..	290	290	
6	5	3	2	1	2	1	..	..	..	39		
93	155	96	102	55	37	21	3	..	..	1,123		
..	..	..	..	..	..	..	..	..	..	..		
..	..	..	..	..	..	..	..	..	..	..		
..	..	..	..	..	..	..	..	..	..	..		
99	160	99	104	56	39	22	3	..		1,162	1,162	

28

Castes.	Names of Villages.	No. of Houses.	Males according to Age. Birth to 10 Years.	11 to 20 Years.	21 to 30 Years.	31 to 40 Years.	41 to 50 Years.	51 to 60 Years.	61 to 70 Years.	71 to 80 Years.	81 to 90 Years.	91 to 100 Years and upwards.
	1	2	3	4	5	6	7	8	9	10	11	12
	Turuf Huwelee.											
Bramins	16. Pingoolee.	42	35	28	29	9	12	8	4	2	1	..
Hindoos of other castes		150	180	93	100	72	33	21	13	7	3	..
Musulmans		11	15	5	6	5	3	2	2	..	1	..
Native Christians		..	..	..	..	..	..	..	..	..	..	..
Seedees		..	..	..	..	..	..	..	..	..	..	..
		203	230	126	135	86	48	31	19	9	5	..
Bramins	17. Kulsoolee.	3	4	3	1	1	..	1	1	..	..	..
Hindoos of other castes		319	371	192	107	100	69	56	29	35	..	..
Musulmans		..	..	..	..	..	..	..	..	..	..	..
Native Christians		..	..	..	..	..	..	..	..	..	..	..
Seedees		..	..	..	..	..	..	..	..	..	..	..
		322	375	195	108	101	69	57	30	35	..	..
Bramins	18. Pokhrum.	11	9	8	5	3	3	3	3	..	..	..
Hindoos of other castes		230	267	175	165	82	68	40	22	11	1	..
Musulmans		..	..	..	..	..	..	..	..	..	..	..
Native Christians		..	..	..	..	..	..	..	..	..	..	..
Seedees		..	..	..	..	..	..	..	..	..	..	..
		241	276	183	170	85	71	43	25	11	1	..
Bramins	19. Bamberde.	15	22	15	11	10	5	1	4	1	..	..
Hindoos of other castes		169	167	98	80	62	41	16	13	4	..	..
Musulmans		7	13	7	3	3	1	2	1	..	..	..
Native Christians		..	..	..	..	..	..	..	..	..	..	..
Seedees		..	..	..	..	..	..	..	..	..	..	..
		191	202	120	94	75	47	19	18	5	..	..
Bramins	20. Sewdow.	1	4	..	1	1	..	..	1	..	..	..
Hindoos of other castes		225	290	135	100	77	65	36	16	11	..	..
Musulmans		..	..	..	..	..	..	..	..	..	..	..
Native Christians		..	..	..	..	..	..	..	..	..	..	..
Seedees		..	..	..	..	..	..	..	..	..	..	..
		226	294	135	101	78	65	36	17	11	..	..

Females according to Age.										Total of each Caste.	Grand Total.	Remarks.
Birth to 10 Years.	11 to 20 Years.	21 to 30 Years.	31 to 40 Years.	41 to 50 Years.	51 to 60 Years.	61 to 70 Years.	71 to 80 Years.	81 to 90 Years.	91 to 100 Years and upwards.			
13	14	15	16	17	18	19	20	21	22	23	24	
25	21	25	14	10	4	5	1	1	..	234		
24	82	112	38	19	37	23	9	2	..	868		
..	4	8	2	3	2	1	1	..	..	60		
..	..	..	..	..	..	..	..	..	..	..		
..	..	..	..	..	..	..	..	..	..	..		
49	107	145	54	32	43	29	11	3	..	1,162	1,162	
3	2	1	1	1	..	..	..	..	..	19		
325	167	145	90	60	50	43	66	..	..	1,905		
..	..	..	..	..	..	..	..	..	..	..		
..	..	..	..	..	..	..	..	..	..	..		
..	..	..	..	..	..	..	..	..	..	..		
328	169	146	91	61	50	43	66	..	..	1,924	1,924	
8	5	3	3	5	4	..	..	..	..	62		
231	148	170	78	65	41	27	9	2	..	1,602		
..	..	..	..	..	..	..	..	..	..	..		
..	..	..	..	..	..	..	..	..	..	..		
..	..	..	..	..	..	..	..	..	..	..		
239	153	173	81	70	45	27	9	2	..	1,664	1,664	
23	8	6	2	5	2	5	..	..	..	120		
166	78	74	32	33	31	26	25	..	..	946		
6	5	5	2	4	..	..	..	..	..	52		
..	..	..	..	..	..	..	..	..	..	..		
..	..	..	..	..	..	..	..	..	..	..		
195	91	85	36	42	33	31	25	..	..	1,118	1,118	
4	2	1	..	..	..	..	..	..	..	14		
267	119	129	72	54	38	13	7	..	..	1,429		
..	..	..	..	..	..	..	..	..	..	..		
..	..	..	..	..	..	..	..	..	..	..		
..	..	..	..	..	..	..	..	..	..	..		
271	121	130	72	54	38	13	7	..	..	1,443	1,443	

Castes.	Names of Villages.	No. of Houses.	Males according to Age.									
			Birth to 10 Years.	11 to 20 Years.	21 to 30 Years.	31 to 40 Years.	41 to 50 Years.	51 to 60 Years.	61 to 70 Years.	71 to 80 Years.	81 to 90 Years.	91 to 100 Years and upwards.
	1	2	3	4	5	6	7	8	9	10	11	12
	Turuf Hewulle.											
Bramins	21. Wurde.	14	17	6	4	8	3	4	4	..	..	..
Hindoos of other castes		161	160	113	100	60	41	26	11	..	..	..
Musulmans		..	..	..	..	..	..	..	..	..	..	..
Native Christians		..	..	..	..	..	..	..	..	..	..	..
Seedees		..	..	..	..	..	..	..	..	..	..	..
		175	177	119	104	68	44	30	15	..	..	..
Bramins	22. Bhudgaum Boodrookh.	5	11	4	5	1	3	2	1	..	..	..
Hindoos of other castes		102	107	80	61	29	27	20	7	..	..	..
Musulmans		..	..	..	..	..	..	..	..	..	..	..
Native Christians		..	..	..	..	..	..	..	..	..	..	..
Seedees		..	..	..	..	..	..	..	..	..	..	..
		107	118	84	66	30	30	22	8	..	..	..
Bramins	23. Koosgaum.	..	..	..	..	..	..	..	..	..	..	..
Hindoos of other castes		42	45	22	22	8	6	5	1	..	..	..
Musulmans		..	..	..	..	..	..	..	..	..	..	..
Native Christians		..	..	..	..	..	..	..	..	..	..	..
Seedees		..	..	..	..	..	..	..	..	..	..	..
		42	45	22	22	8	6	5	1	..	..	..
Bramins	24. Kindlos.	..	..	..	..	..	..	..	..	..	..	..
Hindoos of other castes		29	39	17	21	11	11	8	2	..	..	..
Musulmans		..	..	..	..	..	..	..	..	..	..	..
Native Christians		..	..	..	..	..	..	..	..	..	..	..
Seedees		..	..	..	..	..	..	..	..	..	..	..
		29	39	17	21	11	11	8	2	..	..	..
Bramins	25. Geergam.	..	..	..	..	..	..	..	..	..	..	..
Hindoos of other castes		42	30	17	24	17	5	8	4	..	2	..
Musulmans		..	..	..	..	..	..	..	..	..	..	..
Native Christians		..	..	..	..	..	..	..	..	..	..	..
Seedees		..	..	..	..	..	..	..	..	..	..	..
		42	30	17	24	17	5	8	4	..	2	..

Females according to Age.										Total of each Caste.	Grand Total.	Remarks.
Birth to 10 Years.	11 to 20 Years.	21 to 30 Years.	31 to 40 Years.	41 to 50 Years.	51 to 60 Years.	61 to 70 Years.	71 to 80 Years.	81 to 90 Years.	91 to 100 Years and upwards.			
13	14	15	16	17	18	19	20	21	22	23	24	
10	9	3	4	5	8	1	..	..	..	86		
157	128	86	57	45	30	11	6	..	..	1,031		
..	..	..	..	..	..	..	..	..	..	..		
..	..	..	..	..	..	..	..	..	..	..		
..	..	..	..	..	..	..	..	..	..	..		
167	137	89	61	50	38	12	6	..	..	1,117	1,117	
3	1	7	1	..	2	1	..	..	..	42		
29	78	52	34	25	15	7	..	..	..	571		
..	..	..	..	..	..	..	..	..	..	..		
..	..	..	..	..	..	..	..	..	..	..		
..	..	..	..	..	..	..	..	..	..	..		
32	79	59	35	25	17	8	..	..	..	613	613	
..	..	..	..	..	..	..	..	..	..	..		
50	23	23	8	6	6	1	..	..	..	226		
..	..	..	..	..	..	..	..	..	..	..		
..	..	..	..	..	..	..	..	..	..	..		
..	..	..	..	..	..	..	..	..	..	..		
50	23	23	8	6	6	1	..	..	..	226	226	
..	..	..	..	..	..	..	..	..	..	..		
38	22	13	14	4	4	6	..	..	..	210		
..	..	..	..	..	..	..	..	..	..	..		
..	..	..	..	..	..	..	..	..	..	..		
..	..	..	..	..	..	..	..	..	..	..		
38	22	13	14	4	4	6	..	..	..	210	210	
..	..	..	..	..	..	..	..	..	..	..		
34	21	17	9	6	4	4	6	3	..	211		
..	..	..	..	..	..	..	..	..	..	..		
..	..	..	..	..	..	..	..	..	..	..		
..	..	..	..	..	..	..	..	..	..	..		
34	21	17	9	6	4	4	6	3	..	211	211	

29

Castes.	Names of Villages.	No. of Houses.	Males according to Age.									
			Birth to 10 Years.	11 to 20 Years.	21 to 30 Years.	31 to 40 Years.	41 to 50 Years.	51 to 60 Years.	61 to 70 Years.	71 to 80 Years.	81 to 90 Years.	91 to 100 Years and upwards.
	1	2	3	4	5	6	7	8	9	10	11	12
	Turuf Huwelee.											
Bramins	26. Deegus.	3	3	1	..	1	2	..	..	..	..	..
Hindoos of other castes		182	180	139	71	84	45	31	8	4	..	..
Musulmans		..	..	..	..	..	..	..	..	..	..	..
Native Christians		..	..	..	..	..	..	..	..	..	..	..
Seedees		..	..	..	..	..	..	..	..	..	..	..
		185	183	140	71	85	47	31	8	4	..	..
Bramins	27. Dariste.	..	..	..	..	..	..	..	..	..	..	..
Hindoos of other castes		79	84	51	20	28	16	7	9	7	..	..
Musulmans		..	..	..	..	..	..	..	..	..	..	..
Native Christians		..	..	..	..	..	..	..	..	..	..	..
Seedees		..	..	..	..	..	..	..	..	..	..	..
		79	84	51	20	28	16	7	9	7	..	..
Bramins	28. Ghotge.	6	2	3	4	2	1	..	1	..	..	1
Hindoos of other castes		139	98	59	73	51	27	24	16	3	..	..
Musulmans		..	..	..	..	..	..	..	..	..	..	..
Native Christians		1	..	1	1	1	..	..	..	..	..	..
Seedees		..	..	..	..	..	..	..	..	..	..	..
		146	100	63	78	54	28	24	17	3	..	1
Bramins	29. Jambourе.	18	12	15	4	9	6	4	1	1	..	..
Hindoos of other castes		184	131	104	77	69	66	24	25	4	..	..
Musulmans		..	..	..	..	..	..	..	..	..	..	..
Native Christians		..	..	..	..	..	..	..	..	..	..	..
Seedees		..	..	..	..	..	..	..	..	..	..	..
		202	143	119	81	78	72	28	26	5	..	..
Bramins	30. Sonowre.	7	5	2	6	7	2	..	2	..	..	..
Hindoos of other castes		158	90	77	77	57	39	41	16	10	..	..
Musulmans		6	4	3	3	4	2	2	1	1	..	..
Native Christians		1	..	..	2	..	1	..	..	..	..	..
Seedees		..	..	..	..	..	..	..	..	..	..	..
		172	99	82	88	68	44	43	19	11	..	..

Females according to Age.										Total of each Caste.	Grand Total.	Remarks.
Birth to 10 Years.	11 to 20 Years.	21 to 30 Years.	31 to 40 Years.	41 to 50 Years.	51 to 60 Years.	61 to 70 Years.	71 to 80 Years.	81 to 90 Years.	91 to 100 Years and upwards.			
13	14	15	16	17	18	19	20	21	22	23	24	
2	1	..	2	..	..	..	..	..	..	12		
194	103	64	74	38	32	18	2	..	..	1,087		
..	..	..	..	..	..	..	..	..	..	..		
..	..	..	..	..	..	..	..	..	..	..		
..	..	..	..	..	..	..	..	..	..	..		
196	104	64	76	38	32	18	2	..	..	1,099	1,099	
..	..	..	..	..	..	..	..	..	..	..		
87	46	38	30	22	8	12	10	..	..	475		
..	..	..	..	..	..	..	..	..	..	..		
..	..	..	..	..	..	..	..	..	..	..		
..	..	..	..	..	..	..	..	..	..	..		
87	46	38	30	22	8	12	10	..	..	475	475	
4	4	5	2	1	2	..	..	..	..	32		
87	66	64	32	35	35	17	4	..	..	691		
..	..	..	..	..	..	..	..	..	..	..		
..	2	..	..	..	..	1	..	..	..	6		
..	..	..	..	..	..	..	..	..	..	..		
91	72	69	34	36	37	18	4	..	..	729	729	
16	3	9	10	5	2	3	..	..	..	100		
108	86	114	41	48	29	24	3	..	..	953		
..	..	..	..	..	..	..	..	..	..	..		
..	..	..	..	..	..	..	..	..	..	..		
..	..	..	..	..	..	..	..	..	..	..		
124	89	123	51	53	31	27	3	..	..	1,053	1,053	
6	5	5	2	2	1	1	1	..	..	47		
58	67	79	34	34	29	27	6	1	..	742		
3	1	3	3	2	2	..	..	..	..	34		
2	1	2	..	..	..	..	..	..	..	8		
..	..	..	..	..	..	..	..	..	..	..		
69	74	89	39	38	32	28	7	1	..	831	831	

Castes.	Names of Villages.	No. of Houses.	Males according to Age. Birth to 10 Years.	11 to 20 Years.	21 to 30 Years.	31 to 40 Years.	41 to 50 Years.	51 to 60 Years.	61 to 70 Years.	71 to 80 Years.	81 to 90 Years.	91 to 100 Years and upwards.
	1	2	3	4	5	6	7	8	9	10	11	12
	Turuf Huwelee.											
Bramins	31. Koosbe.	5	6	2	1	..	3	3	..	..	..	..
Hindoos of other castes		90	53	33	45	32	30	17	11	12	13	7
Musulmans		..	..	..	..	..	..	..	..	..	..	..
Native Christians		..	..	..	..	..	..	..	..	..	..	..
Seedees		..	..	..	..	..	..	..	..	..	..	..
		95	59	35	46	32	33	20	11	12	13	7
Bramins	32. Bhurnee.	3	6	3	7	2	2	..	..	..	..	..
Hindoos of other castes		86	94	49	42	35	26	9	8	4	..	..
Musulmans		..	..	..	..	..	..	..	..	..	..	..
Native Christians		..	..	..	..	..	..	..	..	..	..	..
Seedees		..	..	..	..	..	..	..	..	..	..	..
		89	100	52	49	37	28	9	8	4	..	..
Bramins	33. Hirlok.	1	1	1	1	1	1	..	..	1	..	..
Hindoos of other castes		93	90	52	38	26	32	17	11	9	10	2
Musulmans		..	..	..	..	..	..	..	..	..	..	..
Native Christians		1	1	..	..	1	..	..	1	..	..	..
Seedees		..	..	..	..	..	..	..	..	..	..	..
		95	92	53	39	28	33	17	12	10	10	2
Bramins	34. Koopowde.	..	..	..	..	..	..	..	..	..	..	..
Hindoos of other castes		61	59	36	31	12	15	9	7	..	..	..
Musulmans		..	..	..	..	..	..	..	..	..	..	..
Native Christians		..	..	..	..	..	..	..	..	..	..	..
Seedees		..	..	..	..	..	..	..	..	..	..	..
		61	59	36	31	12	15	9	7	..	..	..
Bramins	35. Pangrud.	11	16	13	12	6	4	3	1	..	..	..
Hindoos of other castes		154	153	125	109	45	45	19	3	..	..	..
Musulmans		..	..	..	..	..	..	..	..	..	..	..
Native Christians		..	..	..	..	..	..	..	..	..	..	..
Seedees		..	..	..	..	..	..	..	..	..	..	..
		165	169	138	121	51	49	22	4	..	..	..

Females according to Age.												
Birth to 10 Years.	11 to 20 Years.	21 to 30 Years.	31 to 40 Years.	41 to 50 Years.	51 to 60 Years.	61 to 70 Years.	71 to 80 Years.	81 to 90 Years.	91 to 100 Years and upwards.	Total of each Caste.	Grand Total.	Remarks.
13	14	15	16	17	18	19	20	21	22	23	24	
7	4	2	1	2	..	..	..	..	..	31		
50	40	38	32	28	20	20	13	3	1	498		
..	..	..	..	..	..	..	..	..	..	..		
..	..	..	..	..	..	..	..	..	..	..		
..	..	..	..	..	..	..	..	..	..	..		
57	44	40	33	30	20	20	13	3	1	529	529	
7	5	3	..	2	2	..	..	..	..	39		
88	48	51	26	19	14	7	2	..	..	522		
..	..	..	..	..	..	..	..	..	..	..		
..	..	..	..	..	..	..	..	..	..	..		
..	..	..	..	..	..	..	..	..	..	..		
95	53	54	26	21	16	7	2	..	..	561	561	
2	1	1	1	..	1	1	..	..	..	13		
83	46	43	38	27	21	12	10	6	1	574		
..	..	..	..	..	..	..	..	..	..	..		
1	..	..	1	..	..	1	..	..	..	6		
..	..	..	..	..	..	..	..	..	..	..		
86	47	44	40	27	22	14	10	6	1	593	593	
..	..	..	..	..	..	..	..	..	..	..		
52	38	30	24	12	9	5	1	..	..	340		
..	..	..	..	..	..	..	..	..	..	..		
..	..	..	..	..	..	..	..	..	..	..		
..	..	..	..	..	..	..	..	..	..	..		
52	38	30	24	12	9	5	1	..	..	340	340	
5	10	13	7	1	..	..	..	..	..	91		
52	101	110	45	23	17	2	..	..	..	849		
..	..	..	..	..	..	..	..	..	..	..		
..	..	..	..	..	..	..	..	..	..	..		
..	..	..	..	..	..	..	..	..	..	..		
57	111	123	52	24	17	2	..	..	..	940	940	

30

Castes.	Names of Villages.	No. of Houses.	Males according to Age. Birth to 10 Years.	11 to 20 Years.	21 to 30 Years.	31 to 40 Years.	41 to 50 Years.	51 to 60 Years.	61 to 70 Years.	71 to 80 Years.	81 to 90 Years.	91 to 100 Years and upwards.
	1	2	3	4	5	6	7	8	9	10	11	12
	Turuf Huwelee.											
Bramins	36. Bhudyam Khoord.	1	1	..	..	..	..	1	..	..	..	..
Hindoos of other castes		47	48	39	20	11	10	8	6	2	1	..
Musulmans		..	..	..	..	..	..	..	..	..	..	..
Native Christians		..	..	..	..	..	..	..	..	..	..	..
Seedees		..	..	..	..	..	..	..	..	..	..	..
		48	49	39	20	11	10	9	6	2	1	..
Bramins	37. Neerookhe.	4	6	5	2	2	2	..	2	..	..	..
Hindoos of other castes		100	86	61	62	35	18	12	3	2	1	..
Musulmans		..	..	..	..	..	..	..	..	..	..	..
Native Christians		..	..	..	..	..	..	..	..	..	..	..
Seedees		..	..	..	..	..	..	..	..	..	..	..
		104	92	66	64	37	20	12	5	2	1	..
Bramins	38. Oros Khoord.	4	3	..	4	3	3	..	..	..	..	..
Hindoos of other castes		29	21	14	17	7	7	6	1	1	..	..
Musulmans		..	..	..	..	..	..	..	..	..	..	..
Native Christians		..	..	..	..	..	..	..	..	..	..	..
Seedees		..	..	..	..	..	..	..	..	..	..	..
		33	24	14	21	10	10	6	1	1	..	..
Bramins	39. Kudawul.	3	7	3	..	2	1	..	..	..	..	..
Hindoos of other castes		97	114	44	38	24	16	14	4	..	..	..
Musulmans		..	..	..	..	..	..	..	..	..	..	..
Native Christians		..	..	..	..	..	..	..	..	..	..	..
Seedees		..	..	..	..	..	..	..	..	..	..	..
		100	121	47	38	26	17	14	4	..	..	..
Bramins	40. Awlegam.	10	14	7	7	2	2	5	..	1	..	..
Hindoos of other castes		157	142	133	122	61	33	37	14	1	2	..
Musulmans		..	..	..	..	..	..	..	..	..	..	..
Native Christians		..	..	..	..	..	..	..	..	..	..	..
Seedees		..	..	..	..	..	..	..	..	..	..	..
		167	156	140	129	63	35	42	14	2	2	..

FEMALES according to Age.										Total of each Caste.	Grand Total.	REMARKS.
Birth to 10 Years.	11 to 20 Years.	21 to 30 Years.	31 to 40 Years.	41 to 50 Years.	51 to 60 Years.	61 to 70 Years.	71 to 80 Years.	81 to 90 Years.	91 to 100 Years and upwards.			
13	14	15	16	17	18	19	20	21	22	23	24	
..	..	1	..	..	..	..	..	..	..	3		
6	11	17	13	10	3	2	2	..	..	209		
..	..	..	..	..	..	..	..	..	..	..		
..	..	..	..	..	..	..	..	..	..	..		
..	..	..	..	..	..	..	..	..	..	..		
6	11	18	13	10	3	2	2	..	..	212	212	
1	4	2	1	2	1	..	..	1	..	31		
65	56	57	34	29	15	2	3	..	..	541		
..	..	..	..	..	..	..	..	..	..	..		
..	..	..	..	..	..	..	..	..	..	..		
..	..	..	..	..	..	..	..	..	..	..		
66	60	59	35	31	16	2	3	1	..	572	572	
1	5	1	2	1	1	..	..	..	..	24		
10	23	6	10	10	5	4	..	..	..	142		
..	..	..	..	..	..	..	..	..	..	..		
..	..	..	..	..	..	..	..	..	..	..		
..	..	..	..	..	..	..	..	..	..	..		
11	28	7	12	11	6	4	..	..	..	166	166	
4	3	3	2	1	..	..	..	..	..	26		
85	34	38	24	16	19	7	..	..	..	477		
..	..	..	..	..	..	..	..	..	..	..		
..	..	..	..	..	..	..	..	..	..	..		
..	..	..	..	..	..	..	..	..	..	..		
89	37	41	26	17	19	7	..	..	..	503	503	
5	2	6	4	1	2	3	1	..	..	62		
142	98	116	59	44	32	5	1	1	..	1,043		
..	..	..	..	..	..	..	..	..	..	..		
..	..	..	..	..	..	..	..	..	..	..		
..	..	..	..	..	..	..	..	..	..	..		
147	100	122	63	45	34	8	2	1	..	1,105	1,105	

Castes.	Names of Villages.	No. of Houses.	Males according to Age. Birth to 10 Years.	11 to 20 Years.	21 to 30 Years.	31 to 40 Years.	41 to 50 Years.	51 to 60 Years.	61 to 70 Years.	71 to 80 Years.	81 to 90 Years.	91 to 100 Years and upwards.
	1	2	3	4	5	6	7	8	9	10	11	12
	Turuf Bordwe.											
Bramins	41. Bordwe.	1	1	4	..	..	1	1	..	..	..	..
Hindoos of other castes		151	155	90	86	69	44	17	4	..	..	..
Musulmans		17	17	7	9	8	2	2	..	..	..	..
Native Christians		1	..	..	..	1	..	..	..	..	..	..
Seedees		..	..	..	..	..	..	..	..	..	..	..
		170	173	101	95	78	47	20	4	..	..	..
Bramins	42. Tulnode.	1	4	1	..	..	1	..	..	..	..	..
Hindoos of other castes		43	35	23	23	21	10	4	2	..	..	..
Musulmans		1	1	..	1	..	1	..	..	..	..	..
Native Christians		..	..	..	..	..	..	..	..	..	..	..
Seedees		..	..	..	..	..	..	..	..	..	..	..
		45	40	24	24	21	12	4	2	..	..	..
Bramins	43. Bamboolee.	5	14	2	1	1	4	1	..	..	..	..
Hindoos of other castes		71	70	28	33	28	17	10	3	2	..	..
Musulmans		..	..	..	..	..	..	..	..	..	..	..
Native Christians		1	2	2	..	..	1	..	..	..	..	..
Seedees		..	..	..	..	..	..	..	..	..	..	..
		77	86	32	34	29	22	11	3	2	..	..
Bramins	44. Wakde.	..	..	..	..	..	..	..	..	..	..	..
Hindoos of other castes		89	120	54	44	36	18	11	5	..	..	..
Musulmans		..	..	..	..	..	..	..	..	..	..	..
Native Christians		..	..	..	..	..	..	..	..	..	..	..
Seedees		..	..	..	..	..	..	..	..	..	..	..
		89	120	54	44	36	18	11	5	..	..	..
Bramins	45. Hulwul.	6	4	2	4	2	..	..	..	..	..	..
Hindoos of other castes		93	55	54	43	32	28	8	4	4	..	..
Musulmans		..	..	..	..	..	..	..	..	..	..	..
Native Christians		..	..	..	..	..	..	..	..	..	..	..
Seedees		..	..	..	..	..	..	..	..	..	..	..
		99	59	56	47	34	28	8	4	4	..	..

Females according to Age.										Total of each Caste.	Grand Total.	Remarks.
Birth to 10 Years.	11 to 20 Years.	21 to 30 Years.	31 to 40 Years.	41 to 50 Years.	51 to 60 Years.	61 to 70 Years.	71 to 80 Years.	81 to 90 Years.	91 to 100 Years and upwards.			
13	14	15	16	17	18	19	20	21	22	23	24	
6	1	1	1	..	..	..	..	..	..	16		
118	74	88	48	34	26	10	4	..	..	867		
17	10	10	4	5	2	..	..	..	..	93		
1	..	1	..	1	.	..	..	..	..	4		
..	..	..	..	..	..	..	..	..	..	..		
142	85	100	53	40	28	10	4	..	..	980	980	
2	..	..	1	..	..	..	..	..	..	9		
43	26	27	15	9	6	4	1	..	..	249		
1	1	1	..	..	..	..	..	..	..	6		
..	..	..	..	..	..	..	..	..	..	..		
..	..	..	..	..	..	..	..	..	..	..		
46	27	28	16	9	6	4	1	..	..	264	264	
9	1	5	3	1	..	1	..	..	..	43		
58	37	41	26	23	6	6	3	1	..	392		
..	..	..	..	..	..	..	..	..	..	..		
1	..	..	1	..	..	..	..	..	..	7		
..	..	..	..	..	..	..	..	..	..	..		
68	38	46	30	24	6	7	3	1	..	442	442	
..	..	..	..	..	..	..	..	..	..	..		
108	37	61	22	10	6	2	1	..	..	535		
..	..	..	..	..	..	..	..	..	..	..		
..	..	..	..	..	..	..	..	..	..	..		
..	..	..	..	..	..	..	..	..	..	..		
108	37	61	22	10	6	2	1	...	..	535	535	
3	3	2	1	..	..	..	..	..	..	21		
36	40	55	36	21	6	5	3	..	..	430		
..	..	..	...	..	..	..	..	..	..	..		
..	..	..	..	..	..	..	..	..	..	..		
..	..	..	..	..	..	..	..	..	..	..		
39	43	57	37	21	6	5	3	..	..	451	451	

Castes.	Names of Villages.	No. of Houses.	Males according to Age. Birth to 10 Years.	11 to 20 Years.	21 to 30 Years.	31 to 40 Years.	41 to 50 Years.	51 to 60 Years.	61 to 70 Years.	71 to 80 Years.	81 to 90 Years.	91 to 100 Years and upwards.
	1	2	3	4	5	6	7	8	9	10	11	12
	Turuf Bordwe.											
Bramins	46. Ambrud.	9	8	7	4	4	2	3	..	..	..	..
Hindoos of other castes		237	284	160	125	104	74	13	1	..	..	..
Musulmans		22	30	19	11	20	9	14	..	..	..	..
Native Christians		..	..	..	..	..	..	..	..	..	..	..
Seedees		..	..	..	..	..	..	..	..	..	..	..
		268	322	186	140	128	85	30	1	..	..	..
Bramins	47. Seerwul.	13	13	6	11	6	8	1	..	..	..	..
Hindoos of other castes		180	141	124	130	52	34	22	2	..	..	..
Musulmans		..	..	..	..	..	..	..	..	..	..	..
Native Christians		..	..	..	..	..	..	..	..	..	..	..
Seedees		..	..	..	..	..	..	..	..	..	..	..
		193	154	130	141	58	42	23	2	..	..	..
Bramins	48. Satrul.	..	..	..	..	..	..	..	..	..	..	..
Hindoos of other castes		61	56	44	39	17	13	7	7	..	..	..
Musulmans		..	..	..	..	..	..	..	..	..	..	..
Native Christians		..	..	..	..	..	..	..	..	..	..	..
Seedees		..	..	..	..	..	..	..	..	..	..	..
		61	56	44	39	17	13	7	7	..	..	..
Bramins	49. Kasrul.	2	1	2	1	1	..	..	..	..	..	..
Hindoos of other castes		32	27	14	20	15	11	6	1	..	2	..
Musulmans		1	..	..	..	..	1	1	..	..	..	..
Native Christians		1	1	..	..	..	..	..	1	..	..	..
Seedees		..	..	..	..	..	..	..	..	..	..	..
		36	29	16	21	16	12	7	2	..	2	..
Bramins	50. Pudwe.	..	..	..	..	..	..	..	..	..	..	..
Hindoos of other castes		64	78	46	38	19	19	9	6	..	..	..
Musulmans		..	..	..	..	..	..	..	..	..	..	..
Native Christians		..	..	..	..	..	..	..	..	..	..	..
Seedees		..	..	..	..	..	..	..	..	..	..	..
		64	78	46	38	19	19	9	6	..	..	..

Females according to Age.										Total of each Caste.	Grand Total.	Remarks.
Birth to 10 Years.	11 to 20 Years.	21 to 30 Years.	31 to 40 Years.	41 to 50 Years.	51 to 60 Years.	61 to 70 Years.	71 to 80 Years.	81 to 90 Years.	91 to 100 Years and upwards.			
13	14	15	16	17	18	19	20	21	22	23	24	
13	4	3	3	5	1	..	..	..	..	57		
251	142	145	124	156	17	6	3	2	..	1607		
23	9	21	10	1	2	1	..	..	..	170		
..	..	..	..	..	..	..	..	..	..	..		
..	..	..	..	..	..	..	..	..	..	..		
287	155	169	137	162	20	7	3	2	..	1,834	1,834	
11	13	7	2	5	6	..	..	..	..	89		
161	129	126	60	31	15	2	2	..	..	1,031		
..	..	..	..	..	..	..	..	..	..	..		
..	..	..	..	..	..	..	..	..	..	..		
..	..	..	..	..	..	..	..	..	..	..		
172	142	133	62	36	21	2	2	..	..	1,120	1,120	
..	..	..	..	..	..	..	..	..	..	..		
57	42	24	17	15	20	5	1	..	..	364		
..	..	..	..	..	..	..	..	..	..	..		
..	..	..	..	..	..	..	..	..	..	..		
..	..	..	..	..	..	..	..	..	..	..		
57	42	24	17	15	20	5	1	..	..	364	364	
1	2	..	1	..	..	1	..	..	..	10		
29	16	21	14	10	3	3	1	..	..	193		
1	..	1	..	..	..	..	..	..	..	4		
1	..	1	..	..	..	..	..	..	..	4		
..	..	..	..	..	..	..	..	..	..	..		
32	18	23	15	10	3	4	1	..	..	211	211	
..	..	..	..	..	..	..	..	..	..	..		
75	35	42	21	16	6	1	3	..	..	414		
..	..	..	..	..	..	..	..	..	..	..		
..	..	..	..	..	..	..	..	..	..	..		
..	..	..	..	..	..	..	..	..	..	..		
75	35	42	21	16	6	1	3	..	..	414	414	

Castes.	Names of Villages.	No. of Houses.	Males according to Age. Birth to 10 Years.	11 to 20 Years.	21 to 30 Years.	31 to 40 Years.	41 to 50 Years.	51 to 60 Years.	61 to 70 Years.	71 to 80 Years.	81 to 90 Years.	91 to 100 Years and upwards.
	1	2	3	4	5	6	7	8	9	10	11	12
	Turuf Bordwe.											
Bramins	51. Koonde.	2	4	2	..	..	..	2	..	..	..	..
Hindoos of other castes		142	165	88	62	20	24	28	18	..	..	..
Musulmans		..	..	..	..	..	..	..	..	..	..	..
Native Christians		..	..	..	..	..	..	..	..	..	..	..
Seedees		..	..	..	..	..	..	..	..	..	..	..
		144	169	90	62	20	24	30	18	..	..	..
Bramins	52. Gowraee.	8	7	6	9	1	5	2	..	..	..	..
Hindoos of other castes		99	94	62	45	65	16	10	4	1	..	..
Musulmans		..	..	..	..	..	..	..	..	..	..	..
Native Christians		..	..	..	..	..	..	..	..	..	..	..
Seedees		..	..	..	..	..	..	..	..	..	..	..
		107	101	68	54	66	21	12	4	1	..	..
Bramins	53. Kuswun.	7	3	4	5	1	2	1	1	..	..	..
Hindoos of other castes		75	88	48	54	30	20	6	3	..	..	..
Musulmans		..	..	..	..	..	..	..	..	..	..	..
Native Christians		..	..	..	..	..	..	..	..	..	..	..
Seedees		..	..	..	..	..	..	..	..	..	..	..
		82	91	52	59	31	22	7	4	..	..	..
Bramins	54. Orus Boodrook.	6	1	7	5	6	..	2	1	..	..	..
Hindoos of other castes		223	192	141	120	65	48	25	8	1	..	..
Musulmans		..	..	..	..	..	..	..	..	..	..	..
Native Christians		1	3	..	..	2	..	..	..	..	..	..
Seedees		..	..	..	..	..	..	..	..	..	..	..
		230	196	148	125	73	48	27	9	1	..	..
Bramins	55. Wusurcam.	3	4	2	..	2	2	..	..			..
Hindoos of other castes		208	228	128	92	73	38	24	8	4	..	..
Musulmans		..	..	..	..	..	..	..	..	..	..	..
Native Christians		2	1	..	..	..	..	..	..	..	..	..
Seedees		..	..	..	..	..	..	..	..	..	..	..
		213	233	130	92	75	40	24	8	4	..	..

Females according to Age.										Total of each Caste.	Grand Total.	Remarks.
Birth to 10 Years.	11 to 20 Years.	21 to 30 Years.	31 to 40 Years.	41 to 50 Years.	51 to 60 Years.	61 to 70 Years.	71 to 80 Years.	81 to 90 Years.	91 to 100 Years and upwards.			
13	14	15	16	17	18	19	20	21	22	23	24	
5	..	..	1	1	..	..	..	..	..	15		
153	77	60	24	31	27	14	1	..	..	792		
..	..	..	..	..	..	..	..	..	..	..		
..	..	..	..	..	..	..	..	..	..	..		
..	..	..	..	..	..	..	..	..	..	..		
158	77	60	25	32	27	14	1	..	..	807	807	
5	6	6	4	..	..	..	1	..	..	52		
79	48	57	46	18	17	7	8	..	..	577		
..	..	..	..	..	..	..	..	..	..	..		
..	..	..	..	..	..	..	..	..	..	..		
..	..	..	..	..	..	..	..	..	..	..		
84	54	63	50	18	17	7	9	..	..	629	629	
6	3	4	2	5	..	..	..	..	..	37		
70	56	55	20	19	11	8	..	..	..	488		
..	..	..	..	..	..	..	..	..	..	..		
..	..	..	..	..	..	..	..	..	..	..		
..	..	..	..	..	..	..	..	..	..	..		
76	59	59	22	24	11	8	..	..	..	525	525	
6	2	6	1	1	1	1	1	..	..	41		
189	110	117	77	56	37	34	10	..	..	1,230		
..	..	..	..	..	..	..	..	..	..	..		
..	..	2	..	..	..	..	..	..	..	7		
..	..	..	..	..	..	..	..	..	..	..		
195	112	125	78	57	38	35	11	..	..	1,278	1,278	
3	1	2	..	1	1	..	..	..	..	18		
232	100	105	83	34	32	1	2	..	..	1,184		
..	..	..	..	..	..	..	..	..	..	..		
1	..	2	1	..	..	..	..	..	..	5		
..	..	..	..	..	..	..	..	..	..	..		
236	101	109	84	35	33	1	2	..	..	1,207	1,207	

32

Castes.	Names of Villages.	No. of Houses.	Males according to Age. Birth to 10 Years.	11 to 20 Years.	21 to 30 Years.	31 to 40 Years.	41 to 50 Years.	51 to 60 Years.	61 to 70 Years.	71 to 80 Years.	81 to 90 Years.	91 to 100 Years and upwards.
	1	2	3	4	5	6	7	8	9	10	11	12
	Turuf Bordwe.											
Bramins	56. Kusal.	6	9	5	4	3	2	1	1	1	..	..
Hindoos of other castes		223	220	160	122	71	45	46	13	7	..	..
Musulmans		..	..	..	..	..	..	..	..	..	..	..
Native Christians		1	1	..	..	1	..	..	..	..	..	..
Seedees		..	..	..	..	..	..	..	..	..	..	..
		230	230	165	126	75	47	47	14	8	..	..
Bramins	57. Pat.	65	86	71	37	23	26	12	6	4	..	..
Hindoos of other castes		266	250	180	154	106	80	5	35	11	..	..
Musulmans		..	..	..	..	..	..	..	..	..	..	..
Native Christians		1	2	..	3	..	1	..	1	..	..	..
Seedees		..	..	..	..	..	..	..	..	..	..	..
		332	338	251	194	129	107	17	42	15	..	..
Bramins	58. Tendolee.	52	32	39	29	11	14	..	9	2	1	..
Hindoos of other castes		170	150	110	110	41	52	23	17	8	1	2
Musulmans		..	..	..	..	..	..	..	..	..	..	..
Native Christians		..	..	..	..	..	..	..	..	..	..	..
Seedees		..	..	..	..	..	..	..	..	..	..	..
		222	182	149	139	52	66	23	26	10	2	2
Bramins	59. Chendwun.	19	13	14	7	6	5	1	4	3	..	..
Hindoos of other castes		173	157	111	102	47	57	35	13	5	..	..
Musulmans		..	..	..	..	..	..	..	..	..	..	..
Native Christians		..	..	..	..	..	..	..	..	..	..	..
Seedees		..	..	..	..	..	..	..	..	..	..	..
		192	170	125	109	53	62	36	17	8	..	..
Bramins	60. Kowtee.	14	18	7	5	7	7	5	1	..	..	..
Hindoos of other castes		80	109	57	48	40	19	14	2	..	..	..
Musulmans		..	..	..	..	..	..	..	..	..	..	..
Native Christians		..	..	..	..	..	..	..	..	..	..	..
Seedees		..	..	..	..	..	..	..	..	..	..	..
		94	127	64	53	47	26	19	3	..	..	..

Females according to Age.												
Birth to 10 Years.	11 to 20 Years.	21 to 30 Years.	31 to 40 Years.	41 to 50 Years.	51 to 60 Years.	61 to 70 Years.	71 to 80 Years.	81 to 90 Years.	91 to 100 Years and upwards.	Total of each Caste.	Grand Total.	Remarks.
13	14	15	16	17	18	19	20	21	22	23	24	
7	3	1	6	2	1	1	1	..	..	48		
159	137	118	82	53	40	15	6	1	..	1,295		
..	..	..	..	..	..	..	..	..	..	..		
..	..	1	1	..	..	..	..	..	..	4		
..	..	..	..	..	..	..	..	..	..	..		
166	140	120	89	55	41	16	7	1	..	1,347	1,347	
85	38	36	33	16	11	5	5	..	..	494		
195	125	174	105	73	54	31	15	..	..	1,593		
..	..	..	..	..	..	..	..	..	..	..		
3	..	4	..	1	..	..	..	..	..	15		
..	..	..	..	..	..	..	..	..	..	..		
283	163	214	138	90	65	36	20	..	..	2,102	2,102	
31	29	25	17	17	8	4	1	1	1	271		
165	107	88	51	42	23	16	10	3	1	1,020		
..	..	..	..	..	..	..	..	..	..	..		
..	..	..	..	..	..	..	..	..	..	..		
..	..	..	..	..	..	..	..	..	..	..		
196	136	113	68	59	31	20	11	4	2	1,291	1,291	
19	14	7	6	8	4	3	1	..	..	115		
170	109	96	53	47	44	15	6	..	..	1,067		
..	..	..	..	..	..	..	..	..	..	..		
..	..	..	..	..	..	..	..	..	..	..		
..	..	..	..	..	..	..	..	..	..	..		
189	123	103	59	55	48	18	7	..	..	1,182	1,182	
10	4	5	3	5	2	..	..	..	..	79		
106	42	52	33	28	15	3	..	..	..	568		
..	..	..	..	..	..	..	..	..	..	..		
..	..	..	..	..	..	..	..	..	..	..		
..	..	..	..	..	..	..	..	..	..	..		
116	46	57	36	33	17	3	..	..	..	647	647	

Castes.	Names of Villages.	No. of Houses.	Males according to Age.									
			Birth to 10 Years.	11 to 20 Years.	21 to 30 Years.	31 to 40 Years.	41 to 50 Years.	51 to 60 Years.	61 to 70 Years.	71 to 80 Years.	81 to 90 Years.	91 to 100 Years and upwards.
	1	2	3	4	5	6	7	8	9	10	11	12
	Turuf Bordwe.											
Bramins	......	688	744	508	389	252	223	129	71	23	3	1
Hindoos of other castes	......	7,898	7,993	5,128	4,199	2,769	1,981	1,085	533	208	40	13
Musulmans	......	101	124	71	51	58	29	31	10	4	2	..
Native Christians......	......	14	16	7	7	7	5	2	4	..	..	..
Seedees..................	......	..	..	..	..	..	..	..	..	..	..	..
	Grand Total of the Koodal Division....	8,701	8,877	5,714	4,646	3,086	2,238	1,247	618	235	45	14

Sawunt Waree, Political Superintendent's Office, Camp Belgaum, 30th October 1852.

Females according to Age.										Total of each Caste.	Grand Total.	Remarks.
Birth to 10 Years.	11 to 20 Years.	21 to 30 Years.	31 to 40 Years.	41 to 50 Years.	51 to 60 Years.	61 to 70 Years.	71 to 80 Years.	81 to 90 Years.	91 to 100 Years and upwards.			
13	14	15	16	17	18	19	20	21	22	23	24	
684	388	367	243	207	134	72	23	6	1	4,468		* Grand Total..52,055 { Males ....26,720 / Females..25,335
7,007	4,528	4,381	2,688	1,945	1,315	666	303	28	3	46,813		
99	52	70	31	27	13	5	2	..	..	679		
13	4	15	6	5	1	3	..	..	..	95		
..	..	..	..	..	..	..	..	..	..	..		
7,803	4,972	4,833	2,968	2,184	1,463	746	328	34	4	52,055	*52,055	

(Signed) H. L. ANDERSON,
Political Superintendent.

Census of the Town of Waree,

Castes.	Names of the Wadas.	No. of Houses.	Males according to Age.									
			Birth to 10 Years.	11 to 20 Year.	21 to 30 Years.	31 to 40 Years.	41 to 50 Years.	51 to 60 Years.	61 to 70 Years.	71 to 80 Years.	81 to 90 Years.	91 to 100 Years and upwards.
	1	2	3	4	5	6	7	8	9	10	11	12
Bramins	1. Khaskilwara.	17	16	10	17	13	6	7	5	2	1	..
Hindoos of other castes		210	174	111	97	97	57	34	6	..	1	..
Musulmans		9	5	4	5	3	2	2	1	..	..	..
Native Christians		6	10	5	5	1	2	..	..	1	..	..
Seedees		22	15	5	6	9	8	2	..	2	..	..
		264	220	135	130	123	75	45	12	5	2	..
Bramins	2. Beerwad Kurachee Temb.	2	..	2	1	..	..	..	1	..	..	..
Hindoos of other castes		22	25	10	7	9	5	1	2	..	..	..
Musulmans		..	..	..	..	..	..	..	..	..	..	..
Native Christians		4	6	3	4	2	1	1	..	..	..	..
Seedees		..	..	..	..	..	..	..	..	..	..	..
Jews		..	..	..	..	..	..	..	..	..	..	..
		28	31	15	12	11	6	2	3	..	..	..
Bramins	3. Wada Salnee.	22	15	15	18	12	8	8	6	..	..	..
Hindoos of other castes		132	122	69	73	61	46	29	14	..	2	..
Musulmans		45	43	28	19	26	13	11	2	2	..	..
Native Christians		13	24	5	5	6	3	2	1	..	..	..
Seedees		..	..	..	..	..	..	..	..	..	..	..
		212	204	117	115	105	70	50	23	2	2	..
Bramins	4. Joona Bazar.	11	18	7	9	7	7	3	1	..	..	..
Hindoos of other castes		52	48	24	32	20	13	14	5	1	..	..
Musulmans		22	24	16	15	12	8	5	1	..	..	..
Native Christians		24	29	9	8	11	7	2	3	..	..	..
Seedees		..	..	..	..	..	..	..	..	..	..	..
		109	119	56	64	50	35	24	10	1	..	..
Bramins	5. Wada Mathia Kurbel.	38	41	35	34	26	24	10	6	4	..	..
Hindoos of other castes		83	71	48	51	44	28	19	13	..	..	..
Musulmans		17	11	12	14	10	8	2	3	..	..	..
Native Christians		4	3	2	2	..	1	1	..	..	..	..
Jews		..	..	..	..	..	..	..	..	..	..	..
		142	126	97	101	80	61	32	22	4	..	..

for the Year 1851.

Females according to Age.										Total of each Caste.	Grand Total.	Remarks.
Birth to 10 Years.	11 to 20 Years.	21 to 30 Years.	31 to 40 Years.	41 to 50 Years.	51 to 60 Years.	61 to 70 Years.	71 to 80 Years.	81 to 90 Years.	91 to 100 Years and upwards.			
13	14	15	16	17	18	19	20	21	22	23	24	
22	17	12	13	6	4	1	..	..	..	152		
195	101	149	101	63	52	18	6	..	1	1,263		
5	1	5	3	3	..	1	..	..	..	40		
6	2	5	4	1	..	3	..	..	..	45		
17	11	9	8	4	5	..	..	..	..	101		
245	132	180	129	77	61	23	6	..	1	1,601	1,601	
1	1	..	..	1	..	1	..	..	..	8		
15	5	5	12	5	4	3	..	..	..	108		
..	..	..	..	..	..	..	..	..	..	..		
7	5	5	5	1	1	2	..	..	..	43		
..	..	..	..	..	..	..	..	..	..	..		
..	..	..	..	..	..	..	..	..	..	..		
23	11	10	17	7	5	6	..	..	..	159	159	
17	20	12	10	9	6	2	..	1	..	159		
113	84	90	64	53	35	22	6	..	..	883		
37	24	28	17	16	13	2	..	..	..	281		
15	7	9	3	2	1	3	1	..	..	87		
..	..	..	..	..	..	..	..	..	..	..		
182	135	139	94	80	55	29	7	1	..	1,410	1,410	
15	15	9	8	3	3	3	..	..	..	108		
44	24	32	37	15	19	13	3	..	..	344		
22	9	19	6	4	11	6	..	..	..	158		
24	12	14	8	10	5	2	2	..	..	146		
..	..	..	..	..	..	..	..	..	..	..		
105	60	74	59	32	38	24	5	..	..	756	756	
36	28	30	28	13	20	4	6	1	..	346		
56	40	49	52	42	21	18	2	..	..	554		
26	5	6	11	8	3	5	1	..	..	125		
3	3	2	..	4	..	1	..	..	..	22		
..	..	..	..	..	..	..	..	..	..	..		
121	76	87	91	67	44	28	9	1	..	1,047	1.047	

Castes.	Names of the Wadas.	No. of Houses.	Males according to Age. Birth to 10 Years.	11 to 20 Years.	21 to 30 Years.	31 to 40 Years.	41 to 50 Years.	51 to 60 Years.	61 to 70 Years.	71 to 80 Years.	81 to 90 Years.	91 to 100 Years and upwards.
	1	2	3	4	5	6	7	8	9	10	11	12
Bramins	6. Oobha Bazar.	21	23	12	16	21	10	6	5	1	1	..
Hindoos of other castes		227	146	75	94	96	66	43	10	4	..	..
Musulmans		13	15	8	7	5	6	3	..	1	..	..
Native Christians		19	19	4	5	8	10	2	1	..	..	..
Seedees		..	..	..	..	..	..	..	..	..	..	..
		280	203	99	122	130	92	54	16	6	1	..
Bramins	7. Wanee Wuthar.	3	1	..	..	2	1	..	2	..	..	..
Hindoos of other castes		74	85	58	54	49	38	17	5	3	..	..
Musulmans		10	11	2	2	1	6	2	..	..	..	..
Native Christians		23	23	10	5	13	6	..	2	1	..	..
Seedees		..	..	..	..	..	..	..	..	..	..	..
Jews		..	..	..	..	..	..	..	..	..	..	..
		110	120	70	61	65	51	19	9	4	..	..
Bramins	8. Subnees Wada.	28	22	16	11	22	14	10	1	1	..	..
Hindoos of other castes		62	29	17	26	23	13	11	5	..	..	..
Musulmans		..	..	..	..	..	..	..	..	..	..	..
Native Christians		..	..	..	..	..	..	..	..	..	..	..
Seedees		..	..	..	..	..	..	..	..	..	..	..
		90	51	33	37	45	27	21	6	1	..	..
Bramins	9. Bákercha Wada.	18	15	10	6	11	5	4	2	1	..	..
Hindoos of other castes		62	54	24	29	25	22	11	5	1	..	..
Musulmans		49	53	22	19	26	14	16	4	..	..	..
Native Christians		8	13	5	5	1	2	3	1	..	..	..
Seedees		..	..	..	..	..	..	..	..	..	..	..
		137	135	61	59	63	43	34	12	2	..	..
Bramins	10. In Fort.	..	..	..	1	..	3	..	..	..	..	..
Hindoos of other castes		..	6	5	6	7	2	2	..	..	..	..
Musulmans		..	..	..	2	..	1	..	1	..	..	..
Native Christians		..	1	1	1	1	..	1	..	..	..	..
Jews		..	1	..	..	1	..	..	..	..	..	..
		..	8	6	10	9	6	3	1	..	..	..

FEMALES according to Age.										Total of each Caste.	Grand Total.	REMARKS.
Birth to 10 Years.	11 to 20 Years.	21 to 30 Years.	31 to 40 Years.	41 to 50 Years.	51 to 60 Years.	61 to 70 Years.	71 to 80 Years.	81 to 90 Years.	91 to 100 Years and upwards.			
13	14	15	16	17	18	19	20	21	22	23	24	
12	14	12	13	6	5	1	2	..	..	160		
134	92	106	126	65	65	37	26	2	..	1,187		
12	3	8	6	5	3	1	..	..	..	83		
13	4	6	9	5	5	2	..	..	..	93		
..	..	..	..	..	..	..	..	..	..	..		
171	113	132	154	81	78	41	28	2	..	1,523	1,523	
3	..	..	2	1	..	..	..	..	..	12		
90	47	60	54	43	21	16	6	..	..	646		
3	1	3	8	2	4	..	..	..	..	45		
19	5	11	11	3	4	2	2	..	..	117		
..	..	..	..	..	..	..	..	..	..	..		
..	..	..	..	..	..	..	..	..	..	..		
115	53	74	75	49	29	18	8	..	..	820	820	
26	15	15	21	5	13	4	1	..	..	197		
30	19	27	27	29	16	11	2	..	..	285		
..	..	..	..	..	..	..	..	..	..	..		
..	..	..	..	..	..	..	..	..	..	..		
..	..	..	..	..	..	..	..	..	..	..		
56	34	42	48	34	29	15	3	..	..	482	482	
20	2	9	10	7	3	5	1	..	..	111		
45	25	24	28	20	18	11	2	..	..	344		
49	23	15	34	16	9	6	..	1	..	307		
5	2	1	4	2	2	..	..	..	..	46		
..	..	..	..	..	..	..	..	..	..	..		
119	52	49	76	45	32	22	3	1	..	808	808	
3	1	1	1	..	..	..	..	..	..	10		
5	6	5	3	2	3	2	..	..	..	54		
..	2	..	..	..	1	..	..	..	..	7		
..	..	..	1	1	..	..	..	..	..	7		
2	1	2	..	..	..	1	..	..	..	8		
10	10	8	5	3	4	3	..	..	..	86	86	

34—35

Castes.	Names of the Wadas.	No. of Houses.	Males according to Age. Birth to 10 Years.	11 to 20 Years.	21 to 30 Years.	31 to 40 Years.	41 to 50 Years.	51 to 60 Years.	61 to 70 Years.	71 to 80 Years.	81 to 90 Years.	91 to 100 Years and upwards.
	1	2	3	4	5	6	7	8	9	10	11	12
Bramins	11. In the Lines of Local Corps.	..	..	..	1	1	..	..	..	..	..	..
Hindoos of other castes		..	27	5	105	56	6	..	..	..	..	..
Musulmans		..	4	3	64	36	4	2	..	..	..	..
Native Christians......		..	1	..	4	2	..	..	..	..	..	..
Seedees................		..	..	..	..	..	..	..	..	..	..	..
		..	32	8	174	95	10	2	..	..	..	..
Bramins	......	160	151	107	114	115	78	48	29	9	2	..
Hindoos of other castes	......	924	787	446	574	487	296	181	65	9	3	..
Musulmans	......	165	166	95	147	119	62	43	12	3	..	..
Native Christians......	......	101	129	44	44	45	32	12	8	2	..	..
Seedees................	......	22	15	5	6	9	8	2	..	2	..	..
Jews....................	......	..	1	..	..	1	..	..	..	..	..	..
	Grand Total of the Town of Waree	1,372	1,249	697	885	776	476	286	114	25	5	..

Sawunt Waree, Political Superintendent's Office, Camp Belgaum, 30th October 1852.

Females according to Age.												
Birth to 10 Years.	11 to 20 Years.	21 to 30 Years.	31 to 40 Years.	41 to 50 Years.	51 to 60 Years.	61 to 70 Years.	71 to 80 Years.	81 to 90 Years.	91 to 100 Years and upwards.	Total of each Caste.	Grand Total.	Remarks.
13	14	15	16	17	18	19	20	21	22	23	24	
..	..	..	..	..	..	..	..	..	..	2		
23	28	31	4	..	..	..	..	..	..	285		
5	3	4	3	..	..	..	..	..	..	128		
1	..	3	..	..	..	..	..	..	..	11		
..	..	..	..	..	..	..	..	..	..	..		
29	31	38	7	..	..	..	..	..	..	426	426	
155	113	100	106	51	54	21	10	2	..	1,265		
750	471	578	508	337	254	151	53	2	1	5,953		
159	71	88	88	54	44	21	1	1	..	1,174		
93	40	56	45	29	18	15	5	..	..	617		
17	11	9	8	4	5	..	..	..	..	101		
2	1	2	..	..	..	1	..	..	..	8		
1,176	707	833	755	475	375	209	69	5	1	9,118	*9,118	

*Grand Total......9,118 { Males.........4,513 / Females ......4,605 }

(Signed) H. L. ANDERSON,
Political Superintendent.

General Census of the Sawunt Waree State, for the Year 1851.

Castes.	No. of Houses.	Males according to Age. Birth to 10 Years.	11 to 20 Years.	21 to 30 Years.	31 to 40 Years.	41 to 50 Years.	51 to 60 Years.	61 to 70 Years.	71 to 80 Years.	81 to 90 Years.	91 to 100 Years.	Females according to Age. Birth to 10 Years.	11 to 20 Years.	21 to 30 Years.	31 to 40 Years.	41 to 50 Years.	51 to 60 Years.	61 to 70 Years.	71 to 80 Years.	81 to 90 Years.	91 to 100 Years.	Total of each Caste.	Grand Total.	Remarks.
	1	2	3	4	5	6	7	8	[illegible]	10	11	12	13	14	15	16	17	18	19	20	21	22	23	
Waree Division.																								
Bramins	583	500	302	274	213	179	131	45	20	9	3	390	292	250	221	184	124	58	26	8	6	3,235		
Hindoos of other castes	8,346	6,862	[illegible],698	3,950	3,422	2,472	1,589	752	322	143	83	6,461	4,236	3,661	3,204	2,580	1,794	848	369	158	83	47,687		
Musulmans	225	190	141	110	86	66	27	13	1	1	..	153	95	119	86	60	28	7	4	..	..	1,187		
Native Christians	93	81	50	49	39	28	11	3	3	2	1	83	66	44	32	19	17	5	2	3	1	539		
Seedees	4	..	1	1	2	1	..	..	..	..	..	1	1	3	..	..	..	..	..	..	..	10		
Total	9,206	7,633	5,192	4,384	3,762	2,746	1,758	813	346	155	87	7,088	4,690	4,077	3,543	2,843	1,963	918	401	169	90	52,658	52,658	
Banda Division.																								
Bramins	382	330	233	215	143	138	84	29	9	1	2	311	186	209	143	101	80	40	11	1	1	2,267		
Hindoos of other castes	5,992	[illegible],105	3,252	2,937	2,217	1,572	819	332	111	24	3	4,416	2,643	2,83[illegible]	2,111	1,485	984	483	136	39	10	31,511		
Musulmans	145	126	88	72	62	39	16	11	1	..	..	109	62	7[illegible]	57	40	19	12	10	1	..	795		
Native Christians	140	125	65	68	58	28	10	3	..	..	..	108	57	5[illegible]	48	36	23	10	4	2	..	704		
Seedees	7	8	4	5	2	1	..	1	..	..	..	6	1	[illegible]	2	..	1	1	..	..	1	40		
Total	6,666	[illegible],694	3,642	3,297	2,482	1,778	929	376	121	25	5	4,950	2,949	3,17[illegible]	2,361	1,662	1,107	546	161	43	12	35,317	35,317	
Koodal Division.																								
Bramins	688	744	508	389	252	223	129	71	23	3	1	684	388	367	243	207	134	72	23	6	1	4,468		
Hindoos of other castes	7,898	[illegible],99[illegible]	5,128	4,199	2,769	1,981	1,085	533	208	40	13	7,007	4,528	4,381	2,688	1,945	1,315	666	303	28	3	46,813		
Musulmans	101	12[illegible]	71	51	58	29	31	10	4	2	..	99	52	70	31	27	13	5	2	..	..	679		
Native Christians	14	1[illegible]	7	7	7	5	2	4	..	..	..	13	4	35	6	[illegible]	1	3	..	..	..	95		
Seedees	..	..	..	..	..	..	..	..	..	..	..	..	..	..	..	..	..	..	..	..	..	..		
Total	8,701	[illegible],87[illegible]	5,714	4,646	3,086	2,238	1,247	618	235	45	14	7,803	4,972	4,853	2,968	2,184	1,463	746	328	34	4	52,055	52,055	
Town of Waree.																								
Bramins	160	15[illegible]	107	114	115	78	48	29	9	2	..	155	113	180	106	5[illegible]	54	21	10	2	..	1,265		
Hindoos of other castes	924	787	446	574	487	296	181	65	9	3	..	750	471	578	508	337	254	151	53	2	1	5,953		
Musulmans	165	165	95	147	119	62	43	12	3	..	..	159	71	38	88	54	44	21	1	1	..	1,174		
Native Christians	101	129	44	44	45	32	12	8	2	..	..	93	40	36	45	29	18	15	5	..	..	647		
Seedees	22	15	5	6	9	8	2	..	2	..	..	17	11	9	8	4	5	..	..	..	..	101		
Jews	..	1	..	..	1	..	..	..	..	..	..	2	1	2	..	..	..	1	..	..	..	8		
Total	1,372	1,249	697	885	776	476	286	114	25	5	..	1,176	707	833	755	475	375	209	69	5	1	9,118	9,118	
Tunkha Villages.																								
Bramins	1	..	..	2	..	..	..	..	..	..	..	2	1	..	1	1	..	..	..	..	..	7		
Hindoos of other castes	205	129	112	115	65	53	13	5	2	..	..	114	87	83	54	49	19	6	..	..	..	906		
Native Christians	1	..	1	1	..	..	..	..	..	..	..	1	1	..	..	..	..	..	..	..	..	4		
Total	207	129	113	118	65	53	13	5	2	..	..	117	89	83	55	50	19	6	..	..	..	917	*917	

* Grand Total......150,065 { Males... 76,956 / Females... 73,109 }

(Signed) H. L. ANDERSON,
Political Superintendent.

Sawunt Waree, Political Superintendent's Office, Camp Belgaum, 30th October 1852.

36

Abstract of the Census of the Sawunt Waree State, showing the Total Amount of each Caste, for the Year 1851.

Castes.	No. of Houses.	Males according to Age.										Females according to Age.										Total.	Remarks.
		Birth to 10 Years.	11 to 20 Years.	21 to 30 Years.	31 to 40 Years.	41 to 50 Years.	51 to 60 Years.	61 to 70 Years.	71 to 80 Years.	81 to 90 Years.	91 to 100 Years.	Birth to 10 Years.	11 to 20 Years.	21 to 30 Years.	31 to 40 Years.	41 to 50 Years.	51 to 60 Years.	61 to 70 Years.	71 to 80 Years.	81 to 90 Years.	91 to 100 Years.		
Bramins	1,769	1,725	1,150	994	723	618	392	174	61	15	6	1,542	980	926	714	544	392	191	70	17	8	11,242	Grand Total .. 150,065 { Males .. 76,956 Females 73,109
Hindoos of other castes	23,365	20,876	13,636	11,775	8,960	6,374	3,687	1,687	652	210	99	18,748	11,965	11,535	8,565	6,396	4,366	2,154	861	227	97	132,870	
Musulmans	636	606	395	380	325	196	117	46	9	3	..	520	280	347	262	181	104	45	17	2	..	3,835	
Native Christians.. ..	349	351	167	169	149	93	35	18	5	2	1	298	168	174	131	89	59	33	11	5	1	1,959	
Seedees..	33	23	10	12	13	10	2	1	2	..	..	24	13	19	10	4	6	1	..	..	1	151	
Jews	..	1	..	..	1	..	..	..	..	..	..	2	1	2	..	..	..	1	..	..	..	8	
Total.. ..	26,152	23,582	15,358	13,330	10,171	7,291	4,233	1,926	729	230	106	21,134	13,407	13,003	9,682	7,214	4,927	2,425	959	251	107	150,065	

(Signed) H. L. ANDERSON,
Political Superintendent.

Sawunt Waree, Political Superintendent's Office, Camp Belgaum, 30th October 1852.

MEMOIR

ON

THE SAWUNT WAREE STATE.

BY THE LATE

CAPTAIN GIDEON HUTCHINSON,

10TH REGT. BOMBAY N. I.,

ON SPECIAL DUTY AT SAWUNT WAREE, IN THE YEAR 1818.

Submitted to Government on the 13*th December* 1818.

SAWUNT WAREE.

Previous to the conquests of Shivajee Raja,* the celebrated founder of the Muratha empire, the country now denominated the Sawunt Waree State consisted of the Koodal province,† sub-divided into twelve districts, each under a petty

* Shivajee, descended from the Patels of Hingway, near Seroor, was born in the era Shalivahan 1549, year Akshuee, month Vyshakh, on the 2nd day of the moon's increase (A. D. 1627); was crowned about the year A. D. 1674, and died in the era Shalivahan 1602, year Rowdru, month Chuitru, on the day of the full of the moon (A. D. 1680).

† The Koodal province contains twelve districts (Turuf), two extra districts (Kureat), one sub-division (Wilayut), and one port:—

1.	Musooree, containing eleven villages, yielding a revenue of	Rs. 25,000
2.	Wurad, containing ten villages, yielding a revenue of	17,000
3.	Páth, (a) with ten villages, and a revenue of	15,000
4.	Huwélee (a) has fifteen villages, and a revenue of..	20,000
5.	Maloondee has seventeen villages, paying a revenue of	5,000
6.	Mangaum has fourteen villages, and a revenue of..	25,000
7.	Tulwar has twelve villages, and a revenue of	7,500
8.	Azgaum has twelve villages, and a revenue of	25,000
9.	Satary has twelve villages, and a revenue of	15,000
10.	Munohur or Sangélee has twenty-four villages, and a revenue of ..	12,000
11.	Boruree has sixteen villages, and a revenue of	12,000
12.	Kulsoolee has twenty-two villages, and a revenue of	13,000

Extra Districts.

Pathgaum has twelve villages, and a revenue of..	Rs. 6,000
Naroor has fourteen villages, and a revenue of	7,500
Wilayut contains forty-eight villages, and a revenue of	14,000
Banda Wilayut, Vingorla, the port (duties excluded)	10,000
	Rs. 2,29,000
Duties collected at the Ghaut, port customs, peaceable times, presents, fines, &c. may be estimated at	90,000
	Rs. 3,19,000

Deductions from the Sawunt Waree Revenue.

Vingorla, revenue of	Rs. 10,000	
Customs of the port of Vingorla	3,000	
The Musooree revenue	25,000	
The revenue of Wurad	17,000	
The revenue of Maloondee	5,000	
		60,000
Amount of the present revenue of the Sawunt Waree State		Rs. 2,59,000

(a) From the revenue of these two districts Rs. 6,623 were paid to the Government of Sindhoodoorg.

chief, collectively styled the Bara Naiks, and the five Purgunas* of Dichoolee, Phonda, Pedna, Sanklee, and Munéree, under as many several Desaees, all subject to the superior authority of the Desaee of Koodal, by birth a Bramin, himself tributary to the Nuwabs of Beejapoor on the Krishna.

As circumstances aided, the several chiefs and Desaees, until overpowered or awed, used to resist the payment of their respective quotas. Of these, Lukum Sawunt, the Mangaum Naik, was the most distinguished, by his enterprising and turbulent disposition; during the course of a successful resistance, in a predatory incursion he made captive the Desaee of Koodal, and subsequently assumed his authority through the inability of the Beejapoor Durbar to oppose this usurpation. Vigorous measures shortly reduced to his submission the other Desaees and petty chieftains, and fixed his power on a basis so firm as to have been transmitted to his descendants.

It is the popular tradition that the Desaee, after a short imprisonment, fell a victim to the ambition of his conqueror, and died a violent death. In the Hindoo code, the murder of a Bramin is branded as a crime heinous in the highest degree, and the family of the present rulers of Waree has ever since been considered obnoxious to the implacable vengeance of the vindictive spirit of the murdered Desaee, particularly excited by using the seal of the Koodal province; and which is assigned as the reason of its being never affixed by them, but by the hand of another person, in general a Bramin, who, by his sanctity, is supposed less liable to the spirit's revengeful malice.

During the conquests of Shivajee in the north of the Konkun, Lukum Sawunt had established his authority. On their approach to his own frontiers, he assembled a force of 12,000 Murathas, and promised the Beejapoor Durbar a sufficient aid to stop the further progress of the enemy's arms.

Of the troops granted, under the command of Ghorepuray, 2,000 descended to the town of Koodal, whilst Lukum Sawunt advanced to the northward. A picked body of Shivajee's troops, eluding Lukum Sawunt, attacked and defeated Ghorepuray, who hastily retreated to the upper camp at the Ghauts, and thence to Beejapoor. Though thus deserted, Lukum Sawunt risked the fate of a battle, and was routed with severe loss by Shivajee's Sirdar, Namnath. Unable to rally his troops, Lukum Sawunt sought refuge in the Portuguese territories; but not finding the expected protection, as the Portuguese were fearful of displeasing Shivajee, he sent Peetambur, a Shenvee, to implore the conqueror's clemency. Political, as well as family reasons, (Lukum Sawunt being also a Bhonslay,) induced Shivajee to grant him protection and safety.

* *Purgunas.*

Dichoolee contains twenty-four villages.
Phonda contains twenty villages.
Pedna contains twenty-four villages.
Sanklee contains seventy villages.
Muneree contains twenty-five villages.

After the sole conference permitted to Lukum Sawunt, he was reinstated in his possession under the restrictions—*1st*, of confining his residence to the town of Koodal; *2nd*, not to repair or erect any fortified places; *3rd*, to entertain no considerable body of troops.

Lukum Sawunt was succeeded by his son Khem Sawunt, who first assumed the title of Desaee of the Koodal province.

Shivajee, carrying his arms against the Portuguese, captured the ports of Murdumgur, Seewéswar, and Kurwal.

During these transactions, Anunt Rao Shénvee, in the employ of Khem Sawunt, ingratiated himself with Shivajee, and, in concert with the Viceroy at Goa, planned a sudden attack on his camp.

These intrigues were disclosed to the Raja by Gunojee Ram, lately appointed to adjust the amounts of the collections of the Koodal province and the five Purgunas, which settlements in principal and material points are even now not unfrequently referred to.

Conducted by Anunt Rao Shenvee, the projected attack took place at dawn of day. The first fire was the signal to the ambuscade to sally out, led on by the Raja in person. So impetuous and unexpected was the charge, as instantly to disperse the column, which suffered much in this pursuit. Shivajee gave up the Bardese district to unrestrained plunder as a reward to his soldiery.

Khem Sawunt having secretly aided the above attempt, Shivajee, to prevent a similar recurrence, stationed strong detachments in the principal towns and places in his possession.

Shivajee had experienced the most determined and successful opposition to his arms from the fortified islands on the pirate coast, especially at Dunda Rajpoor, held in Jageer and defended by the Hubshees, the Abyssinian slaves of the Emperors of Dehli.

Anxious to possess a similar fortified island to protect his vessels, and be a stronghold in adversity, he ordered a survey of the coast to be made by his Sirdars Tamrojee Manojee, Gungajee, and Shivajee Kolee.

After much research, the mass of rocks opposite to Malwan was fixed on in Shalivahan 1586 (A. D. 1664) as the site of Sindhoodoorg (the sea-girt rock). The superintendence of the works being committed to the Sirdar Wiswanath, and to one of the descendants of the Koodal Desaee, Shivajee re-ascended the Ghauts.

Unable to refuse, Khem Sawunt was necessitated to furnish the supplies demanded, and to assist in the erection of a fortress, which was to become so great a check upon him and his successors.

Shivajee, desirous to view Sindhoodoorg, which he fondly hoped would extend his fame and power, descended the Baiwése Ghaut, and on his arrival at the town of Musooree (A. D. 1670) surveyed the hill, the present site of Bhurutgur, but was deterred from fortifying it from the total want of water.

At this period were built the small forts of Pudmagur Rajkote, and that of Sezeekote, at the mouth of the Musooree river or Gurunhee (fort-studded river), which, though at present choked with a large accumulation of sand, was at that time navigable for vessels to the town of Maloondee, in the ruins of which, as monuments of its former trade and commerce under the Musulman government, the quay, and the paved ascents of the high road leading to the Ghauts *viá* Kulsoolee, are still to be traced.

Overawed by the troops at Sindhoodoorg, and the many principal stations of his country, Khem Sawunt, however reluctant, was compelled to bow to the terms imposed upon him.

Phond Sawunt succeeded to his father's authority, and taking advantage of the dissensions which arose between the two sons of Shivajee at his death, recovered, in Shalivahan 1602 (A. D. 1680), notwithstanding the troops at Sindhoodoorg and other stations, nearly the whole of the lands possessed by his grandfather, Lukum Sawunt, to the south of the Koodal or Karlee river.

The collections in the districts to the north of the Koodal river were in proportion to the effective strength of each in arms, thus giving existence to that state of anarchy and confusion so productive of oppression and exaction in their worst forms.

To secure these advantages, much attention was paid to the repair of the defences of the several hill forts, especially to those of Eshwuntgur, erroneously called Réree, the name of an adjoining village.

The province of Salsee at this period was held in divided authority, two-fifths of the revenue being paid to the Waree State, one-and-a-half-fifth to Angria, and one-and-a-half-fifth to Bowrekur, clogged with the payment of an annual sum to the fort of Sindhoodoorg.

Wanee Purub, the Patel of the town of Musooree, discovered that Bowrékur intended to fortify the present site of Bhurutgur, and apprehensive a new power would lead eventually to heavier impositions of tribute, communicated the design to Phond Sawunt.

The Sirdar Krishnu Rao Heejaeeree was immediately sent to discover water if possible, failing in which after much labour, an abandonment had nearly taken place; yet, with repeated injunctions not to relax in any exertions, water was at last found at a very great depth.

His desire thus obtained (A. D. 1700), Phond Sawunt in person superintended the erection, then consisting of four bastions, joined by a curtain.

It is currently reported that the water in the wells disappears on the firing of a few guns from the works. The garrison having wooden reservoirs, such as used in Patamars, in which their supply of water is kept, would warrant this report.

To render nugatory any influence Phond Sawunt might have obtained by the possession of Bhurutgur, so immediately on the Salsee frontier, Bowrékur, exactly on the opposite bank, and also on an eminence, erected the fort of Bhugwuntgur (A. D. 1701), commanded by some high ground on the north, overlooking the whole of its interior. The two places may be within the range of a long cannon-shot of each other.

To secure the district of Maloondee, Phond Sawunt also built the small fort of Sadgur on a commanding situation, about the year 1708 A. D.

Phond Sawunt, who was married to several wives, had a numerous issue. Of these it will be only necessary to name Naroba Sawunt, Koot Sawunt, Som Sawunt, Jyram Sawunt, and Nag Sawunt.

It was during this long and extended government that the Waree State appears to have attained its greatest celebrity; the abilities and prowess of Jyram Sawunt preserved in the Konkun the superiority in arms over the Kolhapoor (or Kurweer) Raja, and the daring enterprise of Nag Sawunt obtained for him the Waree (or Chundrugur) province from the Nuwab of Beejapoor about the year 1724 A. D.

The latter days of Phond Sawunt were embittered by the conspiracy of his eldest son, Naroba Sawunt, by whom for a short time he was deposed and imprisoned.

Phond Sawunt brought the guard placed over him to their allegiance, and in the consequent skirmish between the adherents of the father and the rebellious son, the latter was mortally wounded by a musket ball.

This event was much deplored by the unfortunate father, who, as somewhat in atonement to the manes of his deceased son, and in prevention of similar domestic treason, nominated his infant grandson Ramchundru Sawunt (the son of Naroba Sawunt) to be his successor about 1728 A. D., and in his name held the reins of government until his own death.

Affairs were principally conducted by Jyram Sawunt during the minority of Ramchundru Rao Sawunt, at an early period of which the celebrated Angria extended his acquisitions by the capture of Bhugwuntgur and Bhurutgur, which latter place he retained for three years, adding to its several defences, and the ditch around at the base of the hill.

Thus successful, he advanced, and crossing the Koodal river, defeated Jyram Sawunt at Bamburdee, and took prisoner Sheoram Sawunt.

In a treaty then entered into, the Waree State ceded to Angria its two-fifths of the revenue of Salsee.

Peace between two such predatory powers could be but of short continuance. Hostilities soon commenced, and Angria, near the scene of his former victory, experienced a signal overthrow (A. D. 1748), in remembrance of which, his State Nobut is daily beaten at the palace at Waree.

This defeat led to the recovery of Bhurutgur, and the districts between the Koodal and Gurnar rivers.

By his vigilance and promptitude Jyram Sawunt repelled the third and final attempt made by Angria.

The Waree troops thus occupied, the Portuguese seized the five Purgunas, which, in consequence of the predatory irruptions of Jyram Sawunt, carried even into the Portuguese territories, were speedily relinquished and evacuated, as was also Eshwuntgur, which two years previously (A. D. 1746) had fallen into their hands, by surprise, and a breach of friendship.

Affairs thus remained until his father's death, which occurred prematurely during a journey to Bhurutgur, when Khem Sawunt, a minor, succeeded (A. D. 1750), the government, during his minority, being conducted by Jyram Sawunt, assisted by Jewajee Vishram Subnis, who, to secure the advantage of a powerful alliance, procured for him in marriage Luxoomee Baee, the daughter of Mahadajee Sindia; Doorga Baee, the daughter of Dhar Rao Khanvilkur, then a Sirdar in the Waree service; Nurmuda Baee, a daughter of Mansing Rao Sookwee; and Savitree Baee, daughter of Hunmunt Rao Ghatgay, at that time a Poona Sirdar.

In the course of the minority (Shalivahan 1686, A. D. 1764), after nine days' hostilities, the fort of Sindhoodoorg surrendered to an English fleet, which, after an occupation of sixteen months, was restored to the Kolhapoor Raja; to the same fleet also did Eshwuntgur lower its flag, which, after a space of two years, was exchanged for the possession of Vingorla.

On assuming the direction of affairs, in order to counteract the too great influence of Jewajee Vishram Subnis, Khem Sawunt assembled his relations around him. Notwithstanding his favourable sentiments in regard to his relatives, domestic dissensions arose, causing his uncle Jyram Sawunt to retire to the town of Koodal, in which he exercised his authority until his death.

The disasters which have reduced the Waree State to its present weakness and insignificance commenced in this reign (A. D. 1781), by the capture by the Portuguese of Dichoolee, Phonda, Sanklee, and Munéree.

The Waree troops, under the Sirdar Bhaskur, taking advantage of the absence of Mr. Henshaw, the Company's Agent at Goa, recovered possession of Vingorla in the year 1781 A. D.

The expedition to recover the four districts under Som Sawunt was attended with considerable success (A. D. 1782), but a sudden retreat without adequate cause has given rise to surmises injurious to his fame.

The long subsisting contrariety of interests between the Kolhapoor and Waree Durbars seldom broke out into open hostility; mutual petty attempts to surprise and gain by treachery the hill forts each possessed being only essayed by either party.

This contemptible warfare did not materially affect the general tranquillity of the inhabitants, as the two powers, fully sensible of the detriment each sustained by arbitrary collections of the revenues, mutually agreed that one-third of the revenue of Maloondee and Wurad, with the fixed annual sum from Páth and Huwelee, should continue to be paid regularly to the Kolhapoor Raja.

Matters remained thus situated, with only the appearance of peace, until Luxoomee Baee, through her influence with Sindia, procured from the Delhi Durbar for her husband the regal honour of the peacock's feather in Shalivahan 1705 (A. D. 1783).

The pride of the Kolhapoor Raja, as a descendant of Shivajee, ill brooked the accession of royal privileges by the Desaees of Waree. With this rankling in his breast, causes of remonstrances with Khem Sawunt were not long wanting, which ended in an irruption into the Waree territory, as far as the post of Akeree. Unable to carry this post, the troops, after some devastations, were recalled.

Short was the interval before hostilities recommenced, by the taking of Nursingur (since called Seedgur), commanding the Ghotgha pass, in Shalivahan 1709 (A. D. 1787), by the Kolhapoor forces.

To preserve Seedgur from capture, it was in Shalivahan 1709 (A. D. 1787) put into the possession of the troops of Madhow Rao Peshwa, and after a period of six years it was restored by him to the Waree State.

Aided by artillery from Malwan, Bhurutgur was carried, and with it undisputed possession of the districts north of the Koodal river. Newtee and Vingorla were taken with little resistance.

In this distress, Khem Sawunt sent Kooshaba Nana Subnis as ambassador to Goa, to negotiate for assistance; and as security for the payment of the troops, gave the district of Phonda, in which the fort of Tirakole was immediately built.

The troops from Goa landed near Vingorla, and on their juncture with those from Waree the Raja retired to Malwan, evacuating both Newtee and Vingorla.

As Bhurutgur and the district north of the Koodal river were still retained by the Raja, he, previous to ascending the Ghauts, made the necessary arrangements for their defence. In the interim Khem Sawunt, instead of resorting to arms for their recovery, had recourse to the interference of Sindia and Purushram Bhow, by whose remonstrances, not unaccompanied by threats, Bhurutgur and the districts were restored (A. D. 1793), the revenue payable as heretofore, the Waree Durbar relinquishing its collection within ascertained limits around, and in the town of Malwan itself.

Sensible of his approaching dissolution (Shalivahan 1725, A. D. 1803), Khem Sawunt was desirous of a last interview with Rao Saheb, but was thwarted by Som Sawunt (in charge of the palace and city guards), who was desirous his own son should be nominated to the succession in preference to Rao Saheb.

A few hours previous to his decease, at the age of fifty-five years, Khem Sawunt appointed Luxoomee Baee regent, delivering the seals into her hands.

Rao Saheb and Som Sawunt, in a very few months broke out into undisguised opposition, each essaying his utmost to procure his own son's public nomination as successor to be made by Luxoomee Baee, who called in the aid of procrastination to secure to herself the sole direction of affairs, during the vacancy in the succession, in which she was much assisted by Vishnoo Kamut, her minister.

To accomplish his purpose, Som Sawunt resorted to the extreme measure of imprisoning Luxoomee Baee and Doorga Baee. As the first step, Phond Sawunt, his son, was sent to Eshwuntgur, of which he was Killedar, there to collect a number of men, a party of whom were to be at Waroo soon after break of day, at which time Som Sawunt was to secure the gate of the new fort

38

or palace, situated near the centre of the city, the residence of the widows. On the day appointed, Som Sawunt executed his part of the plan. This coming to the knowledge of Rao Saheb at his country seat, he without delay took post at the old fort, near the outer boundary of the city. The aid from Eshwuntgur arrived not until the afternoon was far advanced. Som Sawunt's party was attacked, and routed with considerable loss by Rao Saheb, who thus was able closely to blockade the entrances to the new fort.

Undismayed at these violent proceedings (Shalivahan 1726, 1st Chuitru, A. D. 1804), Luxoomee Baee refused compliance with the demands of Som Sawunt. Rao Saheb in the interim hastily assembling his own and Luxoomee Baee's adherents, stormed the new fort, gave liberty to the female captives, and compelled Som Sawunt to retire to his own fortified house, accompanied by 400 followers.

Under the dread of falling into the hands of his enraged enemies, who refused all terms, Som Sawunt adopted the desperate resolution of destroying himself and family, which was carried into execution by springing a mine, and thus, besides the destruction of his wealth, which he had collected for that purpose, himself, his pregnant wife Joyuwuntee Baee, a young son, Bawa Saheb or Jyram Sawunt, a daughter's son Baboo Rao Ghatgay, and menials, in all amounting to eighteen souls, made a miserable exit (Shalivahan 1726, A. D. 1804), Phond Sawunt, then at Eshwuntgur, and a sister, alone surviving.

Luxoomee Baee still resisted the importunities of Rao Saheb to adopt and appoint to the succession his son, Bhow Saheb, fearing that her influence in the State would be lessened in consequence.

Phond Sawunt, by the death of his father, unable to oppose Rao Saheb, solicited aid from Kolhapoor, from whence Rutnakur Appa Rajadnu was ordered to Malwan, and proceeded from thence to Eshwuntgur, where he personally conferred with Phond Sawunt, who, previously strengthening the garrison with a considerable number of Rutnakur Appa's troops, and settling the necessary arrangements for their regular supply from Sindhoodoorg, accompanied him to Malwan.

Shortly after Rutnakur Appa returned to Kolhapoor, Phond Sawunt visited that capital, and was received with much respect by the Raja (Shalivahan 1726, A. D. 1804), who gave him strong assurances of aid after the rains. The monsoon had no sooner passed by, than Rutnakur Appa descended and seized on the town of Koodal. From thence, the country was laid waste until Luxoomee Baee consented to Phond Sawunt's return to Waree, and to the restoration of his father's rights. This accomplished, Rutnakur Appa re-ascended the Ghauts.

Phond Sawunt soon obtained such influence with Luxoomee Baee and the ministers, that Rao Saheb, securing Hunmuntgur and Banda, by putting Jugutoba* in possession of the former, and Chundroba of the latter, abandoned Waree.

* Jugutoba and Chundroba were illegitimate sons of Rao Saheb.

To oppose Rao Saheb, a force was speedily collected, with which the Ranee Doorga Baee, Jan Rao Nimbalkur, Phond Sawunt,* and many of the chief ministers, marched to Ensolee and Wagdota (Shalivahan 1727, A. D. 1805). Here they were attacked and routed by Rao Saheb, with 500 men. Phond Sawunt with much difficulty escaped to Akeree in disguise. Jan Rao Nimbalkur and others, the principal Sirdars, became pirsoners to Rao Saheb, who the next day entered Waree in triumph.

At this distracted period the garrison of Seedgur fell much in arrears, which in the intestine broils remained unliquidated. Chitko Punt, Amuldar of Salsee, insidiously supplied their wants, and latterly gained possession of the fort, and somewhat appeased the disunited Waree Durbar, in representing that under the protection of the Peshwa it would be free from any attacks of the Kolhapoor Raja.

Rao Saheb stained his victory by several acts of cruelty at Waree, and subsequently constrained Luxoomee Baee publicly to acknowledge his son as the heir to the government, which ceremony took place with much pomp in A. D. 1805, and at which Doorga Baee was present, having previously been released from confinement at Hunmuntgur, her prison since the action of Wagdota.

Phond Sawunt had taken refuge at Koodal, and, aided by Chitko Punt in person, with a party drawn from Seedgur, and Ranojee Naik Nimbalkur, Killedar of Rangna or Prusidgur, had penetrated to Akeree, when the seizure by Ranojee Naik of Cheetko Punt, and his subsequent confinement at Malwan, stopped all further progress.

In the rains of this year (A. D. 1806) Seedgur was blockaded by Ranojee Naik for upwards of a month. The place was found too strong for the party, though reinforced from Malwan.

Phond Sawunt, with the present Sirdars Babna Gopal and Sumbhajee Sawunt,† passed the monsoon at Walowlee and Koodal, in the course of which Rao Saheb died; and ere the monsoon was over, the Raja of Kolhapoor descended with a considerable force to Malwan.

The Raja, seeing the distractions of the Waree State, attacked and carried the forts of Bhurutgur and Newtee, and established the port of Nandooguree previous to his return to Kolhapoor.

Phond Sawunt, brother to Sumbhajee Sawunt, the Portuguese, at last was set at liberty, and obtained the command of a considerable body of the Waree troops, and, aided by Luxoomee Baee, was enabled to reduce the too great power of both Chundroba and Jugutoba, and to imprison Esha Soobhedar, an illegitimate son of Koot Sawunt, who shortly afterwards died in confinement.

Whilst affairs were taking this turn, Phond Sawunt had returned to Waree (Shalivahan 1729, A. D. 1807). The Government, though in the name of the

* Phond Sawunt was son-in-law to Luxoomee Baee.

† Sumbhajee Sawunt's grandfather was the son of Phond Sawunt by a female slave.

young Bhow Saheb, was chiefly directed by Ramchundru Rao (the brother of Doorga Baee), who surprised and put to the sword the garrison of Namdoor Ghunbee, and compelled the other posts to take shelter in Sindhoodoorg.

After the rains, these incursions were carried even to the gates of Malwan, where the Waree troops received a severe check. At a second attack, eight days subsequent, the village at the bottom of the Malwan pagoda pass was laid in ashes by the Ranee's troops. The cruelties committed on this occasion in the districts north of the Koodal river are still fresh in the remembrance of the inhabitants.

To repel similar attacks, 1,000 picked men were immediately detached from Kolhapoor. These, and a reinforcement from Malwan, raised the siege of Bhurutgur, just begun by Chundroba.

By cutting off the communication with Newtee and Eshwuntgur, the latter still in the possession of the garrison placed by Phond Sawunt, these two forts again reverted to the Waree State.

The Kolhapoor Raja, having detached in advance Hybut Rao Gaikwar Sirkhuwas, and 200 horse, descended the Munohur Ghaut with Rutnakur Appa Rajadnu at the head of 3,000 infantry, and gained a victory at Chowkool (A. D. 1807). Pursuing his success with considerable caution, he in a few months encamped before the gates of Waree.

These disasters compelled Luxoomee Baee to call in foreign aid. Appa Desaee Nepaneekur and Venkut Rao Tambooleekur being applied to, the former granted 1,000 men, chiefly Arabs, and the latter 400 Murathas.

A considerable body of men from Nepanee had on the same day that the Raja came in sight of Waree thrown themselves into the fort, and rendered it too strong to be stormed. A few houses in the suburbs were, however, destroyed by fire. On the arrival of the whole of the auxiliaries, a retreat (not unattended with loss) became necessary (A. D. 1808), as Nepaneekur, to create a diversion, had threatened the Kolhapoor territories above the Ghauts.

The auxiliary troops, too powerful to be resisted, shortly seized on the country they had been called on to deliver. In this extremity, the widows fled to the district of Paindné. Ramchundru Rao Khanvilkur, with the young Bhow Saheb, took refuge at Eshwuntgur, and Phond Sawunt retired to Wulowlee. The promises and representations of Appa Soobrao induced their return to Waree, where, however, the semblance of authority they soon found was all that remained to them. Ere the rains commenced, in the name of Luxoomee Baee, Appa Soobrao, without whose approbation nothing was transacted, possessed himself of Eshwuntgur, Vingorla, Newtee, and the other forts.

Affairs remained thus situated, until Luxoomee Baee (Doorga Baee not unconsulted) and Phond Sawunt conspired to murder the young Bhow Saheb, in order to cut off on the part of Daee Baee (Bhow Saheb's mother) and Chundroba all opposition to Phond Sawunt's succession, who became by the death of Bhow Saheb the next male heir to the government.

Previous to perpetrating the murder, Bhow Saheb's Arab guard, placed by

Appa Soobrao, was exchanged for one composed of men devoted to the interest of Phond Sawunt (Shalivahan 1731, A. D. 1809). Those most particularly branded as actors in the murder were Kaloo Bhikajee, hereditary Patel of Baree, afterwards Killedar of Belgaum, and Vishnoo Kamut, who subsequently enjoyed much consideration at Waree.

On the arrival at Waree, from Nepanee, of Maun Sing Rao Patunkut, Phond Sawunt took alarm, and leaving the Koodal province, fled towards Mahar (eastward of Bankote), pursued by Maun Sing Rao as far as Rajapoor, on which town Maun Sing Rao levied a very heavy contribution. On his return, at Seedgur, he received information of a projected attack, which accelerated his march to Kolhapoor.

At this period, party feuds being swallowed up in general distress, Sumbhajee Sawunt, Chundroba, and other Waree chiefs, who, apprehensive of their personal safety, had fled to the neighbouring fastnesses, or to the Paindne district, collected their several forces, and commenced operations against, and gained great advantage over Appa Soobrao, who, in the true Muratha spirit, extorted from Luxoomee Baee and the wealthy inhabitants large sums of money. This persecution brought on an illness, which carried Luxoomee Baee to her grave.

Amongst other operations, Chundroba had laid siege to Hunmuntgur, which became much straitened for provisions. Appa Soobrao determined in person to relieve the place, by marching a strong detachment from Waree. Chundroba, apprised of this, seized the opportunity of possessing himself of Waree, by throwing in a party stronger than that left to defend it. On Appa Soobrao's arrival at the Phookeree Ghaut, close to Hunmuntgur, he was surrounded, and compelled to surrender by Chundroba (Shalivahan 1732, A. D. 1810). This was followed by the fall of Hunmuntgur and Banda, the recovery of Eshwuntgur and Newtee, with the evacuation of the whole of the country by the Nepanee troops before the setting in of the monsoon.

In order that the Government should have an acknowledged head, Sumbhajee Sawunt, Chundroba, and the other chiefs of Waree, had an interview with Phond Sawunt, to whom, on his being invested with the authority of the State, they paid homage, he on his part promising oblivion of past occurrences.

It was at this time the desire of the British Government to annihilate the system of piracy which for many years had been carried on by the Waree and Kolhapoor States, from Sindhoodoorg, Eshwuntgur, and the neighbouring forts, and had been highly detrimental to the interest of the coasting trade of Bombay. It was resolved that this object should be attained by the same measures which were then to be employed to enforce a compliance, on the part of the Poona Southern Jageerdars, to such revision of their tenures as the interests of the Peshwa required, and which it was the Governor General's wish should be accomplished by negotiation, which was rendered the more efficient by the march of two detachments of the Bombay and Madras armies, under the command of Colonels Montresor and Dowse.

Raja concluded a Treaty, on the 1st October 1812, in which, to put a final stop to his piratical depredations, Sindhoodoorg, Pudumgur, Rajkote, Serjékote, and their dependencies, were ceded to the Honorable Company, who in return guaranteed the integrity of his dominions. Phoud Sawunt, in a Treaty negotiated* at Mardoor by the British envoy at Goa, relinquished as a security against further piracies the fort and fortified factory house of Vingorla, and the adjoining land within a boundary of 600 yards, inclusive only of a part of the town, the Treaty conferring on the British Government the right to station on the south bank of the Newtee creek a party to watch the egress and ingress of vessels.

In consequence of these cessions, a battalion of Native infantry, under the command of Major Webb, was detached from Colonel Montresor's force, and arrived at Malwan, where Colonel Smith, of H. M.'s 65th regiment, already was, to receive on the part of Government possession of the cessions (6th November 1812); to report on the state of the country; and ascertain the disposition of the inhabitants.

It was soon discovered, that excepting the town of Malwan and its boundaries, all the lands ceded were held in divided authority, viz:—

The district of Musooree, divided into the Governments of Sindhoodoorg and Bhurutgur, the latter in the possession of the Kolhapoor Raja, the villages undistributed paying a moiety of the revenue to each.

The district of Maloondee, divided into the two Tunkhas of Sindhoodoorg, with eight, and Seedgur with nine villages. The revenue in the former Tunkha was paid in the proportion of one-third to Sindhoodoorg, and two-thirds to Waree, and of the latter Tunkha (in the possession of the Peshwa), in the proportion of one-third to Sindhoodoorg, and two-thirds to Seedgur.

The district of Wurad paid two-thirds of its revenue to Waree, and one-third to Sindhoodoorg.

The districts of Páth and Huwélee were charged with the payment of an annual sum to Sindhoodoorg.

The distribution of the revenue of the district of Salsee was much divided and very intricate, the principal part being paid in the proportion of three-and-a-half-fifths to the Peshwa, and one-and-a-half-fifth to the Government of Bawaree, from which latter proportion certain sums or shares from each village were payable to the forts of Pudumgur, Rajkote, and Serjékote. In this district, also, fines, fees, and every other emolument were increased by the payment in addition to the original fine, &c. of three-and-a-half-fifths or one-and-a-half-fifth, according as either Government might have had cognizance of the subject in dispute or reference.

The police being chiefly that of Waree, justice was generally administered at that city; a person fined, if at Waree, paying a sum in addition of one-

* On the 3rd October 1812.

third to the Government of Sindhoodoorg, and if at Sindhoodoorg, a sum of two-thirds of the amercement to Waree.

From such a complicated system, never-ending disputes could only arise, the more especially with the Sawunt Waree State, which principally administered justice, thus rendering nugatory that protection the inhabitants looked for from the known generosity and equity of the British Government.

Phond Sawunt died at Waree very shortly after the signing of the Treaty of the 3rd October 1812, leaving two sons, the elder Nana Saheb, by the sister of Toregulkur, the younger Bapoo Saheb, by the sister of Aba Nesreekur. Of the mother of the former, it is related, that during the stay of Phond Sawunt at Malwan, she resided in the Goa territories, and on her return after one year's absence, was pregnant with Bapoo Saheb. This circumstance, Phond Sawunt, to suppress his own and her family's disgrace, was silent upon; but on a visit to Toregul an indignant brother put an end to her existence, by cutting her to pieces with his sword.

The Ranee Doorga Baee, who had assumed the regency (Phond Sawunt's sons being minors), attacked Bhurutgur in January 1813, although well acquainted with the guarantee entered into with the British ally, the Raja of Kolhapoor, and Bhurutgur surrendered to Sumbhajee Sawunt and Chundroba after a short blockade.

To the demand of the British Government for the restoration of Bhurutgur to the Kolhapoor Raja, a refusal was made to relinquish it to any but a British force. Colonel Dowse, in consequence, descended the Ghaut, on whose approach (17th March 1813) the place was evacuated, a party from Malwan garrisoning it until its delivery to the Kolhapoor Raja in April 1813.

These acts of hostility to our ally, with the Ranee's subsequent conduct, were considered as sufficient grounds on which to demand a compensation for the expense and inconvenience incurred, as also a fit opportunity to effect an exchange of the districts on the south for those on the north of the Koodal river, together with the offer of an ample remuneration to the Ranee for any loss of revenue which might be sustained by the proposed State arrangement.

Negotiations continuing even whilst the troops under Colonel Dowse were before Eshwuntgur, the Ranee, as its ransom, relinquished her rights to the unceded part of the vale of Vingorla, and promised, on the retreat of the English from the territory, to return to Waree, and settle every dispute in an amicable manner. After a considerable delay on her arrival, her communications with Colonel Dowse were little else than a string of futile arguments and propositions, most unreasonable and inadmissible. A sudden termination to this correspondence took place on the Ranee expressing her unalterable resolution never to enter into any other Treaty than that which, as already stated, had been concluded at Mardoor on the 3rd October 1812. On this unqualified refusal, Colonel Dowse re-ascended the Ghauts (May 1813), previously intimating that Vingorla would be considered a conquest, and not a cession.

In the monsoon, sprung up a domestic enemy, Daee Baee, who, since the death of her son Bhow Saheb, and husband Rao Saheb, in right of the latter had received the usual annual sums and emoluments for furnishing a proportion of men for the service of the State, as Rao Saheb had possessed in the lifetime of Khem Sawunt. Her demands, supported by Chundroba, were, that one of the children of Phond Sawunt should be nominated the heir to the government, assume the name of her murdered son, Ramchŭndru Rao Sawunt, and be adopted as her son. These propositions were rejected by the Ranee, who was well aware a compliance would be but a surrender of her authority.

In pursuance of arrangements on account of the Ranee's refusal to exchange her rights in Wurad and Maloondee for those of the Honorable Company's in Páth and Huwélee, the two former were, on the 27th January 1813, taken possession of by the 2nd Battalion 7th Regt. Bombay N. I. and Artillery from Malwan, and a similar detachment from Colonel Dowse's force. To this force no resistance was made, though the population on the south of the Koodal river was raised *en masse*, and daily threats made of the recovery of the district by force of arms. On this occasion a proclamation was issued, assigning this occupation of the districts by the British Government to be an act absolutely necessary to put an end to the miseries entailed on the inhabitants by a divided authority, the same instrument containing a formal renunciation of Páth and Huwélee.

On Sumbhajee Sawunt suffering under an attack of the palsy, he accused Chundroba as inflicting it by means of magic, and vowed revenge on a return to health. On this occasion so violent were the expressions and determined the enmity of Sumbhajee Sawunt and the Ranee, that Daee Baee, whose sole reliance was on Chundroba, left Majgaum and joined him at Banda on the 19th April 1815. The breach, by a repetition of outrages and insults, was so evident, that hostilities between the parties seemed not improbable.

After much ill health, Nana Saheb by his death left his brother undisputed successor to the government, in May 1815.

The hasty marriage about this time of Bapoo Saheb to the daughter of Narayen Rao Patunkur, in opposition to the decided and unqualified disapprobation of all at Waree, caused great dissatisfaction, the general wish and desire being an alliance with Sindia, who was himself extremely anxious on this head, and had more than once proposed it to the Ranee. Her objection to this alliance chiefly arose from the taint in Sindia's blood, whose grandfather, admitted to the rights of a husband by the female he was to have espoused, before the celebration of the marriage, had by her a son, Sindia's father. This prevented the ceremony ever taking place, as the Sindia caste could not be prevailed on to give their consent.

Two parties at this time divided Waree—the Ranee, supported by the Sirdars Sumbhajee Sawunt, Ramchundru Rao Khanvilkur, chief minister, in opposition to Daee Baee, and Chundroba; the demands of the latter party still being the assumption by Bapoo Saheb of the name of Ramchundru Rao Sawunt, and by Daee Baee to adopt him as her son. In the event of a refusal to the above being still persisted in, she threatened to adopt and nominate to the succession the son of Nag Sawunt Ooruskur, distantly related to the Waree family.

These feuds, it was expected, would eventually lead to hostilities, for which both parties prepared by adding to their respective forces. The Ranee was computed to have in her own personal pay 1,000 men; under Sumbhajee were exclusive of the garrison at Eshwuntgur, consisting of 300 men, 400 Konkunees, 400 Deccan Murathas and Musulmans, and 250 Purdasees. With Babna Gopal, inclusive of the garrison at Newtee, were 300; with Tatoo Khem Sawunt 200; with Dajee Pednakur 200; and with Apa Nesreekur, lately retained in the service, 200; making a total of 3,250. Daee Baee and Chundroba were reckoned to have 800 men, with a promise of aid from Tambooleekur in case of extremity, who was adverse to Nesreekur, having become a party in the family quarrels.

These troops were entertained at a less expense than might generally be supposed, a very large proportion possessing land for their services, and, to cultivate it, were permitted to be absent, but ready at the call of their chiefs. The Purdasees and some of the Deccan Murathas only, were in receipt of full pay from the treasury.

A considerable agitation took place in the Waree Durbar owing to a frequent correspondence with Poona. Although the subject of the letters was kept secret, it was generally surmised they were of a hostile tendency, as consultations were held on the necessity of coming to an immediate agreement with Daee Baee and Chundroba. Arrangements were made for the assembling a considerable body of troops at Nepanee, to be at Waree after the breaking up of the monsoon, and much activity prevailed in the making of field gun-carriages, and in the preparation of military stores.

TREATIES, AGREEMENTS, &c.

ENTERED INTO

BETWEEN THE HONORABLE EAST INDIA COMPANY AND THE SAWUNT WAREE STATE,

Between the 12*th January* 1730 *and the* 29*th November* 1843.

SAWUNT WAREE.

Treaty with the Sawunt Waree State, dated the 12th January 1730.

Articles of Peace and Friendship, agreed on and concluded by ROBERT COWAN, *Esq., President and Governor of Bombay, for and in behalf of the Honorable English East India Company, and* BAPOOJEE NAIK, *Chief Commander at Sea, for* PHOND SAWUNT, *Sir Desaee of Koodal, for and in behalf of the said Sir Desaee.**

ARTICLE I.

That there shall henceforward, for ever, be a firm peace and friendship betwixt the said Honorable English East India Company, their servants and subjects, and the said Sir Desaee, his subjects and vassals, by land and sea, under the following conditions :—

ARTICLE II.

That in case the fleet of the said Sir Desaee shall at any time meet at sea any ships or vessels under English colours, whether of war or merchandize, they shall not molest them, but on discovery that they belong to the English, give them all the assistance they can ; and in case of meeting with a single vessel, they shall not, after showing her colours, chase her with more than one gallivat, to be certainly informed that she is really English. In like manner, when the vessels of war of the said Honorable Company shall meet at sea the fleet or vessels of the said Sir Desaee, they shall permit them to pass unmolested, on showing their colours, and sending a gallivat or other small embarkation, to certify who they are.

ARTICLE III.

If at any time, through stress of weather, or any other accident, any vessels belonging to the English should be drove ashore, and shipwrecked, in the ports or territories of the said Sir Desaee, they shall not be forfeited ; on the contrary, all aid and assistance shall be given the people belonging to them, in saving and preserving the said vessels and their cargoes, and free liberty granted to transport or dispose of what is so saved, as they shall think proper, without paying any salvage, custom, or duty whatever for the same ; and the like shall be observed with all vessels belonging to the subjects of the said Sir Desaee, that shall meet with the like misfortune in the ports or territories of the said Honorable Company.

Article IV.

The ports, places, and settlements of the said Honorable Company and the said Sir Desaee shall be free and open to the subjects and servants of both, to navigate and trade in, on paying the respective duties that are usually paid at the said ports and places, or that shall be hereafter stipulated and agreed on.

Article V.

The sons of Kanojee Angria being professed enemies to the Honorable Company and the said Sir Desaee, it is agreed that the joint endeavour of both shall be exerted to destroy the said enemy, the Honorable Company by their vessels of war, by sea, distressing them as much as possible, and the Sir Desaee both by land and sea, as much as in his power ; and when a proper opportunity offers, the said President and Governor, in behalf of the said Honorable Company, promises to give the said Sir Desaee what assistance he can to destroy the said enemy, by uniting one or more of the Honorable Company's vessels of war with the fleet of the Sir Desaee, the better to obtain the end desired ; but in case of such an union of the marine force of both parties, the chief command of the united force shall remain to the English Commander.

Article VI.

That the Honorable Company shall supply the Sir Desaee with such artillery and warlike stores as he may want, and they can conveniently spare, at reasonable prices.

Article VII.

That these Articles, agreed on and concluded, shall be exchanged and ratified by the said President and Governor, under the seal of the said Honorable Company, and by the said Sir Desaee under his proper seal, in six months from the date hereof, or sooner if opportunity offers.

Done in Bombay Castle, the 12*th day of January* 1729-30.

Memorandum.—*This Treaty was ratified by the Government of Bombay, on the* 17*th April* 1730.

Treaty with the Bhonslay (Sir Desaee of Sawunt Waree), dated the 7th April 1765.

Articles of Agreement with the Bhonslay, concluded at the Fort of Reree, the 7*th April* 1765.

Article I.

There shall be perpetual peace and friendship re-established between the Honorable Company and Khem Sawunt, the Bhonslay, their successors and heirs; and for the stricter observance of the following Treaty of Peace, Khem Sawunt, the Bhonslay, agrees to send two hostages of note, with their families, to reside at Bombay, and to be maintained at his charge.

ARTICLE II.

The Bhonslay renounces all pretensions which he has heretofore formed, or might form, to the lands and tenements situated between the rivers Karlee and Salsee, from the sea shore up to the foot of the Ghauts, which he cedes and guarantees to the Honorable Company, in full right, and will put them in possession of the same; as likewise the sovereignty of the said river and the islands therein; but the Bhonslay requests and hopes the Honorable Company will cause the amount of one-third of the annual revenues of the said lands and tenements to be paid him, either in money, or Europe staples, or in grain. In consideration of his agreeing to, and fulfilling the X. Article, the Honorable Company, on their part, renounce all pretensions to the lands, rents, revenues, and tributes, which now or heretofore did pay obedience, rents, or tributes, to the Malwans, in any part of this country to the south of the river Karlee, and cedes and guarantees the same in full right to the Bhonslay.

ARTICLE III.

The Bhonslay agrees to pay to the Honorable Company one lakh of rupees, as the restitution for the expenses they have been at, during the troubles subsisting between the contracting parties; half to be paid in eight days from the time in which this Treaty is concluded; 25,000 rupees within twelve months of this date; and the remainder, 25,000 rupees, within three years from the date hereof.

ARTICLE IV.

The Bhonslay will not, by any menaces or otherwise, directly or indirectly, deter the inhabitants of the different districts or villages ceded to the Honorable Company, from living in them peaceably; and, furthermore, will oblige all the inhabitants, with their families, who belonged to or lived in the aforesaid districts, who have quitted them, or may hereafter leave them, to return to their habitations.

ARTICLE V.

The English subjects, and the subjects of the Bhonslay, shall have free liberty of trade and commerce with each other, without any hindrance or molestation.

ARTICLE VI.

The Bhonslay will permit the Honorable Company to build a factory or factories, on any part of his territories, adjacent to the sea shore, for vending their commodities, and to keep there such servants and people as they shall think necessary for conducting the same ; and should any of the merchants or others, his subjects, become debtors to the English, they shall have liberty to imprison their persons, or seize their effects, and vend them, till satisfaction is obtained.

Article VII.

The Bhonslay grants to the Honorable Company an exclusive right (except to the Portuguese nation) of importing and vending all Europe cloths, lead, iron, steel, copper, and Europe commodities, in his territories, and to pass the same through his country.

Article VIII.

The Bhonslay will allow all merchants or Vunjaras free liberty to pass and repass his territories, to and from Fort Augustus, with their effects, merchandize, carriages, and beasts of burden, they paying the accustomed duties, and no more, on any pretence whatever.

Article IX.

The Bhonslay agrees to deliver up all the effects which have been carried away from Fort Sundero, in the Malwan gallivats, with guns, and all kinds of stores belonging to them, if any such can be proved to be in his possession now, or at any other time.

Article X.

If Jeeja Baee Maharaj, the Ranee, shall offer to invade the territories of either of the contracting powers, or that she hinders the merchants from passing the Ghauts, and the Honorable Company should find it necessary to attack her, in such case the Bhonslay agrees to assist and aid the Honorable Company with his whole force, and furnish a sufficient number of draught and pack oxen, to carry ammunition, provisions, and stores.

Article XI.

The Bhonslay shall not keep any fleet, or have any vessels or gallivats equipped for war.

Article XII.

If ever the Honorable Company should think proper to demand of the Murathas the lands in the districts of Salsee, which formerly belonged to the Malwans, in such case, they will likewise demand, for and in behalf of the Bhonslay, the lands in the said districts formerly belonging to him. The Bhonslay to pay an adequate share of the expenses that may accrue to the Honorable Company, in making these demands.

ARTICLE XIII.

The fort of Musoora, with all the guns, shot, carriages, and stores therein, shall be delivered up to the Honorable Company, in its present situation, within eight days from this date; in lieu whereof, the Honorable Company shall, at the same time, deliver up to the Bhonslay the fort of Réree, with all the guns and carriages found on the walls, when conquered by the English.

ARTICLE XIV.

The Bhonslay will not entertain in his service any people belonging to the English, whether Europeans or others, nor suffer any European deserters to pass through his districts; but on the contrary, give strict orders to all his officers to seize such as may be seen in his dominions, and return them to the chief of Fort Augustus, on promise of pardon, whether they are applied for or not. The English will observe the same in respect to the subjects of the Bhonslay; and slaves to be returned on both sides.

ARTICLE XV.

If any vessels or boats belonging to the English, their subjects or dependents, shall at any time be drove ashore, or wrecked in any part of the Bhonslay's dominions, he agrees to afford all suitable assistance for the preservation of such vessels and their cargoes; and whatever part thereof may be saved, to be delivered up to their right owner, without any salvage whatever, except the labourers' hire. The English on their parts to observe the same in respect to the vessels belonging to the Bhonslay.

ARTICLE XVI.

If at any time the Bhonslay should have occasion for powder and ball, and military stores, the Honorable Company will supply him with what they can spare, at the usual rates.

ARTICLE XVII.

The Honorable Company agree, if convenient to them, to furnish the Bhonslay with troops, to go against his and their enemies.

ARTICLE XVIII.

The Bhonslay agrees to fulfil the I. II. III. and XIII. Articles, within eight days from the signature of this Treaty; in default of which, he agrees to pay all the charges of maintaining the garrison of the fort of Réree, till they are fulfilled, at which time the Honorable Company will deliver up the fort of Réree.

ARTICLE XIX.

In witness of these articles of Agreement between the contracting parties, we, the underwritten agents, and Ministers Plenipotentiary, have signed with

40

our hands, and in their name, and in virtue of our full powers, the present definitive Treaty, and have caused the seals of the Honorable Company and the Bhonslay to be put thereto.

Done at the Fort of Réree, the 7th day of April 1765.

MEMORANDUM.—*The foregoing Treaty was superseded by the conclusion, on the 24th October* 1766, *of the following "Articles of Agreement."*

Treaty with the Sawunt Waree State, dated the 24th October 1766.

Articles of Agreement made and entered into by and between the Honorable United Company of MERCHANTS OF ENGLAND, *trading to the East Indies, and* KHEM SAWUNT, *the Bhonslay, concluded at the Fort of Réree, the twenty-fourth day of October* 1766.

ARTICLE I.

There shall be perpetual peace and firm friendship re-established between the Honorable Company and Khem Sawunt, the Bhonslay, their successors and heirs; and for the stricter observance of the following Treaty of Peace, the Bhonslay agrees to send (should the Company require it) two hostages of note, with their families, to reside at Bombay, and to be maintained at his charge.

ARTICLE II.

The Bhonslay agrees to pay the Honorable Company two lakhs of rupees (2,00,000), as restitution for the expenses they have been at, from the time the troubles subsisted between the respective parties, and maintaining the fort of Réree; eighty thousand (80,000) rupees to be paid in three months from the 24th October 1766, that is, fifty thousand (50,000) the first month, and thirty thousand (30,000) within the three months; the remaining one lakh and twenty thousand (1,20,000) to be paid in two years from the said 24th of October 1766, at equal payments of sixty thousand (60,000) each year, for the performance of which the Bhonslay agrees to give Vitojee Cammotim, of Goa, as security, and the amount to be paid in Peerkhanee and Hookeree rupees, and as security to Vitojee, the Bhonslay agrees to lodge in the Honorable Company's hands two hostages, by name Dowlut Dulvee and Surzum Bawa, who are to reside at Bombay, and to be maintained at his expense.

ARTICLE III.

The Honorable Company, in consideration of the Bhonslay's fulfilling the foregoing Article, do agree, on the payment of the first sum, viz. 80,000 rupees, to deliver him, the said Bhonslay, the fort of Reree, and do further renounce all claims or pretensions to the lands and tenements belonging thereto.

ARTICLE IV.

The Honorable Company will carry away all guns, carriages, mortars, shot, shells, powder, stores, &c. of what kind soever they may have brought here, and they do give up to the Bhonslay such guns and carriages as are here, that were belonging to Fort Réree.

ARTICLE V.

Khem Sawunt, the Bhonslay, will permit the Honorable Company to build a factory, &c. with warehouses at Réree, at such place as may be most convenient for them, at which place they will hoist their flag, or on any part of his territories adjacent to the sea shore, for vending their commodities, and to keep there such servants and people, also vessels and boats, as they shall think necessary for conducting the same; and should any of the merchants, or others, his subjects, become debtors to the English, they shall have free liberty to imprison their persons, seize their effects, and vend them, till satisfaction is made and obtained.

ARTICLE VI.

The English subjects, and the subjects of the Bhonslay, shall have free liberty to trade and commerce with each other, without any hindrance or molestation.

ARTICLE VII.

Khem Sawunt, the Bhonslay, will not directly nor indirectly give any hindrance or molestation to any vessels or boats with English colours and passes, or any vessels or boats going under English convoys; in like manner the English will not molest any boats or vessels belonging to Khem Sawunt, the Bhonslay, or his subjects, provided they have passes or certificates, with the Bhonslay's seal affixed.

ARTICLE VIII.

The Bhonslay grants to the English nation an exclusive right (except the Portuguese) of importing and vending all Europe commodities, as lead, iron, steel, cloths, copper, &c. in his country, and to pass the same through his territories.

ARTICLE IX.

Khem Sawunt, the Bhonslay, will allow all merchants or Vunjaras free liberty to pass and repass his territories, to and from the English factory, with their effects, merchandizes, packages, carriages, and beasts of burthen, they paying the accustomed duties, and no more, on any pretence whatever.

Article X.

Khem Sawunt, the Bhonslay, will not entertain in his service any people belonging to the English, whether Europeans or others, but, on the contrary, give strict orders to his officers to seize such as may be seen in his dominions, nor suffer any European deserters to pass through his country, but return them to the Resident of the English factory, whether they are applied for or not, on promise of pardon; the English will observe the same in respect to the subjects of the Bhonslay, &c. and slaves to be returned on both sides.

Article XI.

If any vessels or boats belonging to the English, their subjects or allies, or those trading under their protection, at any time be drove ashore or wrecked in any part of the Bhonslay's dominions, he agrees to afford all suitable assistance for the preservation of such vessels and their cargoes, and whatever part thereof may be saved to be delivered up to the lawful owners, without any salvage whatever, except the labourers' hire. The English on their parts to observe the same in respect to any vessels belonging to Khem Sawunt, the Bhonslay.

Article XII.

Khem Sawunt, the Bhonslay, will not, by menaces or otherwise, directly nor indirectly, plunder, or in any shape molest the inhabitants or others thay may have served or lived under the protection of the English, during the time they were in possession of Fort Réree, but permit them to enjoy peaceably their houses, lands, and tenements, in the same free and ample manner as when the Bhonslay's Government subsisted, before the English conquered this place. The least infringement of this Article will be highly resented by the Honorable Company.

Article XIII.

Khem Sawunt, the Bhonslay, agrees, should the Honorable Company be attacked, and they should require his assistance, to provide them with what troops they may want, they supplying them with provisions only. The Honorable Company in like manner agrees to assist the Bhonslay, should it be convenient for them.

Article XIV.

Khem Sawunt, the Bhonslay, in consideration of Vitojee Cammotim's standing his security to the Honorable Company for the amount of this Treaty, does make over to the Honorable Company in his behalf, and for his use, the village and district of Vingorla, with all its oarts, farms, rents, customs, &c. of any kind or sort whatsoever, for the term of thirteen (13) years, at which place the Honorable Company will hoist their flag, and keep there such servants and people as they may think proper; and should Khem Sawunt, the Bhonslay, not have satisfied Vitojee Cammotim for the amount of the Treaty at the expiration of the term of 13 years, the Honorable Company will continue to keep it in their hands until he has received full satisfaction, at which time it will be returned to Khem Sawunt, the Bhonslay, but the Honorable Company will still continue their factory, if they think proper.

ARTICLE XV.

In witness of these Articles of Agreement between the contracting parties, I, the underwritten Agent, for and in behalf of the Honorable United East India Company, and Khem Sawunt, the Bhonslay, for himself, have signed with our hands and in virtue of our full power, the present definitive Treaty, and have caused the seals of the respective parties to be affixed thereto.

Done at Fort Réree, this 24th day of October 1766.

(Signed) THOMAS MOSTYN.

MEMORANDUM.—*The above Treaty was signed by the Sir Desaee of Sawunt Waree, on the 28th October 1766, and was approved and confirmed by the Government of Bombay on the 3rd of the following month, with the exception of that part of Article XIV. which stipulated that the Honorable Company's flag should be hoisted at Vingorla, and which stipulation Mr. Mostyn was directed to have cancelled, if practicable. For reasons, however, subsequently explained by Mr. Mostyn, this Article was permitted to remain unaltered.*

Treaty with the Sir Desaee of Sawunt Waree, dated the 3rd October 1812.

Articles of Agreement concluded between the Raja PHOND SAWUNT BHONSLAY, *Bahadoor, Sir Desaee of Koodal and its dependencies, on the one part, and* COURTLAND SCHUYLER, *Esq., Captain of His Britannic Majesty's 84th Regiment of Foot, and British Envoy at Goa, under instructions from the Right Honorable* GILBERT, LORD MINTO, *Governor General of British India, on behalf of the Honorable East India Company, on the other part.*

ARTICLE I.

There shall be perpetual peace and friendship between the Honorable Company and the Raja Phond Sawunt Bhonslay, and their Successors and Heirs, for ever.

ARTICLE II.

In order to the effectual suppression of the piracies which have hitherto been practised by the subjects of the Raja Phond Sawunt Bhonslay, it is hereby agreed upon, on the part of the Bhonslay, that the fort of Vingorla, and the battery of Gunaram Tembe, with the port and proper limits thereof, shall be ceded, in full right and sovereignty, to the Honorable Company, for ever; and the British troops shall be put in immediate possession of the same.

ARTICLE III.

It is further agreed, on the part of the Raja Phond Sawunt Bhonslay, that he will deliver up to the Honorable Company all gallivats, patamars, and other vessels of every description that may hereafter be found equipped in a warlike manner, and that the same shall become lawful prize to the Honorable Company.

ARTICLE IV.

It is further agreed upon, on the part of the Raja Phond Sawunt Bhonslay, that no vessel of any description whatever, belonging to the Sawunt Waree State, shall be allowed to proceed to or from the port of Newtee, without first being examined by a person or persons, who will be appointed for that purpose by the British authority, and also, that a guard of British troops shall be stationed at the port of Newtee, for the same purpose.

ARTICLE V.

It is also agreed upon, on the part of the Raja Phond Sawunt Bhonslay, his heirs and successors, that if at any time hereafter, any of his subjects shall be guilty of piratical acts, the forts of Réree and Newtee shall be given up to the Honorable Company, in like manner with Vingorla.

ARTICLE VI.

It is further agreed, on the part of the Honorable Company, that as soon as the British troops shall be put in possession of the fort of Vingorla, the blockading squadron shall be withdrawn, and the ports in the Sawunt Waree State shall be opened for the free trade of the subjects of the Honorable Company and the Raja Phond Sawunt Bhonslay.

ARTICLE VII.

British merchants shall be allowed the free liberty of passing and repassing the territories of the Raja Phond Sawunt Bhonslay, with their effects, merchandizes, carriages, and beasts of burthen, upon paying the same land tolls as paid by the natural subjects of the Raja, and no more, upon any pretence whatever.

Article VIII.

The British troops and subjects, residing within the territory of the Raja Phond Sawunt Bhonslay, shall not be obliged to pay a greater price for the produce of his country than the natural subjects of the Raja.

Article IX.

That British subjects residing within the territories of the Raja Phond Sawunt Bhonslay shall be solely amenable to the British authority, and any offences they may commit shall, on a representation from the Raja to the officer commanding, be duly attended to; and the like to be observed, on the part of the British, towards the subjects of the Raja.

Article X.

All military stores of every denomination, and all supplies of provisions and Europe articles, imported for the use of the British officers and troops residing in the Sawunt Waree State, to be allowed to pass duty free.

In witness hereof, we, the undersigned, Raja Phond Sawunt Bhonslay, Bahadoor, Sir Desaee of Koodal and its dependencies, and Courtland Schuyler, Esq., Captain in His Britannic Majesty's 84th regiment of foot, and British Envoy at Goa, have signed the present Agreement, and have caused our respective seals to be set thereto.

Done at the village of Mardoor, in the District of Saturda, Sawunt Waree State, on the 3rd day of October 1812.

(A true copy)

(Signed) Courtland Schuyler, Envoy.

Additional Article.

It is further agreed upon, that private property of every description belonging to subjects of the Raja Phond Sawunt Bhonslay, within the limits of the fort of Vingorla and battery of Gunaram Tembé, ceded to the British, shall be respected; and further, that the British authority will not afford its protection to any of the subjects of the Bhonslay who may be guilty of offences against the Sawunt Waree State: the latter part of this Article to be observed by the Raja Phond Sawunt Bhonslay towards British subjects.

The Governor General's Small Seal.

(Signed) Minto.
„ N. B. Edmonstone.
„ A. Seton.

Memorandum.—*This Treaty, with the Additional Article, was ratified by the Right Honorable the Governor General of India in Council, at Fort William, on the 15th January* 1813.

Deed of Cession, dated the 29th April 1813, transferring the Village and Bunder of Vingorla to the Honorable East India Company, and Mandate to the Villagers and Inhabitants, to attend to and obey the orders of the Honorable East India Company, from the period of such Transfer.

This is the order from the presence, (in the year) Soorsun Sullas Ushur Mya Tyne wu Uluf (corresponding with A. D. 1813).

The above-mentioned village and bunder, except (what appertains to) temples, charities, Bramins, and Inams (formerly allowed as deductions from the Dust, or dues), Sirkar's oarts, grain-land, and salt-pans, and claimants or Hukdars; with these deductions all the rest of the village is given, from the beginning of next year, to the Honorable Company's Sirkar, whose orders you must attend and obey, and pay their dues.

Dated on the 27th day of the Moon, or Month Rubee-ool-Akhir, (corresponding with the 29th April 1813, A. D.).

Treaty with the Sawunt Waree State, dated the 17th February 1819.

Treaty between the Honorable East India Company and the Regency of Sawunt Waree, on the part of RAJEY KHEM SAWUNT BHONSLAY, *settled by Major General* SIR WILLIAM GRANT KEIR, K. M. T., *on the part of the British Government, and by* RAJEY KHEM SAWUNT BHONSLAY, *on the part of the Government of Sawunt Waree, by virtue of full powers from the British Government, on the one part, and with the concurrence and consent of the Regency of Sawunt Waree, on the other.*

ARTICLE I.

There shall be perpetual peace and friendship between the British Government and the State of Waree.

ARTICLE II.

The British Government engages to protect the principality and the territory of Sawunt Waree.

ARTICLE III.

The Regency, on the part of Rajey Khem Sawunt Bhonslay, agrees to act in subordinate co-operation with the British Government, and acknowledge its supremacy, and will not have any connection with other chiefs and States.

ARTICLE IV.

The Regency, on the part of Rajey Khem Sawunt, agrees not to enter into negotiations with any chief or State without the knowledge or sanction of the British Government.

ARTICLE V.

The Regency, on the part of Rajey Khem Sawunt Bhonslay, agrees not to commit aggressions on any one; if by accident disputes arise with any one, they shall be submitted to the arbitration and award of the British Government.

ARTICLE VI.

The Raja, and his heirs and successors, shall remain absolute rulers of the country, and the jurisdiction of the British Government shall not be introduced into that principality.

ARTICLE VII.

The Treaty of X. Articles concluded at Mardoor, between Captain Courtland Schuyler and Rajey Phond Sawunt Bhonslay, on the 3rd October 1812, is hereby confirmed; but Rajey Khem Sawunt Bhonslay, having perfect confidence in the justice of the British Government, agrees, that if any of his subjects be guilty of crimes within the territories of the British Government, they shall be tried and punished by the officers of the British Government.

ARTICLE VIII.

Whereas frequent depredations have been committed in the British territory by subjects of the State of Sawunt Waree, the Regency, on the part of Rajey Khem Sawunt Bhonslay, agrees never to employ in the service of the Government of Sawunt Waree, Sumbhajee Sawunt, or Babna Gopal, the principal instigators of these depredations. The Regency further engages to deliver up to the British Government such of the perpetrators of those depredations as it may be in their power to apprehend, and whose names have been given in by Major General Sir William Grant Keir, K. M. T. It is further stipulated and agreed, that all subjects of the State of Sawunt Waree, who may in future be guilty of plundering the territories of the British Government, or any of its allies, are to be given up to the British Government, to be punished according to the laws of that Government; and in the event of the real criminals not being given up, the amount of the property plundered is to be paid by the Government of Sawunt Waree to the British Government.

ARTICLE IX.

The Regency, on the part of Rajey Khem Sawunt Bhonslay, cedes, in perpetuity, to the British Government, the forts of Réree (Eshwuntgur) and Newtee, together with the lands round those forts which have hitherto

41

belonged to their jurisdiction, comprehending the districts of Páth and Azgaum, and the whole line of sea coast from Karlee river to Vingorla, and from Vingorla to the Portuguese territory; and as Sumbhajee Sawunt and Babna Gopal are unable to reimburse the claims of the British Government, out of consideration to the Rajey Khem Sawunt Bhonslay, those claims are expressly relinquished on the part of the British Government.

ARTICLE X.

As a further security against a renewal of the depredations committed by the subjects of the Sawunt Waree Government, the Regency, on the part of Rajey Khem Sawunt Bhonslay, agrees to admit any British detachment that may be thought necessary by the British Government, into any part of the territory of Sawunt Waree, and to afford it every assistance in seizing plunderers and freebooters.

Concluded at Mazgaum, the 17th February 1819.

(Signed) WILLIAM GRANT KEIR,
Major General.

The above Treaty, consisting of X. Articles, was agreed to by Rajey Khem Sawunt Bhonslay, Bahadoor, Sir Desaee, with the approval of Nurbuda Baee, and Savitree Baee.

(A true translate of the last paragraph)

(Signed) G. HUTCHINSON,
Interpreter.

Treaty with the Regency of Sawunt Waree, dated the 17th February 1820.

Articles of Agreement stipulated and agreed upon between the Honorable East India Company and the Regency of Sawunt Waree, on the part of RAJEY KHEM SAWUNT BHONSLAY, *Bahadoor, Sir Desaee of Koodal and its dependencies, settled by Captain* GIDEON HUTCHINSON, *in charge of the Political duties, on the part of the British Government; and by* RAJEY KHEM SAWUNT BHONSLAY, *Bahadoor, on the part of the Government of*

Sawunt Waree, by virtue of full powers from the British Government on the one part, and with the concurrence and consent of the Regency of Sawunt Waree on the other.

ARTICLE I.

The British Government, in token of its friendship towards the Sawunt Waree State, and to evince that it demanded the cession of the Azgaum and Páth districts, ceded by the Treaty concluded on the 17th February 1819, for the sole purpose of putting an effectual stop to the depredations committed in the Honorable Company's territories, by the subjects of the Sawunt Waree State, does hereby restore to Rajey Khem Sawunt Bhonslay, Bahadoor, the Azgaum and Páth districts, with the exception of the forts of Eshwuntgur (Réree) and Newtee, and the villages forming the line of sea coast, and the undermentioned villages, in perpetuity, viz:—

In Turuf Azgaum.

1 Muoje Azgaum.
1 „ Asolee.
1 „ Nanos.
1 „ Aruvdé.
1 „ Tuluvné.
1 „ Tiruvré.
1 „ Kinlé.
1 „ Gooldoové.
8

In Turuf Boordave.

1 Muojé Véras.
1 „ Vusurgaum.
1 „ Koonde.
1 „ Kansrul.
1 „ Kusvun.
1 „ Kusal.
1 „ Purve.
1 „ Gaonraeeteerowre.
8

In Turuf Path.

1 Muojé Path.
1 „ Terolee.
1 „ Chendvun.
1 „ Kuvthee.
4

ARTICLE II.

It is expressly agreed and stipulated, on the part of the Regency, for and in behalf of Rajey Khem Sawunt Bhonslay, Bahadoor, that no person of or belonging to the above-named places, and others that may be hereafter given, on any account or cause whatsoever, shall be responsible, or punished for any acts committed or done by the order, sanction, or cognizance of the Honorable Company, prior to the date of their being delivered to the possession of the Sawunt Waree State.

The above Treaty, consisting of II. Articles, was agreed to and concluded by Rajey Khem Sawunt Bhonslay, Bahadoor, Sir Desaee of Koodal and its dependencies, with the approval of Nurbudu Baee and Savitree Baee, at

Sawunt Waree, the 17th day of February 1820 (corresponding to Thursday, the third of Rubee-ool-Akhir, in the year Soor Sun Ushreen Mya Tyne wu Uluf).

(Signed) GIDEON HUTCHINSON, Captain,
In Charge Political Duties.

MEMORANDUM.—*This Treaty was confirmed by the Bombay Government, on the 9th March* 1820.

Engagement entered into by the Sir Desaee of Sawunt Waree, dated the 25th December 1832.

Memorandum agreed to by RAJEY KHEM SAWUNT BHONSLAY, *Bahadoor, Sir Desaee Prant Koodal, and Mahals—Soor Sun Sullasheen Mya Tyne wu Uluf.*

My country has been thrown into disorder and confusion more than once, through my own misconduct, and the Honorable Company now, at my request, undertakes to restore my authority : I therefore engage to act up to the following conditions, on which alone the assistance of the Honorable Company is extended to me :—

ARTICLE I.

I will appoint Witul Rao Mahadeo Subnis, my Karbharee, to manage the affairs of my State, and I will not remove him without the consent of the British Government.

ARTICLE II.

Whatever measures of reform, for the reduction of my expenses, or those of my State, and whatever arrangements, for the satisfaction of those whom my misgovernment has rendered discontented, the said Karbharee may advise, and the British Government may sanction, I will authorise, and act up to and enforce, and I will offer no obstructions whatever; and I will engage, to the utmost of my ability and power, always to support the said minister in the discharge of the duties entrusted to him.

ARTICLE III.

If I fail in either of these conditions, I shall have deservedly forfeited the friendship and confidence of the British Government, with whom it will then remain to make a suitable arrangement for the State, preserving the Musnud to my son, according to the Treaty.

ARTICLE IV.

Whatever extra expenses are required on account of the troops, or for any other causes relative to the settlement of the principality, I agree to defray.

The above IV. Articles I agree to. Dated 2nd Chundru Shaban, corresponding with 3rd Poush Shood Shuk 1754, *Mundunnam Sumwutsur* (25*th December* 1832). *The Memorandum executed on the* 19*th instant did not contain the name of the Karbharee appointed, in consequence of which this Memorandum is drawn up, and the first destroyed.*

(True translation)

(Signed) G. GIBERNE,

Principal Collector.

MEMORANDUM.—*This Agreement was approved by the Bombay Government on the* 15*th January* 1833.

Agreement with the Sir Desaee of Sawunt Waree, dated the 15*th September* 1838.

Agreement entered into between ALEXANDER ELPHINSTON, *Esq., Collector of Zilla Rutnagherry, and* UJUM RAJEY KHEM SAWUNT BHONSLAY, *Bahadoor, Sir Desaee of Prant Koodal, Suwusthan Soondur Waree (Sawunt Waree), dated* 25*th Jumadee-ool-Akhir, Soor Sun Tissa Sullaseen Mya Tyne wu Uluf (corresponding with the* 15*th September* 1838, A. D.).

ARTICLE I.

Ujum Rajey Bahadoor does hereby renounce all claim to the sea and land customs, including the fee for stamping piece goods, which he has hitherto levied within, as well as on the borders of the territory of the Waree Suwusthan; hereafter the Rajey Bahadoor has no claim to the above-mentioned items of customs.

Article II.

Ujum Rajey Bahadoor does hereby make over to the British Government the right of establishing Nakas on the frontier of the Waree Umul, and the territory, consisting of Perné, and other Mahals now held by the Portuguese of Goa, and of levying customs there, as also of levying sea customs at the port of Banda. The British Government can levy the customs according to its own rules, and in any manner it pleases, to which levy the Rajey Bahadoor is not to raise any objection, on any account.

Article III.

With the exception of the places mentioned in Article II. of this Agreement, the levy of land customs, including the fee for stamping piece goods, at all other places in the Waree Suwusthan Umul, is abolished.

Article IV.

The British Government shall annually make a certain payment to the Rajey Bahadoor, in lieu of the sea and land customs, including the fee for stamping piece goods, which the Waree Suwusthan hitherto levied, and of the Huks which the Hukdars received direct after examining the collections for the three years, viz. 1834-35, 1835-36, and 1836-37, and after fixing the average or a third of the total thereof, the amount of the average shall be annually paid to the Rajey Bahadoor.

Article V.

The Rajey Bahadoor having signified his wish to the British Government, that articles imported from Goa, for his own use, and for the use of his Durukdars, might be exempted from customs as long as the customs did not exceed rupees five hundred, the British Government complied with the request, and with a view to avoid constant trouble, the British Government agrees to pay annually to the Rajey Bahadoor, on account of the remission, a sum of rupees five hundred, in cash, in addition to the amount of average alluded to in Article IV., and therefore the Rajey Bahadoor is not to raise any dispute on account of the above exemption.

Article VI.

If the British Government should give orders to re-establish the levy of land customs in its own dominions, the Rajey Bahadoor is at liberty to levy customs within his territory at all land Nakas, with the exception of the above-mentioned Nakas, on the Waree and Goa frontier and sea-ports, which have been made over to the British Government for the purpose of establishing Nakas. If the British Government should not issue orders to levy land customs in its own dominions, the Rajey Bahadoor is not at liberty to levy them within his own territory. But should a decision (for levying) be passed (by the British Government), then the difference between the average of the customs of the frontier and sea-port Nakas, and the average agreed to be paid to the Rajey Bahadoor, in Article IV., (that is) the average of the customs of the Nakas at which the Rajey Bahadoor may commence levying customs, is not to be paid to him by the British Government.

The above are the VI. Articles agreed upon.

Dated 25*th Jumadee-ool-Akhir* (15*th September* 1838 A. D.).

(True translation)

(Signed) C. J. Erskine,
Deputy Secretary to Government.

Memorandum.—*This Agreement was confirmed by the Bombay Government, on the* 12*th October* 1838

Proclamation against the performance of the Rite of Sutee, *in the* Sawunt Waree Territory.

Dated the 29*th November* 1843.

Proclamation.

The rite of Sutee is a sinful and unjustifiable taking of human life, and has, in consequence, been entirely abolished in all the territories subject to the Honorable Company's Government, since the year A. D. 1829-30; and also subsequently to that time many powerful States and princes have, at the advice of the British Government, totally put a stop to it in their respective dominions. In like manner, since the Waree State has been managed through the interposition of the British Government, no Sutee has been permitted to take place; but as yet no formal Proclamation has been issued on the subject.

Notice is therefore hereby publicly given to all the inhabitants of this principality, that the rite of Sutee will not be permitted to take place in this State; but that it is entirely prohibited: let no one therefore now attempt to commit Sutee; and let every one use his best endeavours to prevent any one from attempting it; and should any one attempt it, let information be immediately given to the Sirkar. And be it clearly understood, that any person assisting in the rite of Sutee, or not giving immediate information of any one attempting it, or not using his best endeavours to prevent the rite, shall be considered as guilty, in the eyes of the Sirkar, of the gravest offence, and will render himself liable to the severest punishment.

(Signed) J. P. Willoughby,
Secretary to Government.

Bombay Castle, 29th November 1843.

OBSERVATIONS

ON

INSCRIPTIONS ON COPPER-PLATES

Dug up at Naroor, in the Koodal Division of the Sawunt Waree State, in April 1848 ;

WITH TRANSLATIONS.

BY

MAJOR G. LeG. JACOB,

(LATE) POLITICAL SUPERINTENDENT OF SAWUNT WAREE.

40

No. 158 of 1848.

From Major G. LeG. Jacob,
Political Superintendent of Sawunt Waree,

To Arthur Malet, Esq.,
Chief Secretary to Government, Bombay.

Political Department.

Camp Arondé, 15th November 1848.

Sir,

I have the honour to submit the translations of the copper-plates promised in my letter No. 147, dated the 27th ultimo, together with fac-simile copies and rescripts in modern Sanscrit. Verbatim translations are added, the better to facilitate the correction of mistakes if I have made any, and I have appended a few observations, as the subject-matter is of some historical interest.

I have the honour to be, &c.

(Signed) G. LeG. Jacob,
Political Superintendent.

OBSERVATIONS.

These inscriptions are in what has been termed the cave-character or the old Sanscrit, and are of the sixth and seventh centuries A. D.; but they do not differ much from the Girnar inscriptions of the third century B. C. A table explanatory of, and showing the varieties in these letters, is annexed to the translations.

These plates all refer to the Chulookyu or Chulikyu race—the name is therein spelled both ways. The earliest recorded date is Shalivahan Shuk 627 (A. D. 705-06); the donor, Wijuyadityu, son of Winuyadityu. This plate has been numbered II. The earliest inscription appears to be that numbered I., describing a grant by Wïjuyubhuttarika, the beloved wife of Shreendradityu, elder brother of Wikrumadityu, father of the abovenamed Winuyadityu, and was therefore written three generations previously. Whethor Shreendradityu, or, as would appear the more correct name, Shree Chundradityu,* reigned previous to his younger brother, jointly with him, or not at all, is left in doubt; but from the title applied to him, and from the royal boon bestowed by his wife,

* Since completing these translations, another set of plates has been found, recording a grant by another wife of this same prince, whose name is written Shree Chundradityu; the letter *chu* seems therefore omitted by oversight in this plate.

one of the two first alternatives appears probable; hence, as the era of Wikrumadityu's ascension to the Gadee has been shown by the Canarese inscriptions translated by Walter Elliot* to have been Shuk 514 (A. D. 592-93), this plate must have been written about the close of the sixth century.

Wijuyadityu's grant (Plate No. II.) was made in the tenth year of his reign, thereby corroborating the era assigned for its commencement by Mr. Elliot; but the genealogy of this dynasty slightly differs from his in both these plates, which correspond one with the other as far as the eras reach. They both commence with Poolukeshi, and as they were evidently written when the grants were made, they would scarcely have omitted two whole generations between him and their own period; perhaps, therefore, the "Amuru" and "Adityu Varmu" of the comparatively modern Yeoor Inscription, succeeding Sutyashree,† were, if existing at all, this sovereign's brothers, as Chundradityu was of Wikrumadityu, or otherwise *alias* names, in after years taken for separate rulers.

The genealogy and titles of the family, as gathered from these two plates, are as follows :—

Ancestor of the race HARITEE, descended from
Munoo Shree Poolukeshi Wulubh Maharaj.

|

Shree Keertiwurmu Prithwee Wulubh Maharaj.

|

Sutyashruyu Shree Prithwee Wulubh Maharaj.

|

Udhiraj Purmeshwur.

Left branch	Right branch
Shreendradityu (or the name would more correctly appear to be Shree Chundradityu) Prithwee Wulubh Maharaj.	Wikrumadityu Sutyashruyu Shree Prithwee Wulubh Maharaj Udhiraj Purmeshwur.
	Winuyadityu Sutyashruyu Shree Prithwee Wulubh Maharaj Udhiraj Purmeshwur Bhuttaruk.
	Wijuyadityu Sutyashruyu Shree Prithwee Wulubh Maharaj Udhiraj Purmeshwur Bhuttaruk.
	Wikrumadityu.

* Article I. July 1836, Vol. IV. R. A. S. Journal.

† Throughout these plates written Sutyashruyu (Truth-asylum).

The third set of plates names only two Rajas Mungul (or Mungulă) the donor and his father Wulubh, of the Chulikyu race; but whether of the same branch, or conquerors thereof, is left in doubt. The character appears of the same age as the others: perhaps this Mungulă is Mungulisa, the son of Poolukeshi, also styled Wulubh, the first-named of the dynasty; and if so, this inscription is older than No. I. set by two generations. The only place in these grants that I can recognize is that named in this plate Koondiwaduk, probably the modern village of Koondé, not far from Naroor, where the plates were exhumed.

The most interesting passage is in No. II., where Winuyadityu is described as having conquered the ruler of Kanchi (Conjeveram), forced the lords of the islands Kumer, Parseek, and Sinhuha, to pay him tribute, and subdued all the northern countries, as his father Wikrumadityu previously had the south. Can this dynasty have reached at the same time both Persia and Ceylon, or what are these places? These words may also in the construction of the language imply the names of the island rulers, as well as of the so-called islands.

Being very imperfectly acquainted with Sanscrit, I should not have been able to master these inscriptions, nor have found time to devote to them, but for the aid rendered me by Wasoodeo Ramchundru Shastree, and an intelligent young Bramhun trained in the Elphinstone Institution, by name Anunta Bulal.

I do not understand how Mountstuart Elphinstone, whilst quoting Walter Elliot's researches, should have assigned the tenth century for the rise of the Chulikyu dynasty, nor why Bal Gungadhur Shastree, in his translation, or, I should rather say, Muratha edition of this history, published in 1846, omitted to rectify the mistake, since he had himself translated some inscriptions (published in Nos. V. and VIII. of the Journal of the Bombay Branch of the Royal Asiatic Society) whereby he had verified the names of some of the early kings of this race.

TRANSLATIONS.

Translation of Plate No. I.

Be it peace! Glory be to the boar-like body, in whom Wishnoo was made manifest, who agitated the ocean, and bore the world on his right erect tusk! The prosperous race of the Chulookyus, the sons of Haritee, of the lineage of Munoo; praised by the world; brought up by the mothers (1) of the seven nations; who obtained choice blessings through the protection of Kartik; who brought all kings under their allegiance, from the time of their obtaining the boar's signet through the grace of the divine Narayun. The great King Poolukeshi Wulubh, the ornament of the race, purified himself by the sacrifice of a horse, and consequent abluent rites. His great-grandson, the grandson of Keertiwurmu (lord of the earth, the great king, who, having subjugated and forced his enemies to take refuge in forests, &c. firmly implanted his pure fame amongst them), the beloved son of Sutyashruyu (lord of the earth, king of kings, ambitious of supremacy, devoted to war, to whom all kings paid homage, and who gained by the defeat of Shree Hurshuwurdhun, famous in the northern countries, the name of Purmeshwur), is the unconquerable * * * (2) Wikrumadityu. His elder brother Shreendradityu, lord of the earth, the great king, whose beloved wife, Wijuyubhuttarika, the anointed queen, in the year Purdhoums (3) of her family's reign, on theautumnal equinox, the 2nd day of the waning moon of Ashween (September and October), for the attainment of the virtue of a deed done on this day, bestowed, along with water, the privilege of supervision (*i. e.* benefice) of the eight markets Poliyumuputhu, Adigiriku, &c. in Nurukagahur, on Aryuswami Dikshit (a sacrificer), grandson of Grihuputi, a descendant of Wutsu; and son of * * * (4) The donor says: "He who will continue this privilege to be enjoyed by the future generations of this person, will be, like the donor, an enjoyer of virtue; while, on other hand, whosoever may deprive him of it, will be guilty of the five capital crimes." The same is even prescribed by the omniscient Wyas, who says—"Whosoever resumes what is given by himself or others shall be doomed to pass sixty thousand years in hell."—*Finis.*

(1) The seven divine powers typified by female deities—Brámhí, Maheshwarí. Kaomarí, Waeshnawí, Wáráhí, Indrání, and Chámunda.

(2) A few words before this are illegible.

(3) The letters are plain, but the signification is unknown.

(4) Name is illegible.

PLATE No. 1 *(Facsimile.)*

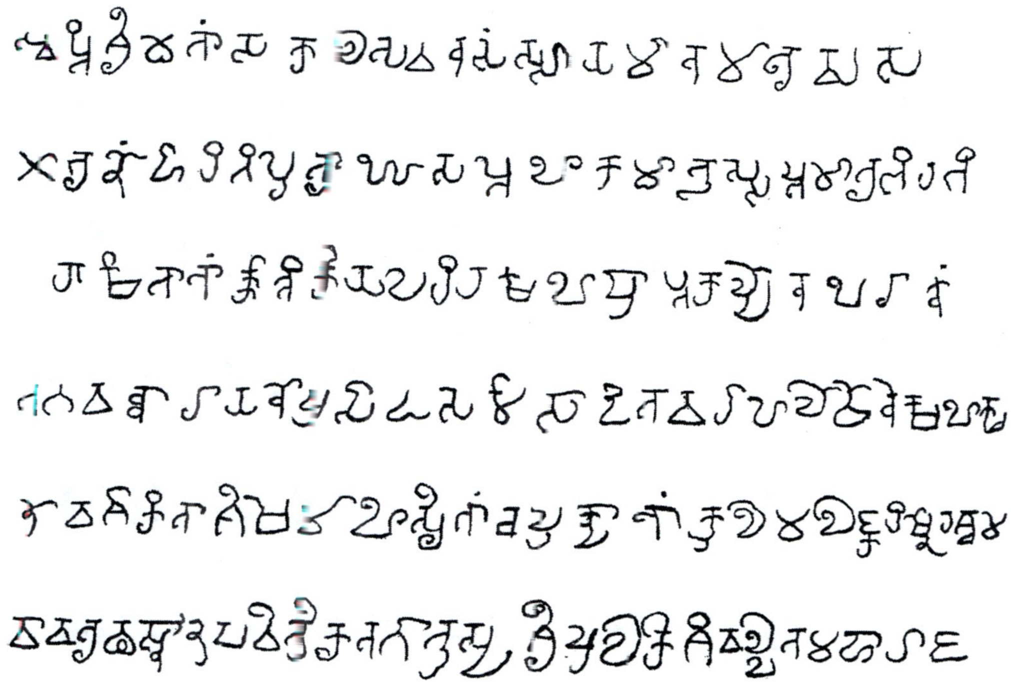

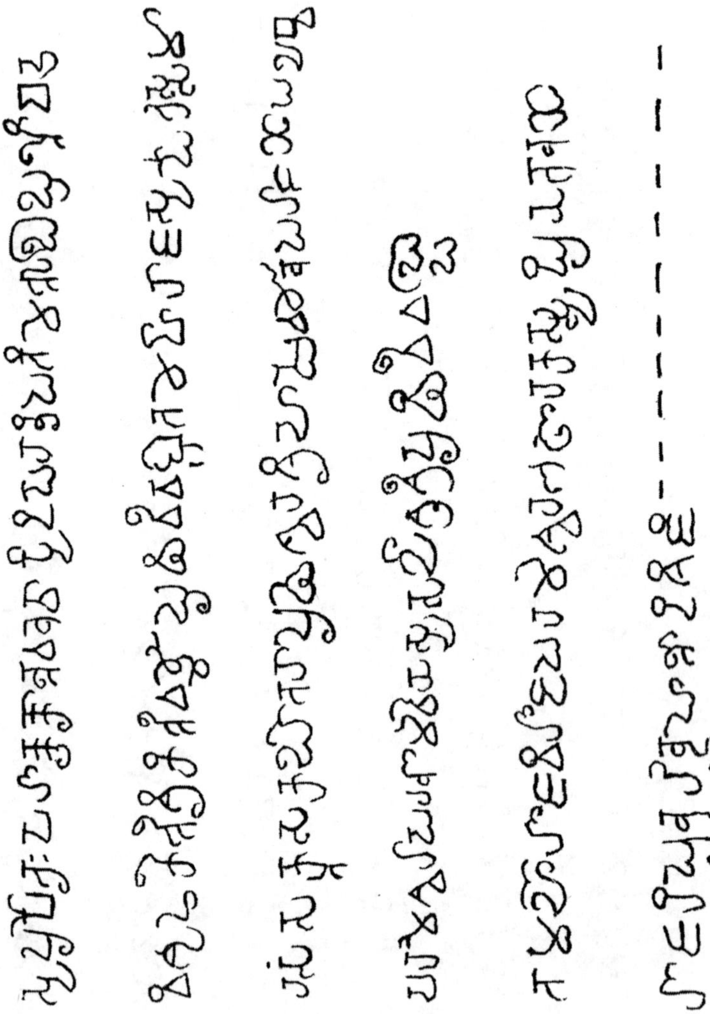

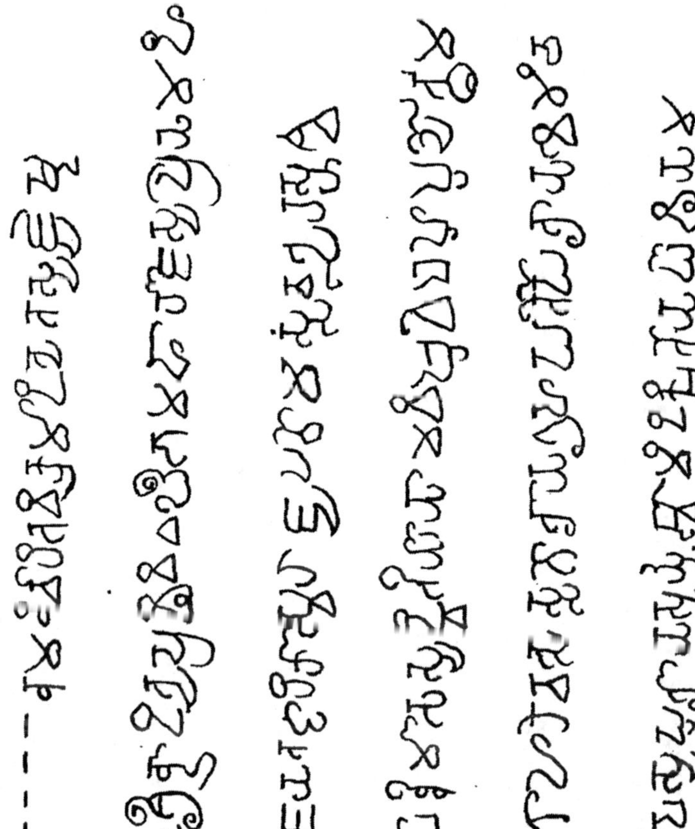

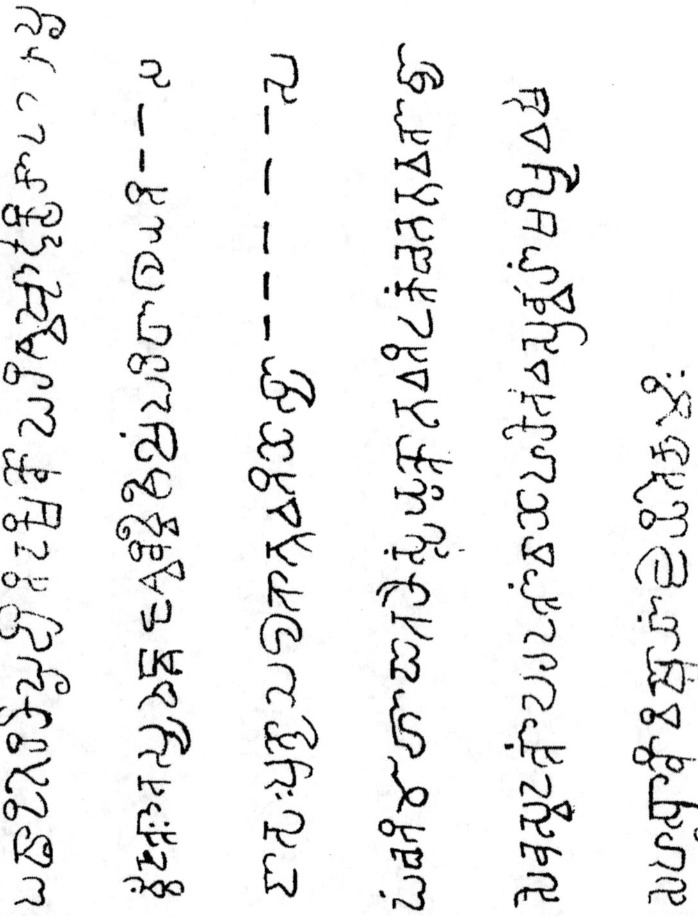

PLATE No. II (*Facsimile*)

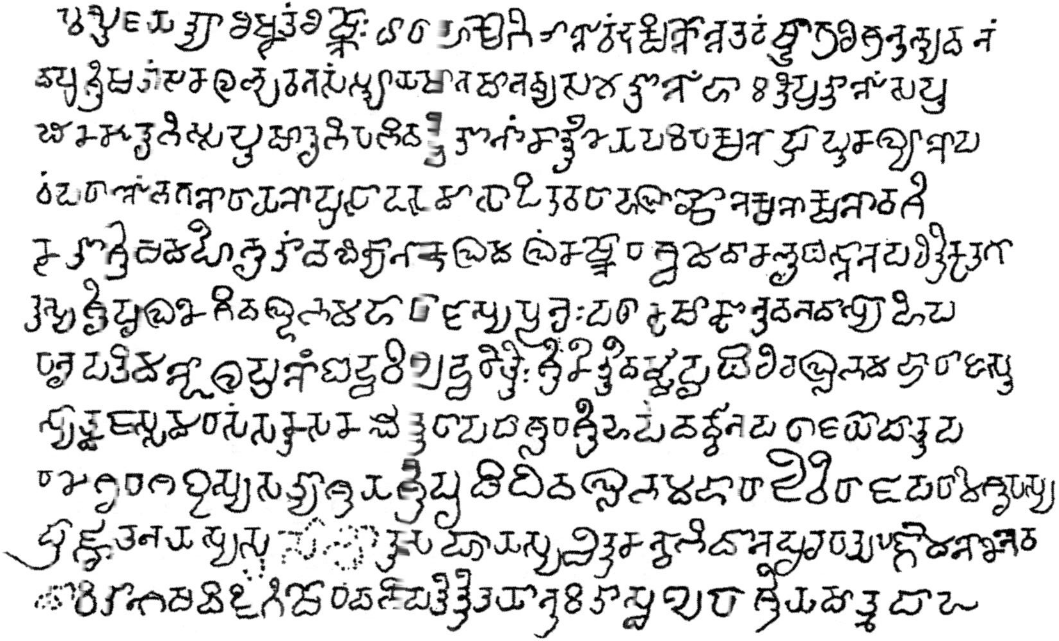

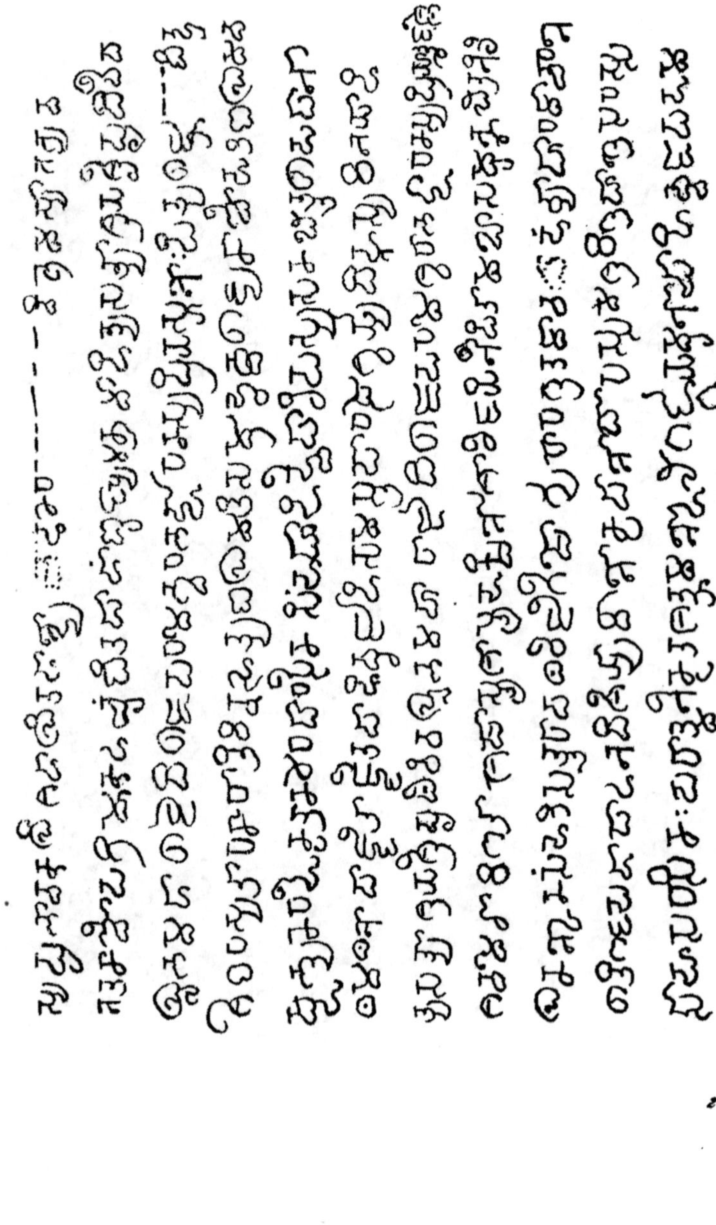

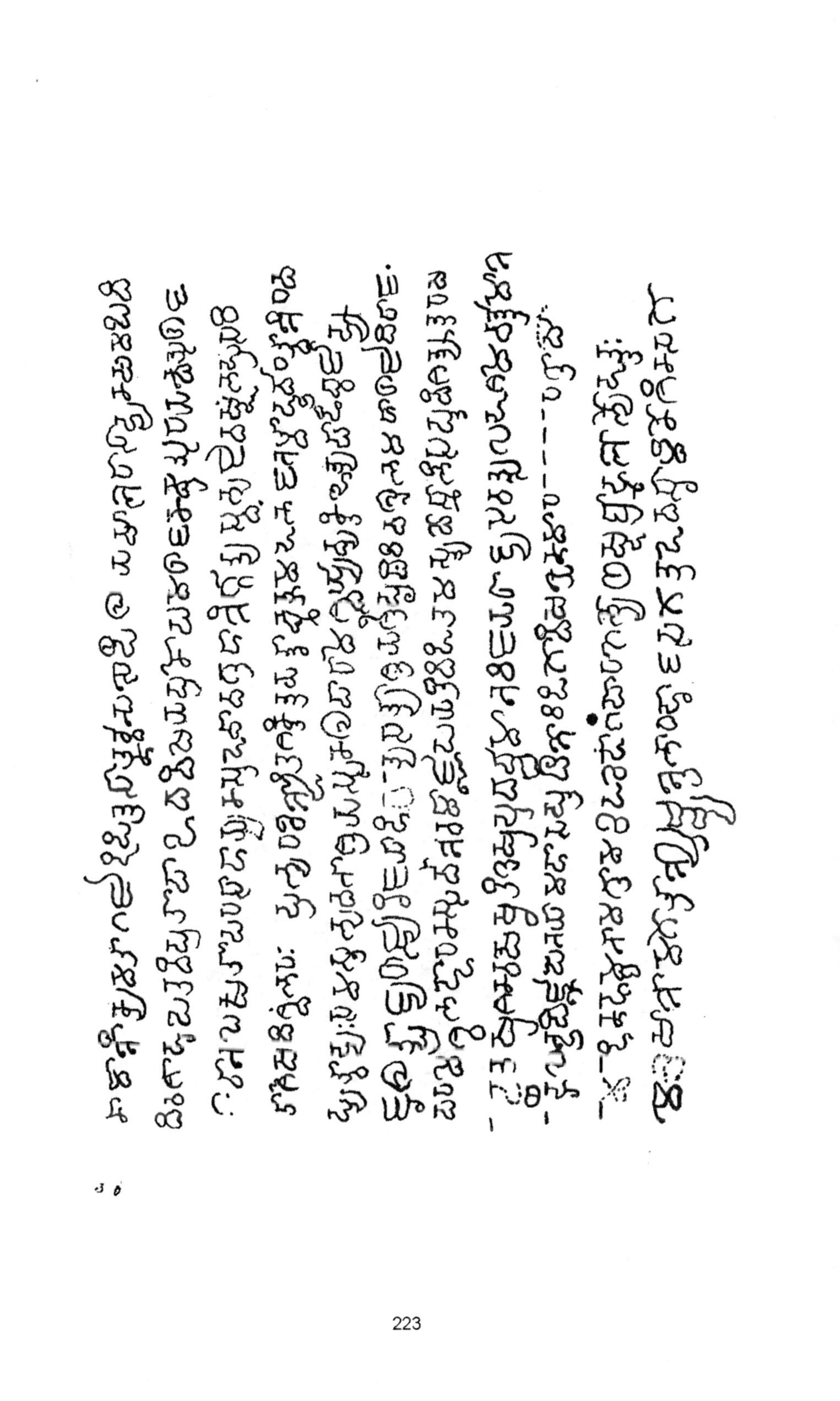

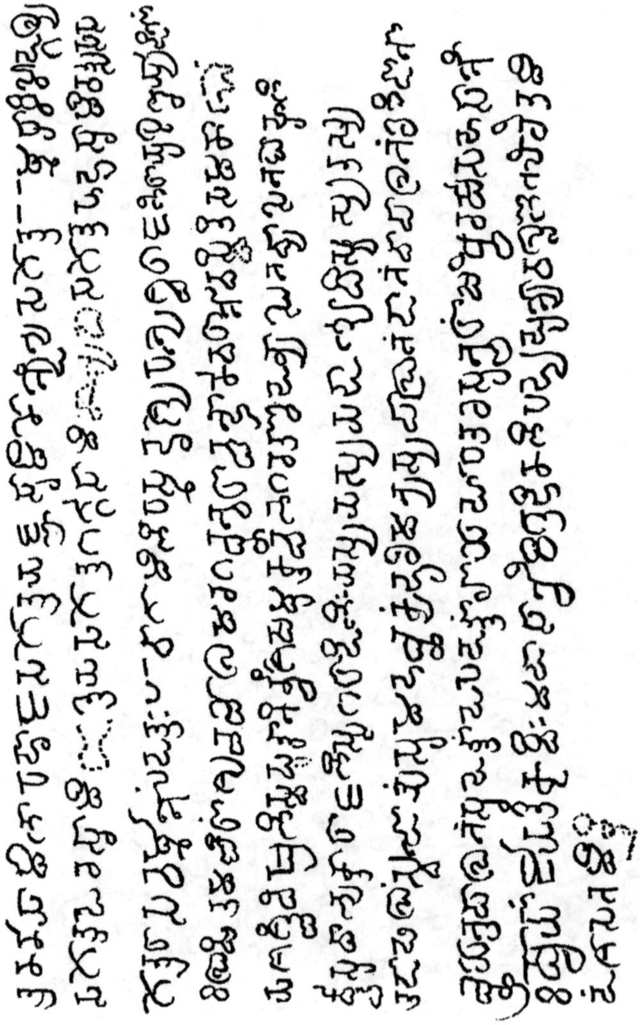

Translation of Plate No. II.

May it be well! Glory be to the boar-like body (1) in whom Wishnoo was made manifest, who agitated the ocean, and on the tip of whose right erect tusk rested the world! The prosperous race of the Chulikyus, (2) sprung from the universally-praised lineage of Munoo; the sons of Haritee; brought up even by the seven nations' mothers (*i. e.* by the seven female deities, Bramhí, Maheshwarí, &c. or by seven mothers like Luxoomee, who obtained a succession of blessings through the protection of Kartik Swamee; (3) who brought all the kings under their allegiance from the time of their obtaining the boar signet through the grace of the divine Narayun. This race was ornamented by the great King Poolukeshi Wulubh, who purified himself by the sacrifice of a horse, and consequent abluent rites. His son, the great King Keertiwurmu, lord of the earth, having subdued and forced all his enemies to take refuge in forests, &c. firmly implanted his pure fame amongst them. His son Sutyashruyu, (4) lord of the earth, and king of kings, much devoted to war, and to whom all kings paid homage, gained by the defeat of Shree Hurshuwurdhun, hero of the northern countries, the name of Purmeshwur. (5) His beloved son, Wikrumadityu, father of intelligent sons, lord of the earth, and king of kings, desirous of supremacy, supported by a harmonious brotherhood, whose lotus-like feet were kissed by the crown of the despotic King of Kanchi, * * * * (6) subdued all his rivals on one horse alone, the excellent Chitru Kundhu. (7) His beloved son Winuyadityu, lord of the earth, and king of kings, desirous of supremacy, disabled as Tarukarati (*i. e.* Skund) did the Dytyas, the insolent forces of Dhuerajyu, King of Kanchi; he made the rulers of the islands Kumer, Parseek, Sinhuha, &c. pay him tribute, and gradually acquired the full symbol of supremacy (Padhidhuruj, &c.) by the overthrow of the kings of the northern countries. His beloved son Wijuyadityu, lord of the earth, and king of kings, desirous of supremacy, attained, even in his childhood, the whole science of rendering weapons efficacious by charms. His grandfather (Wikrumadityu) had conquered the kings of the south, but he exterminated all of them who were inimical to him, and after the death in battle of his father (Winuyadityu), who made conquest of the northern countries, he, moving about at will, got his scymitar's edge blunted by the slaughter of his enemies'

(1) The third incarnation of Wishnoo, for the recovery of the earth from the waters.

(2) In this, and all the plates save Nos. I. and IV., the word is written Chulikyu.

(3) The son of Mahadeo, and Commander in Chief of the Celestial Forces.

(4) Literally, "truth-asylum."

(5) The kings succeeding Sutyashruyu henceforth bear in the plate both his name and the new title acquired by him, in addition to their own.

(6) A few words before this are unintelligible.

(7) Literally means "many-coloured neck."

numerous elephants. He, foremost in battle, (8) ardent in noble enterprises, made all his enemies subject to him * * * * (9) No sooner did he hear of anarchy than he left his home, like Wutsuraj (*i. e.* Ooduyun, of the solar race), relying on his own power, removed this source of misery in the country, the excess of every vice, which had arisen from the oppression of Bramhuns, a royal calamity; giving protection to all his subjects by the strength of his arms. He is arbitrary, at all times possessed of the three royal attributes (*i. e.* bravery, policy, and energy). He humbled the pride of his enemies, but he himself cannot be mastered. He is spotless, and for all this is become all the world's support. His dominions adorned by all the symbols of supremacy (Padhidhuruj, &c.) are extensive. He commands thus :—" Be it known to you that we, in Shuk 627, the tenth current year, Pruwurdhuman, of Wijuyadityu's reign, at the request of * * * Doopendru, (10) granted Koomaru * * * * (11) in the country Muhasuptuminuwidigo, (12) to the best and amiable Bramhuns, inhabitants of the village of Hikoodhumbu * * * (13) who have penetrated through the Veds and their branches. We mention their names and lineage, viz. Dewu Swami, a descendant of Bharudwaj; Kurku Swami, a descendant of Kuoshik; Yudun Swami, a descendant of Bharudwaj; * * * Swami, (14) a descendant of Kuondinuyu; Dewu Swami, a descendant of Muodgulyu; Gurggu Swami, a descendant of Atreyu; Roodru Swami, a descendant of Kashyup; and Rasunwommun, a descendant of Wutsu. Knowing that life and wealth are transient as glittering sun-beams, our successors or other kings, who may thirst for fame, enduring as long as the world, the moon, and the sun exist, should protect this grant as their own child. It is prescribed by the omniscient Wyas too, that many kings, Sugur and others, have enjoyed the earth; to whomsoever the earth belongs, to him belongs the fruit thereof. It is easy for the great to grant wealth once, but it is difficult to preserve what others have given; therefore the latter is a more meritorious act than the former. He who resumes what is given, either by himself or others, stays sixty thousand years as a worm in hell. The unblemished Poonyu (15) Wulubh, most prudent in suggesting the time of peace and war, wrote this edict.—*Finis.*

(8) The words also imply " first in beauty."
(9) Some words being entirely effaced, the connexion is here broken.
(10) One letter preceding Doopendru is illegible.
(11) Four letters following Koomaru are illegible.
(12) Two letters, *nu* and *go*, in Muhasuptuminuwidigo, are doubtful.
(13) Three letters preceding Hikoodhumbu are illegible.
(14) Three letters preceding Swami are unintelligible.
(15) Or Poonyu may be the epithet of Wulubh.

PLATE No. III (Facsimile.)

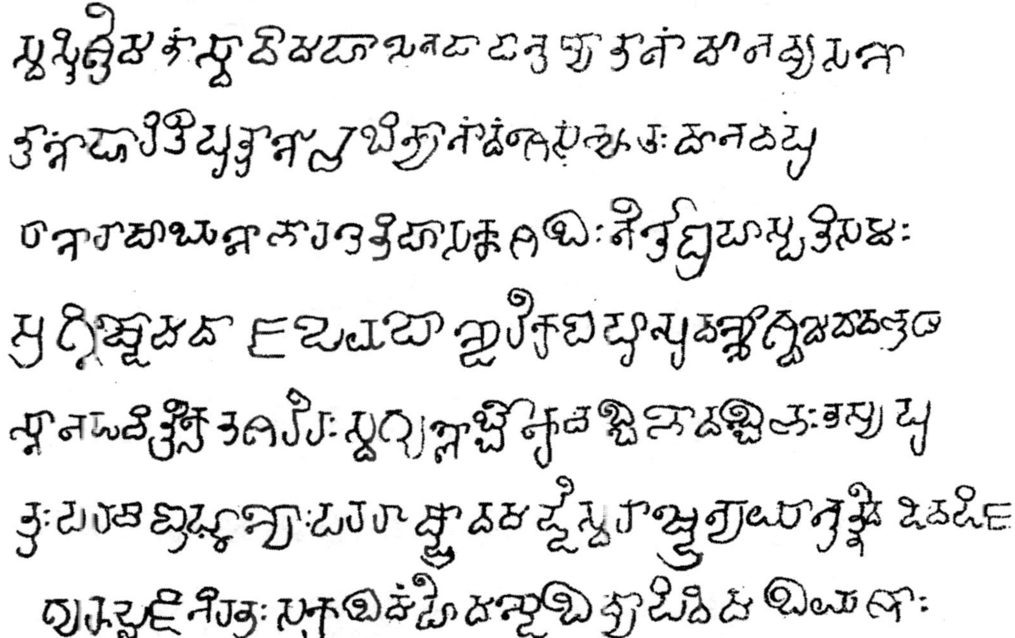

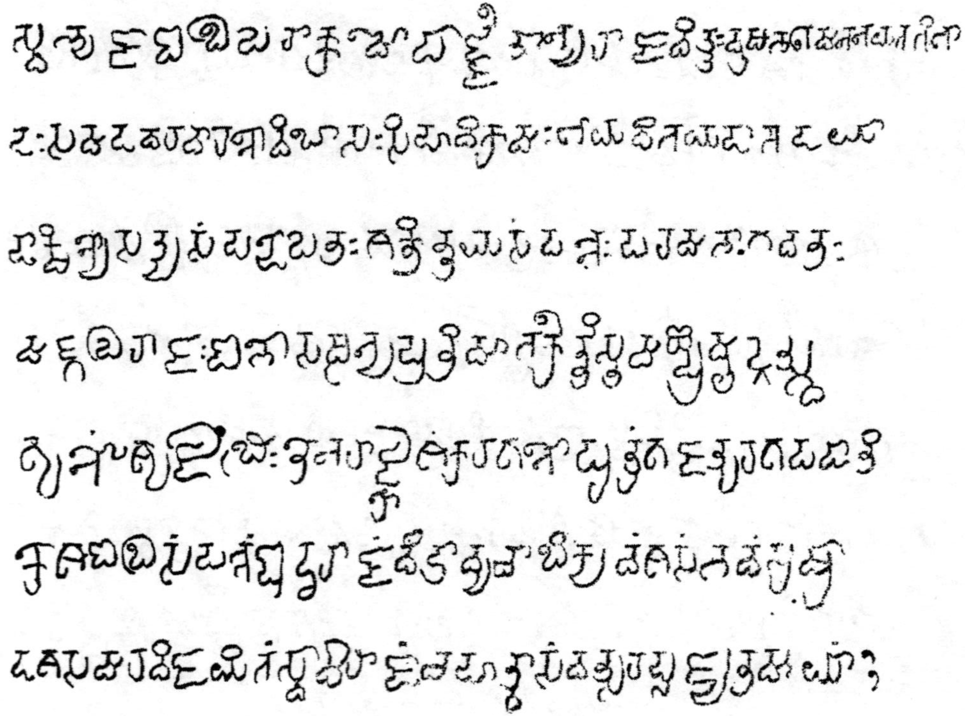

2c

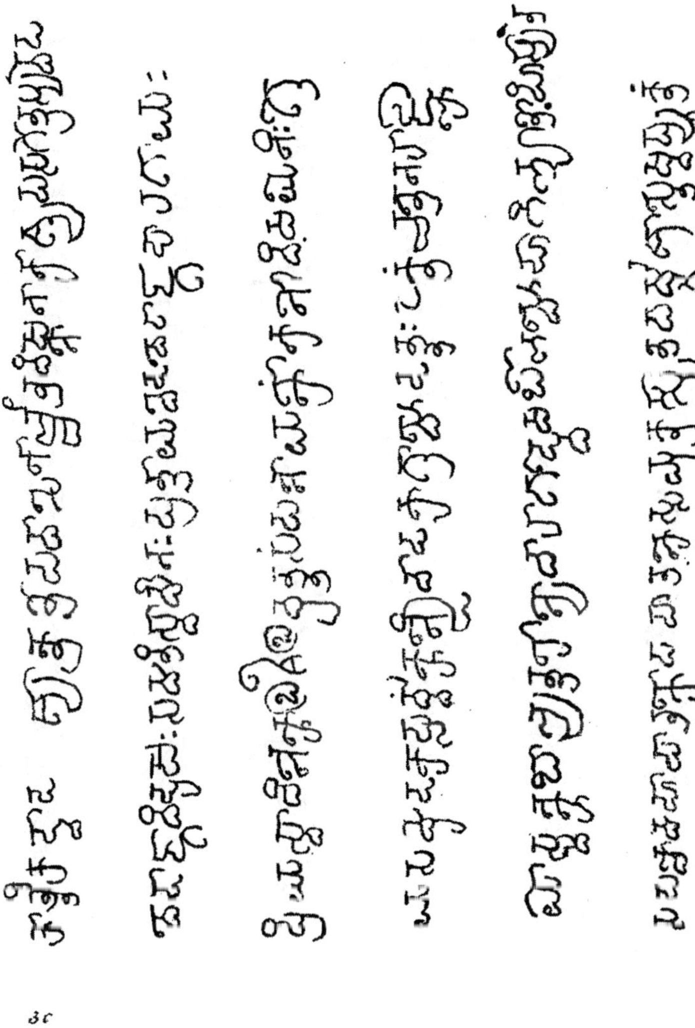

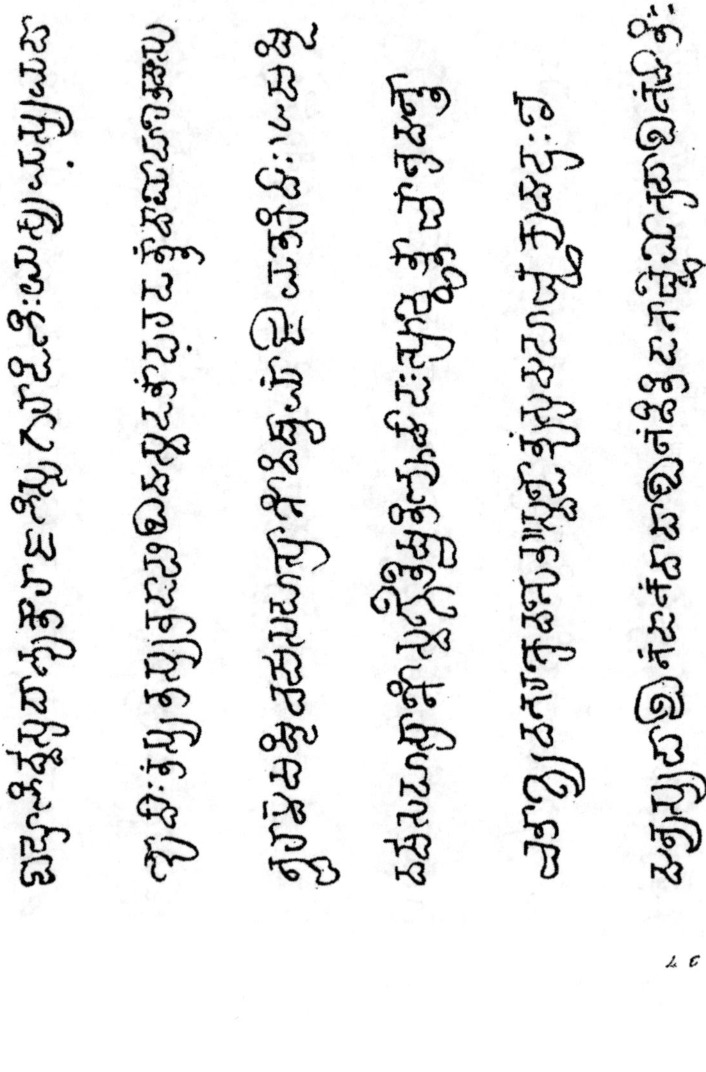

Translation of Plate No. III.

May it be well! The King Wulubh, belonging to the wealthy Chulikyu race, the offspring of Haritee, descended from the children of Munoo, and constantly meditating on the feet of Swami Muhasew (*i. e.* Kartik), well versed in the institutes of Munoo, the eighteen Poorans, Valmeek's Ramayun, Vyas's Muhabharut (ancient history), like Brihusputi in ethics, purified himself by the ablutions made after the Ugnishtome, Wajupeyu, Puondureek, and a costly Ushwumedh (a sacrifice of a horse) sacrifice, and rendered himself popular by his qualities. His son Mungul Raj is most attached to the Bramhuns, a subduer of other's territories, equitable in his own dominions, and devoted to the worship of God (the gods), Bramhuns, and his preceptor. His pure fame pervades the world. He, by his personal prowess, made other kings submissive, and obtained tribute from them. His gait, sight, and voice are like those of a bull; he is uncontrollable as a lustful and high-mettled elephant; brave as a lion, full of justice, humility, charity, mercy, modesty, and truth; possessed of the three attributes (*i. e.* bravery, policy, and energy); most pious, inimitable in good qualities—by the lustre of whose virtues the darkness of opprobrium is repelled. This illustrious king expelled Shuukurugun's son, Boodh Raj, strong in elephants, horses, infantry, and treasure. He slew Swami Raj, a descendant of the Chulikyu race, who had been victorious in eighteen battles. After this, the king, fasting on the most hallowed day in the year, the 12th day of (the waxing moon) Kartik, and worshipping Vishnoo, spiritual-mindedly granted with water (1) Koondiwaduk, a village in the Konkun, to Priyuswami, descended from a respectable family, versed in the Veds and their parts, good-tempered, well-behaved, the son of Soomuti Swami, who understood the Veds, and their parts, and was descended from Kashyup. Mungul Raj said: "Any one, either of my or other's family, that may angrily, or maliciously, or avariciously, or foolishly, withdraw the grant, will be guilty of the five capital (2) and also minor crimes." It is not he only that says so, but even the religious code prescribes the same. Many kings, Sugur and others, possessed the land. All rulers reap the fruits of their acts. Any one who takes back the land given by himself or others, stays as a worm sixty thousand years in hell. The land-donor remains sixty thousand years in heaven; on the contrary, the depriver and his abettor dwell the same number of years in hell. It is easy for the great to grant wealth, but it is difficult to preserve what others have given. Granting and preserving are both virtuous deeds, but the latter is more so than the former.—*Finis.*

(1) A ceremony observed previous to any donation, intimating the entire relinquishment of right over the thing given.

(2) 1*st*, Slaughter of a Bramhun; 2*nd*, Drinking of wine; 3*rd*, Stealth of gold; 4*th*, Incest with father's or Gooroo's wife; and 5*th*, Drinking and eating with the perpetrator of any of these crimes.

16

No. IV. is entire, having three plates, like the others, in the set. From the first leaf, which is greatly corroded, to the word Purmeshwurusyu on the first line of the second leaf, is a repetition of a part of Plate No. II. Priyutunuyusyu, which follows it, an adjective of Wikrumadityu, is evidently wanting on Plate No. II. From that, however, Plate No. IV continues up to the words Widitam-astu-wosmábhi*h*, in the first and second lines of its last page, the same as Plate No. II., and then follows thus:—Soonoo Wikrumadityu-sutyáshruyu-shree-príthwee-wulubhu-muhárájádhi [son] Wikrumadityu [titles] * * * * Rája-Purmeshwuru surwájnápuyuti * * * * (1) to all commands.

No. V. has lost its third leaf. Its first leaf is greatly corroded. The few words that are legible from Swusti to Wurtumáne are a repetition of a part of Plate No. II., followed by Rásuwunugure, the last word. The donor is Wijuyadityu. The grant is conferred in Shuk 622, in the 5th year of his reign.

No. VI. has two leaves, almost eaten away, the middle one wanting. The few words decipherable convey no meaning.

No. VII. is the upper part of one leaf. It contains the final Shloks of the other plates.

(1) Five lines come next, which are full of omissions of several words, as is obvious from the last Shloku, and are therefore unintelligible. There is no Shuk found in it. This plate is very badly written, and abounds in numerous orthographical errors. Wijuyadityu is the donor, but he gives it in his son's name.

No 1 *(Transcript)*

1d.

स्वस्ति श्रीमतां सकल भुवन संस्तूय मान मानव्यस

गोत्राणां हारितिपुत्राणां सप्तलोकमातृभि⁑स्सप्त मातृभि⁑र्भि

रक्षितानां कार्तिकेय परिरक्षण प्राप्तकल्याण पराणां

भगवन्नारायण प्रसाद समासादितवराह लाञ्छनेक्षणक्ष

णवशीकृताशेषमहीभृ⁑तां चलुक्यानांकुलमलंकरिष्णोरश्वमे

धावभृथस्नान पवित्रीकृतगात्रस्य. श्रीपुलकेशिवल्लभमहाराज

⁑ यत्रैतच्चिन्हंतत्राधस्तात्रपट्टेऽक्षराभावोबोध्यः

स्यप्रपौत्रः पराक्रमा⁂क्रान्तवनवास्यादिपरनृपतिमण्डलप्रणिबध्द

विशुध्दकीर्तिश्रीकीर्तिवर्म्मपृथिवी⁂वल्लुभमहाराजस्यपौत्रस्सम

रसंसक्तसकलो⁂त्तरापृ⁂थिवी⁂श्वरश्रीहर्षव⁂र्ध्दनपराजयोपलब्ध

परमेश्वरापरनामधेयस्य· सत्याश्रयश्रीपृथिवीवल्लु

भमहाराजाधिराजपरमेश्वरभट्टा⁂रकस्य⁂ प्रियतनयो

राजरिपुनरेन्द्रहन्ता दिशिजि - - - - - - - - - - -

⁂ यत्रेतच्चिन्हं तत्राधस्ताम्रपट्टेऽक्षरभेदलेखनानभिज्ञत्वंबोध्ये.

2d

3d

माप्य — — — — नमनिवारितविक्रमादित्यः* तस्यज्येष्ठं

भ्रातुः श्रीन्द्रादित्य* पृथिवीवल्लभ महाराजस्यप्रियमहि

षीविजय भट्टारिकास्वराज्यपर्धोमस्संवत्सरे* आश्व

युजपौ*र्णमासंस्यद्वितीयायाम् विषुवेबहुपुण्यार्थम्

नरकागाहरेवत्स*सगोत्रायगृहपतिपौत्रायस्वामिच

—रैवि—स्यपुत्रायआर्य्यस्वामिदीक्षितायपोलियम

पश्चादिगिरिकाप्रभृतिदक्षिणोपरिश्च श्टट्रक्षिका उदकपू

र्व्वंदत्ताः तस्यवङ्गजेष्वनिर्व्विशेषं परिपालयति — — स

दातुः पुण्यफलभाग्भवतियो यस्य — — — — - स

पंचभिर्महापातकैस्संयुक्तोभवति उक्तंच भगवताव्या

सेन. स्वदत्तांपरदत्तांवा योहरेत वसुन्धरां षष्ठिवर्ष

सहस्राणिविष्ठायां जायंते कृमिः

Literal Verbatim Translation of Transcript No. I.

Swusti shrímutám sukulu-bhoowunu sunstooyumanu Mánuwyusugotru-
Be peace prosperous the universe by praised (and) Munoo's offspring

nám Háriti-pootránám sapta-loku mátribhi (1) ssuptu- mátribhi*h*
lineage of Haritee's sons the seven nations' mothers by (such) seven mothers

abhiru (2) kshitáuám Kártikeyu- purirukshunu- práptu- kulyánu
nourished Kartik Swami by (made) protection from obtained welfare of

puráṇám Bhuguwun Náráyuṇu- prusádu- sumásáditu wuráhu lanchhan-e-
best (who have) the divine Narayuṇ's blessing by procured the boar's signet's

kshuṇe kshuṇu wushíkrit-á- sheshu- muhíbhritám Chulookyánám
appearance's time (from) subjugated all the kings (such) the Chulookyus

koolum- alunkurishṇo*h* ashwumedh-á-wuhhrithsnánu-
to the family adorner sacrifice of a horse (belonging to) formal ablution by

puwitrikritu- gatrusyu Shrí-poolukeshi-wulubhu- muháráju
purified body (who has) Shree Poolukeshi Wulubh the great king

---

sya prupuo-tra*h* purákrum-á- (3) krántu- wunuwásy-á-di-
of a great-grandson by prowess deposed (therefore) forest inhabitants, &c. (such) ini-

puru-nripati muṇḍulu- prunibudhu- wishoodhu keerti Shree-keerti-
mical kings of circle in firmly established pure fame (who has) (such) Keertiwur-

wurmu-prithwee-(4) wulubhu- muhárájusyu puotra*h* sumuru- sunsuktu
mu earth- lord the great king of a grandson to war devoted

sukul- o-tturá- pru (5) theshwuru Shri-hurshuwurdhu- nu purá-
if prith (6) wee-(7) shwuru
the whole northern notorious king Shree Hurshuwurdhdhun of defeat
or landlord

juy-o-pulubdhu Purumeshwur-á- puru- namudheyusyu Sutyáshruyu
from got Purumeshwur (such) other name (who has) (such) Sutyashruyu
or truth-asylum

Shrée-prithwee-wulubhu- muháraj-á-dhiráju- purumeshwuru
landlord the great king of kings Purumeshwur (the Supreme Being)

Bhuttá-(8) rakasyu priyutunuyu : Rájuripoouurendruhuntá dishiji
(who) saves by the speech dear son : [ten letters illegible]
or (who) desires mastership

---

(1) bhi is omitted on the plate.
(2) rá written on the plate.
(3) má is omitted on the plate.
(4) wi is written on the plate.
(5) pri written on the plate.
(6) the is written on the plate.
(7) wi is wanting on the plate.
(8) ḍhá is written on the plate.

Prápyu [five letters illegible] mu-aniwáritu Wikrumádityah (9) tusyu jeshṭhı
unconquered (such) Wikrumadityu his elder

bhrátooh Shreendráditya- pri-(10) thwee- wulubhu- muhárájusyu priyu muhishí
brother Shreendradityu earth- lord the great king of beloved queen

Wijuyubhuṭṭáriká- swurájyu- Purdhomus-sunwutsure A'shwuyooja-
Wijuyabhuṭṭarika own (or family's) reign Purdhomus in year Ashwin (September-

puorṇṇu-(11)-masusya dwitíyá- yám Wishmoe bahu-
October) ending month of 2nd day of the moon on autumnal equinox much

poonyár thum Nurukágahure Wutsusu-(12) gotruyu Grihuputi- puotrayu Swámi cha
virtue for in Nurukagahur Wutsu of lineage Grihuputi's grandson Swami

[one letter illegible] rae wi [one letter illegible] syu pootráyu A'ryyuswami-
of son Aryyuswami

díkshitáya- poliyumu.
sacrificer for Poliyum.

Puth-á-digiriká- prubhri-(13)ti-dukshn-o-pari shwashṭ-á-ttekshiká ooduku-poorwum
road Adigirika and others eight marts of supervision water before

dutt'áh tusyu wunshujushyu nirwi-(14)-sheshum puripáluyuti [two letters
gave his the family begotten in indiscriminately (who) preserves

illegible] su-dátuh poonyu-phulu-bhak bhuwuti yosyu [five letters illegible]
that donor of virtue fruit's enjoyer becomes who of this

su-punchubhih muhá- pátukweeh sunyooktuh bhuwuti ooktunchu Bhuguwutá
that the five capital crimes with mixed becomes (it) is said even omniscient

Wyásénu
Wyas by

Swu-duttám puru-duttam wá yo-haret wus oondhurám.
Shushṭi-wurshu-suhusıáni wishṭháyám jáyuté kri- (15) mih iti.

---

(9) ah wanting on the plate.
(10) pra is written on the plate.
(11) una written on the plate.
(12) ssa written on the plate.
(13) bhri written on the plate.
(14) wí written on the plate.
(15) krí written on the plate.

Nº II. (*Transcript.*)

स्वस्ति जयत्याविष्कृतं विष्णोर्वाराहं क्षोभिताऽर्णवं दक्षिणोन्नतदंष्ट्राग्रविश्रान्तभुवनं
वपुः श्रीमतांसकलभुवनसंस्तूयमानमानव्यसगोत्राणांहारितीपुत्राणां सप्त
लोकमातृभिस्सप्तमातृभिरभिवार्धितानां· कार्तिकेयपरिरक्षणप्राप्तकल्याणप
रंपराणां· भगवन्नारायणप्रसादसमासादितवराहलाञ्छनेक्षणक्षणवशी
कृताशेषमहीभृतां· चलिक्यानांकुलमलङ्कः ष्णोरश्वमेधावभृथस्नानपवित्रीकृतगा
त्रस्य· श्रीपुलकेशिवल्लभमहाराजस्यसूनुः पराक्रमाक्रान्तवनवास्यादिप
रनृपतिमण्डलप्रणिबद्धविशुध्दकीर्तिः श्रीकीर्तिवर्म्मपृथिवीवल्लभमहाराजस्त
स्यात्मजस्समरसंसक्तसकलोत्तरापथश्वरश्रीहर्षवर्धनपराजयोपात्तप
रमेश्वरशब्दस्य· सत्याश्रयश्रीपृथिवीवल्लभमहाराजाधिराजपरमेश्वरस्य
प्रीज्ञतनयस्यसुसौभ्रात्रसहायस्य· चित्रकन्धाभिधानप्रवरतुरङ्गमेणैकेनैव
वारिताशेषविजिगीषोरवनिपतित्रितया गुर्जित्वा स्वगुरोश्श्रीयमात्मपाद

स्यप्रभाव कुलिशदालित पाण्ड्य --------- विभ्रमस्यानन्याव

वनतकाञ्चीपति मुकुटच्चुंबित पादांबुजस्य· विक्रमादित्य सत्याश्रयश्री पृथिवीव

ल्लभ महाराजाधिराज परमेश्वर भट्टारकस्य प्रियसूनोः पितुराज्ञा --- बिन्दु

शेखरस्य तारकारातिरिव दैत्यबल मतिसमुत्थतन्धै राज्य काञ्चीपति बलमव

ष्टभ्य· करदीकृतक मेर पारसीकसिंहहादिद्वीपाधिपस्य· सकलोत्तरापथना

थ मथनोपार्ज्जितार्ज्जित पादि ध्वजादि समस्त पारमैश्वर्य्य चिन्हस्य· विनयादि

त्य सत्याश्रयश्री पृथिवीवल्लभ महाराजाधिराज परमेश्वर भट्टारकस्य· प्रियात्मजश्शै

शव एवाधिगताशेषास्त्रशस्त्रो· दक्षिणाशाविजयिनि पितामहे समुन्मूलित निखि

लकण्टकसहइतिरुत्तरापथविजिगीषोर्गुरोरग्रत आवधाहव्याहार माचरन्न

रातिगज घटापाटनविशीर्य्यमाणकृपाणधारस्समग्र विग्रहाग्रेसरस्स

त्साहसरसिकः परात्मनीकृतशत्रुमंण्डलोगंगायमुनापादि ध्वजपद रू:

2.0

3.v. कामाणिक्यमतागजादिपितृसात्कुर्वन्वैरैः पलायमानैरासाद्यकथमपिवि

धिवंशादुपेतबिप्रतापादेवविषयप्रकोपमराजकमुत्सारयन्वत्सराज

इवानपेक्षितापरसाहाय्यकस्तदेवावग्रहान्निर्गत्यस्वभुजावष्टम्भप्रसवि

ताशेषविश्वंभरः प्रभुरखण्डितशक्तित्रयत्वाच्छत्रुमदभंजनत्वादुर्धरत्वान्निरव

द्यत्वाद्यः समस्तभुवनाश्रयस्सकलपारमैश्वर्यव्यक्तिहेतुपादिध्वजाद्यु

ज्वलत्प्राज्यराज्योविजयादित्यसत्याश्रयश्रीपृथिवीवल्लभमहाराजाधिराज

परमेश्वभट्टारकस्सर्वानेवमाज्ञापयतिविदितमस्तुवोस्माभिस्सप्तविंशत्युत्तरष

ट्छतेषुशकवर्षेष्वतीतेषुप्रवर्धमानविजयराज्यसंवत्सरेदशमेवर्तमाने

— दुपेन्द्रविज्ञापनयामहासप्तगि [illegible] विदि [illegible] विषयेकुमार --- रग्रामो

— [illegible] — हिकुटम्बनामग्रामवेदवेदांगपारगेभ्योग्रेष्टब्राह्मणेभ्योदत्तः

ए तेषान्नामगोत्राण्युच्यन्ते· भारद्वाजसगोत्रदेवस्वामिकौशिकसगो

त्र कर्कस्वामिभारद्वाजसगोत्रयज्ञस्वामिकौण्डिन्यसगोत्र — — म्मस्वामिमौद्गल्य

सगोत्रदेवस्वामिआत्रेयसगोत्र.गर्गस्वामिकाश्यपसगोत्ररुद्रस्वामिवत्ससस

गोत्रासवर्म्मणांदत्तः — — आगामिभिरस्मद्वंश्यैरन्यैश्चराजभिरायुरैश्वर्य्यादीनां

विलसितमचिरांशुचंचलमवगछन्धिराचंद्रार्कवरार्णवस्थितिसमकालं

यशश्चिचिषुभिस्वपुत्रनिर्व्विशेषमुक्तंच भगवतावेदव्यासेन.बहुभि

र्बसुधाभुक्ताराजभिस्सगरादिभिः यस्ययस्य यदा भूमि स्तस्य तस्य

तदाफलं.स्वन्दातुंसुमहच्छक्यंदुःखमन्यस्यपालनंदानंवापालनंवेतिदाना

च्छ्रेयोनुपालनं.स्वदत्तांपरदत्तांवायोहरेतवसुंधरां षष्ठिवर्षसहस्राणि

विष्ठायांजायतेकृमिः संहासान्धिविग्रहीकनिरद्यपुण्यवल्लभेनलिखितमि

दंशासनमिति.

Literal Verbatim Translation of Transcript No. II.

Swusti juyuti awishkritum Wishṇo*h*
May it be well may live victorious (in whom) made the appearance of Wishṇoo

wáráham kshobhitárṇuwum dukshiṇonnutu- dunshṭrágru-
relating to (the) boar (who has) agitated the sea right erect tusk's tip

wishrántu- bhoowunum wupoo*h* ‖ shrímutám sukulu- bhoowunu sunstooyu-
rests the world (such) body prosperous the whole universe by prais-

mánu Mánuwyusugotru-ṇám Harití- pootránám suptu-(1) loku
ed begotten of the offspring of Munoo Haritee's sons seven nations'
or seven lokamatas

mátribhi- ssuptu- mátribhi*h* abhiwurdhdhitánám Kártikeyu puri-
mothers seven mothers by nourished Kartik Swami's pro-
(*i.e.* Lukshmee's) (such) seven mothers by

rukshuṇu- praptu kulyáṇu- purumpuráṇám Bhuguwu-(2) Náráyuṇu prusadu-
tection from obtained welfare's continuity the divine Narayun of grace by

sumásáditu wuráhu- lanchhun-e- kshuṇu- wushíkrit-á-sheshu
gained (the) boar's signet of appearance's time from (who have) subjugated all

-muhíbhritám Chulikyánám koolum alunkuri (3) shṇo*h* ashwu
the kings of the Chulikyus to the family an adorner sacrifice of a

medh-á-wubhrithusnanu- puwitri kritu- gátrusyu Shrí-poolukeshi-
horse (belonging to) formal ablution by (who has) purified the body Poolukeshi

wulubhu- muhárájasyu soonoo*h* purákrum-á- krántu- wunuwá-
Wulubh the great king of a son by (whose) bravery deposed (therefore) forest in-

syádi puru-nriputi- muṇḍulu- pruṇibuddhu- wishooddhu-
habitants, &c. inimical king's circle in (who has) firmly established pure

kírti*h* Shrí-keertiwurmmu- prithwee-wulubhu- muhárája*h* tusyu átmujusyu-(4)
fame Keertiwurmu landlord the great king his a son (who is)

su (5) muru- sunsukta sukul- o-tturá- puthu- shooru- Shrí-hurshuwurdhdhunu
to war devoted in whole northern country brave Hurshuwurdhdhun's

purájuy-o-páttu Purumeshwuru- shubdusyu
defeat from (who has) procured Purumeshwur (the Supreme Being) name

Sutyáshruyu- Shrí-prithwee-wulubhu-muháráj-á-dhiráju-
(such) Sutyashruyu (truth-asylum) the world-lord the great king's lord (therefore)

---

(1) The Shastree Wasoodeo Ramchundru Goórjur, assisting me in the translation of the plate, gives a third meaning to these words, *i. e.* that the seven mothers are understood to imply Brámhí, Máheshwarí, Kaomarí, Waeshnawí, Wáráhí, Indrání, and Chámundá.

(2) wa is omitted on the plate. (3) ri is wanting on the plate.

(4) ayu is wanting on the plate. (5) written ssa.

Purumeshwurusyu * * *(6) prájnu tunu yusyu soosaobhrátru
Purumeshwur's (whose) intellectual sons (are) harmonious brotherhood

suháyusyu Chitru-kundh-á-bhidhánu- pruwura- toorungumeṇu eke-
(whose) help (is) Chitrukundha (whose) name (is) the best steed by

nuewu wárit-á-sheshu-wijigíshoh awunée-puti-trituyánriwitá-
one only (who has) removed all the lovers of conquest

swu- gooroh- shríyumátmupádu [unintelligible]

-syu prubháwu- koolishu- dulitu Pandyu [eleven letters illegible]
by bravery (that is) thunderbolt-pelted Pandyu

Wibhrumusyu anuny-á-wunutu- Kanchí-puti- mookooṭu-
not to other bending down (such) Kanchi's ruler of crown by

choombitu- pudámboojusyu Wikrumádityu Suty-á-shruyu- shree-prithwee-
kissed the feet lotus-like (such) Wikrumadityu truth-asylum land-

wulubhu- muháraj-á-dhiráju- purumeshwuru- bhuṭṭ árukusyu priyul
lord the great king's king Purumeshwur (who) by the speech saves of dear
or (who) desires mastership

soonoh pitoorájáná [three letters illegible] bindooshekhurusyu
son • father's command a drop (who has) on the crown of head

Tárukáráti-riwu Duetyu-bulum uti- sumooddhutum Dhuerájyu
Taruka's enemy (*i. e.* Skundu) like Duetya's forces very insolent Dhuerajyu

Kánchí- puti-bulum awushṭubhyu kuradí- kritu Kumeru-Párusík
Kanchi's ruler of forces having disabled tribute givers (who) made Kumer Parseek

Sinhuh- á-de- dwíp-á-dhipusyu sukul-o-tturá- puthu- náthu- muthun-o-
Sinhuha and also islands of kings the whole northern country of master's defeat by

• párjjit-á-rjjitu- pádhidhwuj-á-di sumusta- párumushwuryyu- chinhusyu
gained (and) gained flags of supremacy, &c. entire supremacy of marks (such)

Winuyádityu Suty-á-shruyu Shree-prithwee-wulubhu- muháráj- á-dhiráju-
Winuyadityu truth-asylum landlord great king's king (therefore)

urumeshwuru bhuṭṭ árukusyu priyá-tmuju- shshaewe ew-ádhigut-
urumeshwur (who) by the speech saves of dear son childhood in even (who) attained
or (who) desires mastership

á sheshu- á-strushástru dukshu in-áshá-
the whole science of rendering weapons efficacious by charms the south direction of

wijuyuni pitámuhe sumoonmoolita- nikhilu- kuṇṭuku- sunhutih- oottará-
conqueror (being) grandfather eradicated all enemies' multitude northern

puthu wijigíshoh- gooroh agra áwadhá-
heaven of a desirer of going (such) father (*i.e.* Winuyudityu) of after from
or country of a desirer of conquest

---

(6) The sense is incomplete, and the words priyu tunu yusyu, inserted in the duplicates of this passage, repeated in Plates Nos. IV. and V., appear to have been omitted.

hum wyáhárum- áchurun áráti- guju- ghuṭá- páṭunu
death's (day) at will moving about enemies' elephants number of slaughter by
conversation maintaining

wishíryyumáṇu- kripáṇu- dháraḥ sumugru- wigruh-á-gresuruḥ
blunted (whose) scymitar's edge (during) the whole battle foremost
(amongst) all forms (the) first

sutsáhusu-rusikuḥ purátmuní-kritu shutroo- muṇḍuluh Gungá-
in duteous enterprises ardent (who) dependent upon made enemies circle

yamooná- páḍhi dhwuju pudumu [eleven letters gone]

Káməṇi kyumutá gujádi pitrisuṭ-koorwun paraeḥ- puláyumánaeḥ ásí-
father-like having made by enemies fugitives having
or by others

dyu kuthumupi widhiwushát oopetu Wipru táp át-ewu wis-
established whatsoever by chance happened to Bramhuṇs, oppression for the

huyu- prukossum arájukum ootsáryun Wutsu-raju-iwu
five senses in excess which brings anarchy (who has) removed. Wutsuráj (*i.e.* Ooda-
or in country molestation which brings [yun of solar race) like

anupekshit-á-puru- sáháyukaḥ tuda (7) ewagruhát nirggutyu
(who has) unexpected others aid at that time house from having set out

swu-bhooju-á- wushtumbhu prusuwit-á- sheshu Wishwunibhuraḥ
own arm's support (who has) rendered all Wishṇoo (*i. e.* protector)

prubhooḥ akhuṇḍitu- shukti-truyutw át
absolute (with whom) permanently (are) the attributes three (*i. e.* prubháwu,

shutroo- mudu- bhunjunutwát
muntru, and utsáhu) enemies of pride of (who has) agency of breaking down (therefore)

doordhurutwát. niruwudyutwát yaḥ sumustu-bhoowun-á- shru-
difficult to be mastered without blemish (therefore) who all the world's sup-

yaḥ sukulu- purumeshwurya- wyukti-hetoo- pádhidhwuj-á-di
port the whole of the supremacy appearance cause (is) flags of supremacy and others by

oojwulut- prájyu- rájyaḥ- Wijuyádityu- suty-á-shruyu- shrí-prithwee-
resplendent, extensive dominion (such) Wijuyadityu truth-asylum landlord

wulubhu-muharaj- ádhiráju Purumeshwuru (8) Bhuṭṭárukḥu
great king's king Purumeshwur (the Supreme Being) (who) by the speech saves
or (who) desires mastership

surnwan- ewum ájnápuyuti widitumustoowaḥ usmábhiḥ suptu-winshutyoot-
to all thus commands known let it be to you (we) by us seven (&) twenty (whose)

turu- shuṭchhuteshoo Shuk-warsheshoo atiteshoo
latter part six hundred (years) (so many) Shalwan's epoch's years in having passed

---

(7) wawa written on the plate. (8) ra is omitted on the plate.

Pruwurdhdhumánu- Wijuyu-rajyu- Sunwutsuré dushumyam wurttumáné
Pruwurdhdhuman Wijuyudityu's reign's year in tenth current
or accession to the throne from the reigning year

[one letter illegible] doopendru- wijnápunuyá- Muhá-suptuminawidigo wishuye Koo-
by supplication Mahasaptaminuwidigo in country Koo-
máru [four letters illegible] rugrámah [one letter illegible] ma [one letter illegible] Hikoo-
máru a village Hikoo-
dhumba- namu- grámu- Wedu- wedángu- parugebhyah agre-
dhumb name (of whose) village the Veds (and) the parts in versed best (and)
shtu- Brámhunebhyah duttah eteshum námu- gotrán-yu- chchyante
amiable (such) Bramhuns for granted of these names lineage (we) pronounce
Bháru-dwájusugotru- Dewuswámi Kuoshiku sugo.
a descendant of Bharudwaj Dewuswami a descendant of Kuoshik.

tra-Kurkuswámi Bharudwajusugotru Yujnuswámi Kuondinyusagotru
Kurkuswami a descendant of Bharudwaj Yudnuswami a descendant of Kuondinyu
[two letters unintelligible] Mmaswámi Muodgulyusugotru- Dewuswámi A'tre-
Mmaswami a descendant of Muodgulyu Dewuswami a de-
yusugotru- Gurgguswámi Kushyupusugotru- Roodruswámi Wut-
scendant of Atreyu- Gargguswami a descendant of Kashyup Roodruswami a de-
sa- (9) sugotru (10) rusuwarmmanund duttá [two letters illegible] ágámibhih as-
scendant of Wutsu successors (such)
mut wunshyae- ranyaescha rájubhih áyoorueshwury yádí nám wilusitum
our-belonging to family others or by kings age, wealth, &c. of existence
achir-anshoo-chanchulum awagachchhandhará chundr-á-rku- wurárnuwu-
moving rays (like) transient having known the world the moon, the sun, the ocean of
sthiti- sunu- kalum yushushchichishubhih swu-pootru- nirwwishesh-
existence (till) the same time celebrity of gainers by own son (from) is gone distinc-
um ooktanchu Bhuguwutá Veduwyásenu Wyásenu.
tion (in which deed) (it) is said also omniscient the Ved's divider by Wyas.

Buhubhir-wusoodhá bhooktá rájubhir-sugurádibhih yusyu yusyu yudá bhoomih tusyu tusyu tudá phulum swundátoom soomuhuch chhukyum dookhum unyusyu pálunum dánum wá palunum we-ti dánách chhreyo noopálunum, swuduttám puruduttám wá yo hureta wusoondhurám shushti-wurshu-suhusráni wishthayám jáyuté krimih.—[Vide Translation of Transcript No. III.]

Mubásandhiwigruhiku- nirawa (11) dya Poonyu-wulubhena
Well peace (and) dissension knowing the season of unblemishable Poohyu Wulubh
or pure virtue (whose is) Wulubh
or pure virtue of lord (is he)
likhitam-idam shasanam-iti.
by is writted this command in this manner.—*Finis.*

(9) sasa written on the plate.

(10) All these names are the same as mentioned in the Sootru Prawur.

(11) wa is omitted on the plate.

Nº III (*Transcript.*)

स्वस्ति॰ श्रीमतां स्वामिमहासेनपादानुध्यातानां॰ मानव्यसगो
त्राणां॰ हारितीपुत्राणां चलिक्यानां॰ वंशेसंभूतः मानव पु
राण रामायणभारतेतिहासकुशलः नीतौ बृहस्पतिसमः
अग्निष्टोम वाजपेय पौण्डरीकबहुसुवर्णाश्वमेधावभृथ
स्नानपवित्रीकृतशरीरः स्वगुणैर्लोकवल्लभोवल्लभः तस्यपु
त्रः परमब्रह्मण्यः परराष्ट्रावमर्दीस्वराष्ट्रन्यायानुवर्त्तीदेवद्विज
गुरुपूजानिरतः सकलहीमंण्डलव्यापिविमलयशाः

स्वभुजबलपराक्रमोपार्ज्जितान्यराजवित्तः वृषभगमननयननिना

दः समदवरवारणविलासःसिंहविक्रमः नयविनयदानदया

दाक्षिण्यसत्यसंपदोपेतः शक्तित्रयसंपन्नः परमभागवतः

मङ्गलराजः बभौसत्वेन्यप्रतिमानकीर्तिस्तम ऽ प्रभृन्दन्त्व

गुणांशुजालैः तेनराज्ञाशकरगणपुत्रंगजतुरगपदाति

कोशबलसंपन्नं बुध्धराजविद्राव्यचालिक्यवंशसंभवं अष्टा

५ दशसमरविजयिनं स्वामिराजंचहत्वासंवत्सरपूज्यतमायां

3f

कार्तिकद्वादश्याकृतोपवासेनार्च्चितविष्णुनाकाश्यपगोत्रस्यवेद

वेदाङ्गविदुषः सुमतिस्वामिनःपुत्रायवेदवेदांङ्गपारगायः ※

त्रियस्वामिनेकुळशीलवृत्तसंपन्नायकोंकणविषयेनिःश्रे

यसमुदकपूर्व्वकुण्डिवादकग्रामोदत्तः उक्तंचतेनराज्ञा

योस्मत्कुलाभ्यन्तरोन्योवारागद्वेषलोभमोहाभिभूतोहिंस्यात्

सपंचमहापातकोपपातकैस्संयुक्तस्यात् धर्म्मशास्त्रेष्वप्युक्तं

※ एतच्चिन्हाधोविसर्गोस्तिसलेखकदोषइतिमन्मनीषा

बहुभिर्वसुधाभुक्ता राजभिस्सगरादिभिः यस्य यस्य यदा

भूमिः तस्य तस्य तदा फलम् स्वदत्तां परदत्तां वा योहरेत वसु

न्धराम् षष्ठिवर्षसहस्राणि विष्ठायां जायते क्रिमिः षष्टि

वर्षसहस्राणि स्वर्गे तिष्ठति भूमिदः आच्छेता चानुमन्ता

च तान्येव नरके वसेत् ।। स्वन्दातुं सुमहच्छक्यम् दुःख

मन्यस्य पालनं दानं वा पालनं वेति दानाच्छ्रेयोनुपालनमिति

Literal Verbatim Translation of Transcript No. III.

Swusti shrímutám Swámi-mahásenu- pádánoodhyá-
May it be well wealthy Swami Muhasen (*i.e.* Kartik) constantly meditating on

tánám Manuwyusu-gotráṇám Háriti-pootráṇám Chulikyánám wunshe sum-
the feet of descended from Munoo Haritee's sons of the Chulikyus in a race begot-

bhoota*h* Mánuwyu Pooráṇu Rámáyuṇu Bhárutu
ten the institutes of Munoo the Poorans the Ramayuṇ (by Valmeek) the Muha-

itihásu kooshulu*h* nituó Brihusputi-suma*h* Agnishṭo-
bharut (by Vyas) ancient history well versed in ethics Brihusputi-like a particular

mu wajupeyu puoṇḍuríku buhoosoo-
Yudnu or sacrifice [a particular sacrifice] [a particular sacrifice] much gold (expended in

wurṇṇáshwumedhu awubhritasnánu puwitrí-
which) a sacrifice of a horse by the ablutions made at the end of sacrifices purified

kritu-shuríra*h* swugooṇue*h* lokuwullubho Wulubhu*h* pusyu pootra*h* purumu-
body own qualities by popular Wulubh his son most attached

Brumhuṇyu*h* puru-ráshṭráwumurddí swu-rashṭru-myáyánoo-wurtí
to the Bramhuns other's dominions of a subduer (his) own kingdom in, equity guided by

dewu-dwiju-gooroo-poojan iruta*h* sukulu-muhí-muṇḍulu
God (or gods) Bramhuns and preceptor of worship devoted to the whole globe

wyápi-wimulu-yushá*h*.
(whose) (is) pervaded pure fame by.

Swu-bhooju-bulu- purákrumopárjjitá-nyu-rajuwitta*h*
(Who has) by his personal prowess obtained from other kings riches (tribute) (whose)

wrishabha-gumunu-nuyunu ninádah sumudu-wuruwárunuwilá-
bull-like-gait-eyes voice (are) (as) lustful high-mettled elephant uncon-

sa*h* sinhu-wikruma*h* nuyu-winuyu-dunu-dyá- dákshiṇyu- sutyu-
trolled lion's like bravery, justice, humility, charity, mercy, modesty, truth, (these)

sumpudo-peta*h* shukti-truyu-
riches, full of powers, three (*i. e.* prabháva, muntra, utcháha, that is bravery,

sumpunnu*h* purumu-bháguwutu*h* Mangulu-raja*h* bu-
policy, and energy) plentifully possessed of most pious Mungul the king be-

bhuo satwenya-pratimána-kírtístauma ⊖⊖(1) pramrindanswa-
came illustrious inimitable in good qualities (& one) the darkness of opprobrium re-

guṇánshujálue*h* tenu Rájna Shunkuruguṇu-pootrum guju-
pelled, by the lustre of (whose) virtues that by King Shunkurguṇ's son to elephants,

(1) This mark is used instead of a preceding skeurg.

44

toorugu-pudáti-kosha bulu-sumpunnam Booddhu-rájum widráwyu
horses, infantry, treasure (this) strength possessed of Booddh the king having driven out

Chulikyu wunshu-sumbhuwum Ashṭádushu-sumuru-wijuyinum Swamirájum chu
the Chulikyu race in begotten eighteen battles in victorious to Swamiraj also

hutwa sunwutsuru-poojyutumáyám.
having slain in the year hallowed most in.

Kartíku-dwádushyám krito-puwásen Archchitu-wishṇooná Káshyupu-
On the 12th day of Kartik (who has) fasted worshipped Wishṇoo a descendant

sugotrasyu Wedu-wedangu-widooshaḥ Soomuti-swáminaḥ pootrayu
from Kashyup the Veds (and their) parts, understanding of Soomuti Swami for the son

Wedu-wednága-párugáyaḥ (2) Priyuswámine koolu-shílu-writtu-
the Veds (and their) parts (who has) passed over for Priyuswami one of a respectable

sumpunnayu Konkuṇu-wishuye nishreyusum ooduku
family, good-tempered, well-behaved in the Konkuṇ country spiritual-mindedly with

poorlawum Koonḍiwáduku-grámo duttaḥ ooktunch tenu rájná yo smatkoo-
water Koondiwaduk village gave said also by that king who our fami-

álbhyunbtaronyowá raga-dwesha- lobha mohabhibhooto hinsyátu su-puncha-
ly in any other or anger, malice, avarice, folly, subdued by will deprive that the five

mahápátukopupátkue sunyookt- syátu dhurmmashástreshwupi-ooktum.
capital crimes minor crimes will be guilty of in the code of religion even (it is) said.

Buhoobbhir- wusoodhá bhooktá rajubhi Sugur-adibhiḥ yusyu yusyu yudá
By many land enjoyed by kings Sugur and others whose whose when

bhoomiḥ tusyu tusyu tuda phulum swuduttám puruduttám wá yo huretu
land his his then fruit self-given by others given or who deprives

wusoodhuram shushṭi-warshu-suhusráṇi wishṭháyám jayute krimiḥ(3) 1€ shushṭh
land (world) sixty years thousands in hell becomes a worm sixty

wurshu-suhusráṇi swurgge tishṭhuti bhoomidaḥ achchhettá chá-noomunta-chu
years thousands in heaven stays land-donor depriver and abettor also

tanyewu naruke wuset‖ swun-dátum soo-muhuch-chhakyum dookhum an-
those same in hell dwells wealth to give for the great very easy difficulty of

yusyu pálunum dánum wá pálunum we-te danach-chhreyo- noopálu-
others to preserve granting or preserving or in this than a grant virtue con-

num iti.
tinued preservation in this manner.—*Finis.*

---

(2) It ought to be páragáya.

(3) krí written on the plate.

No. 11 of 1849.

From Major G. LeG. Jacob,
Political Superintendent of Sawunt Waree,

To A. Malet, Esq.,
Chief Secretary to Government, Bombay.

Political Department.

Sawunt Waree, 8th January 1849.

Sir,

With reference to the observations accompanying my letter No. 158, dated 15th November last, I have the honour to send (Enclosures Nos. 1 to 4) a fac-simile copy, with transcript in modern Sanscrit, and English translation, of the set of plates mentioned in note to the 2nd paragraph as just found, and as giving the correct name of the elder brother of Wikrumadityu. The owner, a Bramhun of Kochré, the village to which the grant refers, would only part with it whilst being copied, and that most grudgingly, conceiving it to possess some talismanic virtue. For reasons already advanced, the inscription must have been written in the sixth century of our era.

I have the honour to be, &c.

(Signed) G. LeG. Jacob,
Political Superintendent.

Translation of Enclosure No. 3 to Letter to Chief Secretary, No. 11, *dated 8th January* 1849, *as literal as is consistent with the sense in English.*

May it be well! The prosperous race of the Chulookyus, the sons of Haritee, of the lineage of Munoo, praised by the world; brought up by the mothers of the seven nations; who obtained a succession of blessings through the protection of Kartik; who brought all kings under their allegiance from the time of their obtaining the boar's signet through the grace of the divine Narayun. The great king Poolukeshi Wulubh, the ornament of the race, purified himself by the sacrifice of a horse, and consequent abluent rites. His great-grandson, the grandson of Keertiwurmu (lord of the earth, the great king, who, having subjugated and forced his enemies to take refuge in forests, &c. firmly implanted his pure fame amongst them), the beloved son of Sutyashruyu (lord of the earth, king of kings, devoted to war, to whom all kings paid homage, and who gained by the defeat of Shree Hurshuwurdhun, lord of the northern countries, the name of Purmeshwur), is Wikrumadityu. He, having subdued all the hostile kings of every quarter, and inherited his family's property, (throne, &c.) rendered himself invincible by his paramount power. His elder brother was Chundradityu, lord of the earth, and king of kings, whose beloved wife, Wijuyu Mahadevee * * * (1) the anointed queen, an enemy to the Kuliyoog (iron age), thus publicly ordains:—Be it known to you, that on the 12th day of the waxing moon of Vyshakh (April and May), I, having fasted, bestowed, along with water, the Thikan Wukoolukuchchhu, together with a salt marsh in Kochchooruku village (modern Kochuré), on * * * Goluswami, (2) a descendant of Wutsu. Any one, * * * (3) either of our or other's family, who will preserve the grant, will be an enjoyer of virtue; while, on the other hand, he who will resume it will be guilty of the five capital crimes. The land donor enjoys heaven for sixty thousand years; while, on the contrary, the resumer, and the one who approves of the resumption, are doomed to pass the same number of years in hell. Whosoever resumes land, given by himself or others, stays sixty thousand years as a worm in hell. * * * (4)

(1) Four following letters are unintelligible.
(2) Four letters preceding the name are unintelligible.
(3) A few letters before this are plain, but their signification is unknown.
(4) The final ten letters are unintelligible.

Table explanatory of the several Plate characters.

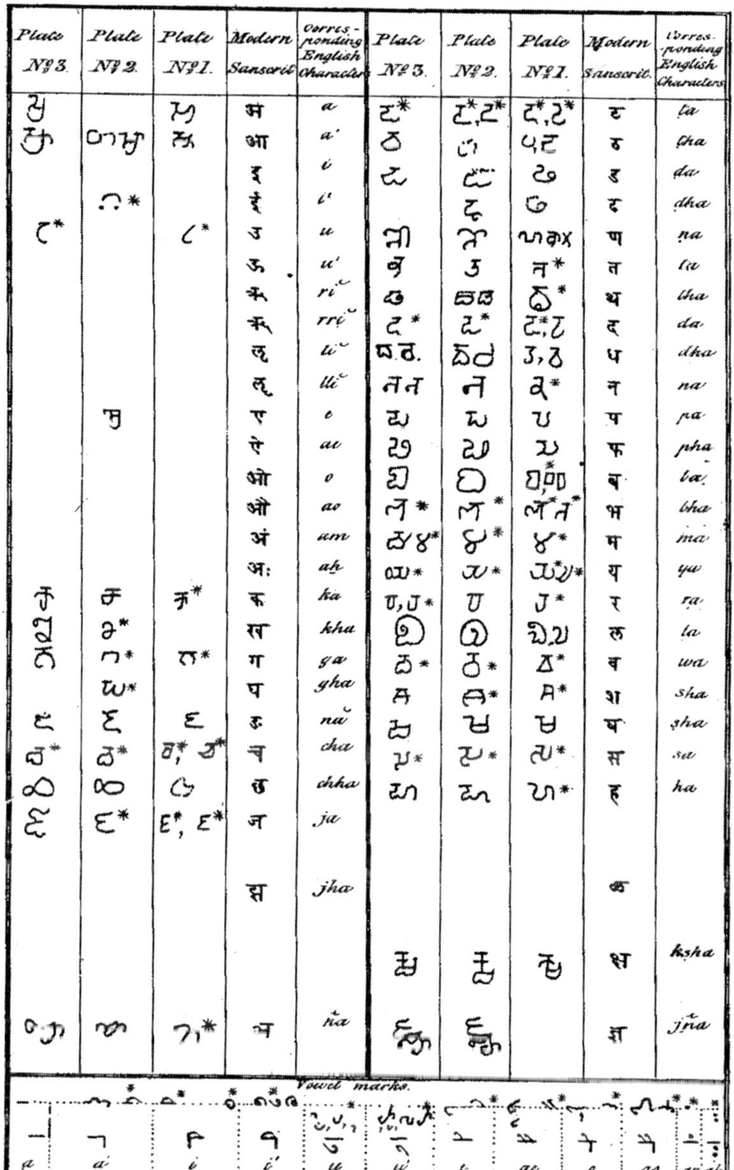

Modern Sanskrit	Corresponding English Characters	Modern Sanskrit	Corresponding English Characters
अ	a	ट	ta
आ	a'	ठ	tha
इ	i	ड	da
ई	i'	ढ	dha
उ	u	ण	ṇa
ऊ	u'	त	ta
ऋ	ri	थ	tha
ॠ	rri	द	da
ऌ	lri	ध	dha
ॡ	llri	न	na
ए	e	प	pa
ऐ	ai	फ	pha
ओ	o	ब	ba
औ	ao	भ	bha
अं	am	म	ma
अः	ah	य	ya
क	ka	र	ra
ख	kha	ल	la
ग	ga	व	wa
घ	gha	श	sha
ङ	nă	ष	ṣha
च	cha	स	sa
छ	chha	ह	ha
ज	ja		
झ	jha	ळ	
		क्ष	ksha
ञ	ña	ज्ञ	jña

Vowel marks: a, a', i, i', u, u', e, ai, o, ao, am ah

(···) Dotted letters are doubtful.

*Letters and vowel marks agreeing with those given in Prinsep's Tables are marked with an asterisk.

Inscription on a set of Copper Plates (Facsimile)

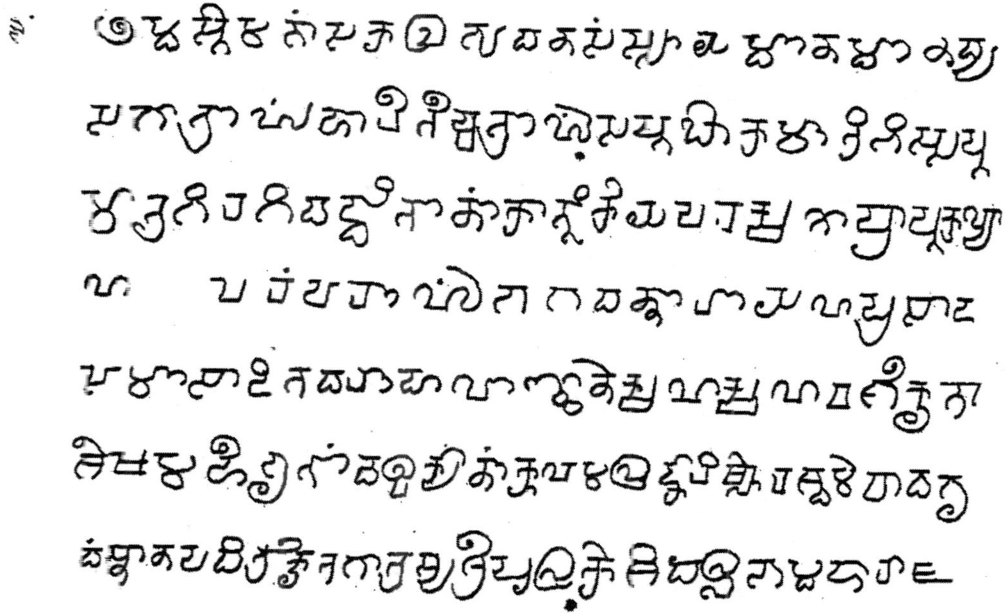

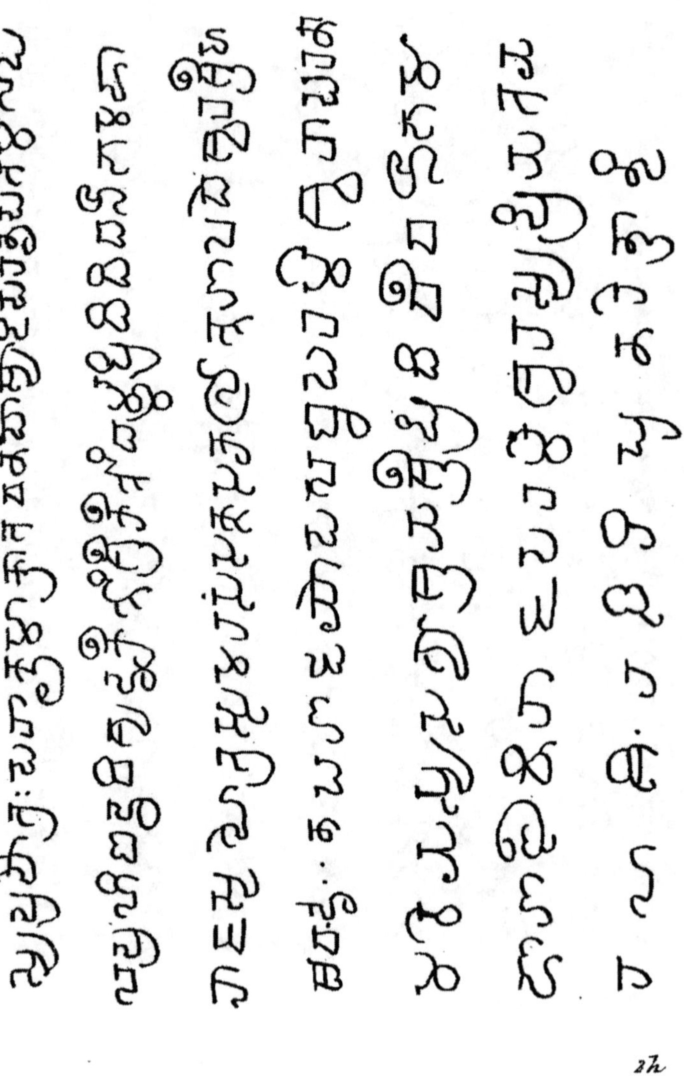

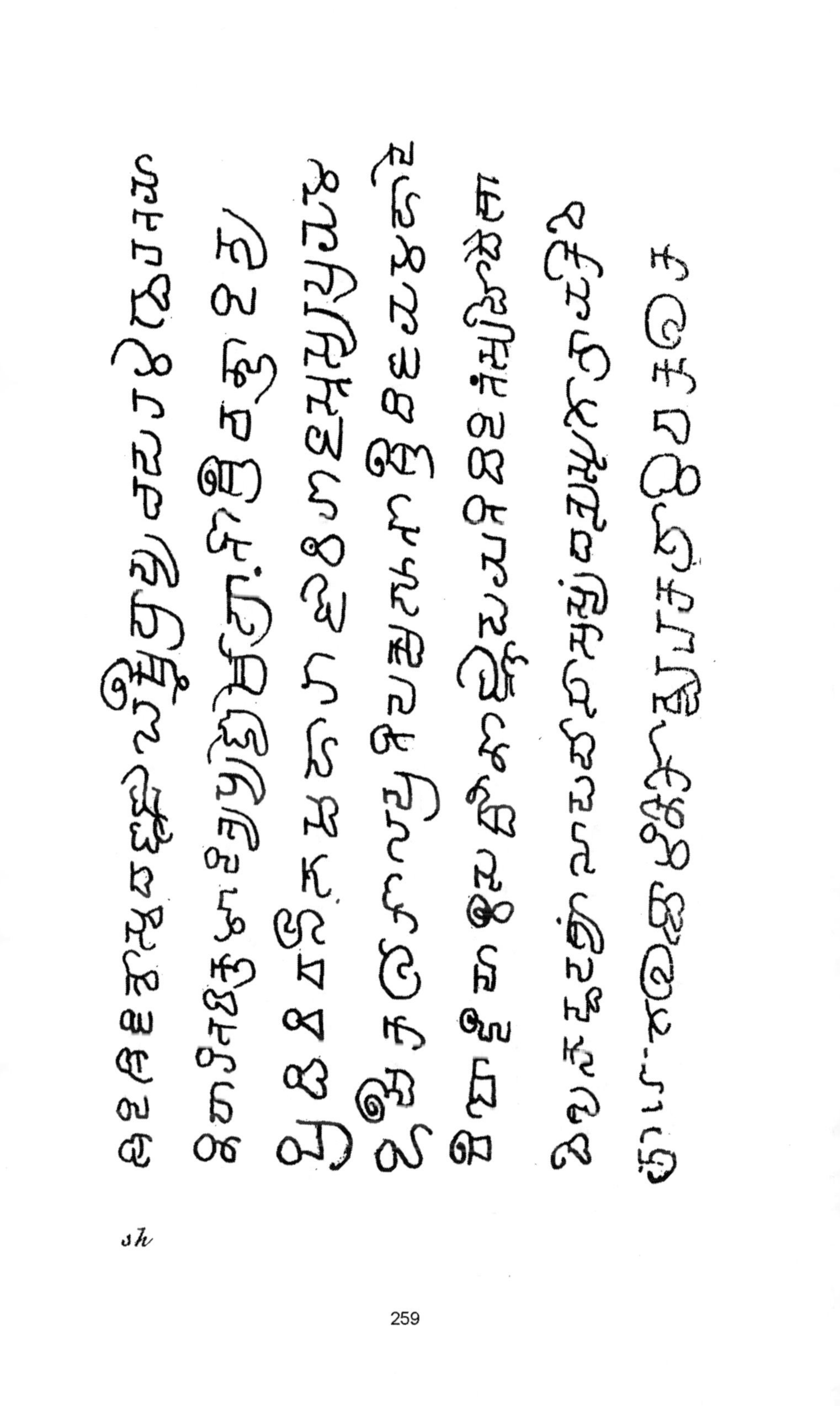

sh

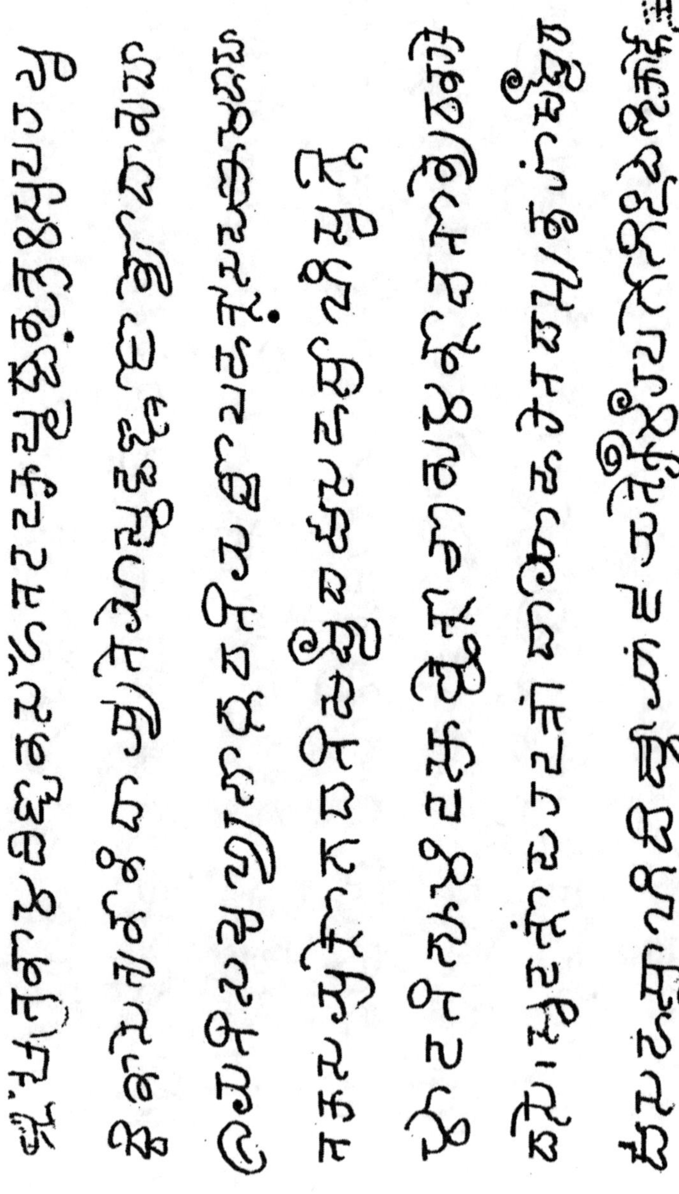

5h

Transcript in Modern Sanscrit of Copperplate Inscription

स्वस्ति श्रीमतां सकलभुवनसंस्तूयमान मानव्य

सगोत्राणां हारीती पुत्राणां सप्तलोकमात्रिभिस्सप्त

मातृभिरभिवर्द्धितानां कार्तिकेयपरिरक्षणप्राप्तक

ल्याण परंपराणांभगवन्नारायणप्रसादसमासा

दितवराहलाञ्छनेक्षणक्षणवशीकृताशेषमहीभृतां

चलुक्यानां कुलमलंङ्करिष्णोरश्वमेधावभृथस्नानपवि

स्यत्र पात्रः पराक्रमाक्रात वनवास्यादि परनृपातमण्ड

लप्रणिबद्ध विशुद्ध कीर्ति-श्री कीर्तिवर्म्म प्रिथिवि वल्लुभ

महाराजस्य पौत्रस्स मर संसक्त सकलोत्तरापथेश्वर-श्री

हर्षवर्द्द नपराजयोपंलब्धपरमेश्वरापरनामधे

यस्य सत्याश्रयश्री प्रिथिवीवल्लुभ महाराजाधिराज

परमेश्वरस्य प्रियतनय रणशिरसि रिपुनरेन्द्रान्दि

7h

शिदिशिजित्वा स्ववङ्शजां लक्ष्मीं प्राप्य च परमेश्वरतया
निवारितविक्रमादित्यस्तस्य ज्येष्ठोभ्राताश्रीचंद्रादित्य
प्रिथिवीवल्लभमहाराजाधिराजस्तस्यप्रियमहि
षीकलिकालप्रतिपक्षभूताश्रीविजयमहादे
वी [illegible] सर्व्वानाज्ञापयतिविदितमस्तुवोवैशाख
शुक्लद्वादश्यांसोमवासा [illegible] वत्सस्सगोत्रायकेरव
ठा [illegible] गोलस्वामिनेकोच्चुरकग्रामेचकुंडलक

च्छ दात्रना न रवज्जन ताहत उदकमूब न्दत्त४लुपउ च्व

द्वैक सेतुनानिवार्य्यते यो स्म ह्रूंड: शा जो न्यो वा नुपाल

यति स पुण्यभाग्भवति षष्टिवर्षसहंस्राणि स्वर्गे

मोदति भूमिद आच्छेत्ता चानुमन्ता च तान्येव नरके व

से। स्वदत्तां परदत्तां वा यो हरेत वसुन्धरां षष्टिवर्ष

सहस्राणि विष्ठायां जायते क्रिमिः ॥ लेपे ॥ १२८४ ...

Literal Verbatim Translation of Enclosure No. 4 *to Letter to Chief Secretary, No.* 11, *dated 8th January* 1849.

Swusti shrimutám sukulu-bhoowunu sunstooyumánu Mánu-
May it be well prosperous the whole universe (by) praised (who) are lineage of

wyusu- gotránám Hárítí-pootránám suptu-loku-mátri (1) bhi*h*- suptu- mátri-
Munoo descendants Haritee's sons seven nations (of) mothers seven (such)

bhi*h* abhiwurdhitánam Kártikeyu- purirukshunu- praptu- kulyánu-
mothers by brought up Kartik (by) protection (from) obtained blessings (of)

purumpuránám bhuguwun Náráyunu- prusádu- sumásáditu- wurábu
succession the divine Narayun (of) grace (from) gained the boar (of)

lánchhhun- e-kshunu- kshunu- washíkrit-a-sheshu- muhíbhritám
mark (of) appearance (of) time (since that) subjugated all kings

Chulookyánám koolum- alunkuris*h*no*h* ashwumedh-á- Wubhrithu-
Chulookyus to the race an adorner the sacrifice of a horse (of) Awubhrithu

snanu- puwitrikritu- gátrusyu Shree-poolukeshi-wulubhu- muhárája-
ablution (by) purified body Poolukeshi Wulubh the great king

---

syu prupuotru*h* purakrum-á- krántu- wunuwásyádi- puru-
of a great grandson bravery (by) subdued (therefore) forest inhabitants, &c. hostile

uriputi- mundulu prunibuddhu- 'wishooddhu- kírti- Shree-kírtiwurmu-
kings (of) circle in fixed pure fame Keertiwurmmu

pri-(2)thwee-(3) wulubhu- muhárájusyu puotrá*h* sumuru- sunsuktu- su-
earth lord the great king of a grandson war (to) devoted the

kul-o- thurá- puth-e-shwuru Shree Hurshuwurdhdhunu- purajuy-o-
whole northern country (of) lord Hurshuwurdhdhun (of) defeated (from)

pulubdhu Purumeshwur- á-puru- námudheyusyu Sutyashruyu- shree-prithwee- wulubhu
got Purumeshwur other name Sutyashruyu earth lord

muharájádhiráju Purumeshwurusyu priyu tunuya*h* (4) runu-
the great king (of) kings Purmeshwur (lord paramount) of dear a son war

shirusi ripoo-nurendrám di-
in inimical kings to

---

shidishi jitwa swu-wunshujám lukshím prapyu-
in (all) directions having conquered own family (in) sprung wealth having obtained

chu purumeshwurutuyá aniwáritu- Wikrumádityа*h* tusyu jeshtho bhrátá Shree-
also supremacy from unsubdued Wikrumadityu his elder brother Chun-

---

(1) tri written on the plate.
(2) Throughout the plate pree is written instead of pri in the word Prithwee.
(3) wi written on the plate. (4) a*h* wanting on the plate.

chundrádityu- prithwee-(5) wulubhu- muháráj-á- dhirája*h* tusyu pri-(6)yu
draditya land- lord the great king (of) kings his beloved

muhishí Kulikálá prutipukshubhootá Shree Wijuyu-ma-
anointed queen the Kuliyoog (iron age) to enemy* (who) is become Wijuyu Má-

hádewí  surwuwán ájnápuyuti widitumu (7) stoowa*h* Wue-
hádevee to all commands be it understood to you Wue-

[unintelligible]

shákha- Shooklu dwádushyám sopu-
shakhu (April-May) Shooddhu (white or waxing) 12th day on (who has been) with

wásá 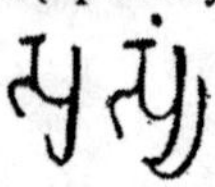 Wutsusu(8)gotrayu kekha  Goluswámine
fast the descendant of Wutsu Goluswami for

[unintelligible] [doubtful]

Kochchooruka gráme Wukooluku-
Kochchooruku village in

chchhu kshetru- námu khajjunusuhi-
Wukoolukuchchhu a piece of land (a thikan) (of) name a salt marsh along

tum oodukupoorwum duttum 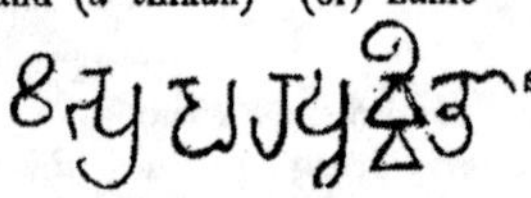 setooná niwaryate ya*h*
with water before granted bridge prohibits who

[unintelligible]

asmudwunshuja*h* anyowá anoo- paluyuti sa*h* poonyubhak bhuwuti
our descendant other or after preserves that virtue (of) participator becomes

yushchu upuhurttá sa*h* punchu mahápátuku- sunyookta*h* bhuwuti
who and resumer that the five capital crimes with (blended) becomes

Shushti-wurshu-suhusrani swurgge moduhti bhoomida*h* (9) áchchhettá
[Vide translation of Transcript No. III.]* enjoys

chánumuntáchu tanyewu nurukewuset (10) swuduttám puruduttám wá yoharet
wusoondhurám shushti-wurshu-suhusráni wishtháyám jáyute kri(11) mih

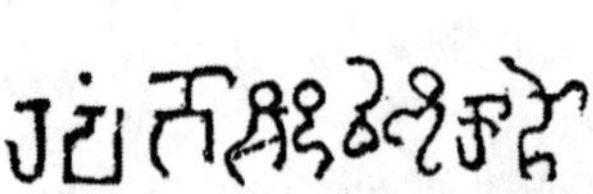 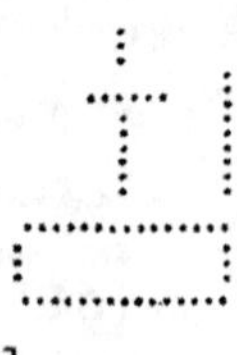

[unintelligible]

---

(5) wi written on the plate. (6) pra written on the plate.
(7) ma wanting on the plate. (8) ssa written on the plate.
(9) a*h* wanting on the plate. (10) t wanting on the plate.
(11) kri written on the plate.

* Accompanying letter to Chief Secretary, No. 158, dated 15th November 1848.

To A. Malet, Esq.,

Chief Secretary to Government.

Sir,

With reference to your letters Nos. 5329, 279, and 681, dated the 21st December 1848, 18th January and 15th February last, we have the honour to return the enclosed papers regarding the copper-plates forwarded by Major Jacob.

These plates have been carefully examined, as also the transcripts in the old characters and the Devunuguree. We are of opinion that these transcripts are generally faithful and correct: a few instances of partial inaccuracy are noted on the margin in pencil; they do not exceed half a dozen.

As to the English versions, we regard them likewise as generally correct, that is to say, they generally give a correct notion of the meaning of a passage on the whole, though not perhaps literally or verbally.

We had begun to mark on the margins of these also the variations which we traced from the original, but finding this would lead into greater detail than might be required by Government, and that the translations are sufficiently correct for all practical purposes, we thought it better merely to report our opinion of their general accuracy.

The common invocation has inadvertently been prefixed to the translations of Plate I.

We have the honour to be, &c.

(Signed) J. Stevenson.

" C. J. Erskine.

Bombay, 5th April 1849.

No. 152 of 1849.

From Major G. LeG. Jacob,
Political Superintendent of Sawunt Waree,

To A. Malet, Esq.,
Chief Secretary to Government, Bombay.

Political Department.

Sawunt Waree, 16th November 1849.

Sir,

As on a former occasion His Lordship in Council expressed a desire to obtain ancient inscriptions found in this district, I do myself the honour to transmit additional ones of a subsequent date to the Naroor plates, referred to in correspondence as per margin, but still of some historical interest. They are respectively of the years A. D. 933 to 1261, and 1391. Of the two first, the copper-plates exist in excellent preservation, but their owners decline parting with them, supposing them to contain some mystic virtue; as I annex fac-similes, whereby the variety of character is exhibited, this seems a matter of no moment. Inscription No. III. is taken from a copy in possession of a descendant (named Ram Krishn Tengsé) of one of the grantees, who says the plates are in possession of another descendant, now residing at Belgaum. Ram Krishn Tengsé lives in Kochré, the same village that was thus bestowed nearly five centuries ago, under the Sanscrit name of Koochchur, and the limits of this village, as described in the grant, appear the same to this day. This inscription was brought to me whilst engaged last year in ascertaining the boundaries of the adjoining villages of Pât and Mhapun, but I have found no time to make a correct translation of this and the others till now, and should have been unable to do so at all, but for the assistance given by Wasoodeo Ramchundru Shastree, and a young Bramhun named Anunta Bulal.

No.	Political Superintendent to Government.	No.	Replies.
93	13th July 1848...	3114	28th July 1848.
147	27th October „ ..	{ 5328	21st Dec. „
158	15th November „ ..		
		2260	25th May 1849.

The eras of the plates so referred to were—
No. I. set shortly after A. D. 592-93, date inferred.
„ II. set A. D. 705-06, date given.
„ III. set doubtful, but probably two generations prior to No. I.

The enclosures are fac-simile transcripts in modern Sanscrit, verbatim, and free translation of the oldest plates, with a table explanatory of their character; fac-simile transcript and translate of No. II.; copy and translation of No. III.; with a paper of observations on the points they severally offer worthy of note.

I have the honour to be, &c.

(Signed) G. LeG. Jacob,
Political Superintendent.

Observations on three Inscriptions on Copper-plates, referred to in a Letter to the Chief Secretary, No. 152, *dated* 16*th November* 1849.

On No. 1, of A. D. 933.

This records the grant in the Shalivahan year 355, by a sovereign of the Yudoo race, Gowind Raj, of the village Lohugrám, in the district of Rampoor,* to Keshow Dikshit, son of a Bramhun fellow-student. The language is pure Sanscrit, but inflated with gigantic hyperbole, puerile conceits, and far-fetched metaphors, containing little matter to compensate the labour of digging out the meaning.

The plates belong to a Bramhun family residing near Sanglee, but to what quarter the grant may pertain I know not: the seven places recorded may help to fix this—1*st,* Lohugrám, the village given away ; 2*nd,* Rampoor, the Talooka; 3*rd,* the four villages bounding the grant, viz. Ghodégrám, Wunjoolco, Winchuwihurubh, and Sonuuhee ; and 4*th,* Poonduwurddhun, the birthplace of the grantee. From a passage alluding to the Ganges and Jumna as "watering his kingdom," the Yudoo sovereignty at this era must have been more extensive than is generally supposed.

The following genealogical tree is gathered from the plates, and it will serve to clear up doubts left by previous inscriptions. It differs little from Bal Gungadhur Shastree's attempt to reconcile his and Mr. Wathen's notices, published in No. V. (for April 1843) of the Journal of the Bombay Branch Royal Asiatic Society, page 213. The Roman figures give the order of succession.

* Called Rampoori Suptu Shut, or Rampoor of the seven hundred (villages probably).

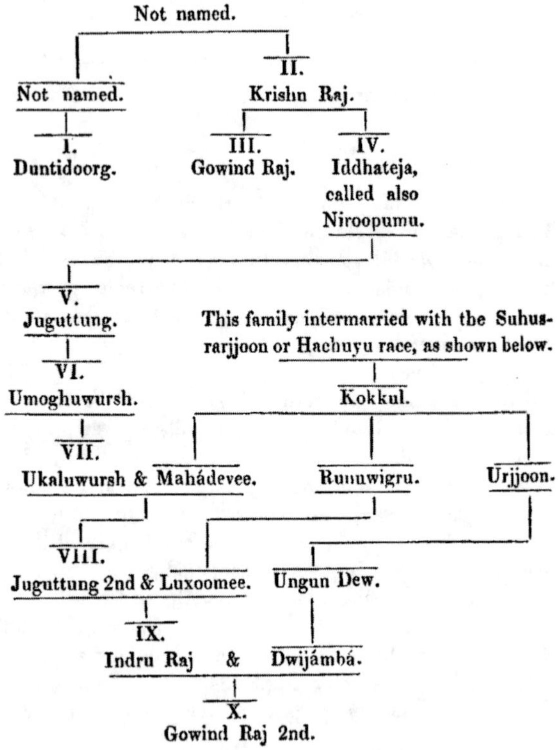

Donor of the grant called also Soowurunwursh and Wulubh Nurendru Dew.

The senior name of the race, second in succession to the Gadee, is described as having overthrown the Chulookyus, the reigning tribe celebrated in the Naroor plates. Supposing the ten reigns to average fifteen years, which, as the fourth Raja was a first cousin to the first, will be nearer the mark than the higher average generally assumed, this would give the year A. D. 783 as the period of the overthrow of the Chulookyu dynasty by the Yudoo.

No. 2, of A. D. 1261.

This inscription shows the Chulookyus again in the ascendant, and reigning at Kulyán, Kunwu Dew the king.* His minister, Keshow Mahajani, bestows the village Terwátuk, the modern Terwun, in the Rajapoor Talooka, on certain Bramhuns, and the deity Vimuleshwur, the latter said still to enjoy

* Boasting also four other high-sounding names.

his portion. The Sanscrit is not grammatical; the character approaches much nearer to the modern type. The inscription is probably the same of which an imperfect copy and translation are given in Vol. V. Royal Asiatic Society's Journal, page 177.

No. 3, of A.D. 1391,

Is an interesting relic of the Beejanuggur dynasty, founded, according to Ferishta, in A. D. 1344, by Bilal Dew, Raja of the Carnatic, who named it after his son Beeja.* I regret not having Wilks to refer to. Hamilton, quoting him and other authorities, dates the commencement of this city A. D. 1336, and completion A. D. 1343, by Aka Hurihur and Bukka Hurihur, and their minister the learned Madhuwu Achariyu. This inscription gives only the following genealogy:—

Achyoot, married to Shree.
|
Bookkuraj.
|
Hurihur.

The first-named is not spoken of as a sovereign, but the second is. The discrepancy between all three—Ferishta, Hamilton, and the plates—remains to be cleared up; but there would evidently seem an error in attributing the foundation of Wijuyu to the parties named, for supposing another and previous Hurihur, there would scarcely have been another and powerful Madhuwu. This person is celebrated in Sanscrit writings as the minister of the Bookkunu race, which, supposing him to retain office under the son, agrees with this genealogy. His different names, according to the Shastree who is my authority on this point, are Madhow Acharyu, and Chutoor Wedacharyu. Later in life he forsook mundane affairs, turned Sunyasee, and received the name of Widyarunyu.† This inscription, alluding to Wijuyu, says that Bookkuráj here lived as an Indru, defying all his enemies; and as no mention is made of Achyoot's deeds, or residence, the inference is that Bookkuráj was the first of the race who established himself in power in this quarter. Hurihur is described as ruling over the whole of the Indian peninsula that is washed by the ocean, and it seems doubtful whether supremacy to the Indus be not claimed. His prime minister, the aforesaid Madhuwu, whom he invested with the sovereignty of Juyuntipoor, conquered Goa from the Tooroosbkas (Turks), and re-established there the worship of the ancient idols, which they had uprooted. This victorious personage, before transferring control over the Goa country to another minister, named Nuruhuri, granted to the parties named in the plates the village of Kuchchur, called also Madhuwupoor. This village, the modern Kochré, is not many miles from the present Goa frontier.

* Properly Wijuyu-nuggur, the City of Victory; called in this inscription Wijuyu only.

† His works are said to be Adhikarunu Nyáyu, Málakulá Madhuwu, Párashuru Madhuwu, and several others much prized.

Free Translation, but as close to the Sanscrit as the Language will admit of. Date of Plate Shalivahan Shuk 855 (A. D. 933).

The melodious Samved songs, in which Suruswutee (1) takes delight, sung by Brumhu, pleased with the creation of the universe, continue in honour ! From the moon [that swan sitting on the lotus of the cerulean lake, surrounded by a numerous train of star-like lotuses ; that silvery parasol of the great king Kam, (2) whose unrivalled sway prevails throughout the creation ; that milky ocean in beauty ; that silvery mountain in resplendence ; that ivory comb of the goddess (3) who rules over the eastern quarter ; that mansion of universal beauty] there sprung a race whence issued forth on earth an ocean-like branch of Yudoos, the abode of riches and fame ; the theatre of policy, prosperity, and deep meditation ; beneficent and renowned for protecting the poor. In this cloudless heaven rose Duntidoorg, skilled in arts, (4) to whom his host of enemies were submissive as the starry spheres to the moon ; the abundant and extensive rays of whose fame, like those of the moon's white light, filled all quarters. (5) His illustrious sun-like paternal uncle Krishn Raj, having ascended the hero's ancient Meroo's crest-like throne, dispelled the dark and insolent Chulookyu race, and sent forth, as the sun does when first rising over the mountain tops, the light of his power over other kings, (6) and diffused his glory throughout the world. His son Gowind Raj, born at Indoobimbushilatul, ornamented by a mark caused by the smoke of his burning enemies, came after him. He was succeeded by his illustrious younger brother Iddhateja, also called Niroopumu, who had a heroic and philanthropic heart, whose dread made the progeny of his numerous enemies to tremble, and whose sway-tracing signet (Moodra) reached to the seas, hence known by the name of Sumoodru (with signet), which they still bear. (7) He was followed by his son Juguttung, whose rivals, bereft of their authority, had become as sapless and impotent as the withered breasts of old women. His son Umoghuwursh, who succeeded him, was of incomparable power. * * * * (8) His spotless fame so wide, that, filling up the whole universe, and finding no outlet, it ultimately over-flowed in the form of water into the deep ocean of the world. Of him was born king Ukaluwursh, to whom experienced shieldsmen, terrified by his prowess, instantly surrendered, throwing down their swords and bucklers.

(1) The Indian Muse. (2) The Hindoo Cupid. (3) Untranslatable.

(4) Here is an untranslatable play upon words, founded on the double meaning of the adjective " Kuláwánu," " possessed of digits," and " possessed of arts" ; the former applicable to the moon, and the latter to the king.

(5) Also " gratified the hearts of mankind."

(6) The play upon the word अट्ट (Uttu), signifying both " light" and " command," admits of no exact translation in English.

(7) Here is a play on the word " Sumoodru," signifying " seas" in one sense, and " with signet" (or power) in the other.

(8) A few words following are unintelligible.

Máhádevee, an ornament of the Suhusrarjjoon race, (9) the daughter of Kokkul, became his queen. Their son, King Juguttung, resembling Dhurm (Ujátu-shutroo), by having no enemies, but glorious for prowess, like Bheemusen and Urjjoon, (10) was married to Luxoomee, (11) the daughter of Kokkul's son Runuwigru, who was able to withstand his rival kings, deep, and holding (like the ocean) precious things. From the King Juguttung arose Luxoomee's son, (12) like the sun from the Ooduyachul, (13) glorious, flourishing, called another sun amongst the kings, and who truly deserved in this world the name of Indru Raj, (14) being one entitled to continual homage, (15) exterminating all iniquitous kings and their adherents by the thunderbolt of his prowess. (16) Dwijámbá (who, like Luxoomee from the ocean, or like Parwuti from the Himaluyas, the lord of the mountains, was born from Ungun Dew, very strong in force, the son of Urjjoon, who became by his virtues the senior son of the aforementioned Kokkul, who was a descendant of the Hachuyu race, that broke down the pride of Rawun) became Queen of Indru Raj. Their son Gowind Raj (who surpassed Kam in beauty; who never committed wicked deeds, although with full opportunity; who never dishonored the elders, nor brought disgrace on himself by perpetrating evil actions, such as going with a brother's wife, &c., nor ever acted the coward's part by assuming derangement to cloak misdeeds; who signalized himself in the world as adventurous only in charity and war), became the next king. He poured forth bounties like rain upon his people, so that he at last was said to have inundated the whole creation with gold. The earth, finding herself rid of her wicked rulers, at the height of his triumph over the world, commenced to dance for joy, raising, as if to gesticulate, her hands, the flapping banners of supremacy. (17) The sun and moon, also, knowing that this victorious king does not bear with any insolent

(9) Afterwards also called Hachuyu.

(10) Dhurm, Bheemusen, and Urjjoon are the first three of the brothers called the "Five Pandoos."

(11) The metaphor is constructed by comparing this princess to Luxoomee the wife of Wishnoo, the goddess of wealth, and also the first of the fourteen precious things produced by the ocean when it was churned by the gods and giants.

(12) The play upon the words "Lukshmyá*h* nunduna*h*" signifies as above given in one sense, and "supporter of splendour" in the other.

(13) The name of the mountain behind which the heavenly bodies are supposed to rise.

(14) The metaphor is constructed by comparing this king with Indru, the chief deity (quite a Jupiter Tonans), supposed to have punished the flying mountains by scorching up their wings with his thunderbolts.

(15) The play upon the term "Animishu-durshunu-yogya*h*" signifies as given above in one sense, and "fit for the visits of the divinities" in the other.

(16) Here is another play upon the term "Sthiti-chulitu-sukulu-bhubhritpukshu-chchhed-a-bhimooktu-bhooju-wujra*h*," signifying as given above in one sense, and also "hurling out of his hand a thunderbolt to deprive all the flying mountains of their wings."

(17) Pali, called also Padhi in some of the previously translated plates.

and inimical ruler, (18) became terrified, and submissively ran, like heralds before him. Princes and authorities bowed themselves down before his ever-victorious palace, shining with his lustre, having its external gateway lofty, and shaped like the moon. Has it actually happened that the Ganges and Jumna have poured themselves into and watered his kingdom because of its superiority over all others in virtue and genius? While this victorious king has been peaceably reigning, his virtuous kingdom has been freed from all enemies, and the expression "Wimanu," an evil character, is understood only as a celestial vehicle, (19) to the truth of which parrots even bear testimony. The soot of the numerous fumes rising from the fire of his great valour in battle produced another heaven of azure clouds, in which the rays, reflected while brandishing the glittering swords, are the flashes of lightning, and the pearls (20) that drop in breaking the temples of the stubborn and hostile elephants, shine like the stars. His fame so pervades and saturates the universe, that the moon, the milky ocean, and the thousand-headed snake, are the produce of its superfluity. It is no wonder that enemies succumbed to his authority when he desired to search out and exterminate all such, (21) for even the conscious lotus, (22) being terrified, but knowing its concealment under water still more dangerous, implored mercy, as it were, by offering Luxoomee to him out of its bud. (23) The *Pandanus odoratissimus* took, as if through fear shelter in a valley under a mist of its own odoriferous particles scattered by the wind, but the jack-tree (24) and cane (25) saved their lives by becoming vassals, and standing at the doors (26) of his palace. The king, by his beauty rivalling that of Kam, has become another Nityukundurp, (27) thus deriding Máhádeo's third fiery eye, for having in vain burned up and made Kam Unityukundurppu. (28) He has been so richly blessed with energy, nursed by council and valour, the other two constituents of royal strength, that he throught little of even Indru's happiness. He, a second Brumha amidst the

(18) The words "Purum-munduládhipum," signifying as above, and also "other lord of circle" (disc or system), such as the sun and moon, a Raja in his Durbar, &c.; hence the allusion to the sun and moon, lost in the translation.

(19) An untranslatable play upon the double meaning of the word "Wimanu."

(20) This metaphor is founded on the popular belief of the elephant's forehead containing a pearl.

(21) Here is an untranslatable play upon the double meaning of the word "Kantuku," which means "thorns" as well as "enemies."

(22) A particular species of red lotus, having thorns.

(23) Here is a play upon the word "Koshu," which means a "bud," and also "treasury." Luxoomee dwells in both the lotus-bud and treasury.

(24) The jack-tree, though itself not thorny, bears a fruit covered with prickles.

(25) Porters and mace-bearers generally stand with their canes at the doors; hence the allusion.

(26) Door-frames are generally of jack-wood.

(27) That is "everlasting" or "imperishable Kam."

(28) That is "transitory" or "perishable Kam."

Chunukyus, (29) a Narayun (30) on account of his being devoted to the welfare of the world, subjugated by his unparalleled valour, became also a Trinetru, (31) living as it were within the inimical breasts (32) that he had himself torn open with his plough. This blessed king of kings [independent, and ever most desirous of maintaining his supremacy, called Soowurunwursh, and also for his universal popularity Wulubh Nurendru Dew, (33) constantly meditating on the feet of the prosperous and independent Nityuwurshu Dew, a great teacher, and a king of kings] orders all ministers, Mankurees, (34) rulers of kingdoms and countries, principal villagers, respectable men, and all who are tenacious of their dignity: " Be it well known unto you, that the king [who, with a view of promoting his own and his parents' virtue and fame, by a long continuance of his capital, shielded by wise counsellers, even restores by-gone grants to gods and Bramhuns, and who daily issues by hundreds innumerable edicts of village grants, on Thursday, while the moon is in the mansion Poorwu Bhadrupudu, the 15th of Shrawun (July-August), in the Shalivahan year Wijuyu, 855 years having passed of that era] has given in Inam, till the sun and moon endure, formally pouring water (35) from the hand, the village Lohugrám, in Rampoori Suptu Shut, with all the trees thereon, exempt from payment of grain or gold, * * * * (36) and from the ingress of the military, to Keshow Dikshit, son of his fellow-student Damodur Bhut, born in the city of Poonduwurddhun, a descendant of Kuoshik, and a Kunwu (37) sectary. The undisputed boundaries of the village so granted as never to be coveted back are Ghodégrám on the east; Wunjoolee village on the south; Winchuwihurubh village on the west; and Sonnuhee village on the north. No one should ever interfere with Keshow Dikshit or his posterity whilst they are cultivating or enjoying, or suffering the village to be cultivated or enjoyed. Future kings (either of my own or other lineage, who may know that wealth is as transient as the waves undulated by a hurricane, life as the summer clouds, and also that preserving an assignment of land is more meritorious than granting it, which is their common duty) should duly observe and protect this our grant. Ram has said—' to give land, and thus build a bridge, to pass, as it were, over an ocean of sin, is a duty common to rulers'; but oh! you future kings, to

(29) May be perhaps the descendants of Chunukyu, the name of a sage, now applied to a man of prudence.

(30) That is Wishnoo.

(31) The Three-eyed, a title of Máhádeo.

(32) One of Shivu's epithets is "Smushanuwasi," or "dweller in cemetery"; hence this far-fetched metaphor.

(33) This, signifying "the darling of kings," is the king's sixth epithet.

(34) The persons entitled to certain honours and presents rendered at courts, councils, festivals, village assemblies, &c.

(35) A practice observed at the time of making a donation, to intimate relinquishment of right over it.

(36) A few words following are unintelligible.

(37) A particular section of the Yujoorwed.

protect this bridge of charity from time to time is the repeated solicitation of your suppliant Ramchundru." It is also said that he who gives land abides sixty thousand years in heaven, but a resumer and an abettor in its resumption are doomed to pass the same number of years in hell. He who takes back land given, either by himself or others, becomes a worm, and rots along with his ancestors in his own hell. Charity given by a single-handful, (38) or resumption of what is given, destroys the merit of all former donations. He that gives land dwells myriads of years in the heaven of Brumha. Be there blessing throughout the creation ! Be our salutation to Shivu !

(38) Giving with a double-handful is held meritorious by the Shastras.

Verbatim Translation. (*Compound words are shown by a connecting hyphen.*)

Juyunti Brumhuṇuh surgu- nishputti moodit- á-tmunah

Live victoriously Brumha of universe (of) creation (by) pleased heart (whose is)

Suruswutí (1) ?? tánundáh mudhooráh Sámugítuyah (2) || tárá-

Suruswutee by (made ?) joy (in which) melodious Samved songs stars (of)

chukr-á-bju- sḥu (3) ṇḍ-á- writu- gugunu- surush- (4)

circle (like) lotuses (of) number (by) surrounded (such) sky (this is) a lake

pudminí- rajuhunsát tree- loky- kádhiputyu- sthitu- Mudunu-

lotus (on) a swan (is it) three worlds (in) (whose) supremacy existed Kam

muhárájụ- shooddh- a-tuputtrar láwunyu kshíru- sindhoh

the great king (of) white parasol (is it) beauty (in) milk (of) ocean (is it)

dyooti- rujutu-gireh digwudhoo-duntuputtrát wunshuh

splendour (in) silver mounted (is it) direction-females (of) an ivory comb (is it) a race

somát uyum yuh tribhoowunu- kumul-á-wásu- suodhát

three worlds

the moon from this which universe (of) fortune (of) living (of) mansion (is it)

upetah || tusmát shriyuh koolu-gruhum bhoowunum muhimnuh kriḍ-á-

originated that from riches of family-house (is it) a house (is it) greatness (of) a diver-

spudum sthiti- muhurddhi- gubhírutánám tráyun usutwu-

sion place (is it) protection great prosperity (and) seriousness of a patron the weak

puripálunu- lubdhu- kirtih wunshoh bubhoowu bhoowi

(of) protection (from) (which) obtained fame (such) a race sprung the world in

sindhoo- nibhoh Yudoonam || purinutu- puru- muṇḍuluh

enemies

an ocean-like Yadoos of (to whom) submissive (is) (of the moon) others (of) circle

kuláwán pruwitutu- buhulu- yush-o-nshoo-

arts (in) skilled fame (of) rays

(of the moon) with (16) digits extensive many (of the moon) white rays

poorit-ashah- shushudhuru iwu Duntidoorgurajoh Yudoo-

by (who has) filled up directions the moon like (such) Duntidoorg king Yudoo

koolu- wimulu wiyuti utho dityáyu || tusyu ádyum nriputeh pitriwyu

(of) race (this) pure heaven in then arose his old king of paternal uncle

ooduyí shreewíru sinhásunum Meroh shringum iwu adhiroohyu

flourishing heroes (of) throne Meroo of horn (or crest) like having mounted

---

1 Wife of Brumha, and the Indian Muse.

2 Sam is the third of the four Veds, always recited in a singing tone.

3 It should be read kha. Sha is usually written for kha, and kha for sha, and pronounced so, in proper names, by the followers of Kunwu-Shákhá of the 2nd Ved Yujoorwed.

4 sha is incorrect. Oopudhmániyu Wisurg is here wanted

46

ruwi-wut Shrí-krshṇurájah tutuh dwust-o-dri (5) ktu- Chulookyu-
the sun-like Krishn Raj then (who has) dispelled insolent Chulookyu

wunshu- timiruh prithweebhritám mustuke nyust-a-ṭṭah
(of the sun) mountains of (of the sun) fixed light
race (this) darkness kings of head over (who has) fixed commands

sukulum jugut pruwitutueeh tejobhih ákrántuwán ‖ tusmát Gowindurájah
the whole world very extensive resplendence by pervaded him from Gowind Raj

abhoot Indoobimbushilátule yusyu ari- ploshu- dhoomron-
was born Indoobimbshilatul in whom to enemies (of) burning (of) smoke (of)

kuh (6) prushastiriwu lukshute ‖ tusya abhawat bhoowunu pálunu-
mark an ornament-like looks his had been the world (of) protection (for)

wiru-booddhih ooddhútu- shutroo- koolu- suntutih
powerful (whose) mind (is) (who) shook enemies (of) races (of) offspring

Iddhatejáh Rájá anoojah Niroopum-á- puru- námudheyah
(such) Iddhateja king younger brother (whose) Niroopumu other name (is)

yunmoodryá amboodhirupi pruthituh sumoodrah ‖ tudunoo Juguttungah
an ocean
whose signet by ocean too became known with signet that after Juguttung

aguni purihutu- niju- sukulu- muṇḍul-a-bhogáh gutu-
was born lost relations (of) whole circle (of) (whose) all enjoyments (are) passed

yaowunu- wunitajunu- koochu- sudrishoh yusyu wueri-wirpáh ‖
youth (such) women number (of) breasts like whose inimical kings

tusmát chu Umoghuwurshah abhuwut- atoolu- bulah yeu
force
that from also Umoghuwursh sprung unequalled (whose) strength (is) whom by

kopát apoorwueeh Chulooky-á-bhy nshukhádyueeh junitu-rutee-yumuh priṇitah
anger by modern [unintelligible] [unintelligible]

wiṇguwullyám Wuerinch-a-nd-o-dur-á-nturbuhih oopuri tule yut na
[unintelligible] Brumha (of) egg (of) belly in (and) out over beneath which (for) not

lubdhwá awukáshum toyu- wyáját wishooddhum yushuh iwu
having attained space water (of) counterfeit by pure renown is it?

nihitum tut jaguttoongu-sindhao ‖ tusmát Ukáluwurshah nriputih
placed that world (in) deep (such) ocean in that from Ukaluwursh king

abhoot yut- purákrumu- trustueeh sdyuh sumuṇḍulágrum kheṭuku- muhi-
was born whose prowess (by) harassed instantly also sword shields (in) the

tueeh purity uktum ‖ Suhusrárjjoonu- wunshusyu bhooshuṇum Kokkul-á-
expert by threw down Suhusrarjjoon (of) race of an ornament Kokkul (of)

tmujá tusyu abhawat Máhádevi Juguttungu-
daughter his (*i. e.* Ukaluwursh's) became anointed queen Juguttung

---

(5) Should be dree. (6) mronkuh written by mistake for mránkuh.

-*h* tutu*h* aguni || gumbhírát rutnu-nidhe*h* bhoobhrit- pruti-
serious
her from was born (of the sea) deep precious things (of) mine kings ene-

pukshu- rukshunu kshumuta*h* Kokbha (7) lu- sootu- Runuwigruhu
mies (from) protection (for) able Kokkul (of) son (such) Runuwigru

juludhe*h* Lukshmí*h* sumootpunná || sá jáyá ajáyutu ajátu-shuttro*h*
dhurm
(this) ocean from Luxoomee was born she wife became not became enemies

tusyu muhibhooja*h* Bhímusen-A-rjjoon-o-
(to whom) that (*i. e.* Juguttung) king of Bheemsen (&) Urjjoon (from) (as if)

patto (8) a- yusho- bhooshunu- shalina*h* || tuttru Jugut-
(of the sun) the
procured renown ornament (by) one who looks handsome there Jugut-

tung- O-duyu-dhuruní dhuruta*h* prutápu- kulit-a-
world (in) high prowess
tung (that is) Ooduyachul mountain from (of the sun) heat by pervaded

tmá Luk (9) myá*h* nundunu*h* oodita*h* ajuni-
(of the sun) splendour of (of the sun) pleaser
(whose) body (is) Luxoomee of son is said to have been

wijuyí ráju- mártunda*h* || sthiti-
morality
born victorious kings (among) the sun (*i. e.* best) (of Indru) situation (from)

chulitu- sukulu- bhoobhrit- pukshu- chchhed-á-bhimooktu-
deviators kings (of) adherents (of)
(of Indru) movers all (of Indru) mountains (of) wings (of) lopping off (for) hurled

bhooju- wujra*h* animishu- durshunu-
prowess thunderbolt constant visit (of)
(who has) (of Indru) arm (by) thunderbolt (of Indru) gods (to) (of Indru) visit (for)

yogya*h* yu*h* sutyum ihu Indruráju*h* iti || yu*h* tasmin dushu-
worthy
worthy (who is) who truly (therefore) here Indru Raj thus who that in the ten-

kunthu durpu- dulune Shréehuchuyánám koole Kokkulla*h*
necked (*i. e.* Rawun) (of) pride (of) destroying Huchuyas (of) race in Kokkul

prutipádita*h* asyu chu goonu- jyeshtha*h* Arjjoona*h* abhoot
previously told this of also qualifications (by) elder (such) Urjjoon had been

sootah tut-pootra*h* Ungunudewa*h* iti utibulu*h* tusmát Dwijámbá ubhuwut
sun his son Ungun Dew thus strongest him from Dwijámbá was begotten

pudm-e-wu amboonidhe*h* Oom-e-wu Himuwaunámnu*h*
Luxoomee-like the sea from Parwutee-like Himachul name (whose is) from

---

(7) It ought to be Kokka. (8) tta badly engraved. (9) sh is here required.

kshumá bhritprubhoh || Shrindrunurendrát tusyám soonooh abhoot bhooputih
mountains (of) lord from Indru Raj from her in son was born a king

Dwijámbáyám Gowinduràja-námá Kám-a-dhiku-roopu-
Dwijámbá in Gowind Raj (whose) name (is) Kam (of) (than) more features (of) (whose)

suonduryah || samurthye suti vinditám (10) pruwihitá nu ewu
beauty (is) power being wickedness (who) committed not surely

agruje kroorutá bundhooh- strí- gumuná-dibhih koochuritueh
elders over cruelty brother (of) wife (with) going, &c. wicked deeds by

awurjitum nu ayushah shuoch-á-shuochu- purángmookhum nu chu
brought no disgrace purity (and) impurity (to) averse not also

bhiyá pueshàchyum augíkritum tyágenu asumu-sáhusueh
fear through devilry owned grant by (and) enemies (towards) adventures by

chu bhoowune yuh sahus-ánkuh abhuwut || wurshun Soowurnuwurshuh
Soowurnuwursh
also world in who hazard (whose) mark (is) became rainer gold-rainer

prubhootu wurshuh api kunuku-dhárabhih jugut akhilum eku-kánchunum
plentifully pourer (being) also gold (of) streams by world whole uniform gold

ayum akurot iti junueh ooktah || yut adhi-digwijuy-a-wus-ure suti
this made thus people by is said whose great directions (of) conquests (of) time being

prusubhu- sumbhrumu- bháwne ewu bhooh supudi urityuti Pali-muhádh-
preparation
great hurry (of) appearance at just the earth instantly dances Pali (11) great

wuj-o- chhritu-kuru anyu- koonáthu- wiwurjjitu ||
lords
flags (these) (who) has raised hands other wicked kings (of) (which is) devoid

suhute hi (12) mundul-á-dhipum purug (13) esh abhyoodují sumooddhutum
circle others
endures for which (not) province (of) lord inimical this prosperous insolent

iti játu-bhiyá dhiya ágrutah ruwi-chundruo upi yusyu dhawu-
thus became fearful (such) mind by forward the sun (and) moon too whose run

te || (14) amunutu- puru- mundul-e-shwurum suha- wijuyu- shtu- (15)
province-lord
(to whom) submissive other petty-kings (are) along with victory (with) fill-

bhi-weshmu shobhitum sumu-himukuru-tornum
ed (such) house looking well high and formed like the moon whose external front gate (is)

---

(10) Unooswar over tá not wanted.

(11) Pali has also been called Padhi in some of the previously translated plates.

(12) na is wanting.

(13) ग is written for म (mu) in a few places in the plates. A little horizontal stroke to complete the letter may inadvertently have been omitted.

(14) tah is required in place of te.

(15) shta required in place of shta.

chirum niju-teju- stuti yusyu rajute || suhute
long while (in which) own light (of) quantity (is) whose looks handsome bears

sumutá (16) hi ní (17) muyum nu pureshám su-wisheshu- shalineem yut
equality for which ingenuity full (of) not others of with prosperity glorious whose

uninditu- raju- (18) mundirum nuņoo Gungá-Yumoonà chu sewute ||
unblemished kingdom (is) mansion really the Ganges (and) Jumna also attend on

yusmin rajuni soorajyum nirjit-a-ri witunwuti
which king good kingdom defeated (whose) enemies (are) reigning (while)

wimánu-sthitiḣ (19) iti áseet nubhoge* sḥoo (20) ku- wachunum ||
the dishonoured (of) existence
celestial vehicle of existence
birds of worth (of) existence thus was heaven in parrots (of) speech

yusyu ooddámu prutápá- nulu- buhulu- shikhá kujjulum
whose overbearing prowess; (this is) fire (of) many fumes (from) soot

nilu- meghaḣ wisphoorjjit- khudgu- dhárá- sphoorunu-
(these are) blue clouds sparkling sword (of) blade (of) brandishing (of)

wisheerņáni ewu widyoodwilásáḣ doorwár-á-rí-
reflected rays (these are) very lightning (of) flashes irrestrainable enemies (of)

bhu- koombhusthulu- dulunu- gulut- muoktikáni (21) ewu
elephants (of) temples (of) breaking (by) dropped pearls (these) very

táráḣ chundru- kshír-á-bdhi-sheshàḣ (22) bhrutu- bhoowunu-
stars the moon milk (of) ocean (&) the thousand-headed snake filled the world (in)

yusho- ráshi- nishrunditani ||
(such) fame (of) heap (of) exudations

yusmin kuntuku- (23) shodhun-o-tsooku- munushi (24) ambhojuná-
who enemies (of) search (about) eager mind being water-born (*i. e.* lotuses)

laeḣ bhi (25) yá iwa oonmugnum nu puyussoo koshu-
treasury (in)
(of) tubes by fear by as if sunk not water in bud (in) (whose)

---

(16) Unooswar over ta omitted. (17) ni written by mistake for dhi. (18) jya badly engraved.

(19) This is a figure of speech called Wirodhábhásu. It is a play on the word "Wimánu," which signifies the dishonoured, a celestial vehicle (and birds of merit). The Pundit states that *nubhoge must be translated as accompanying Wimánu-sthiti, although, for the sake of the verse, separated therefrom.

(20) sḥoo written by mistake for shoo.

(21) In Hindoo belief, the elephant's temples contain pearls.

(22) Yasha, Fame, being supposed to be white, her exudations are represented by the three principal white things of the three worlds, viz. the moon for the upper, the ocean for the centre, and the world-supporting snake Sheshu for the lower world.

(23) The following passage is a far-strained play on the double meaning (thorns and enemies) of this word.

(24) Should be Munusi—shya written by mistake for sya. (25) Should be bhi.

wusuti (26) lukshmi*h* kroota oopayunum ketukyá (27)
(whose) residence (is)
residence (is) (such) fortune made a gift *Pandanus odoratissimus* by

puwun-o- llusun-niju- ruju*h*- poonj-a-ndhukar-o- dure
wind (by) flying its particles (of) number (by) darkness (is whose) stomach in

bhoogurbbhe punusenu (28) wettrulutuyá dwarí átmu-shood-
(such) world (of) interior in jack-tree by rattan by door at bodies (of) purifica-

dhyue sthitum‖ yu*h* chu sumoopuhusitu- Huru- nuyunu- duhune- (29)
tion for stood who also being ridiculed Máhádeo (of) the eye (of) fire (by)

wihit-a-nityu- Kundurppu- roopu- suonduryu- durppu*h* (30)
made perishable (such) Kam (of) person (of) beauty (of) pride (who has) (for

Shree- Nityukundurppa*h* prubhoo- muntru-
which) Shree (is called) Nityukundurppu prowess (and) counsel (these)

shuktyoopubrínhit-o-tsáhu- shukti- sumáksbiptu- Shutumoo- (31)
powers (by) reared up (such energy power (by) (who has) blamed Indru (of)

kha- (32) sookhu*h* Cháṇukyu (33) chutoormookha*h* pruthit-
happiness Chunukyu (race in) four-faced (*i. e.* Brumha) renowned

ue-ku- wikrum-á-kránta- wusoondhurá hitu- kurunu- puráyuna*h*
unrivalled
alone
only prowess (by) subjugated (such) world (of) good doing (to) devoted

Shreewikrántu Náráyuna*h* swukuru- kulitu-
prowess (in Wishnoo)
(who is) (for which) Wikrantu Narayun (is called) own-hand (by) held

heti- hulu- dulitu- wipukshu- wukshusthulu-kshettru*h*
weapon plough (by) broken enemies (of) breasts (in) (whose) abode(is) (for which)

Shreenrooputi- tri(34)ne(35)tra*h* sumubhuwut
kings (in) the Three-eyed (*i. e.* Máhádeo) (is called) had been

su*h* chu Purumu- bhuttáruku- muháráj-a- dhiráju-
saving by speech
he very (who is) greatly desiring supremacy great king (of) kings

---

(26) Luxoomee is supposed to dwell in a lotus-bud. Written wusuti by mistake for wusutirie-wusuti*h*.

(27) These trees are supposed to grow in low places, pits, &c.

(28) The frame of the front-door at least, of a house, is ordained to be of jackwood by the Wustushástru (architecture).

(29) Should be na in place of ne.

(30) This metaphor is founded on the tale of Kam, the Hindoo Cupid, having been burnt up by the fire of Máhádeo's third eye, for interrupting him at his devotions, and existing afterwards only as a spirit.

(31) Should be na.

(32) Shutumookha, signifying "a performer of a hundred sacrifices."

(33) k badly engraved. Chanukyu, an author of a work; a sage.

(34) tri is written for tree. (35) Should be ne.

purumeshwuru- shree- mu-nuityuwurshudew- pád-a-
Purumeshwur (*i. e.* paramount) rich Nityuwurshdew (of) the feet (on)

noo- dhyát- Purumu- bhuṭṭáruku muháráj-a-
who saves by speech
(who has) constantly meditated greatly who desires supremacy great king

dhiraju- purumeshwuru Shreemut- Soowurṇṇuwurshudewu-
of kings Purmeshwur (*i. e.* paramount) rich (such) Soowurunwurshudew

prithwee-wulubhu- shreemut- wulubhu- nurendrudewa*h* kooshulí surwán
earth-lord rich Wulubh Nurendru Dew the blessed all to

ewu yutásu n ह tyu mánukán rashṭruputi-
thus [unintelligible] persons entitled to (certain honours to) kingdom (of) lord

wishuyuputi- grámukooṭu- muhutturu- yooktu- kopu- yooktuká-
country (of) lord villagers to nobles along with angry offi-

dhikárikan sumádishuti astoo wa*h* sunwiditum yutha amát-
cers to well commands be (it) you to well known thus (whose) minis-

yu- (36) kheṭu- rájudhaní sthirutur-am- wusthanenu mátá-
ters (are) shields (such) metropolis (of) constant existing by mother (and)

pittro*h* átmunu*h* chu pooṇyu- yush-o-bhiwridddhuye poorwu- looptán api
father of my also virtue (and) fame (of) progress for before dropped too

dewu-bhog-á- -gruhárán prutipáluyutá pruti- dinun
gods (of) possession (and) a religious grant the one that protects by every day

chu niruwudhi- numusyu- grámu- shásunám shutusa*h* (37) pruyuchchhutá
Inam
also unboundedly reverend (such) village orders (by) hundreds the one that gives by

Shuku-nroopu- (38) kal-a-titu- sunwutsuru- shuteshoo ashṭusoo punchu-
era (of) king (of) time (of) passed years (of) hundreds eight fire (and)

puncháshu-d-dhikeshoo ankuto-pi Sunwutsuránám ८५५ Pruwurt-
fifty more (in which are) number (in) also years of 855 cur-

tumánu- wijuyu- sunwutsur-á- nturgu (39) tu- Shráwuṇu- puorṇumásyám
rent Wijuy year in July and August (of) full-moon in

wáre Gooro*h* Poorwabha- (40) drupudá- nukshuttre (41) pruthumu- kur-
fresh
right
day on Jupiter of Poorwa Bhadrupud lunar mansion in first hand-

o duk-á-ti-surguṇu ‖ Pooṇduwurddhunu- nuguru- winirggutu Kuo-
water (of) much pouring by Poonduwurdhun city (in) was born (such) Kuo-

---

(36) Written nyu by mistake for tyu. (37) sa*h* written by mistake for sha*h*.
(38) *i. e.* Shalivahan. (39) rgga imperfectly engraved. (40) bha is written for bhá.
(41) Supposing this Nukshutru to be correctly stated, the month Shrawun is erroneously written for Bhadrupud, and should the stated month be correct, the Nukshutra is wrongly written.—*Sic dicit Pandit.*

shiku- sugotru- Wajikunwu subrumhuchári Damodurubhuṭṭu- sootáyu
shik (of) lineage (of) Wajikaṇwu- (42) (of) fellow-student Damodur Bhut (of) son

Keshuwu-díkshitáyu Ramupoorisuptushut-á- nturgutu- Lohugrámu*h* suwrik-
Keshow Dikshit to Rampoori Suptu Shut in Lohugrám together with

shu- mal-a-koola*h* sudhanyu-hiruny-a-deya*h* sudunḍu doshu
trees (of) number (by) covered with grain (and) gold not to be given [unintelligible]

dush-á-purádhu subhootopáttu prutyuya*h* awáṭu bhuṭu pruweshu
[unintelligible] [unintelligible]

---

shutotturáya*h* Brumhudáyu- nyayenu á-chundr-á-rkum
[unintelligible] Bramhanical property (of) rule by (43) till the moon (and) the sun

numusya*h* duttu*h* yusyu chu ágháṭá*h* poorwuta*h* Ghodégrámu*h*
Inam
(exist) worthy of reverence granted whose also boundaries the east on Ghodégrám

dukshiṇuta*h* Wunjoolí-namá gráma*h* pushchimuta*h* Winchuwihuru-
the south on Wunjoolee (whose) name (is) a village the west on Winchuwihurubh

námá gráma*h* ootturuta*h* Sonnuhí-námá gráma*h* ewum
(whose) name (is) a village the north on Sonnuhee (whose) name (is) a village thus

chutoor-á- ghátu- wishooddhum Lohugrámum Keshuwu-díkshitusyu
the four boundaries (in) clear (such) Lohugrám Keshow Dikshit to

krishuta*h* kurshuyuta*h* bhoonjuta*h* bhojuyuta*h* wa nu ke (44) chit
(while) cultivating causing culture enjoying causing to enjoy or not any one by

wyághátа*h* kárya*h* mutt- (45)a-nil-a-ndolitu- julu turungu- turulum
interruption should make violent wind (by) undulated water-waves (like) transient

aeshwuryu (46) shurud-ub- bhru-
September-October & October-November
(such) wealth the fourth of the six seasons (of) clouds (of) (like) (whose)

wibbhrumum jiwitum sámányun chu bhoomidunu- phulum uwuguch-
sport (is) (such) life (it is) common also land-grant (of) fruit know-

chhudbhi*h*r (47) ágámi- nrooputibhi*h* usmut wunshue*h* wá uyum asmud- dhur-
ing succeeding kings by our descendants by or this our charitable

mudaya*h* sumunoomuntuwya*h* prutipáluníyu*h* chu|| ooktun chu Rámuchun-
grant duly should be observed should be preserved also (it is) said also Ramchun-

dreuu sámányuh uyum dhurmusetoo*h* nroopánám kále-kále páluniya*h*
dru by common this a charity-bridge kings of time and time in should be preserved

---

(42) A particular section of the Yujoorwed.

(43) Bramhanical property is considered as a great bane to the family of any one that takes it by unfair means.

(44) na is wanting on the plate.

(45) should be ttá.

(46) Unooswar over ya is wanting.

(47) Two Wisurgs written by mistake for one.

bhuwudbhih surwán ewum bhawinuh parthiwendrán bhooyobhooyah yachute
you by all to thus future kings to again (and) again begs

Rámuchundrenuh|| shushti- wurshu suhusráni swurge tishthuti bhoomidah áchch-
Ramchundru sixty years (of) thousands heaven in stays a land-donor a des-

hetá chu anoomuntá chu táni ewu nuruke wuset|| swu-duttám
troyer (of land) also an abettor and those (years) very hell in abides self-given

puru-duttám wá yah huret-too (48) wusoondhurám swu- wishtá (49) yám
others (by) given or who takes away land own hell in

kri (50) mih bhootwá pitroobhih suhu puchchyute|| prusrootyá
a worm having become forefathers by along with lingers a single handful by (51)

sumprudánenu duttusyu áhurunenu chu junmu- prubhrooti yut duttum
granting by given thing (of) resumption by also birth from what (is) given

tut surwum nishphulum bhuwet || kulpu-koti-suhusráni
that all unfruitful becomes 4,320,000,000 × 10,000,000 × 1,000

kulpu-koti-shutani chu niwuset Brumhunoloke bhoomidánum
4,320,000,000 × 10,000,000 × 100 also abides Brumha (of) world in land donation

dudáti yah|| shiwum astoo surwujugutuh Omnumah (52) Shiwáyu. 1
gives who blessing be the whole universe of Om-bow Shivu for.

---

(48) huretu would be better in place of huret-too.

(49) should be wishthá.

(50) kri is written for kree.

(51) giving alms with a double-handful is held meritorious by the Shastras.

(52) Om, a mystic word (representing the Hindoo Trinity), signifies also good, &c. &c., and is always prefixed to the word "Namah," a reverential bow.

Table explanatory of the Plate character (88 ...) A.D. 933.

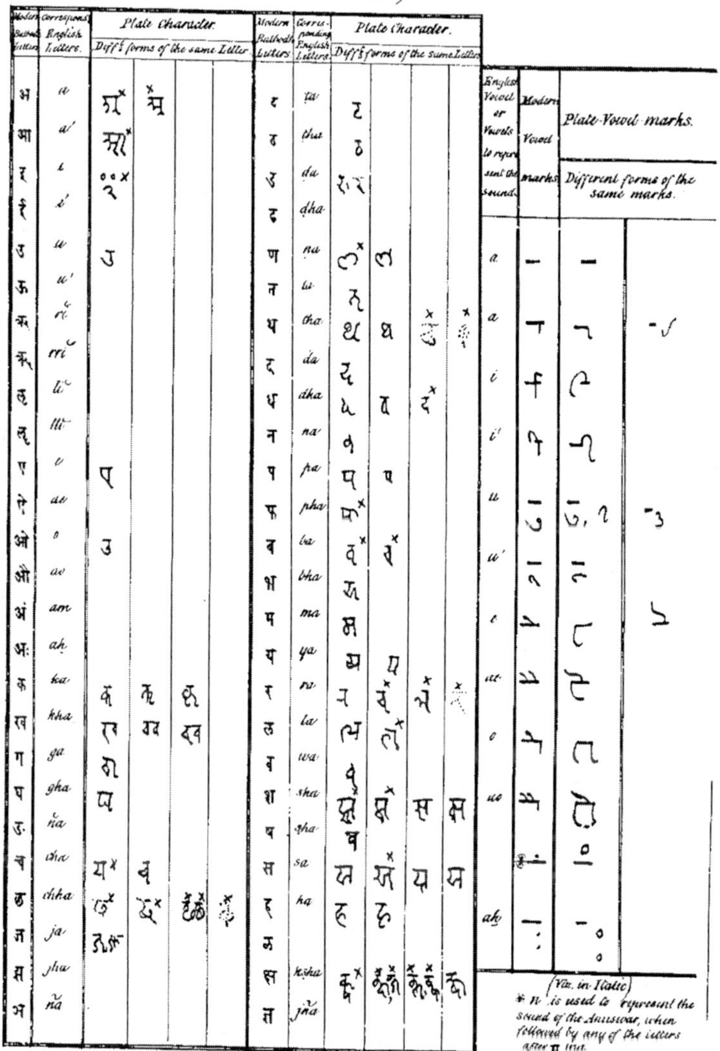

Modern Balbodh Letters	Corresponding English Letters	Modern Balbodh Letters	Corresponding English Letters
अ	a	ट	ta
आ	a'	ठ	tha
इ	i	ड	da
ई	i'	ढ	ḍha
उ	u	ण	na
ऊ	u'	त	ta
ऋ	ri	थ	tha
ॠ	rri	द	da
ऌ	lri	ध	dha
ॡ	llri	न	na
ए	e	प	pa
ऐ	ai	फ	pha
ओ	o	ब	ba
औ	au	भ	bha
अं	am	म	ma
अः	ah	य	ya
क	ka	र	ra
ख	kha	ल	la
ग	ga	व	wa
घ	gha	श	sha
ङ	ṅa	ष	sha
च	cha	स	sa
छ	chha	ह	ha
ज	ja	ळ	
झ	jha	क्ष	ksha
ञ	ña	ज्ञ	jña

English Vowel or Vowels to represent the sound	Modern Vowel marks	Plate Vowel marks: Different forms of the same marks
a		
a'		
i		
i'		
u		
u'		
e		
ai		
o		
au		
*		
ah		

(Viz. in Italic)
* n is used to represent the sound of the Anuswar, when followed by any of the letters after ग &c.

Dotted letter indicates that its exact form is somewhat doubtful.

*Letters thus marked are differed from any to be found in Prinsep's Tables.

Most of the unmarked letters resemble those of the Kutila inscription Table, A.D. 992.)

Fac-simile of three Copper Plates

in possession of a Native Gentleman,

at Sawunt Waree

Shuku 855,

A.D. 933.

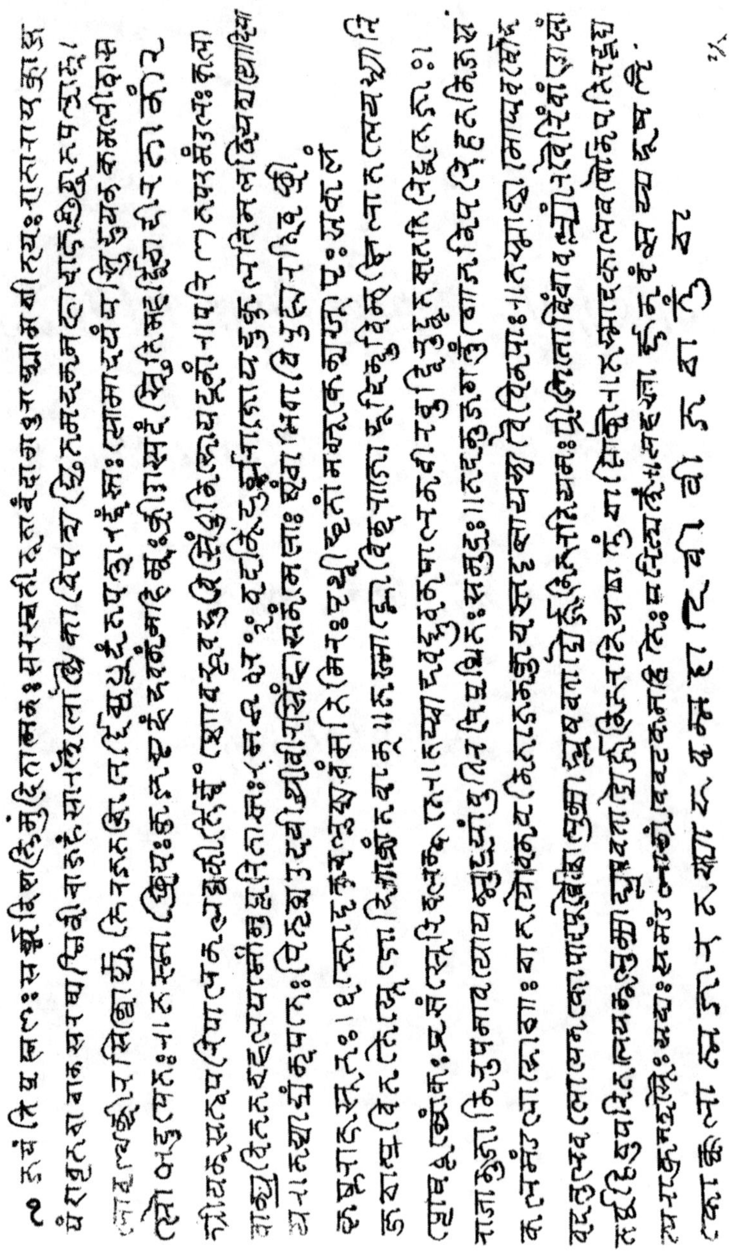

स्तू त्तोकमि॥ वंदीनाद्रुतमि वेर्ह्मरुस्य लिपकद्ध नक्कुराक्कमतः। कोक्कूत्लस्मुतस लब्रह्मकत्लवल्लिकल्लीः स
त्तुत्सक्का॥ या ज्ञाया याज्ञाय ताकात्सक्को स्मुस्य मही दुरः दीम त्सकार्कुकोपाः यत्क्तोदूषणस्य॥ त्विकः॥
तत्कूजबाकुंवोदय्यवरलीयनतः पूतायकलिमात्मात्मक्मामंरमडदीत्ता जकिविदुयीना जमार्कुरेः॥ यिलिव
लितसकत्महूस्मत्मक्का त्कुदादिमुत्कुदुजवकूः यकि मिषदर्शवाया त्वया यः स्तत्मिर्हुदूनाकंः स्मतिव
दर्प्य दत्ल त्कमीर्त्केहस्या सांकुत्लेकोक्कूल्लः सतिपा दिताद्य स्मुण त्कात्षार्ह्मीवा दूस्मुतः तस्मुत्तोक्का लादवक्ष्मतिव
त्तमूरमाद्विरा स्वा रुवसत्मे यांवुकि त्वेनुत्मे वहिमयक्कामूः क्कमादस्मू तोः॥ स्मीकुतल्तुतसीं स्मूकुञ्चदूय तेर्दि
जंष्वायंत्ता विकूनाद्रमामाकामादिसत्रयत्सोकूर्यः नाल्तोवा त्वोरपनाक्मुरवंभ्य दियापे साद्यमंगीन्कनं त्वा
वामना दिदिः कुरनितेनावर्हिर्हनमायद्धाः॥ होवात्योरपनाक्मुरवंवदियापे साद्यमंवीकनं स्मा
वोकासममसाह त्सेष्मुदुवत्मेययता हस्मांकाद्यवतू॥ दर्शक्मनुवल्तुवर्षः प्रदूतपर्षापिकमकश।
ना किः उवादविदत्मत्मेककांहममयमकत्ता दितिरु त्मेनुकुः॥ यद्विदिगिहयावसत्ने तित्रुस्न
दसंडमस्मावमवदूः॥ सयदिकत्सतिषा त्लिमहायूतोष्ठ तककाम्कुयिवर्कितान॥ सहत्तुरि मंडलादिपंय
नत्ग त्योस्मुदयीसमुद्यतंः तिज्ञात दिया ठिपाग्रात्वविवम्मुावपियस्यक्षवाल॥ स्त्र वमत पकमंजले
स्त्रतंसदविज्यश दिवम्म॥ त्साद्विरंसम्महिमकरातान त्लंविरं किजात जसूलियय्या ना डूत्तेना॥ सह
त्मसमताद्विवीनयैवपन्नवांसवितसषमात्विशीं पदविंदितनाजमं दिरं रवुवां सायमुनाव त्सेवते॥
य त्सीनं क्काजकि त्सोनादं मितर्हितानि दितमू तिद्विमाकद्मि तिनिष्पा सीक्कादावोषुकवासंसा यथ्यद्वांमपुता
पात्म्यवहत्म त्सिदवककूतंकीत्म त्मेप्याद्विस्पूर्हिदूल वास्मुण्ग एयिसल त्म्वोवविघ्युदिन्यासाः
दुर्वीनानी स्कुंदस्मु त्मदत्मस्मात्मक्कोक्किकाक्नावतानामूकुद्री नाप्विमेषादरदुवनयस्तारासिरिषं
दितावि श।

3j

यस्मिंश्चंद्रकान्तावमोनुकमनक्षांत्योत्नमाल्लिर्दैप्यवोमयूँमपषुकोमवसवसति लुम्श्मीः ततापायनं के
तक्षापततोल्लसक्रिरुनरुः पुंरुां वकातादतदुत्वाईपनस्वनत्वेकुलतयाद्यायालकुत्वे। स्थितं॥ यमुस मु
पहस्नितहनकयकदहप्रविहितानित्यकन्दर्परूपत्सोदंर्यदर्पः श्रीमित्यकन्दर्पः। प्रद्युम्नं ग्रुमकृप पैहि
त्ला साहसत्कैसमाक्षिपूलस्तमुददसुददम्या ग्पादतक्ष्मुदवः। प्रचितेकविकृयाक्रांतवसुं धनाहितक्यारप
नायणः श्रीविक्रांतनानायण॥ स्वकनकलिताहतिफलदलितविपक्षपक्षस्थलक्षेत्रः श्रीवपतितणरुः॥
समदवसवपरमवयद्भानकमहानाज्ञाविनारुपनत्मेस्वरश्रीमहिथवर्षादिवपादानुध्यातपरमदेव न
कमहानाज्ञाविनाजुपनत्मेस्वरश्रीमनुवल्गुवर्षदेवपथ्वीयवसरश्रीमद्गुल्मदवर्तेन्द्रदेवः कुशलीसर्यालद
ययास्वंववयामकाश्चपतिविषयपतिग्रामकूटमहत्तनयुक्ताकापयुक्तकातिका
निकामगादिसलमनुवः संविदितं यथा माव्यवेवटमाजवारीखिनतनावमूनिकमाता
पिटोर्नात्मनश्च पुण्ययाम्ना क्रिदव्यमूर्व्विनुप्रामपिदवव्योनाशुहानाव्युतिपालय
ताप्रतिदिकं यविनवदिनमथ्याग्रामस्ता सवाविमततः श्रयद्धतास्तकनपका त्यातीतसंवत्सन
सतत्वसूसुपंयपंबास्दविकेषुकातापिसंवत्सना ५०॥ प्रवर्तमानदिरुय सं व सातीत र्म
तश्रीवरगपोर्तुनाथ्यांवावालवपुताः प्रज्ञदिदूपदानसुपुप्रथमकालादकारितसाक्षिणलःपुंउव
दूरवारविविर्क्तरत्को स्निकसलोगतूदारिकाएसवुक्षवानिदामादनदहसुताय
केसवदीक्षितायनामपुनीसपूस्ततांतक्षीतत्म्यादश्रामः सवक्षमालाकुलः स
धान्यहिरण्यादेयः सदएव्योबदसायनावसद्धलापातुप्रत्ययः श्लावादरहदग्रवक्ष
४

स्नातोदनात्याब्रह्मदायमात्यमावंद्रा र्कंमनाम्नादतः पश्चासाघाटाः पूर्वतः प्योाड
ग्रामः दक्षिणतः वंकुलीनामाग्रामः पश्चिमतः विदं विहन्दनाम्ना ग्रामः उत्तरतः
सोकुदीनामाग्रामः एवंचतुराघाट विशुद्धं त्याद ग्रामं केसवदीक्षितस्यात एतः क
र्षयितारुत्तोद्गारयतोवाम के विघ्नाघातः कार्यः मद्रा किसाक्षोलितलतसंवात
पलमेकर्षयंत्रायदस्नु विद्गुमंडी विर्तसामामां यदूमियाकपालमदठाद्भिः नाया
मिकपतिक्रिवस्म दूदेवीयम स्मद्दूर्म्मदायंः सम्नकुमं तव्याः प्रतिपालनीयश्च॥ उक्तं
वनामनुदेरणा॥ सामान्योयं धर्मसेतुर्नृपाणं कालेकालेपालनीयो
भवद्भिः सर्वानेतान्भाविनः पार्थिवेंद्रान्भूयो भूयो याचते
रामचन्द्रः॥ षष्टिं वर्षसहस्राणि स्वर्गे तिष्ठति भूमिदः। आच्छेत्ता चानुम
न्ता च तान्येव नरके वसेत्॥ स्वदत्तां परदत्तां वा यो हरेत वसुंधरां
स विष्ठायां कृमिर्भूत्वा पितृभिः सह पच्यते॥ प्रशस्ता संप्रदाके मद
नुयाहरणामचररूप्यप्रद्युतिपदकेन सर्वे किंचानूनं स्यात्॥ क
ल्पकोटिसहस्राणि कल्पकोटिशतानि च। वसन्ति विष्णुलोके तु ये
च भूमिदा धर्म्मपालकाः॥ शिवमस्तु सर्वदेशवासतः॥ उक्तमः शिवाय नमः

These copper tablets with holes for the usual ring, were received from Atmaram Shiwram Chitnees, of Sawunt Waree, who received them from his relations living at Bagnee, near Sanglee. They are in an excellent state of preservation, and appear never to have been under ground. They bear the Shakiwahun Shuk 855, corresponding with the Christian Era 933. Their dimensions are 13 inches in length, $9\frac{2}{4}$ inches in breadth, and $\frac{3}{10}$ of an inch in thickness.

Transcript in Balbodh of three Copper Plates in possession of a Native Gentleman at Sawunt Waree.

Shuku 855, A.D. 933.

७ अथ तिब्रह्मणः सर्गनिष्पत्तिमुदितात्मनः सरस्वतीहूतानंदा मधुरास्सामगीतयः ॥ ताराचक्राब्ज
षंडावृतगगनसरष्यभिनीराजहंसा ॥ त्रैलोक्यैकाधिपत्यस्थितमदनमहाराजशुद्धातपत्रात्
लावण्यक्षीरसिंन्धोर्द्युतिरजतगिरेर्दिग्वधूदंतपश्चा ॥ हंशः सोमादयं यास्त्रिभुवनकमलावास
सौधादुपेतः ॥ तस्माच्छ्रियः कुलग्रहभवनमहिम्नः क्रीडास्पदं स्थितिमहर्द्धिगभीरतानां ॥
आयन्मसत्वपरिपालनलब्धकीर्त्तिर्वंशो बबूव भुवि सिंधुनिभो यदूनां ॥ परिणतपरमंडलः कला
चान्प्रविततबहलयशोंशुपूरिताशः ॥ शशधर इव दन्तिदुर्णराजो यदुकुलविमलवियत्यथोदिया
य ॥ तस्याद्यं नृपतेः पितृव्य उदयी श्री वीरसिंहासनं मेरोः श्रृंगमिवाधिरुह्य रविवच्छ्रि
कृष्णराजस्ततः ॥ ध्वस्तोद्दृक्तचलुक्यवंशतिमिरः पृथ्वीभृतां मस्तकेन्यस्ताङ्घ्रः सकलं
जगत्प्रथितैस्तेजोभिराक्रांतवान् ॥ तस्माद्गोविंदराजोभूदिन्दुबिम्बशिलातले यस्यारि
प्लोषधूम्रांकः प्रशस्तिरिवलक्ष्यते ॥ तस्याभवन्भुवनपालनवीरबुद्धिरुद्धूतशत्रुकुलसंततिरिद्धतेजाः ॥
राजानुजो निरुपमापरनामधेयो यन्मुद्रयां बुधिरपिप्रथितः समुद्रः ॥ तदनु जगत्तुंगोजनिपरि
हृतनिजमंडलाभोगाः गतयौवनवनिताजनकुचसदृशा यस्य वैरिनृपः तस्माच्चा
मोघवर्षोभवदतुलबलो येन कोपादपूर्वैश्चालुक्याभ्भूषरवाद्यैर्ज्जनितरतियमः प्रीणितोविंग
वल्ल्यां ॥ वैरिस्त्रांडोदरांतर्बहिरुपरितलेयन्नलब्धावकाशं तोयव्याजाद्विशुद्धं यश इव निहितं तज्ज
गत्तुंगसिंधौ ॥ तस्मादकालवर्षो नृपतिरभूद्यत्पराक्रमत्रस्तैः सद्यः समंडलाग्रं खेटकमहि
तैः परित्यक्तं ॥ सहस्रार्जुनवंशस्य भूषणं कोकुलात्मजा ॥ तस्याभवन्महादेवी जगत्तुंग

स्तस्तोजनि ॥ गंभीराद्दलनिधेर्भूभृत्प्रतिपक्षरक्षणक्षमतः । कोकाल्लमुत्तरणविग्रहजलधेर्लक्ष्मीः स
समुत्पन्ना ॥ साजायाजायताजातशत्रोस्तस्य महीभुजः भीमसेनार्जुनोपात्तयशोभूषणशालिनः ॥
तत्रजगत्तुंगोदयधरणीधरतः प्रतापकलितात्मालक्ष्म्यानंदनउदितोजनि विजयी राजमार्त्तण्डः ॥ स्थितिश्च
लितसकलभूभृत्पक्षच्छेदाभिमुक्तभुजवज्रः अनिमिषदर्शनयोग्यो यः सत्यमिहेंद्रराज इति ॥ यस्तस्मिन्दशकंठ
दर्पदलने श्रीहैहयानां कुले कोक्कलः प्रतिपादितोस्य च गुणज्येष्ठोर्ज्जुनोभूत्सुतः तत्पुत्रो ग्गणदेव इत्यतिब
लस्तस्माद्द्विजास्त्वाभवत्पद्मेयांबुनिधरूमे वहिमवन्नाम्नः क्षमाभृत्प्रभोः ॥ श्रीन्द्रनरेंद्रात्स्यां सूनुरभून्नृपतिर्द्वि
जांबायां गोविन्दराजनामकाधिकरूपसौंदर्यः ॥ सामर्थ्ये सति निन्दितां प्रविहितां नैवाग्रजे क्रूरताबन्धुः स्त्री
गमनादिभिः कुचरितैरावर्जितंनायशः । शौचाशौचपराङ्मुखं न च भियापैशाच्यमंगीकृतं त्या
गेनासमसाहसैश्च भुवने यस्साहसांकोभवत् ॥ वर्षन्सुवर्णवर्षः प्रभूतवर्षोपि कनकधा
राभिः जगदखिलनेककांचनैर्मयमकरोदितिजनैरुक्तः ॥ यद्दिग्विजयावसरे सतिप्रस
भसंभ्रमभावनएवभूः । सपदि नृत्यति पालिमहाध्वजोच्छ्रुतकरान्यकुनाथविवर्जिता ॥ सहते हि मंडलाधिपंप
रमेयोभ्युदयी समुद्धृतं । इति जातभियाधियाग्रतो रविचंद्रावपि यस्य धावते ॥ अवनतपरंमंडले
श्वरं सहविजयरट्टभिवेश्मशोभितं समहिमकरतोरणचिरं निजतेजस्तति यस्य राजते ॥ सह
तेसमताहिधीनयंनपरेषां सविशेषशालिनीं । यदनिंदितराजमंदिरं ननु गंगायमुनाच सेवते ॥
यस्मिन्राजनि सौराज्यं निर्ज्जिताशिवितन्वति विमानस्थितिरित्यासीन्नभोगेषु कयाचन ॥ यस्योद्दामप्रता
पानलवहलशिखाकज्जलंनीलमेघाविस्फूर्ज्जत्खड्गधारास्फुरणविसरणान्येवविद्युद्विलासाः ॥
दुर्व्वारारीभकुंभस्थलदलनगलन्मौक्तिकान्येवताराश्चंद्रक्षीराब्धिशेषाभृतभुवनयशोराशिनिष्पं
दितानि ॥

यस्मिन्कंटकशोधनोत्सुकमनस्यंभोजनालैर्भूयेयोन्मग्नंनपयस्तुकोशवसतिलक्ष्मीः कृतोपयनंके
तक्यापवनोल्लसन्निजरजःपुंजांधकारोदरेभूगर्भेप नसेनवेत्रलतयाह्याप्यातमशुद्धेस्थितं ॥ यश्च ससु
पहसितहरनयनदहनेविहितानित्यकंदर्प्परूपसौंदर्यदर्प्पः श्रीनित्यकंदर्प्पः ॥ प्रभुमंत्रशक्त्युपबृंहि
तोत्साहशक्तिसमाक्षिप्तशतमुखसुखश्चाणक्यचतुर्म्मुखः ॥ प्रथितैकविक्रमाक्रांतवसुंधराहितकरणप
रायणःश्रीविक्रांतनारायणः ॥ स्वकरकलितहेतिहलदालितविपक्षवक्षस्थलक्षेत्रःश्रीनृपतित्रिणेत्रः
समभवत्तस्य परमभट्टारकमहाराजाधिराजपरमेश्वरश्रीमन्नित्यवर्षदेवपादानुध्यातपरमभट्टार
कमहाराजाधिराजपरमेश्वरश्रीमत्सुवर्ण्णवर्षदेवपृथ्वीवल्लभश्रीमद्वल्लभनरेंद्रदेवः कुशली सर्व्वानेव
यतासंद त्यमानकान्राष्ट्रपतिविषयप्रतिग्रामकूटमहत्तरयुक्तकोपयुक्तकाधिका
रिकान्समादिशत्यस्तुवः संविदितं यथा मान्यखेटराजधानीस्थिरतरांवस्थानेन माता
पित्रोरात्मनश्च पुण्ययशोभिवृद्धये पूर्व्वलुप्तानपि देवभोगाग्रहारान्प्रतिपालय
ताप्रतिदिनंचानिरवधिनमस्य ग्रामशासनानि शतसः प्रयच्छता शकनृपकलातीतसंवत्सर
शतेष्वष्टसु पंचपंचाशदधिकेष्वंकतोपि संवत्सराणां ८५५ प्रवर्तमानविजयसंवत्सरांतर्ग
तश्रावणपौर्ण्णमास्यांवारे गुरोः पूर्व्वाभद्रपदानक्षत्रे प्रथमकरोदकांतिसर्गेण ॥ पुंडव्र
ईननगरविनिर्गतकौशिक सगोत्रवाजिकण्वसब्रह्मचारिदामोदरभट्टसुताय
केशवदीक्षिताय रामपुरीसप्तशतांतर्ग्गतलोहग्रामः सवृक्षमालाकुलः स
धान्यहिरण्यादेयः सदंण्डदोषदशापराधसभूतोपात्तप्रत्ययः आचाटभटप्रवेश

थतोत्तरायोब्रह्मदायन्याचेनाचंद्रार्क्कनमस्योदत्तः यस्यचाघाटाः पूर्व्वतः घोडे
ग्रामः दक्षिणतः बंजुलीनामाग्रामः पश्चिमतः विंचविहरनामाग्रामः उत्तरतः
सोन्नहीनामाग्रामः एवंचतुराघाटविशुद्धंलोहग्रामंकेशवदीक्षितस्यकृषतः क
र्षयतोभुंजतोभोजयतोवानकेबिहूधाघातः कार्यः मत्दानिलान्दोलितजलतरंगत
रलमैश्वर्यंशरदभ्रविभ्रमंजीवितंसामान्यंचभूमिदानफलमवगच्छद्भिः रागा
मिनृपतिभिरस्मद्वंश्येर्वा यमस्मद्धर्म्मदायः समनुमंतव्यः प्रतिपालनीयश्च ॥ उक्तं
च रामचंद्रेण ॥ सामान्योयंधर्म्मसेतुर्नृपाणांकालेकालेपालनी
योभवद्भिः सर्वानेवभाविनः पार्थिवेंद्रान्भूयोभूयोयाचते
रामभद्रः ॥ षष्टिवर्षसहस्राणिस्वर्गेतिष्ठतिभूमिदः ॥ आच्छेत्ताचानुमं
ताचतान्येवनरकेवसेत् ॥ स्वदत्तांपरदत्तांवायोहरेत्तुवसुंधरां
स्वविष्टायांकृमिर्भूत्वापितृभिस्सहपच्यते ॥ प्रसृत्यासंप्रदानेनद
त्तस्याहरणेनच ॥ जन्मप्रभृतियद्दत्तंतत्सर्व्वंनिष्फलंभवेत् ॥ क
ल्पकोटिसहस्राणि कल्पकोटिशतानिच ॥ निवसद्ब्रह्मणोलो
के भूमिदानंददातियः ॥ शिवमस्तुसर्व्वजगतः ॥ ॐ नमःशिवाय ॥

Free Translation, as close to the Sanscrit as the language will admit of. (Date of Plate, Shalivahan Shuk 1182, A. D. 1261.)

1182 years having passed of the blessed Shalivahan era, Rowdru being the current year, Saturday, the 7th of the fortnight of the waning moon of Puoosh (December-January). He who has been honoured with the title of the five great words, as Rayu Dhurneè, Wurahurayu, Butkaripoorayu, Sahus Mullu, and Shree Kanwudeo Rayu, residing in the best city of Kulyan, a descendant of a Kurn, (1) in the Kuliyoog; a sun causing the bud of the lotus-like Chulookyu race to bloom; whose flag carries the golden boar; the ocean of truth; (2) a fulminating cage for sheltering refugees; a devout worshipper of Muheshwur; (3) lord of the empire gained by propitiating Máhádeo by devotion; a black bee sucking the mellifluous lotus-like feet of Shree Kedardeo: since the time of the accession to the throne of such Kanwudeo, Keshow, surnamed Mahajuni, has been the minister. This noble statesman, who is pious, prudent, skilled in arts, whose advice is the head-ornament of all great counsellors, during the merit-giving time of the sun's entrance into Capricorn, has devoutly and spiritual-mindedly assigned the village of Teruwatuk, (4) which he had obtained by the favour of the Raja, with trees and other usually grant-accompanying things, together with all its produce, with power to punish crimes and correct morals within its boundaries, to Keshow Prubhoo, of the Bharudwaj lineage, who is to supervise the eight sacerdotal duties, (5) and to the following deity and other nineteen Bramhuns, pouring water on their hands, and issuing this edict to Goi Ravol, son of Jalhun Ravol. The land called Rhat Seewar, (6) enjoyed by the Shoodras, is assigned to the deity Wimuleshwur, and the land lying near the temple to Madhow Deo, of the Bharudwaj lineage, for the daily worship of and offerings to the deity. The remaining Bramhuns are—3, Nugde Krumait, of the Bharguw lineage; 4, Withul Paishas, of the Kashyup race; 5, Withul Paishas, of the Bharguw lineage; 6, Ookul Paishas, of the Bharudwaj lineage (on whom is bestowed the Brumhuturi); 7, Govind Bhut, of the Gargyu lineage; 8, Somde Bhut, of the Utri lineage; 9, Somde Krumait, of the Wusishth lineage; 10, Keshow Bhut, of the Wusishth lineage; 11, Madheo Bhut, of the Kashyup lineage; 12, Wasoodeo Bhut, of the Moodgul lineage; 13, Pudmun Bhut, of the Wusishth lineage; 14, Madheo Bhut, of the Gargyu lineage;

(1) The name of the half-brother to the Pandoos, famed for munificence.

(2) Or a mine of precious truth. (3) Máhádeo.

(4) Now called Terwun, near Rajapoor, Talooka Vejedroog.

(5) 1, Sacrifices, &c.; 2, consecration of gods, wells, gardens, &c. &c.; 3, the ceremonies closing and concluding long religious observances; 4, predicting eclipses, interpreting them, telling auspicious seasons for undertaking any work; 5, consulting the religious code of laws and institutes, and prescribing therefrom penances, &c.; 6, preaching the Poorans; 7, administering justice; 8, supervision of the religion of the country.

(6) Perhaps Bhat Seewar.

15, Uchyoot Bhut, of the Utri lineage; 16, Wamun Bhut, of the Kashyup lineage; 17, Narayun Bhut, of the Bharudwaj lineage; 18, Narayun Thakoor, of the Bharudwaj lineage (on whom the office of a Chowdhuree, and of a protector of the village, is bestowed); 19, Hurideo Bhut, of the Bharudwaj lineage; 20, Tikul Bhut, of the Bharguw race. Four orchards, called Kurhatuk, are assigned to the holy purpose of permanently supporting the Muth, (7) which is provided with culinary copper vessels, and situated near the temple. Kings descended either from the present or other ruling race of this country must so piously preserve this village grant, as to become enjoyers themselves, too, of beatitude. Many kings, as Sugur and others, made land grants; but whosoever is the lord of the land, to him belongs the merit of preservation thereof. The resumer of land, given either by himself or others, passing sixty thousand years as a worm in hell, is born a wretched Chandal! He that seizes one tola of gold, or a cow, or a bit of land, even of a finger's breadth, is doomed to remain in hell till the annihilation of the elements. It is recorded that no poison should be named equal to the seizure of Bramhanical property, for the former destroys merely the one that takes it, but the latter also one's posterity. To all future rulers, either of my or other race, who will preserve this my grant, I bow down. This is written by Gowind, the auspicious Maheshwuree.

(7) The nearest word for this is perhaps convent.

Translation, as literal as is consistent with the sense in English. (Date of Plate Shalivahan Shuk 1313, A. D. 1391.)

Be our salutation to Máhádevee, over whom waves, as a Chowree, the lofty head-kissing moon; who is like the Moolustumbhu (1) for the erection of the universe! Be glory to the boar (Wishnoo), who came into existence of his own will, and on whose tusk the globe of the earth looks beautiful as a lotus flower on its tube-like pedicle! The gold mountain Meroo rests elegantly on the flower-like globe as the pericarp of the lotus. Bharut (India) and the other continental divisions form the petals of the globe. The seven mountains Koolachul, &c. that surrounded the pericarp Meroo are the stamens which add to the beauty of this flower. India is one of the petals. In its southern half is situated the country of Kurnatuk, through which flows the well known and great river thereof, Toongubhudra. Even its sacred banks are so efficacious as to burn up a forest of sins. On one of the banks is the place of the great god Wiroopakshu. (2) This place is supposed to have the same degree of sacredness as the Ganges. In its vicinity stands the fortified and impregnable capital city Wijuyu, where the females have lotus petal-like long eyes, and possess such exquisite beauty as to resuscitate and rouse up even Kam, burnt up by Máhádevee. (3) As a divine incarnation in the family of Yudoo, Bookkuráj (4) was born of Shree, wife of Achyoot. He was dreadful in war. He defied all his enemies, and lived here as an Indru (god of gods). His són Hurihur, (5) powerful as Indru, went forth to conquer the world. He is worthy of the name, for his name and virtues are the same as those of Wishnoo and Shivu. He, whilst ruling the region formed by the northern bank (6) of a river heard of but not seen, (7) the Eastern Sea, Rama's pool, and the Western Sea, the great kings of all the world fall at his feet. By his order his prime minister Madhuwu (8) began to rule Juyuntipoor, the effects of whose sound policy are so admirable that his enemies, while living, enjoy not a moment's rest. His name resounds in every quarter. He, at the head of a large army, set out with an intention of subduing countries.

(1) The name of a particular stone column, carved at its capital with various grotesque figures, erected before the undertaking of any structure.

(2) Now called Humpíwiroopakshu.

(3) The Indian Cupid, of whom it is related that one day, when attempting to subdue Máhádevee while absorbed in meditation, he was burnt up by the god's third fiery eye.

(4) Also called Bookunu.

(5) Wishnoo and Shivu.

(6) The original appears to include the river.

(7) Perhaps the river Indus or Attock, which the Hindoos are prohibited by their religious code to cross.

(8) The Hindoo author, who wrote a commentary on the Veds, and works on the laws and institutes of Munoo, on theology, astronomy, physic, and other subjects, which are extant, and held in great estimation.

A capital, surrounded by a sea, in the Konkun, and bearing the name Goa, was environed by an ocean of his forces. This heroic minister banished all the numerous Toorooshkhas (9) infesting the country, and set up again Suptukotishwur, and the other ancient idols that had been rooted up and thrown away by them. But Hurihur, there consulting with his ministers, concluded that his empire would be of short duration if the prime minister were not in his own territory. He therefore recalled the minister, and bestowed on him the throne of Juyuntipoor, of which he was now the anointed ruler. Another minister, Nuruhuri, a descendant of Attreyu, and the son, by Umbika of Brumhursh, a Bramhun well versed in the Veds and Shastras, was sent out to Goapoor in his room. Nuruhuri's younger brother Bhaskur is well known. Nuruhuri, a king-like personage, reared up by the rain of ambrosial satisfaction, derived from the favour of benign knowledge as it were a Shunkur, (10) and thus becoming a Kulputaroo (11) to all the learned of his age. Fame, a bride, previous to her wedding with the minister, presented the renown of all his enemies as the offering of Lahyá (parched rice) to the sacred fire of his prowess. She sat on the marriage slab, (12) then stepped upon the seven continents, and proceeded to the heavens, as if to visit and receive personally a blessing from Wusishtha's wife Uroondhutí. (13) The happy and wealthy Madhuwuraj, the chief of great ministers, and the guide of spiritual worshippers, says:—"On Wednesday, during the time of the solar eclipse, when charitable deeds are highly meritorious, in the month of Wueshakhu (April and May) of the Shalivahan current year Prujaputi 1313 (A. D. 1391), I assign, with the pouring of water into which gold has been dropped, as a religious endowment, the village Kuchchur, called also Madhuwupoor, in the country of the same name, Kuchchur, in twenty-five allotments, to twenty-four Bramhuns who are well versed in the Veds and Shastras. Their names and lineage are as follows:—Two of the allotments, the first and twenty-fifth, are given to Domodur Bhut, son of Unuut Bhut, a descendant of Bharudwaj—the latter is granted to him as supervisor over the other Bramhuns; *2nd*, to the grandson of Mahadeo Bhut, and the son of Ununt Bhut, a descendant of Wusishthu; *3rd*, to Wasoodeo Bhut, son of Narusinhu Bhut, a descendant of Attreyu; *4th*, to Kan Bhut, son of Ununt Bhut, a descendant of Bharudwaj; *5th*, to Damodur Bhut, son of Wasoodeo Bhut, a descendant of Attreyu; *6th*, to Máhádeo Bhut son of Narum Bhut, a descendant of

(9) The Pundit asserts that a tribe of Mahomedans who had established themselves at Goa were so called. The flesh-eating Toorooshkhas are mentioned in a plate found near Attock, assigned to about the eighth century, in the collection published in Vol. VI. Royal Asiatic Society's Journal, the word being translated Turks.

(10) Name of Máhádevee, implying good-doer.

(11) A fabulous tree, nourished by ambrosia, which yields whatever may be desired.

(12) Or the crest of a mountain.

(13) A goddess of chastity. This metaphor is throughout founded on the practise of Wiwa huhomu, a ceremony essential at all weddings.

Attreyu; 7*th*, to Wamun Bhut, son of Máhádeo, a descendant of Jumudugni; 8*th*, to Ram Bhut, son of Damodur Bhut, a descendant of Attreyu; 9*th*, to Kan Bhut, son of Ûnunt Bhut, a descendant of Bharudwaj; 10*th*, to Puomnidewu Bhut, son of Withul Bhut, a descendant of Jumudugni Wutsu; 11*th*, to Ununt Bhut, son of Máhádeo Bhut, a descendant of Kootsu; 12*th*, to Ununt Bhut, son of Keshow Bhut, a descendant of Jumudugni; 13*th*, to Junardun Bhut, son of Govind Bhut, a descendant of Attreyu; 14*th*, to Wishnoo Bhut, son of Ramkrishnu Bhut, a descendant of Jumudugni; 15th, to Huri Bhut, son of Damodur, a descendant of Attreyu; 16*th*, to Gowind Bhut, son of Mandeshi, a descendant of Kuooshik; 17*th*, to Wasoodeo Bhut, son of Withul Bhut, a descendant of Jumudugni; 18*th*, to Puomnidewu Bhut, son of Gowind Bhut, a descendant of Kuooshik; 19*th*, to Máhádeo Bhut, son of Huri Bhut, a descendant of Jumudugni Wutsu; 20*th*, to Tan Bhut, son of Narayun Bhut, a descendant of Wusishthu; 21*st*, to Bhutum Bhut, son of Máhádeo Bhut, a descendant of Jumudugni Wutsu; 22*nd*, to Withul Bhut, son of Namdeo Bhut, a descendant of Bharudwaj; 23*rd*, to Máhádeo Bhut, son of Wamdewu Bhut, a descendant of Bharudwaj; 24*th*, to Keshow Bhut, son of Gowind Bhut, a descendant of Wusishthu.

The boundaries of the so granted village Kuchchur, hence called Madhuwupoor, are as follows:—Pât lies to the east of it; a banian tree and a stone, situate on the summit of the intervening hill, form the eastern boundary line; Mhapun lies to the south; a salt marsh, by the name of Purugulee, (14) in the jungle, forms the southern boundary line, from which runs westward the dam of a smaller marsh. Near this is a ravine, (15) on the beach of the sea. The sea lies exactly to the west, Purualya (16) lies to the north; the Paulote, (17) and the creek beneath it that runs to the sea, form the northern boundary line. The grant of this village, with all its appendages, trees, water, treasure if found, and everything thereon, is made by the consent of the king, his ministers, the chief men of the village, exempt from all sorts of taxation and oppression to the above-mentioned Bramhuns, who may undisturbedly enjoy it. To preserve what has been granted, a common duty incumbent on all kings, is like a bridge for their safety over an ocean of sins. Oh! you monarchs, preserve this bridge at all times, is the constant prayer of your suppliant Ramuchundru. He who resumes what is granted, either by himself or others, is doomed to pass sixty thousand years as a worm in hell.

(14) Now called Purugalwí.

(15) Also ditch, pit, deep hole, chasm.

(16) Now called Purooló, or Puruló.

(17) We have no good English word for this useful term, signifying the line of any ridge or portion of land, from which the water turns in opposite directions.

Transcript of Plate, dated Shuk 1313 (A. D. 1391).

श्रीमहागणाधिपतये नमः ॥ अविघ्नमस्तु ॥ नमस्तुंगशिरश्चुंबि चंद्रचामर
चारवे ॥ त्रैलोक्यनगरालंभ मूलस्तंभाय शंभवे ॥ लीलाकोलः स जयति हरिः कुंद
लक्ष्मीं दधद्य दंष्ट्रानाले नलिनमिव भू मंडलं तद्विभाति ॥ यत्र स्वर्णक्षितिधरपतिः कर्णिका
वर्षपंक्तिः पत्रश्रेणी कुलशिखरिणः केसराणां प्रसारः ॥ तस्मिन्भारत वर्षदक्षिणदले
देशोस्ति कर्णाटकः स्तन्मध्ये सरिदुत्तमा विजयते सा तुंगभद्राभिधा ॥ यत्तीरे दुरिताटवी
हुतवहे देवो विरूपाक्ष इत्यास्ते संततमंतरेण सुमनः स्रोतस्विनी चिंतनं ॥ तस्योपकं
ठे विजयाभिधाना सा दुर्जया राजति राजधानी ॥ यस्यां विरूपाक्षकटाक्ष दग्ध मुज्जी
वयंति स्मरमुत्पलाक्ष्यः ॥ वंशे यदो रभिनवांश इवाच्युतस्य श्रीसंगमादजनिसंगर
रंगभीमः ॥ श्रीबुक्कराज इति धिकृत शत्रुरेष तामध्यतिष्ठदधमध्यम लोकपा
लः ॥ अथ भुवं भवगामिनः सुतं हरिहरिदीशपराक्रमंम् ॥ जगदिनः समजीगमदाद
रा त्स चतुरं चतुरं बुधिमेखलांम ॥ आकर्ण्णस्छ सरिद्वरोत्तरतटा दापूर्वपाथोनिधे
रासेतो रवनिं चिरादवति सत्या पश्चिमांबोनिधेः ॥ स्छाने स्मिन्गुणनामभि हरि
हरो राजाधिराजादिभी राजोर्वीपति मौलिमालितपदां भोजे महीवल्लभे ॥ तस्याज्ञ
या माधवमंत्रिवर्यः प्रशाज्जयंती पुरराज्य मृद्धंम् ॥ यन्मंत्रशक्त्या वपुरुत्सृजंतोप्यरात
यः स्वास्थ्यमंहो भजंते ॥ आशांतविश्रांतयशाः समंत्री दिशो जिगीषु र्मह
ता बलेन ॥ गोवाभिधां कोंकणराजधानीं मन्ये न मन्ये रुणदर्णवेन ॥ प्रतिष्ठितां
स्तत्र तुरुष्कसंघा नुत्पाद्यदोष्णा भुवनैकवीरः ॥ उन्मूलितानां मकरोत्प्रतिष्ठां श्री स
प्तनाथादिसुधा भुजां यः ॥ तस्मिन्नृते क्षितितले सतिकीर्तिशेषं सन्मंत्रिभि र्हरिह
रो नृपतिर्विचार्य ॥ गोवापुरे नृहरिमंत्रिण मादरेण राज्ये पदे समभिषिच्य पुरो
जयंत्याः ॥ आत्रेयान्वय वारिधावुदभव न्मंबांबिका गर्भतः साक्षाद्रूसाभिध
द्विजवरा द्यो भास्करस्याग्रजः ॥ विद्याशंकर सत्कृपामृतरसा सारेण संवर्द्धितो
विद्वत्कल्प महीरुहो नरहरिः क्षोणीपति र्भासते ॥ कृत्वा सप्त पदानि सप्तसु महाद्वा
पेषु भूभृच्छिला मास्थायाथ विमुच्य शात्रव यशो लाजान्प्रतापानले ॥ प्रत्यक्षेण वि
लोकितुं दिवमपि प्राप्ता तथा रुंधती मित्थं कीर्तिवधूः सदा नरहरिं क्षमापं वृणी
ते वरंम् ॥ स्वस्ति श्री शके त्रयोदशाधिक त्रिशतोत्तर सहस्रे गते वर्तमान प्रजा
पति संवत्सरे वैशाखमासे कृष्णपक्षे अमावास्यायां सौम्य दिने सूर्योपराग पु
ण्यकाले स्वस्ति श्रीमन्महा मंत्रीश्वर उपनिषन्मार्ग प्रवर्तकाचार्यः श्रीमन्माधव
राज्ञः कुच्चरविषय वर्तिनं कुच्चरनामानं ग्रामं माधवपुरमिति प्रथितनामदेयं
सर्वमान्यमग्रहारं कृत्वा पंचविंशति वृत्ति कल्पना माकलय्य श्रुताध्ययन
संपन्नेभ्यः चतुर्विंशति ब्राम्हणेभ्यः सहिरण्योदकदान दारापुर्नकं तं ग्रामं सं
प्रदद इति प्रदात्तं धर्मशासनं तेषां ब्राम्हणानां गोत्रनाम विवरणम् ॥ ॥

भारद्वाज गोत्रस्य ऋक् शाखाध्यायिनः अनंतभट्ट पुत्र दामोदरभट्टस्य वृत्ति रेका १ वासिष्ठ गोत्रस्य ऋक् ० महादेव पुत्रानंतभट्ट पुत्रस्य वृत्तिरेका २ आत्रेय गोत्रस्य ऋक् ० नारसिंव्हभट्ट पुत्र वासुदेवभट्टस्य वृत्तिरेका ३ भारद्वा. ज गोत्रस्य ऋक् ० अनंतभट्ट पुत्र दामोदरकानभट्टस्य वृत्तिरेका ४ आत्रेय गोत्रस्य ऋक् ० वासुदेवभट्ट पुत्र दामोदरभट्टस्य वृत्तिरेका ५ आत्रेय गोत्रस्य ऋक् ० नारंभट्ट पुत्र महादेवभट्टस्य वृत्तिरेका ६ जामदग्न्य गोत्रस्य ऋक् ० महादेव पुत्र वामनभट्टस्य वृत्तिरेका ७ आत्रेय गोत्रस्य ऋक् ० दामोदरभट्ट पुत्र रामभट्टस्य वृत्तिरेका ८ भारद्वाज गोत्रस्य ऋक् ० अनंतभट्ट पुत्र कानभट्ट स्य वृत्तिरेका ९ जामदग्न्यवत्स गोत्रस्य ऋक् ० विठ्ठलभट्ट पुत्र पौम्निदेव भट्टस्य वृत्तिरेका १० कुत्स गोत्रस्य ऋक् ० महादेवभट्ट पुत्रानंतभट्टस्य वृत्ति रेका ११ जामदग्न्य गोत्रस्य ऋक् ० केशवभट्ट पुत्रानंतभट्टस्य वृत्तिरेका १२ आत्रेय गोत्रस्य ऋक् ० गोविंदभट्ट पुत्र जनार्दनभट्टस्य वृत्तिरेका १३ जाम दग्न्य गोत्रस्य ऋक् ० रामकृष्ण पुत्र विष्णुभट्टस्य वृत्तिरेका १४ आत्रेय गोत्र स्य ऋक् ० दामोदरभट्ट पुत्र हरिभट्टस्य वृत्तिरेका १५ कौशिक गोत्रस्य ऋ क् ० मांदेशी पुत्र गोविंदभट्टस्य वृत्तिरेका १६ जामदग्न्य गोत्रस्य ऋक् ० विठ्ठलभट्ट पुत्र वासुदेवभट्टस्य वृत्तिरेका १७ कौशिक गोत्रस्य ऋक् ० गोविं दभट्ट पुत्रस्य पौम्निदेवभट्टस्य वृत्तिरेका १८ जामदग्न्यवत्स गोत्रस्य ऋक् ० बाहरिभट्ट पुत्र महादेवभट्टस्य वृत्तिरेका १९ वासिष्ठ गोत्रस्य ऋक् ० नारायणभट्ट पुत्र तानभट्टस्य वृत्तिरेका २० जामदग्न्यवत्स गोत्रस्य ऋक् ० महादेवभट्ट पुत्र भटंभट्टस्य वृत्तिरेका २१ भारद्वाज गोत्रस्य ऋक् ० नामदेव भट्ट पुत्र विठ्ठलभट्टस्य वृत्तिरेका २२ भारद्वाज गोत्रस्य ऋक् ० वामदेवभट्ट पुत्र महादेवभट्टस्य वृत्तिरेका २३ वासिष्ठ गोत्रस्य ऋक् ० गोविंदभट्ट पुत्र केशवभट्टस्य वृत्तिरेका २४ भारद्वाज गोत्रस्य ऋक् ० अनंतभट्ट पुत्र दामोदर भट्टस्य पुनर्महाजनैः अन्या दत्ता वृत्तिरेका २५ एवं पंचविंशति वृ त्तयः कुच्चरिनामधेयस्येदानीं कृतमाधव पुराभिदंतस्या ग्रहारस्य चतुः सीमा विवरणं ॥ पुर्वस्यां दिशि पाटग्रामस्य सीम्नि- पर्वत शिरसि वटवृक्ष पाषाणः ॥ दक्षिणस्यां दिशि म्हापण ग्रामस्य सीम्नि अरण्यमध्यस्थ परगालीति क्षारि क्षेत्रांतर्गतं कृत्वा तत्प्रभृति पश्चिम दिगनुखारीप्रकारं समीपतः समुद्रवेलायां व्हदश्च ॥ पश्चिमस्यां दिशि समुद्रः ॥ उत्तरस्यां दिशि परी ल्य ग्रामस्य सीम्नि प्रवाहादधः समुद्रपर्यंतौ क्षारोदकनदीच ॥ एवं चतुः सी मांतर्गतं माधवपुराग्रहारं सहिरण्योदकदान धारा पूर्वकं सर्व नमस्यं सर्व बाधा विवर्जितं निधि निक्षेप जल पाषाण सिध्यि सहितं चतुर्विंशति ब्राम्ह

णाः सुखेन भुंजीरन् ॥ सामान्योयं धर्मसेतु र्नृपाणां काले काले पाले पालनी यो भवद्भिः ॥ सर्वानेतान् भाविनः पार्थिवेंद्रा न्भुयो भुयो याचते रामचंद्रः स्वदत्तां परदत्तां वा यो हरेत वसुन्धराम् ॥ षष्टि वर्ष सहस्राणि विष्ठायां जायते कृमिः ॥ श्रीशुभमस्तु ॥ ॥

A Facsimile with Transcript in Balbodh,

of three Copper-plates dated Shak 1182 (A.D. 1261.)

॥ स्वस्ति श्री शकु ११८२ वर्षे रौद्र संवत्सरे। पुष्य वदि
सप्तमि शनि दिने। आद्येह समधिगत पंच महाशब्द
महामंडलेश्वर। कल्याणपुरवराधीश्वर। कलियुग
कर्णान्वयप्रसूत। चालुक्य कुलकमलकलिका विकास
भास्कर। सुवर्णवराहलांछन धज सत्य रत्नाकर। शरणाग
त वज्रपंजर। महामाहेश्वर। महेश्वर देव चरण प्रसाद नारा
धर्मोपचारादेवाप्त परमराज्येश्वर। श्री केदारदेवपद
पंकज भ्रमर। रायधरणीवराहराय। बटकाररिपुराय
साहसमल्ल श्री कांवदेव रायविजय राज्योदि। त

द्राज्यभारचालनसमर्थ। आचारनिपुण सारासारविज्ञा

रचतुर। सकलकलाकुशल। महामात्यमंत्रचूडामणि। श्रीकेशवमहा

जनिना। श्रीकांवदेवराय। प्रसादलब्ध। तेरवाटकनाम। धयो

यग्रामः। उत्तरायणसंक्रांतिपर्वणि। परमया भक्त्या। महाधा

मिंढगणभूत्रासखिद्रमाला· कुलासोपरिकर। दंड दोष मा

र्गणसहितचतुःसीमापर्यंतं। निधिनिक्षेपसहितः विंशति

विप्रसहिताय भारद्वाजगोत्रोत्पन्नाय। अष्टभोगसहित

केशवप्रभवे। हस्तोदकेन प्रदत्तः। तदर्थशासनं प्रय

च्छति। तेषामेतानि नामानि। हाटसीवारसंबंधिनी श्रू

द्रप्रजोपजीविनी समग्रा। भूमिं विमलेश्वरदेवस्य। तथा

देवस्य संनिधौ या भूमि। स। भारद्वाज गोत्रस्य। माधवदेवस्य। गं
धधूपनिवेद्यार्थ। भार्गव गोत्र नागदेकमैत। काश्यप गोत्र विठ
लपैशास। भार्गव गोत्र विठलपैशास। भारद्वाज गोत्र। उक
लपैशास। ब्रह्मवसहित। गार्ग्य गोत्र गोइंदभ। अत्रि गो
त्र सोमदेभट। वासिष्ठ गोत्र सोमदेकमेत। वाशिष्ठ गोत्र के
शवभट काश्यप गोत्र। माधवभट। मुद्गल गोत्र। वासुदेवभट
वा·सिष्ठ गोत्र पद्मुमणभट। गार्ग्य गोत्र माधवभट। अत्रि गो
त्र अच्युतभट। काश्यप गोत्र वामनभट। भारद्वाज गोत्र ना
रणभट। भारद्वाज गोत्र नारणठाकुरस्य चौधिविक। सा
ग्रामप्रतिपालकः। भारद्वाज गोत्र हरिदेवभट। भार्गव गोत्र
तिकलभट। एवमेतानिना माभिदेव संनिधौ। तां

ब्रभाजन पूर्वक । शाश्वत मठ धर्मकार्यार्थक ह्लाटकवाटिका
वत्वारि अकसंख्या आह्लेण राउल सुत गोः राउलस्य दातव्य ग्रामो
य मा चान्वय संभूत राज्ञा अपरेण वा धार्मिकेण भूत्वा पालनीयं । य
था दात्रैय भाकुपालका पि भविष्यति । बहुभिर्वसुधा दत्ता राजभिः सगरा
दिभिः । यस्य यस्य यदा भूमिस्तस्य तस्य तदा फलं । स्वदत्तां परदत्तां वा यो
हरेत्य वसुधरां । षष्ठिर्वर्षसहस्राणि विष्ठायां जायते कृमिः । क्रिमि
यो भितततो गत्वा चांडालेष्वभिजायते । हिरण्यमेकं गामेकं भूम्याम
प्येकमंगुलं । हरंनरकमायांति यावदाहुतसंप्लवं । न विषं विषमि
त्याहुर्ब्रह्मस्वं विषमुच्यते । विषामेकाकिनो हंति ब्रह्मस्वं पुत्रपौत्रि
कं । मद्वंशजाताः परवंशजाताः पापादपेतमनसो भुवि भार भूताः । यै
पालयंति मम धर्ममिदं हि सर्वे तेभ्यो मया विरचितांजलिमूर्ध्नि रे
षा । ॥ श्री गोविंदेन विलिखाते । श्री मंगलमाहे श्री ल ट ५

These copper plates, 1 foot long, 7½ inches broad, and 1/30 of an inch thick, composing the Edict dated 1182 (A.D. 1261) are joined by a ring running through them. Wasoodew Ramchundru Shastree procured them, as a loan for deciphering, from Bhaoo Bullal Phunsulkur Khot of the village Bhoon Teruun, and the Manager of Wimuleshwur, the deity thereof. They have been many years in his possession, but once, some years ago, were shewn to the Inam &c. inspecting authorities. The inscription is not in good Sanscrit. This plate would appear to be the same as the one which has been imperfectly translated in English in the Journal of the Royal Asiatic Society of Great Britain and Ireland, Vol. V. Page 177.

No. 96.

From Major G. LeG. Jacob,
Political Superintendent of Sawunt Waree,

To A. Malet, Esq.,
Chief Secretary to Government, Bombay.

Political Department.

Dated 11*th July* 1850.

Sir,

As His Lordship in Council expressed a desire to possess ancient copper-plate inscriptions, I do myself the honour to submit a fac-simile of one written A. D. 1436, together with a translation and key to the character.

2. The original set of plates is in possession of a family residing in the Goa territory, who do not like to part with it, as it is the title-deed to their estate. It is of some historical interest. The establishment in this quarter of a powerful Bramhanical dynasty, in succession to the Chulookyus and Yudoos, seems to be a new bit of history. The numerous conquests, detailed by one of the race, apparently four generations before the grant, were probably mere incursions.

I have the honour to be, &c.

(Signed) G. LeG. Jacob,
Political Superintendent.

Translation of a Sanscrit Inscription on a set of Copper-plates, dated Shuk Shalivahan 1358 (A. D. 1436), *in the possession of the Donee's descendants in the Goa Territory.*

Praise be to Shivu! Glory to the incarnate boar, with whom the deluge of waters was as a pool; on the tip of whose tusk the world looks beautiful as a pearl! The race of the puissant king is thus described:—There was born, on the bank of the Jánhuwí (*i. e.* Ganges) a Bramhun, named Dewu Shurmá, of the lineage of Kashyup, a follower of the Yujoorwed, thoroughly versed in it and the other Veds, the sciences subordinate to them, and the Shastras; true of speech; a subduer of his passions; foremost in knowledge of the deity; humble and devoted to the performance of the six duties. To secure himself from the molestation of the Toorooshkhas, (1) he thence came down to the Konkun, where, in Indul, (2) the best of villages, he was detained and revered by the king. He then obtained the sovereignty, and, by the grace of the Kunukeshwur (3) god Indumanli (*i. e.* Máhádeo), got sons. His sons and grandsons became renowned for their bravery, strength, and other good qualities. From this stock sprung the rich and mighty Jugudeo. Of him was born Ugi, illustrious from his wealth, strong as the gods. From him was born Máyindeo. Victory always attended his war-chariot. After having subdued the rulers of Souráshtru of Lát, of the Dravid country, the powerful Tiling (*i. e.* Tailingan) and Gand (*i. e.* Gour) monarchs, and the descendants of the Yudoo and Hamir races, the hero governs their land. Glory be to him, who lives as long as the world endures; who has conquered all kings, and whose ambrosial fame has filled the world with its never-fading brilliancy. He, by force of arms and power, having expelled the Murathas, (4) who had usurped for twelve years the territory of the Kádumbs, installed on the throne the great Tribhoowunumullu, the son of Wijuyadityu, and out of affection for him undertook to conduct the government. [Here follow three Shloks of inflated verbiage, in praise of the King Bhuiruwu, containing nothing worth translating.] After Máyindeo came Kuidewu, who was succeeded by the powerful Nágudewu, after whom came Bhuiruwu. [Here follows a string of Nágudewu's praises.] Nágudewu, during his stay in the village of Puliku, of which the chief men are Kásars, granted in the month Chuitru, of the Shalivahan year Anal 1358 (*i. e.* A. D. 1436), the village Wurudengí in Inam, with this copper-edict, to Pashum Shetí, the son of Roopu Shetí, obtained through the grace of the goddess Shree Kálíká. It is bounded on the east by Chipolí; on the north by Chándel; on the south by Ojari; and on the west by Wátashandí. [Here follow four Shloks in praise of generosity, and deprecating, as usual, the resumption of Inams.]

(1) A term denoting a cruel people, applied to Mahomedans, or a particular tribe thereof. (*Query* Turkomans?)

(2) Modern Hindlé, in the Salsee Mahal of the Malwan Talooka.

(3) Modern Kunkeshwar, in the same Mahal.

(4) May also mean expelled those who had usurped in Maháráshtrá the power of the Kádumbs, but the Shastree prefers the text.

The following Genealogical Tree is deduced from the foregoing:-

Dewu Shurma'

Jugudewa.

Ugi

Máyinduwu.

Káidewu.

Nagudewu (the donor).

Bhairawa.

Table explanatory of the Plate Character, where the Letters differ from the Modern Sanscrit:

Shalivahan Shuk 2328
1 3 5 8 *(A.D. 1436)*

Modern.	Plate.	Modern	Plate.	Modern	Plate.	Modern	Plate.
अ	अ	ङ	क	म	म	ह	ह
आ	आ	ज	ज	य	य	क्ष	क्ष
उ	उ	ण	ण	ह	प	ज्ञ	ज्ञ
ए	▽	ध	ध	ळ	ह्ल	ि	॥
क	क	न.	न	श	रा,टा	ु	८
च	च	भ	स	स	स	ू	५
						ो	ो

Three Copper Tablets, joined by a ring running through them, and bearing on its handle, as a Seal of the donor, an entire figure of Hanuman, and the mutilated bust of some Deity, most probably Gunuputi,) were received for deciphering from Wamun Ráwu, Chitnis of Sawunt Waree, who obtained a loan of them from Ghír shet, Kásar, living at Mhapsé in the Goa Territory. They are said by the Kasár to have been possessed by his family for some generations. They are in an excellent state of preservation, and appear never to have been under ground. They bear the Shálíwáhun Shuku 1358, corresponding with the Christian Era 1436. They are 9¾ inches long, 7 broad, and 15 cents of an inch thick weighing 8 pounds.

Modern Characters have been written in smaller characters over the old letters, where differing much, to facilitate perusal.

* Precisely as in the Plates themselves, the order of which, it will be seen, is inversed.

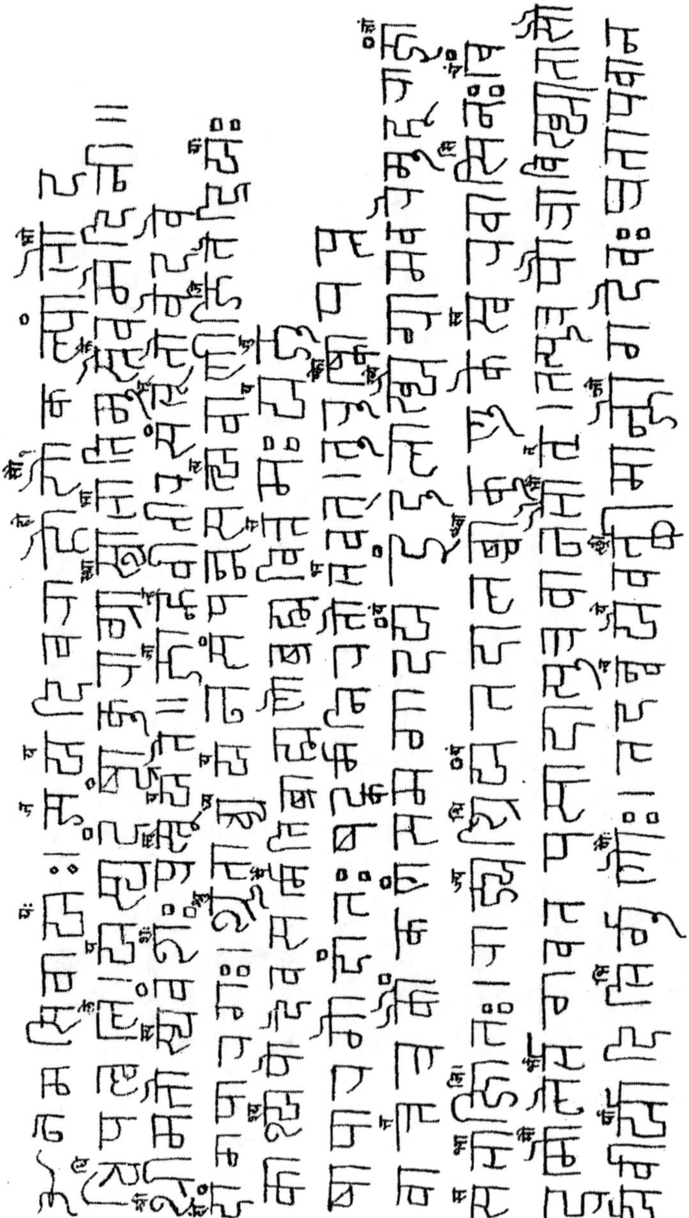

2 m.

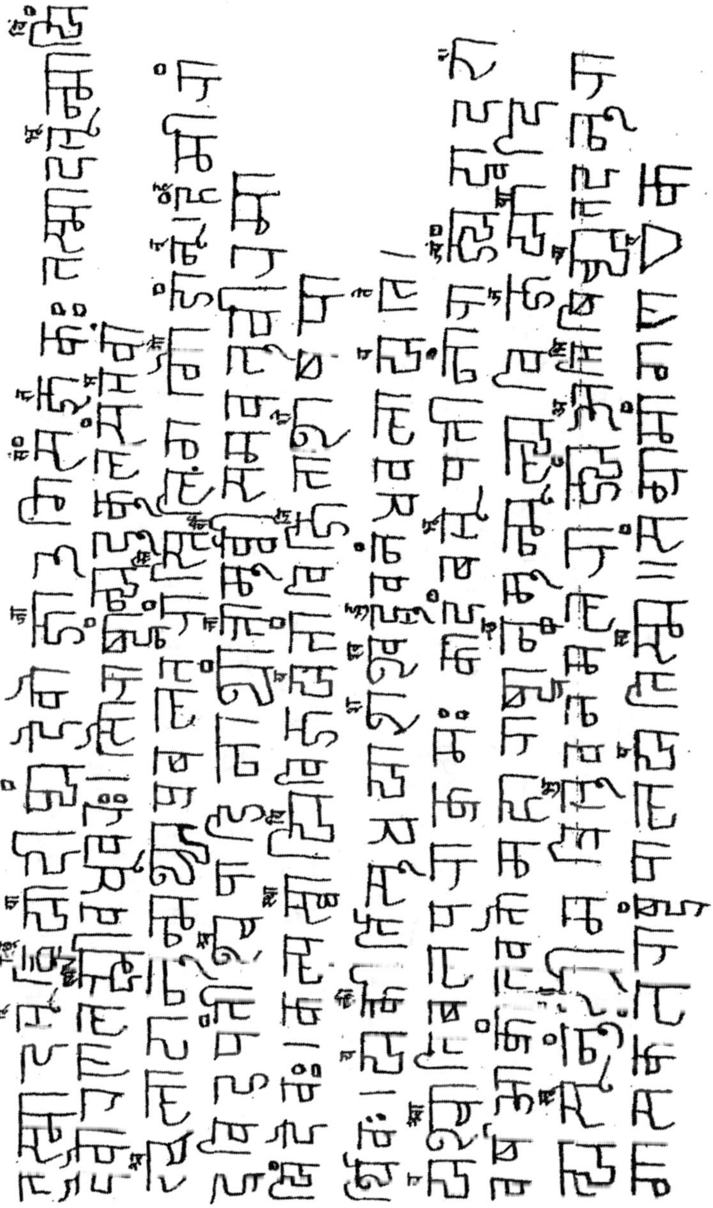

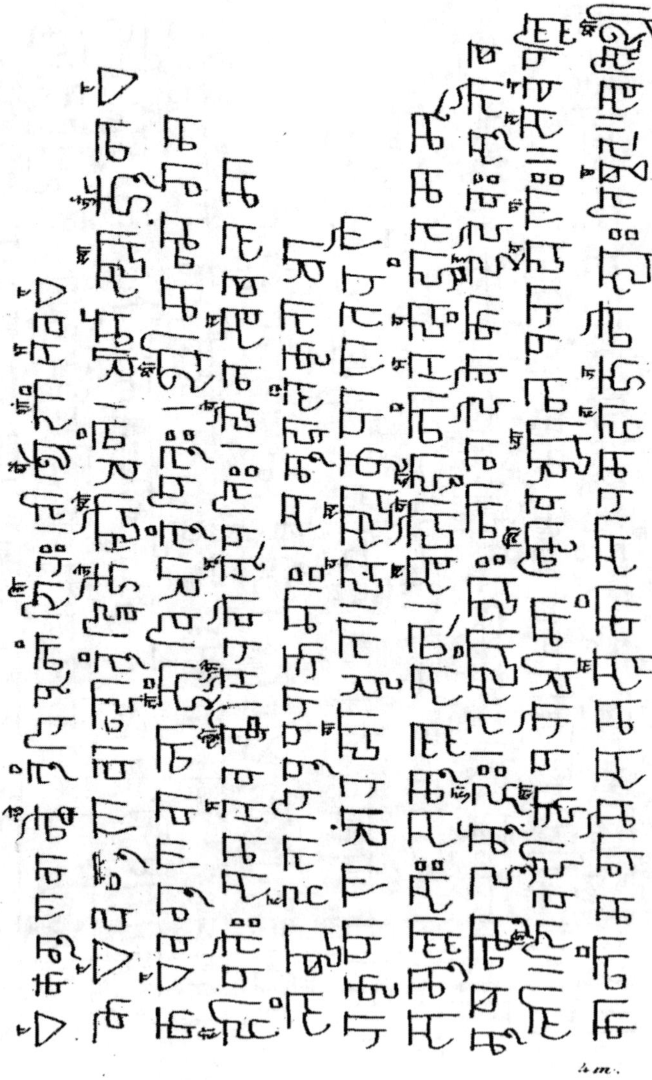

श्री सैंयव देप णेः। वप डुंगी ह्रीमा। स्वर्वन मत्स्य कतु नदी
धले। श्री नह्लु संवत्स्के पे बैत्रे मा से ट२३१४ स कु श्रीका ली
का देवी वप पुत्रेनुप सेठी पुत्रे लषुम सेठी दतं या ह म
तों ह्र सां स लें प्रदातु पुं बंदी सेसी माचीपोली स्रेवीः ३ त्र
दीसे सी माचीं देला वीः टषी। णदी से ३ ऊं टीसे वी
सीमाः पमी मदी से वा टषं डीवीं सीमाः स्रेवं वं तुं प्या

टसीमाः दान पाल्हं न योर्म्भ धो दाना ये योसाल नं दानं स्वर्गमाप्नो
ति। पालनादच्युतं पदं। स्वदत्तं परदत्तं वा। यो हरेत वसुंधरा। सष्टिं वर्ष
सहस्राणि। विष्टायां जायते क्रिमि। स्वर्णमेकं गवामेकं। भूमिरेकमंगुलं
हरं नरक माप्नोति। यावदा भूमि संप्लवं। सामान्यो यं धर्म सेतु र्नृपाणां काले काले
कालेपाल्हन्येयो भवद्भिः। सर्वानेतान् भाविनः पार्थिवेंद्रान् भूयो भूयो याचते रामचंद्र

No. 3891 of 1850.

Political Department.

To the Secretary to the

Bombay Branch of the Royal Asiatic Society.

Sir,

I am directed by the Right Honorable the Governor in Council to transmit to you, for submission to the Bombay Branch of the Royal Asiatic Society, copy of a letter from the Political Superintendent of Sawunt Waree, dated the 11th ultimo, No. 96, with the fac-simile of a Sanscrit inscription which accompanied it, and to request that the Society will favour Government with any remarks on the subject which they may have to offer.

I have the honour to be, &c.

(Signed) J. G. Lumsden,
Secretary to Government.

Bombay Castle, 19th August 1850.

No. 5 of 1851.

To H. E. Goldsmid, Esq.,

Secretary to Government, Bombay.

Sir,

I have the honour to acknowledge the receipt of your letter No. 1214, dated 20th March last, referring me to a former letter, No. 3891, dated 19th August last, and accompaniments, from A. Malet, Esq., Chief Secretary to Government, and, in reply thereto, to acquaint you, for the information of the Right Honorable the Governor in Council, that the fac-simile of the Sanscrit inscription, forwarded with the latter, has been submitted for examination to the Rev. Dr. Stevenson, whose remarks on it are contained in the annexed extract from the Proceedings of the Monthly Meeting of the Society, held on the 24th ultimo.

I am also directed to state, that this fac-simile will be published in the next No. of the Society's Journal.

I have the honour to be, &c.

(Signed) Henry J. Carter,
Secretary B. B. R. A. Society.

Bombay, Town Hall, 8th May 1851.

Extract from the Proceedings of the Bombay Branch Royal Asiatic Society, held on the 24th April 1851.

" This ancient inscription from the Konkun, for which the Society is indirectly indebted to Major LeGrand Jacob, certainly contains rather a curious piece of the ancient history of the Konkun, and deserves to be preserved on that account. As to the date, I should read, instead of Shuk 1358, Shuk 1374; however, the difference is not material. I should also place the last name in the list before the two that now precede it. With these changes, I approve of the view given of the contents of the inscription."

(True copy)

(Signed) HENRY J. CARTER,
Secretary B. B. R. A. Society.

A STATISTICAL REPORT

ON

PORTUGUESE INDIA.

A GENERAL, STATISTICAL, AND HISTORICAL REPORT

ON

PORTUGUESE INDIA;

DESCRIPTIVE OF

THE GEOGRAPHICAL POSITION OF THE PRINCIPAL PORTS; TERRITORIAL DIVISIONS; PERIODS OF ACQUISITION; AND DETAILS RESPECTING AGRICULTURE, COMMERCE, &c.

WITH NOTES,

CONTAINING INFORMATION RELATIVE TO THE DIFFERENT SUB-DIVISIONS, WITH THEIR REVENUE, &c. &c.

TO WHICH IS APPENDED

An Account of the Convents suppressed in 1835;

WITH PARTICULARS RELATIVE TO THEIR FOUNDATION, REVENUES, &c.

EXTRACTED, IN 1850, FROM OFFICIAL DOCUMENTS,

BY

CAPTAIN JOAQUIM JOSE CICILIA KOL,

(LATE) CHIEF SECRETARY TO THE GOVERNMENT OF PORTUGUESE INDIA.

Statistics of the Old and New Conquests, and External Councils of Portuguese India.

	Districts.	Geographical Position. (1) Latitude, North.	Geographical Position. (1) Longitude, East of Greenwich.	Year of Conquest.	Dimensions in Square Miles. (2) Length.	Dimensions in Square Miles. (2) Breadth.	Dimensions in Square Miles. (2) Space.	Divisions. (3) Villages.	Divisions. (3) Parishes.	Houses, and the general Population. Houses.	Houses, and the general Population. Population.	Citizens in Active Service. Electors.	Citizens in Active Service. Eligibles.	Sudder Stations.	Houses and Population. (Sudder Stations.) Houses.	Houses and Population. (Sudder Stations.) Population.	Troops at each Sudder Station.
Old Conquests—three Councils.	Isles of Goa *a*	15°44′30″	73°45′	1510	11½	7	46	35	32	12,545	45,525	400	184	New Goa.	3,600	9,500	Regiment of Artillery, Company of Moors, and Contingent.
	Salsette *b*			1534	21½	10½	104	64	26	25,023	99,243	496	332	Margao	3,249	12,596	1st Battalion of Caçadores.
	Anjediva *b*			1505	¾	..	1	1						Anjediva	117	430	Garrison of the Fort.
	Bardez *c*			1534	12½	11	72	39	26	28,103	97,164	612	136	Mapuça	3,187	11,393	4th Battalion of Caçadores.
	Tiracol *c*			1746	1	1	1	1						Tiracol	67	359	Detachment 1st, and Presidency.
New Conquests—ten Provinces and one Jurisdiction.	Ponda	14°53′30″	74°8′30″	1763	20¼	12¼	81	28	3	7,224	27,615	293	23	Queula	435	2,483	2nd Battalion Infantry.
	Panch Mahal (Five Provinces). Astagrar				17	14½	369	18	1	723	3,807	3	..	Rion	95	394	Detachment 2nd.
	Embarbarcem				24	17½		38		1,360	7,156	9	2	Sanguém	367	1,294	
	Bally				17	6⅔		27		802	4,127	36	..	Bally	71	386	
	Chondravady				17	9		19	1	1,468	7,571	13	4	Amoná	61	235	Detachment 1st.
	Cacora				3	3		2	..	355	1,461			Cacorá	187	995	
	Canacona				20	14	103	7	1	3,706	12,901	60	26	Canacona	572	2,451	Detachment 1st.
	Cabo de Rama							1		357	1,683			Colla	373	1,475	Company of Veterans.
	Bicholim			1781	20⅔	9	69	29	1	4,804	17,618	133	26	Caçabé	270	1,032	3rd Battalion Infantry.
	Sanquelim				20½	17½	144	88	1	2,483	8,568			Sanguelim.	192	1,012	Detachment 3rd.
	Pernem			1783	17½	10	73	26	1	4,081	28,305	37	11	Caçabé	296	1,840	Detachment 4th.
External Councils.	Damaun	20°18′	69°35′	1553	6¾	3¼	22	109	3	8,151	33,159	122	34	Fort	38	160	2 Companies.
	Diu	20°46′	67°25′	1535	1½	½	1¾	3	2	3,017	10,765	49	9	Fort	1,467	4,116	1 Company.

(1) The latitudes and longitudes above given belong—the first to Tiracol, the northernmost point of the coast; and the second to Polem, in the province of Canacona, the southernmost point of the same coast. Our possessions in the interior of Hindoostan extend to 74° 28′ of longitude.

(2) These dimensions have been supplied by a Committee of Engineer Officers.

(3) See next page.

a The Council of the Isles is composed of four principal islands: in the first (Tissuvaly) is situated New Goa, the Capital of Portuguese India.

b, *c* For election purposes, the island of Anjediva forms a part of the Council of Salsette, and the District of Tiracol of that of Bardez, as provided in the General Order in Council No. 574, dated the 11th April 1845.

60

Note (3).

The following are the classified divisions of each district, with the assessments, taxes, and half-taxes paid by each village, and its distance from the Sudder Station in leagues of 18 to a degree :—

Islands of Goa, 35 Villages, included in 32 Parishes.

Parishes.	Villages.	Taxes.			Distances.
Conçeição (Capital)	Taleigão	515	4	48	2/3
Santa Ignez					
S. Miguel					
Santa Cruz	Calapor	618	3	48	1/2
	Cugira	164	4	42	
Santa Maria Magdalena.. ..	Siridao..	109	4	42	1 1/4
Senhora de Belém	Bambolim	78	2	06	1 3/4
Santa Barbara	Morombim o.g.* ..	563	0	51	3/4
Senhora das Mercès ..	Morombim o.p.* ..	325	2	03	1/2
	Murda	116	0	10	
Senhora do Rozario	Curca	116	3	00	1 1/4
S. Joaõ de Sahagu	Corlim	223	4	57	1 3/4
S. Matheus	Azossim	384	3	24	1 2/3
S. Joaõ Baptista..	Carambolim	1,884	2	30	1 3/4
S. Andrè..	Goa-Velha	907	4	51	1 3/4
Senhora de Guadalupe	Batim	937	0	27	1 1/7
S. Lourenço	Mercurim	292	4	33	2
	Agaçaim				
Santa Anna	Telaulim	429	3	27	1 1/4
Senhora de Piedade ..	Navelim	371	4	18	1 3/4
	Goltim..	32	1	51	
S. Mathias	Malar	416	4	57½	1 3/4
Espirito Santo	Naroã	......			2
Senhora da Graça	Chorão	1,032	0	48	1 1/4
S. Bartholomeu					
S. Pedro	Panelim	73	0	00	1 1/4
	Banguenim	78	2	06	
Sé Primacial	Ellà	381	3	17¾	1 1/5
Priorado do Rozario					
Santa Luzia					
S. Estevam	Jua	745	1	50	2
S. Braz	Cumbarjua	Merçè.			2 1/4
	Gandalim ..	20	1	36	2
Senhora do Amparo	Mandur	68	1	24	2
Senhora do Loreto ..	Goalim.	156	4	00	1 1/3
	Moulà				
S. Simão..	Gaunsim	346	4	22	1 2/3
Santa Anna	Telaulim	429	3	27	1 1/4
Senhora d' Ajuda ..	Ribandar	57	2	09	2/3
	Chimbel				

* O'grande (large) and o'pequeno (small).

31

Salsette, 64 *Villages, included in* 26 *Parishes.*

Parishes.	Villages.	Taxes.	Distances.
Sra. dos Martyres	Assolna	National Contract	2½
S. João Baptista	Adsulim	310 3 28	¾
	Benaulim	6,966 2 54	
	Cannà	188 2 49½	
Sra. dos Remedios	Betalbatim	3,347 3 57	1
	Gonsua	208 1 18	1¼
Sra. do Succorro	Carmonà	1,923 0 45	1¾
	Cavelossim	837 1 36	2¼
Sra. de Belém	Cavorim	367 1 46	1⅓
	Guirdolim	1,077 0 03	2
	Chandor	614 1 06	1¾
S. Francisco Xavier	Chicalim	456 4 24	4
Sra. da Esperança	Chinchinim	1,809 2 09	2
	Sarzorà	660 4 39	1¾
	Deussua	579 1 56½	1½
	Darmopor	548 4 28½	1¼
	Sirleim	215 4 31½	1⅛
Sra. dos Mercès	Coluà	1,519 3 57	1
	Sernabatim	1,069 2 17¼	1
	Vanelim	425 2 54	1
	Candaulim	167 3 49½	1
S. Felippe e S. Thiago	Cortalim	922 2 14½	3
	Quelosim	475 0 19½	....
S. Aleixo. S. José	Cortorim	2,987 3 30½	1¼
Sra. da Saude (County)	Conculim	2,195 1 50	2½
	Verodá		
S. Salvador	Loutulim	2,773 2 49½	....
	Racaim	395 2 12	2
S. Francisco Xavier	Macazana	1,617 2 37	
Espirito Santo (Capital)	Margão	4,988 0 08	2
Santo Andrè	Mormugão	1,038 3 09	....
	Vadem	283 0 57	4½
S. Miguel	Orlim	1,511 1 13½	4¼
Sra. das Neves. Sra. das Neves	Raia	2,371 2 30	1½ 1¼
Sra. da Saude	Sancoale	2,025 4 55½	3¾
Sra. do Pilar	Seranlim	1,069 2 47½	3¾
	Doncolim	572 3 32	¾
N. Sra. do Rozario	Telanlim	902 2 51	1
	Aquèm	471 0 06	4
	Davorlim	267 2 00	⅓
	Darmampor	548 4 28½	1⅓
	Navelim	Margão.	¼
Sra. da Gloria	Varca	2,300 4 58½	¼
Sra. de Assumpta	Velção	853 4 42	1¼
	Palle	821 2 19½	2¼
	Hessorsim	221 2 45¾	2½
	Chicolnà	131 1 27¼	3½
S. Francisco Xavier	Velim	National Contract.	3
	Ambelim		2¾

Parishes.	Villages.	Taxes.			Distances.
Sa. Cruz	Verna	3,299	1	$00\frac{1}{2}$	$1\frac{1}{4}$
	Nagoà *	1,009	4	00	2

Bardez, 39 *Villages, included in* 26 *Parishes.*

Parishes.	Villages.	Taxes.			Distances.
S. Thome	Aldona..	2,874	0	42	$1\frac{1}{2}$
S. Miguel	Anjuna..	1,227	1	$33\frac{1}{2}$	$1\frac{1}{4}$
Sto. Caetano..	Assagão	802	0	$50\frac{1}{2}$	1
Sta. Clara...	Assonora	301	0	$07\frac{1}{2}$	2
S. Aleixo..	Calangute	3,561	4	$01\frac{1}{4}$	$1\frac{1}{2}$
Sra. da Esperança .. .. S. Lourenço de Linhares.. ..	Condolim	1,629	3	45	2
S. Francisco das Chagas..	Coluale..	462	3	21	$1\frac{1}{4}$
	Camorlim	705	4	$38\frac{3}{4}$	$1\frac{1}{2}$
S. Diogo..	Guirim..	612	1	00	$\frac{1}{4}$
	Sangolda	589	1	$30\frac{1}{2}$	$\frac{3}{4}$
S. Jeronimo	Mapuça (Capital) ..	582	2	$46\frac{1}{4}$	
	Conchelim	437	2	$10\frac{1}{2}$	$\frac{3}{4}$
	Corlim..	70	2	$51\frac{3}{4}$	$\frac{3}{4}$
Sra. da Conceição	Moirà	622	1	$50\frac{1}{2}$	$\frac{3}{4}$
Bom Jesus	Nachinolà	886	3	$56\frac{1}{4}$	1
Santissima Trindade ..	Nagoà	373	2	$23\frac{1}{4}$	$\frac{3}{4}$
	Saligão..	1,225	3	$59\frac{3}{4}$	1
	Arporà..	675	2	05	$1\frac{1}{4}$
Sra. dos Remedios .. .. Reis Magos	Nellur	816	0	36	$1\frac{1}{2}$
Sra. do Mar	Oxel	337	4	20	$1\frac{3}{4}$
Sta. Anna	Parrà	778	2	$42\frac{1}{2}$	$\frac{3}{4}$
	Verla	249	3	$58\frac{3}{4}$	$1\frac{1}{3}$
	Cancà	178	0	$58\frac{1}{2}$	2
S. João Baptista.. ..	Pilerne..	1,105	0	40	$1\frac{1}{2}$
	Marra	115	4	00	1
Mài de Deus	Pomburpa	1,385	3	$22\frac{3}{4}$	$1\frac{1}{3}$
	Olaulim	495	1	$00\frac{3}{4}$	$1\frac{1}{4}$
Senhora da Victoria ..	Revora..				2
	Nadora..	95	0	16	$2\frac{1}{4}$
	Pirna				$2\frac{1}{2}$
Santo Antonio	Siolim	1,768	2	$49\frac{1}{2}$	$1\frac{3}{4}$
	Marna	417	4	$38\frac{3}{4}$	1
Salvador.. .. .. .. Soccorro.. .. .. .. Penha de França..	Sirula	3,568	0	$50\frac{1}{2}$	$1\frac{7}{3}$
S. Christovam	Tiveim..	699	1	26	$1\frac{1}{3}$
	Sirsaim..	60	0	47	$1\frac{1}{2}$
S. Izabel..	Ucassaim	679	2	39	$\frac{1}{2}$
	Bastorà	550	4	$38\frac{1}{2}$	$\frac{1}{4}$
	Punala..	295	0	12	$\frac{1}{2}$
	Pallem..	241	1	05	$\frac{3}{4}$

* Some of the people on this island credulously maintain that, in 1844, a miraculous cross was found erected in the hollow of a tamarind tree.

Ponda.

Parishes.	Villages.	Taxes.			Distances.
	Adcolna	880	0	00	2¼
	* Bandora	3,700	0	00½	4½
	Betgui	2,773	0	37½	3
	Betodem	446	1	00	5⅓
	*Borim..	5,150	4	23½	5¾
	Boma	807	3	15	2¼
	* Candcapar	1,109	4	45	4¼
	Candolà	1,413	0	00	2¼
	Coddar..	284	1	07½	6
	Conaxem	28	0	00	3
	* Cundaim	4,322	1	48½ *	3¼
	Cumcoliem	47	2	11	3
	Curty	209	1	37½	5¼
	* Marcaim	9,252	1	15	2¾
	Nirancal	98	0	28	7
Parish	Orgão	953	4	41	2¼
	Ponchovaddy	4,448	3	22½	7¾
	* Piriol	2,182	3	45	3⅓
	* Querim	215	2	55	3⅓
Parish	* Quenla	505	0	38	4½
Parish	Sirodà	14,850	4	45	6¾
	Talaulim	1,795	1	00	4¾
	Tivrem..	1,739	0	31	2¾
	Vaddy	133	3	00	5¾
	Vagurmem	769	3	48	3¼
	Velinga..	3,482	1	18	3¾
	Verem	3,323	1	45	3
	Volvoy	2,077	2	00	3¾

Astragahar.

Villages.	Districts.	Taxes.	Distances.
Batty	Districts	The taxes are paid by the Camara, and amount to Xerafins 13,239-4-07½.	6¼
Dongoro			
Naiquinim			6½
Sigonem			9¼
Beliem	....		9¼
† Colomba	....		3
Cumbary..	....		6¾
Cunanga	....		9
† Curddy	....		5¼
Curpem	....		5¾
Neutrauly	....		7¼
Nunem	....		7½

* These villages compose the Camara (Chamber).

Villages.	Districts.	Taxes.	Distances.
* Rivona..	....	The taxes are paid by the Camara, & amount to Xerafins 13,239-4-07½.	$3\frac{1}{2}$
Salguinem	....		$9\frac{1}{4}$
Veliana ..	....		$6\frac{3}{4}$
Verlem ..	....		$8\frac{1}{8}$
Vichondrem	....		7
Zaqui ..	....		$3\frac{1}{2}$
	Embarbarcem.		
Bomba ..	1, Surla.	The Chamber pays the taxes, which amount to about Xerafins 8,127-2-00.	$8\frac{1}{2}$
Dangorly..			$6\frac{1}{2}$
* Muguly			$4\frac{1}{2}$
Oxel ..			7
Surla ..			$6\frac{1}{4}$
* Aglota..	2, Sancorda.		$6\frac{1}{2}$
* Sancorda			6
Sangoddo			8
* Sigão ..			$7\frac{1}{2}$
Cotarly ..	3, Salauly.		$4\frac{1}{2}$
* Salauly..			$6\frac{3}{4}$
* Xelpem			6
Camarconda	4, Codly.		$3\frac{1}{2}$
* Codly ..			$4\frac{1}{7}$
Coproy ..			4
Caranzol..	5, Colem.		$8\frac{1}{4}$
* Colem ..			8
Mollem ..			$8\frac{1}{2}$
Sonaulim..			$8\frac{1}{2}$
* Bamborbarcem	6, Bamborbarcem.		6
Peliem ..			5
Calem ..	7, Calem.		6
Costy ..			$5\frac{3}{4}$
Dudal ..			$5\frac{3}{4}$
Maulinguem			$5\frac{1}{2}$
* Sisodem			$7\frac{1}{2}$
Paliem ..	8, Tudou.		$6\frac{1}{2}$
Potrem ..			$7\frac{1}{4}$
Tudou ..			$6\frac{1}{2}$
* Ugnem			$5\frac{1}{2}$
Atbarcem	9, Atbarcem.		4
Bandol ..			$5\frac{1}{2}$
Cormonem			$8\frac{1}{4}$
Colombossem			$4\frac{1}{4}$
* Moissal			$3\frac{1}{2}$
Rumbodem			$4\frac{1}{2}$
Santon ..			$4\frac{3}{4}$
Sanvordà..			$3\frac{1}{2}$
	Bally.		
* Adnem..	1, Bally.	These districts pay Xerafins 7,892-4-35.	$3\frac{1}{4}$
* Bally ..			$3\frac{1}{2}$
Bendurdem			$3\frac{1}{2}$
Bondol ..			$3\frac{3}{8}$
Fatorpem			$3\frac{1}{4}$

* These villages compose the Camara.

Villages.	Districts.	Taxes.	Distances.
Barcem		These districts pay Xerafins 7,892-4-35.	$5\frac{1}{4}$
Cordem			....
* Quedem	2,		....
Nervantoloy	Barcem.		....
Paddy			$4\frac{3}{4}$
Perla			$5\frac{3}{4}$
Araly			....
Dabem			$5\frac{1}{4}$
Naquelim	3,		4
Quitor	Araly.		$3\frac{1}{2}$
Vangurdem			....
Caurem			4
Casur			$6\frac{1}{4}$
Cotarly			....
Corla			$6\frac{1}{4}$
Dantordy			....
Gocondem	4,		$5\frac{1}{4}$
Maina	Maina.		$4\frac{3}{4}$
Mangal			....
Marigil			....
Quircolna			$5\frac{1}{5}$
Sulcanor			$6\frac{1}{2}$

Chondravady.

Villages.	Taxes.	Distances.
Amboulim	These pay Xerafins 14,396-4-22½.	$2\frac{3}{4}$
Amona		$2\frac{3}{4}$
Assoldem		$2\frac{1}{2}$
* Aviddem		3
Chaili		$2\frac{3}{4}$
Chicaxelven		$2\frac{3}{4}$
* Cothomby		2
Chinchorem		3
* Curmané		..
Messompem		$4\frac{3}{4}$
Molcomem		$4\frac{1}{2}$
Nagavem		$4\frac{1}{4}$
Quepem (Parish)		3
Selvon		$2\frac{1}{2}$
Sirvoy		$3\frac{1}{3}$
Vendorna		5
Veddar		$2\frac{3}{4}$
Xeldem		$3\frac{1}{2}$
Xanodem ..		5

Cacorá.

Villages.	Taxes.	Distances.
Cacora	3,874 1 43	$3\frac{1}{2}$
Soliem		4

* These villages compose the Camara.

Canacona.

Villages.	Taxes.			Distances.
Canacona	7,880	0	05½	6⅔
Cotigão, Maulinguem .. .. .. } Caregále and Bordem .. .. .. }	......			8¾
Gaudongrem	824	2	12	7
Loliem .. .. } Pololem .. .. }	7,275	0	43½	{ 8½ 7¼
Nagaxem and Paldem	....			{ 7⅓ 8¼
Poinguinim	3,503	2	14	....

Bicholim.

Villages.	Taxes.			Distances.
* Amoná	2,061	2	48½	3¼
Advorpale	587	1	15	5
Arvalem	81	1	48	3
Atturly	363	4	40½	3
Bordem	722	0	37½	3
Carapur	....			4
Cassabé (Parish)	556	3	45	3
* Cottomby	570	0	00	5
Cudnem	1,857	2	11½	3¾
Dumaxem	89	2	48¼	3
Salem	.. ...			....
Sarvona	349	1	48¾	....
Sirgão	2,590	3	07½	....
Gangem	45	0	00	5¾
Lasngão	......			3¼
Latambarcem	704	1	15	4
Maulinguem	......			4⅔
Mencurem	1,265	4	48	3¼
Mulgão	1,335	1	15	2⅔
Naroá	709	2	40	2¾
Navelim	2,449	0	00	3¾
* Pally	1,310	0	00	5½
Pesurlem	1,114	4	22½	4¼
Piligão	1,132	4	41½	3½
* Surla	2,957	3	07½	4½
Vainguinim	569	3	26¼	2¾
Velguem	960	1	15	5
Verly	......			4½
Usgão	1,972	0	00	5¾

Sanquolim.

Villages.	Taxes.	Villages.	Taxes.
Ambedem (Parish) ..	150 0 57	Anjuna	....
Ambeli	.....	Aruby	....
Ambedem-Codal	2 0 00	Assodem	....

* These villages compose the Camara.

Villages.	Taxes.	Villages.	Taxes.
Birondem	....	Morlem	....
Bocalim	....	Nadorem	1 0 00
Bondedem..	....	Nagarsem	....
Boriem	....	Nanelim	....
Buimpale	....	Nanus	....
Cadlem	....	Nagargão	110 0 00
Calandem	....	Onda	145 3 45
Caranzal	....	Padeli	9 0 00
Carambolem Bararo. ..	....	Palim	16 2 30
Carambolim	....	Pansuli	....
Chandedem	....	Pendrali	....
Carpur	1 0 00	Podoxem	....
Conquirem	....	Ponxem	93 4 28
Cerivalé	....	Querim	....
Codanly	....	Ravou	....
Codoqui	....	Rivem	....
Compordem	....	Sanquelim	....
Colaundem	170 1 28	Salelim	....
Cumarcon	....	Santordem	....
Curxurem	8 1 54	Sanvorsem	....
Cursum	....	Satari	....
Dabem	....	Senganem	....
Davem	36 1 57	Sonalim	....
Damaxem	1 0 00	Sonus	....
Derodem	....	Surla	....
*Eddodem	63 0 29	Talicol	....
Gabanem	....	Tanal	....
Goelem	....	Vaguriem	14 0 2
Golaulim	....	Vainguinim	....
Gontuly	....	Vantem	271 3 47
Guloly	....	Velguem	....
Jorem Bararuco	....	Velus	4 4 54
Jurem Curdo	....	Volpem	....
Maulinguem	....	Vonoliem	52 0 26
Mattoly	....	Urdem	....
Massordem	....	Vurana	....
Mahus	....	Xelapa-Curdo	....
Mendil, and Quelil ..	....	Xelapa-Cazaruco	....
Melaulim	40 0 00	Zedanim and Pedanim ..	....
Morlem	200 0 00	Zarmem	8 0 00
Molpona	18 0 00		

Pernem.

Villages.	Taxes.	Distances.
Alorna	930 2 30	$3\frac{1}{4}$
Amberem	375 4 00	$3\frac{2}{3}$
Arambol	2,460 0 00	$3\frac{2}{3}$

* These villages compose the Camara.

Villages.	Taxes.			Distances.
Cassabé (Parish)	3,330	3	25	3⅓
Cansarvornem	....			....
Cazanem	720	2	12	3½
Chandel	151	2	08	4
Chaporá	....			....
Chopodem	313	1	52	2
*Corgão	3,709	3	58	4
*Dargale	2,907	3	08	2
Ibrampur	1,482	3	44	3¾
*Mandrem	4,912	3	20	3⅓
Mopa	327	2	48	4
Morgim	2	0	00	....
Ozori	....			3
*Parcem	1,930	1	33	2⅓
Paliem	1,192	4	04	3½
Poroscora	893	3	10	4
Querim	2,106	0	45	4
Tambocem	1,321	3	18	4
Torcem	1,838	0	10	4⅓
Tuvem	684	3	47	....
Vancodà	1,182	2	51	3¾
Vernarà	566	0	18	2½
Uguem	1,664	0	50	3¼

Damaun.

Purguna Naer.

Parish of Bom-Jesus.

Praca.
Campo dos Remedios.
Jumprizes.
Ambavary.
Magarvara.
Patalara.
Damaõ de Cima.
Doler.
Jampor.
Preal.
Jary.
Bamboly.
Tana-Pari.
Devá-Pareri.
Naila-Pareri.
Horta de Van.
Talvary.
Concem.
Bangi Mita.
Horta Gaude.

Purguna Calana Pavary.

Parish of S. Jeronimo.

Forte de S. Jeronimo.
Damaõ pequeno.
Varacunda.
Catrlà.
Marvor.
Caria.
Carivari.
Dabel.
Rignanvara.
Janivancar.
Deucà.
Duntorta.
Bempor.
Calecachigão.

Etly Paty.

Purguna Nagar Avely.

Dadra.
Tigra.
Damuniva.
Sambarvay.
Vagehimpa.
Massat.
Salvassa.
Ambly.
Cudacem.

* These villages compose the Camara.

52

Racoly.
Sily.
Coloname.
Futandy.
Uborcui.
Golonda.
Morcoul.
Bandamem.
Randa grande.
Randa piqueno.

Uply Paty.

Purguna Nagar Avely.

Darhapara.
Noroly.
Aral.
Cavary.
Sonary.
Chopara.
Chicly.
Sorungy.
Dapará.
Vassuna.
Amboly.
Aply.
Parzay.
Paty.
Colam.
Velga.
Cardy.
Caraxigão.
Chauna.
Dolaza.
Umborny.
Cadoly.
Tinolà.
Berdabone.
Goraoparà.
Canol.
Cunta.
Catar.
Talaule.
Rodanum.
Sily.
Chicta.
Cararbary.
Vachaura.
Maudoly.
Medram.
Ambabary.
Carchondam.
Dudonim.
Varadam.
Ruipara.
Jampolpada.
Gourcary.
Sindony.
Chancha.
Gunsá.
Berdam.
Beldapara.
Bespam.
Quespam.

Diu or Dio.

Parishes.

Sé Mariz .. }
Sto. Andre .. } Praca, Muxivara, Bravara, Gogola.

CENSUS

OF THE

DISTRICTS COMPRISED IN THE PORTUGUESE POSSESSIONS IN INDIA;

TAKEN IN THE YEAR 1848.

Details of

Districts.	Population.							
	Sexes.		Married.				Unmarried.	
	Males.	Females.	Males.	Females.	Widowers.	Widows.	Males.	Females.
Isles of Goa	22,656	22,864	12,649	12,658	3,109	4,040	8,218	6,491
Salsette... } Anjediva }	48,644	50,599	17,939	17,944	5,350	8,156	25,355	24,499
Bardez	46,102	5,162	24,534	24,534	5,808	1,162	16,322	4,558
Tiracol	171	188	88	88	4	53	57	69
Ponda...	14,646	12,969	10,387	10,392	327	938	3,922	1,649
Panch Mahal (Five Provinces). Astagrar... ...	1,879	1,928	937	939	102	247	840	742
Panch Mahal (Five Provinces). Embarbarcem..	3,657	3,475	2,438	2,439	114	442	1,105	638
Panch Mahal (Five Provinces). Bally	2,040	2,087	1,530	1,534	105	244	405	309
Panch Mahal (Five Provinces). Chondravady...	3,255	2,535	2,799	2,801	236	222	950	569
Panch Mahal (Five Provinces). Cacora	694	776	355	355	78	103	261	309
Canacona	6,627	6,274	4,868	4,874	182	753	1,582	642
Cabo de Rama	897	786	579	579	45	75	263	142
Bicholim	9,122	8,496	7,439	7,443	149	412	1,534	641
Sanguelim	4,853	3,715	3,124	3,129	174	267	1,555	329
Pernem	14,223	14,082	11,215	11,221	322	1,102	2,676	1,769
Damaun	16,899	16,260	9,286	9,548	1,805	1,622	5,808	5,090
Diu	3,935	3,536	2,134	2,268	591	1,041	2,646	2,085

Population.

AGES.

To a Year old.	From 1 to 5.	5 to 10.	10 to 15.	15 to 20.	20 to 30.	30 to 40.	40 to 50.	50 to 60.	60 to 70.	From 70 upwards.
1,479	1,543	5,018	5,421	6,651	8,584	6,666	5,100	2,817	1,306	515
5,058	9,030	10,041	11,036	11,358	13,824	14,144	11,237	7,426	4,681	1,408
4,637	8,964	10,913	1,032	13,410	15,215	13,021	9,950	6,459	3,121	1,204
22	46	49	39	47	49	49	27	15	11	5
2,330	2,968	2,761	2,153	4,199	7,242	2,012	1,304	1,279	986	301
332	339	418	487	757	701	381	292	102	21	17
648	557	601	702	982	1,074	1,006	1,142	317	112	15
266	244	308	371	749	1,001	552	460	108	75	11
540	816	1,070	1,347	157	1,722	732	643	219	114	9
106	122	74	126	301	262	183	108	121	55	3
,282	1,254	1,241	1,285	2,161	2,674	1,231	1,320	164	228	61
120	175	191	106	235	203	222	272	101	51	7
1,271	1,468	1,548	2,175	2,494	2,305	2,230	2,032	1,101	935	49
849	1,235	769	1,069	1,203	1,161	1,172	755	226	110	21
2,260	2,732	3,348	3,259	5,301	4,847	2,524	2,366	1,098	519	51
1,895	2,630	3,298	3,760	4,147	4,475	4,535	3,535	2,300	1,598	986
688	1,322	1,556	1,177	1,299	1,785	1,288	804	479	243	124

53

Districts.	Races.										Heads of Families.	
	Europeans.		Descendants of Europeans.		Asiatics.		Africans.		Descendants of Africans.			
	Males.	Females.	Males.	Females.	Males.	Females.	Males.	Females.	Males.	Females.	Proprietors.	Non-Proprietors.
Isles of Goa	79	47	236	233	23,353	21,665	96	112	46	62	1,290	9,197
Salsette... } Anjediva. }	14	3	72	58	48,446	50,432	57	78	28	28	3,381	21,642
Bardez	20	10	143	179	45,976	50,537	99	106	45	49	8,426	11,567
Tiracol	..	..	..	..	171	188	..	..	..	..	..	..
Ponda	16	.	51	24	14,605	12,967	3	3	12	9	1,034	6,274
Panch Mahal (Five Provinces). Astagrar ...	..	..	..	..	1,879	1,928	..	..	..	..	107	526
Embarbarcem	..	..	..	..	3,657	3,499	..	..	..	..	115	1,224
Bally	..	..	..	..	2,040	2,087	..	..	..	..	78	703
Chondravady	1	1	..	..	3,981	3,588	..	..	..	..	285	1,432
Cacora ...	..	..	..	..	684	777	..	..	..	..	81	233
Canacona	..	..	..	..	6,627	6,274	..	..	..	..	803	2,323
Cabo de Rama ...	..	...	..	..	897	786	..	..	..	..	43	243
Bicholim	..	..	..	..	9,122	8,496	..	..	..	..	807	3,211
Sanguelim	..	..	..	..	4,837	3,715	8	8	..	..	231	1,106
Pernem	..	..	..	..	14,226	14,079	..	..	..	..	1,742	3,148
Damaun...	25	2	16	10	16,832	16,192	47	72	19	24	4,923	3,228
Diu...	5	..	12	14	5,272	5,291	31	51	39	50	65	1,374

Religion, &c.

Living on their own Landed Property.	Living on their Salaries, except the Military.	Living on their Labour.	Living on their Labour, and other Industrious means.	Mendicants.		Menial Servants.		Free.		Religion.		
				Resident.	Vagrant.	Males.	Females.	Males.	Females.	Christians.	Hindoos.	Moors.
444	2,718	7,599	575	126	126	526	442	80	42	36,384	10,033	104
189	121	21,642	3,192	323	1,075	2,119	2,086	..	..	93,229	5,934	80
671	1,295	6,167	3,468	158	280	567	477	..	..	83,459	13,691	14
..	1	66	..	..	..	..	..	..	..	289	70	..
112	12	6,274	934	203	331	921	603	..	..	4,451	22,730	408
64	..	526	87	46	17	98	98	..	..	405	3,370	22
28	..	1,224	114	58	14	102	87	..	..	888	6,195	75
21	..	703	68	27	41	62	33	..	..	778	3,275	110
101	..	1,232	274	12	13	279	127	..	..	3,726	3,651	88
22	..	233	83	5	6	27	54	..	..	429	1,025	5
150	..	2,334	834	112	140	721	632	..	..	2,235	10,636	30
29	..	243	55	12	6	42	31	..	..	286	1,379	
237	7	3,211	792	247	234	782	637	..	..	985	16,461	165
85	5	1,106	215	78	39	116	147	..	..	58	8,384	141
377	5	3,148	731	228	111	1,083	947	..	..	3,381	24,702	219
112	261	1,221	485	89	127	527	481	..	..	1,093	27,792	4,274
110	130	3,176	102	95	27	103	203	63	84	419	9,575	771

Districts.	Clergy.				Men			
	Priests.	Deacons.	Sub-Deacons.	Minorists.	Full Solicitors.	Country-trained Barristers.	Medical Men and Surgeons qualified in Europe.	Ditto ditto in Goa.
Isles of Goa	133	8	1	53	3	18	3	30
Salsette .. } Anjediva.. }	293	34		292	1	26	..	44
Bardez	171	5	14	251	..	24	..	40
Tiracol	1	..	..	..	..	..	..	1
Ponda	4	..	..	1	..	..	..	2
Panch Mahal (Five Provinces). Astagrar	..	..	..	..	..	..	..	..
Panch Mahal (Five Provinces). Embarbarcem ..	..	..	..	..	..	..	..	..
Panch Mahal (Five Provinces). Bally	..	..	..	..	..	..	..	..
Panch Mahal (Five Provinces). Chondravady ..	1	..	..	..	..	..	..	..
Panch Mahal (Five Provinces). Cacorá	..	..	..	..	..	..	..	..
Canacona	1	..	..	..	..	..	..	..
Cabo de Rama	1	..	..	..	..	..	..	..
Bicholim	2	..	..	..	..	..	..	..
Sanguelim	1	..	..	..	..	..	..	..
Pernem	2	..	..	..	..	..	..	..
Damaun	3	..	1	1	..	4	..	4
Diu	2	..	..	..	..	3	..	2

Callings, &c.

OF LETTERS.								MERCHANTS.		
Druggists qualified in Europe.	Ditto ditto in Goa.	Naval Architects, qualified in Europe.	Ditto, Practical.	Schoolmasters of 1st Lessons.	Citizens able to Write.	Midwives.	Herbalists.	Pedlars.	Coasting Traders.	Commercial Company.
1	11	2	..	21	3,332	44	29	26	23	1
..	3	..	..	41	7,675	47	16	356	1,130	..
..	19	..	..	36	6,617	60	20	952	90	..
..	..	..	..	..	5	1	..	2	..	..
..	..	..	..	4	2,116	12	12	64	..	..
..	..	..	..	.	132	14	2	11	..	..
..	..	..	..	1	83	6	3	23	..	..
..	..	..	..	..	52	5	2	..	..	..
..	..	..	..	..	747	8	..	32	..	..
..	..	..	..	..	42	2	..	3	..	..
..	..	..	..	2	833	8	..	..	..	..
..	..	..	..	..	65	2	..	..	..	..
..	..	..	..	3	724	11	..	87	..	..
..	..	..	..	1	183	4	..	52	..	..
..	..	..	..	2	644	9	..	..	..	..
..	1	..	1	3	2,191	96	30	88	329	..
..	1	..	..	1	1,124	13	8	70	46	..

54

Artificers,

Districts.	Painters.	Goldsmiths.	Wax Chandlers.	Ironsmiths.	Bricklayers.	Carpenters.	Bakers.	Shoemakers.	Washermen.	Potters.	Braziers.	Hatters.	Musicians.	Sugar and Jagree Manufacturers.	Cocoa and Toddy Jagree Manufacturers.
Isles of Goa..	34	210	11	138	89	142	71	72	234	60	12	11	114	35	38
Salsette .. } Anjediva.. }	27	283	41	175	268	313	209	56	395	396	43	18	217	45	340
Bardez	14	209	21	81	336	141	..	25	..	227	..	1	179	565	
Tiracol..	..	..	..	..	..	..	..	..	..	..	..	..	..	..	..
Ponda	..	140	..	112	15	28	..	5	37	28	..	..	..	12	
Panch Mahal (Five Provinces). Astagrar	..	33	..	10	..	..	..	..	10	..	..	..	..	2	
Embarbarcem ..	..	44	..	16	..	..	..	..	15	..	..	..	..	5	
Bally	..	16	..	9	..	..	..	..	8	..	..	..	..	6	
Chondravady ..	..	78	..	22	..	..	..	..	21	51	..	..	..	11	
Cacorá	..	11	..	7	..	..	..	..	5	..	..	..	..	2	
Canacona	..	31	..	16	..	..	..	..	19	20	..	..	..	9	
Cabo de Rama	..	10	..	7	..	..	..	..	3	..	..	..	..	2	
Bicholim	..	112	..	27	40	..	..	..	11	12	..	..	..	11	
Sanguelim	..	21	..	22	..	..	..	..	4	..	..	..	..	....	
Pernem	..	63	..	28	..	..	..	..	18	14	..	..	..	12	
Damaun	..	65	..	52	20	42	..	138	116	35	8	.	3	46	
Diu	..	52	..	19	21	46	...	6	31	19	..	..	..	....	

(4) (Derrubadores) cocoanut tree and leaf cutters are employed in clearing the trees, &c.

(5) Boyas or Boiazes are bearers, or people engaged to convey Machillas (Palkees): there are generally four to each Machilla, and they carry it either on their heads or shoulders.

Labourers, &c.

Spirit Distillers.	Oil-men.	Salt-men.	Cocoanut Leaf Cutters, &c. (4)	Stone Diggers.	Toddy-drawers.	Barbers.	Bangle Sellers.	Sailors.	Fishermen.	Chunam Manufacturers.	Sawyers.	Dyers.	Bearers. (5)	Low Caste. (6)	Moochies. (7)	Agriculturists.
285	24	299	90	13	439	95	..	742	909	33	26	22	121	140	29	10,368
535	289	226	435	231	688	98	25	546	879	120	375	29	797	405	48	10,413
935	55	112	472	278	1,431	49	..	542	877	8	74	5	209	443	61	10,948
42	..	..	..	..	88	1	..	4	1	..	..	..	..	..	1	9
187	..	..	134	31	199	103	..	348	155	..	..	..	42	141	25	6,273
41	..	..	43	..	43	14	..	..	..	..	..	..	..	14	4	525
59	3	..	27	..	64	3	..	..	..	..	..	..	..	28	6	1,224
112	5	..	28	..	118	5	.	4	70	..	..	..	..	21	3	703
121	4	..	26	..	132	15	..	..	..	..	..	..	..	31	8	1,232
9	2	..	13	..	11	8	..	..	..	..	..	..	..	12	7	227
127	6	..	102	..	136	14	..	20	360	..	..	..	..	18	8	2,314
20	1	..	33	..	22	3	.	..	..	..	..	..	..	23	1	456
140	7	..	144	10	151	48	.	21	..	..	..	..	18	62	13	2,211
..	..	..	54	..	..	7	..	..	..	..	..	..	..	47	4	1,016
230	6	21	58	..	242	26	..	4	55	..	..	..	..	85	21	3,148
202	43	84	202	..	1,192	60	..	..	1,393	8	3	51	38	376	60	8,834
	10	28	..	..	58	42	.	12	403	14	6	77	108	149	8	406

(6) Farazes; people of very low caste, bamboo basket-makers, &c.
(7) Shoemakers; those who make shoes of the kind worn by Hindoos.

Districts.	Principal Agricultural Products. Those paying Tithes. Rice.	Cocoanuts.	Salt.	Grain, &c. (in Candies). Nachinim.	Woorid.	Mugo.	Beans.	Savom.	Round Pepper.	Girgilim.	Cultu.	Tury.	Orio.	Hemp.	Cotton.	Beetlenuts.	Fruit, &c. Jacks.	Mangoes.
Island of Goa	98,929	6,433,640	44,670	1,200	176	[illegible]	328	8	2½	7	12	94	2	20½	4	32	161,065	8,328,000
Salsette } Anjediva }	147,960	15,000,000	12,000	1,118	250	..	8	..	13	100	280	62	..	10	4	75	150,000	2,736,000
Bardez } Tiracol }	121,389	4,301,300	27,061	3,433	770	27	37½	38	5	178½	247½	4	..	13½	0½	37	250,717	3,364,300
Ponda	85,294½	6,989,353	2,134½	10,074½	621	31	60	645½	61	388	830	1,458	7,042	28	20	1,031½	23,741,204	42,228,483
Panch Mahal (Five Provinces). Astagrar ..																		
Embarbaroem																		
Bally																		
Chondravady.																		
Cacorá ..																		
Canacona																		
Cabo de Rama ..																		
Bicholim																		
Sanguelim																		
Pernem																		
Damaun	3,540	20,700	161	41	..	3	4	..	..	4	..	11	..	17	..	..	....	....
Diu	....	100,000	..	..	..	..	..		..	..	..	..	..	..	..	..	....	75,000

and Finance.

Navigation.			State Revenue.						
Bunder-boats.	Cargo-boats.	Fishing-boats.	Customs Duties, &c.	Taxes on Property.	Imposts (direct).	Imposts (indirect).	Miscellaneous Receipts.	Expenditure.	Deficit.
)	81	705	369,274 3 10¼	529,018 1 58	423,218 3 04	361,414 3 52	236,018 3 29	Estimated. 1,509,101 4 24 Actual. 1,584,575 2 03¼	Estimated. 12,521 2 01 Actual. 14,904 4 40¼
5	36	96	39,649 1 58	64,146 0 26	3,782 2 22	39,849 1 58	5,329 2 43	87,758 0 02	....
3	31	203	21,443 3 56	14,049 1 21	12,805 0 51	20,1[illegible] 0 17	10,450 0 18	55,306 0 19	170 2 36

54

State

Districts.	Highest Authority of the State.	Judicial. Chief.	Judicial. Magistrates.	Judicial. District Magistrates.	Judicial. Their Substitutes.	Judicial. Justices of the Peace.	Judicial. Justices Elect.	Public Ministry. Chiefs.	Public Ministry. Delegates.	Ecclesiastical. Chief.	Ecclesiastical. Primatial See.	Ecclesiastical. Parishes.	Ecclesiastical. Chapels.	Ecclesiastical. Extinct Religious Institutions. (8)	Ecclesiastical. Expelled Members.	Ecclesiastical. Priests.	Revenue.
Isles of Goa	The Governor General.	The Chief Justice.	There are three, including the President, but the two remaining are also Military Judges.	1	1	15	15	Clerk of the Crown and Revenue.	1	Archbishop, Primate of the East.	One.	32	40	8	102	675	Committee of Public Revenue.
Salsette .. .. .. }				1	1	25	25		1			{ 26	56				
Anjediva .. .. .. }												{ 1	..				
Bardez .. .. .. }				1	1	26	26		1			{ 26	57				
Tiracol .. .. .. }												{ ..	1				
Ponda				These Provinces are apportioned into three Judicial Circuits, viz. 1st, the Isles of Goa; 2nd, Salsette; and 3rd, Bardez. This division is under a decree dated the 7th December 1836.		These are not under any special Rules or Regulations.			These form part of the Judicial Circle.			3	1				
Panch Mahal (Five Provinces). Astagrar												} 2 {	..				
Embarbarcem ..													1				
Bally..													..				
Chondravady ..													..				
Cacorá													1				
Canacona												2	..				
Cabo de Rama												..	..				
Bicholim												1	..				
Sanguelim												1	..				
Pernem..												1	..				
Damaun	Govr.			Judge.		The Judges.			1	Vicars General.		3	2	2	2	3	Committees.
Diu	Govr.			Judge.					1			2	..	2	..	..	

(8) For Notes (8), (9), (10), and (11), see page 338.

Management.

Civil.				Municipal.		Agricultural.		Pious Institutions.			Public Schools.						Military.						
Administrators.	Their Substitutes.	Parish Governors.	Parish Committees.	Municipal Chambers.	Ditto Councils.	Agrarian Chambers.	Village Committees.	Houses of Mercy.	Hospitals. (9)	Confraternities. (10)	Elementary. (11)	Advanced.	English.	French.	Murathee.	Superior.	Forts.	Fortresses.	Marine Establishments.	Engineer Ditto.	Troops.		
																					Regular.		Irregular.
1	1	15	15	1	1	1	28			26	9	1				3					Artillery, 474; 1st Battalion of Infantry, 467; 2nd, 630; 3rd, 606; 4th, 469; Moors, 79; Total 2,725.		Sunudee Soldiers, whose number is uncertain.
1	1	26	26	1	1	1	60	1	2	24	11	1	1	1	1	1	4	12	4	12			
						..	..					..											
1	1	26	26	1	1	1	39			24	9	1											
						..	..					..				..							
1 Financial Administrator.	One.	..	..	The Agrarian Chambers attend to Municipal duties, and to the election of Delegates and Agents to Public Committees.	..	9	28	..	..	..	4	..	..	..	..	..	..	..	..	..		Veterans, 188; in Garrison, 97.	
		..	..		.		17	..	..	..	3	..	..	..	..	..	..	..	..	..			
		..	..		..		9	..	..	..		..	..	..	..	..	..	..	..	..			
		..	..		..		4	..	..	..		..	..	..	..	..	..	..	..	..			
		..	..		..		9	..	..	..		..	..	..	..	..	..	..	..	..			
		..	..		..		1	..	..	..		..	..	..	..	..	..	..	..	..			
		..	..		..		5	..	..	..	..	..	..	..	..	..	..	..	..	..			
		..	..		..		..	..	..	..	2	..	..	..	..	..	..	..	..	..			
		..	..		.		29	..	..	..	4	..	..	..	..	..	..	..	..	..			
		..	..		..		..	..	..	..	1	..	..	..	..	..	..	..	..	..			
		..	..		..		26	..	..	..	4	..	..	..	..	..	..	..	..				
Governors.		1	1	1	1	..	..	1	1	..	2	..	..	..	..	..	1	1	1		1 Comp.	64	..
		1	1	1	1	..	..	1	1	..	2	..	..	..	..	..	..	1	..	..	1 Comp.	..	..

(8) The following is the account of the extinct Convents in 1835, their foundation, edifices, funds, and rents :—

Religious Orders.	Year of Foundation	Houses.	Inmates of each Order.	Funds.			Rents.		
Franciscans	1,510	4	27	94,631	0	00	638	2	30
Dominicans	1,548	10	41	......			23,127	1	00
Franciscans (Reformed)..	1,566	7	3	86,793	0	00	980	0	00
Augustins	1,572	8	59	72,646	0	00	18,292	1	00
S. Caetano	1,640	1	16	20,838	0	00	2,936	2	30
S. João de Deus	1,681	4	15	19,983	1	40	721	0	00
S. Filippe Nery	1,682	2	36	65,938	4	00	8,579	0	00
Carmelites	1,751	1	23	10,510	0	00	5,074	0	00
Total.. 8	....	37	248	371,340	0	40	60,348	2	00

(9) The Military Hospital in Goa is supported by Government, and in it are admitted, by special sanction, their civil employés, and others known to be poor ; the former, on admission, forfeit a portion of their pay. The other hospital is supported by the Caza de Misericordia (House of Mercy). In Damaun and Diu the hospitals are military.

(10) These are pious associations, which have their own laws and funds.

(11) First rudiments. These schools are supported, some by funds subscribed for literary purposes, and others, viz. those of parishes (denominated those of singing and music) by the Village Committees, and by Church and Confraternity funds. Schools of languages are those of Latin, French, English, and Murathee. The superior schools are those for mathematical, military, and medico-chirurgical studies, and the seminaries of Rachol and Chorão for ecclesiastical studies.

The distances in the following Polymetrical Table are calculated in leagues of 18 to the degree, and by the most frequented roads:—

Examples.

From New Goa to	Canacona..	.. ..	12½
,, ,,	Mapuça ..	.. ..	2½
,, ,,	Ponda ..	.. ..	5
From Alorna to	Margão..	.. ..	10¼
,, ,,	Nanus ..	.. ..	7

	Nova Goa	Agoada	Alorna	Baga	Betul	Bicholim	Cabo de Rama	Canacona	Chapora	Doddomarogo	Gaspar-Dias	Mapuça	Margao	Mormugao	Nanus	Pernem	Ponda	Quepem	Reis-Magos	Sanguelim
Nova Goa, Pangim.																				
Agoada.	1½																			
Alorna.	5⅜	5⅝																		
Baga.	2⅓	1¾	4¾																	
Betul.	9¼	10¼	14½	11¼																
Bicholim.	3¾	4¼	2½	4¼	11															
Cabo de Rama.	10⅛	12¼	16¼	13	1¾	12¼														
Canacona.	12½	11	16½	14⅞	3¾	3¾	3½													
Chapora.	3	2⅞	4½	1	12	5	14	15½												
Doddomarogo.	5⅓	5	1	4¾	12½	1⅓	13½	15¼	4½											
Gaspar-Dias.	⅜	2	6	2¾	9¼	4⅜	11	12½	3¾	5¾										
Mapuça.	2½	2⅓	3¼	1½	11⅞	3	13½	15	1¾	3¼	3¼									
Margao.	5¾	7¼	10½	8	3½	7¼	5	6⅞	8¾	8½	5¾	8¼								
Mormugao.	2⅓	3⅞	7⅞	4½	8	7⅞	9½	11	3⅓	9	1⅞	4¾	4½							
Nanus.	7¾	9¼	7	9	10¾	4½	11¾	13	9½	6	8¼	7½	7¼	8¾						
Pernem.	5½	5⅞	2¾	3¾	14⅞	4½	16⅜	18	3	3¾	6¼	3⅜	11¼	7⅜	9⅓					
Ponda.	5	6½	7	7¾	6¾	4½	7¾	9¾	9	6	5½	6¼	3¼	4¾	4	9				
Quepem.	8⅓	10	11⅔	10½	3½	9	5¼	4¾	10½	10½	8½	11	2¾	7¼	7	13½	4½			
Reis-Magos.	⅝	⅞	5⅓	2¼	9¾	3¾	11½	13⅛	3	4½	1¼	2¼	6¼	3	8¼	5½	5⅝	9		
Sanguelim.	4½	6	3⅔	5¾	10½	1⅓	12	13½	6⅛	2⅞	8⅛	4⅓	7	7½	3¼	6	3¾	8¼	5	
Tiracol.	6	5⅞	5½	4	15	6½	17	18⅜	3	3¾	6⅝	4½	11¾	8⅛	10¾	2¾	11	14½	6¼	7⅞

56

Quality of the Soil.—Except in the limited possessions of Diu and Damaun, the ground is mountainous, and intersected by rivers. The newly conquered lands are the most fertile, but, generally, a deficiency of water in any portion of these possessions is rare.

Mountains.—The highest mountains are the " Chandarnate," at Paroda in Chondravady, the "Sidnato" at Borim in Ponda, the " Consid" in Astagrar, the " Vaquerim" at Gutulem in Sattary, and the " Dudsagor" at Sonaulim in Embarbarcem.

Water-falls.—There are three in this State : the first, at Dudsagor in Sonaulim, in the province of Embarbarcem, descends 500 feet ; the second in order is at Sanguelim, and the third at Pernem.

Rivers ; their Names, Length, Course, and the Principal Islands thereon.—There are eight principal rivers—

1st, that of *Tiracol* or *Araundem,* 14 miles in length, forms the northern border of Pernem, and at its mouth is situated the village and fortress of the same name.

2nd, that of *Chaporá* or *Coluale,* 18 miles long, separates the provinces of Bardez, Bicholim, and Sanguelim, from that of Pernem, and takes a zig-zag course through the villages of Chaporá, Coluale, Mencurem, and Salem. On the left margin are situated Bardez, Bicholim, Pernem, Vaidongoro, Arabo, and Alorna.

3rd, that of *Baga ;* length one mile. It passes a redoubt of the same name, and penetrates the province of Bardez.

4th, that of *Sinquerim ;* length $3\frac{1}{8}$ miles. It enters the province of Bardez, and helps to form the peninsula of Agoada.

5th, that of *Mandovi* ;* length from its remotest origin, $38\frac{1}{2}$ miles. It runs a great distance north of the island of Goa, and south of the provinces of Bardez, Bicholim, and Zambaulim. Its many branches penetrate the said provinces, and it extends south of the province of Ponda. On its margins there are various villages of note. Its chief branches enter the villages of Mapuça (capital of the province of Bardez), Tivim, and Assonora ; also Bicholim, Sanguelim, Candiapar, Embarbarcem, and Zambaulim, besides the arm which joins the Zuary river of the Isles of Goa.

6th, that of *Zuary*† ; length 39 miles. On the south it skirts the island of Tissuvady, and on the north the province of Salsette. It separates Salsette from Ponda, and runs along the coast of Zambaulim, as far as Uguem [Portugal and Castro] ; a small branch runs into the island of Goa as far as the village of St. Anna (Telaulim), passing, in its course, the principal villages in

* Since the abandonment of the old city, this name has been extended to the whole river, whereas it was formerly used only to distinguish the portion near the Custom House (Mandovi).

† Zuary is a spot in the village of Goa Velha (Old Goa), very much apart from the river.

the provinces of Salsette and Zambaulim on its left side, and on the right the principal villages on the island of Tissuvady and the province of Ponda. It crosses the river Mandovi between Marcaim and St. Lourenço, to form the island of Tissuvady, and thence at a small distance it separates itself so as to form the island of Quelossim; and after this it unites and runs as far as Lontulim, where it divides again, and forms the islet Vanxy or Vanxo, and runs in a direct line thence to Netorlin.

7th, that of *Sal*, 15 miles long. It runs into the province of Salsette; passes by Betul and Assolna, and reaches the neighbourhood of the district of Margão, at a place called Careacholiando. Its branches are small, of which some run into the same province, and others into that of Zambaulim.

8th, that of *Talpona*, 7 miles long. It enters the province of Canacona, and reaches within a short distance of Portagale.

Outlets.—The three rivers of Sinquerim, Zuary, and Mandovi discharge themselves into the port of Goa; the others at different places along the coast.

The Port of Goa.—The harbour of Goa is formed by the extremities of two peninsulas, namely Salsette and Bardez, and it is divided by the projection from the island of Goa called Cabo (cape), which leaves space on both sides, at Agoada and Mormugão, for ships to anchor.

Anchorages.—There are only two, those of Agoada and Mormugão. In that of Agoada ships may lay without any danger, either by day or night, and in 5 fathoms, from September to the end of May; in that of Mormugão in 3½ and 4 fathoms near land. In the rainy season it is difficult to remain in the former, owing to high winds and seas; it is also difficult to go up the river Mandovi, owing to the sand-bank which obstructs the bar, which on full and new moons has scarcely 2 fathoms water. Notwithstanding this, however, in urgent cases, with the NW. wind, ships can remain at the anchorage of Mormugão.

Prevailing Winds.—These are various. From the latter end of May till the end of September the weather is damp, and often tempestuous, and the winds from the S. and W. and WNW. render the coast navigation difficult. In March NW. winds prevail, which in April and May are accompanied by heavy thunder-storms. In the months of December and January the land winds commence, and continue until the middle of February.

Islands.—There are 20 islands formed by the eight rivers already named. These are the islands of Goa, (Tissuvady, 30 villages), Choraõ, Divar, Cumbarjua, Jua or St. Estevam (St. Stephen), Ratos, Mota or Accaro, Tolto, Dongorim, Capao or Vanxim, St. Venancio, Ponelem, Corjuem, Arabo, the Ranes, St. Jacintho or the *Secretary* (Dantas), Quelossim, the little island of Lontulem, Vanxy or Vanxo, and that of Rochol (at present become almost an island).

Ferries, Boats, &c.—The communication across the eight rivers and their branches, as well as with the islands, is by means of canoes, commonly called Passagens. There are upwards of 104 of these; 35 belong to Government.

Fish.—The rivers and their branches contain various kinds of palatable fish and shell-fish, such as Saltoens (a kind of fish that leaps), Tainhas (Pomphrets), sturgeons, sole-fish, Bagres (a kind of long fish), Munjes, prawns, crabs, muscles, cockles, oysters, &c. &c.

Inhabitants.—The inhabitants of the country are divided into three classes—Europeans, their descendants, and Natives. These, again, are sub-divided into four classes—Bramins, Charados, Sudros, and Musulmans.

Languages.—Besides the Portuguese, there are those of the country, which vary not only in provinces, but also in villages.

Religion.—The Roman Catholic is the dominant religion; the others are tolerated. Notwithstanding this toleration, however, only the Hindoos and the Moors have their temples. In Old Goa (Conquista Velha) the Hindoos have two temples (Pagodas), and the Moors one mosque (in the Islands of Goa). All the rest are in New Goa (Novas Conquistas).

Houses, Population, and Land.—The houses in the Isles, in relation to the population, are 1 to $3\frac{672}{1000}$, giving to each square mile 989 souls. In Salsette the houses are 1 to $3\frac{968}{1000}$, giving to each square mile 945 souls. In Bardez, the most cultivated and populous territory, 1 to $3\frac{157}{1000}$, giving 1,331 souls to each square mile. In the new conquests,—the most extensive, and least populous and cultivated,—the inhabitants are mostly Hindoos, and live after their own fashion, many families in a house. The houses to the population are 1 to $4\frac{598}{1000}$, thus giving scarcely 144 souls to the square mile. The houses in Damaun are as 1 to $4\frac{088}{1000}$, giving 1,507 souls the square mile. In Diu, a small place, but well peopled, the houses are as 1 to $3\frac{568}{1000}$, giving 6,151 souls to each square mile.

Average of Births.—In healthy villages the average number of births to each marriage is from 6 to 8 children, and in the unhealthy from 2 to 4. Barren people are rare.

Time of Marriage.—Christian females generally marry between the ages of 13 and 18, and males between the ages of 20 and 30. The Hindoo males marry at any age, and even two or more wives, provided they support them all, when they live in the same house; but the Hindoo women generally consummate their marriages immediately on their attaining puberty. The marriages of Hindoos are always arranged by the parents; the contracting parties only become acquainted with each other at the marriage ceremony.

Duration of Human Vigour.—The men from the ages of 20 to 45 years, and the women from 15 to 40, enjoy all their physical power, except in the case of artizans and agriculturalists, whose troubles commence early.

Agricultural Products.—The principal articles are five: rice, salt, cocoanuts, betelnuts, and Nachinim; those of the second class are Woorid, Coolit, Tory, Pacolo, Mugo, beans, Sanvom, potatoes, chillies round and long, onions, Girgilim, coffee, cotton, and hemp.

Agricultural Implements.—The implements used in culture are few, namely the plough, rake, hatchet, mattock, Divolo (a mallet to break lumps of earth), and Oloi or Guto, a board used for levelling the ground.

Agricultural Charges.—The expense of growing rice, in sweet and salt ground, is calculated generally at one-third of the value of the produce, but in high sandy lands half the produce; in cocoanut oarts at one-fifth, in betelnut oarts in some places at a half, and in others at one-third.

Fruit.—Fruit are of two kinds, wild and garden. Amongst the first are the bull's-eye, Jagomas, white Jambos, Babolans, Carandans, Belcas, Guava, Cajus, Jambolans, Churnas, &c. Amongst the second are custard-apples, melons, Moguins, pomegranates, water-melons, papays, citrons, oranges, Tangerinas (Sonaringas), pumeloes, Malacca Jambos (Churnas).

Wild and Garden Flowers.—The indigenous flowers are various; some are wild, and others are produced in gardens; they are both much in demand in the markets, particularly by the Hindoos. The most common of the wild flowers are Cul-Champins, Nac-Champins, Onvolans, Surgans, Madercilvas, Candolans, Abolins (sky-blue, white, yellow, and purple), Undans, Coassó, or Ató, Comolans, Salcans, &c. From gardens, Zaiznios, Nentios, Mogarins, Bui-Champins (these grow like mushrooms), Dore-Mogarins, Xiuntins (various), roses (various), Buttons (white and purple), Perpetua, Abolins (carmine and light red, also gold colour), Pat or Pach, Alexandria (various), &c. &c.

Vegetables.—Vegetables are various and abundant, especially in the rainy season. They form the principal food of the Hindoos. Those most cultivated are Blites, Bretalhas, radishes, parslane, tendulins, pumpkins, Bendas, cucumbers, yams, Caratins, Cualengas, nole-kole, salad, &c. &c. Besides these there are several others, proper for the use of animals, and also for dyeing purposes.

Shrubs and Medicinal Plants.—Many of these known, and advantageously used by herbalists; some are already in use in medicine, and, if medical men do not use them more freely, it is because the former try to conceal their virtues, notwithstanding the rewards which await publicity.

Exotics.—The soil can produce almost all the fruits and flowers which are not indigenous, but however luxuriant these shrubs grow, their fruit is always inferior in size and quality, and have no seed: it is strange, however, that the vines produce beautiful grapes biennially.

Forests.—The country produces varied and magnificent timber, well adapted for ship-building and civil architecture. The most abundant are the jack, Mareta, Benteca, blackwood (holy wood), chair-wood (Edu), rosewood, Puna (timber used for masts), teakwood, sandal-wood, ebony (iron-wood), &c. &c. The last three qualities are rare. Generally the timber is dear, and the stupid method of conveying the timber from the forests (Novas Conquistas, where abundance of trees exist untouched), viz. dragging it all the distance by means of men or bullocks, is the cause of making it dearer than the timber brought from the south (Calicut and Cochin).

Animals of the Forests.—There are many species of them, but the common ones are the Tiger (Vago) of different sorts,—Royal, Bibio, Vagantis dos Salqueiros,—and the buffalo, the stag, the chamois, the white and black bear, (bears are rare, except at Canacona), the hare, the wild hog, the porcupine, the dog, the monkey, the fox, the cat, the winged cat, the rat, the weasel, the jackal, the dormouse, the squirrel, the chameleon (some winged), Talagora (a large kind of lizard), Tirio, &c. &c.

Reptiles and Insects.—There are different kinds of reptiles, of which the following are the principal :—the Cobra de Capello,—Naguine is the male and Giboia (the female ?),—which are sometimes seen in the jungles of Sonaulim, in Embarbarcem ; the Divodo, Aguio (carpet-snake), viper, water-snake, rat-snake, green-snake, and the boa. Insects are of very many kinds, particularly in the rainy season, and their classification is very extensive.

Game Birds.—These are of various kinds, and the following are the most known :—partridge, quail, snipe, paddy-bird (white, brown, Boquem or Bolar, Cudem Boquem, Royal Camardongo), Concari, woodcock, Maçarico, Telio or Buddi (diver), dove (of different sorts, sizes, and colours), jungle woodcock, peacock, pigeons of various kinds, &c. &c. &c.

Manufactures.—A few people employ themselves in Bardez, in weaving cotton tiaras, and in dyer's work : generally the arts are exercised only by families to supply their own wants, or in execution of special orders.

External Commerce.—The principal articles exported are betelnuts, salt, cocoanuts, rice, round pepper, saltpetre, cinnamon, coir work, and gums. The inferior articles are dry cocoanut used for oil, fruit of all kinds, cocoanut oil, cocum oil, vinegar, spirits (of cocoanut and Caju), Jagree, Caju, chillies, dry cocum, dry mango slices, hemp, stockings, wax, cinnamon, butter, chunam, firewood, sewing-thread, fishing-nets, shells, tamarind, preserves, salt fish, fish-fins, fish-maws, fowls, geese, turkeys.

Internal Commerce.—Nearly the whole of the internal commerce is like that of Bombay, and the neighbouring places subject to the British dominion.

Imposts.—The three provinces (Concelhos das Ilhas, Salsette, and Bardez) are subject to the following imposts :—Tithes on the three articles, rice, cocoanuts, and salt, at 10 per cent. (except to the members of village committees, who are excused half dues for the trouble their public duties entail) ; excise of 10 per cent. on cocoanut trees producing toddy ; seal and stamp duties, customs dues, tobacco licenses, the snuff monopoly, and monopoly for the sale of spirituous liquors, jack seeds, duties on copra and betelnut, on rents in kind, duties on spices and silk manufactures, land and sea postage, custom house seal, paper seal, charitable institutes, literary subsistence, &c. &c.

TREATIES, AGREEMENTS, &c.

ENTERED INTO

BETWEEN GREAT BRITAIN AND PORTUGAL,

Between the 23rd June 1661 *and the 19th November* 1850.

PORTUGAL

Grant by the King of Portugal *of the* Island of Bombay *to His Majesty* Charles II., *King of Great Britain.*

Extract, Articles XI. and XII. of Treaty concluded on the 23rd June 1661, between His Majesty Charles II., *King of Great Britain, and* Alfonsus VI., *King of Portugal.*

Article XI.

That for the better improvement of the English interest and commerce in the East Indies, and that the King of Great Britain may be better enabled to assist, defend, and protect, the subjects of the King of Portugal in those parts, from the power and invasion of the States of the United Provinces, the King of Portugal, with the assent and advice of his Council, gives, transfers, and by these presents grants and confirms, to the King of Great Britain, his heirs and successors, for ever, the port and island of Bombay, in the East Indies, with all the rights, profits, territories, and appurtenances whatsoever thereunto belonging, and, together with the income and revenue, the direct, full, and absolute dominion and sovereignty of the said port, island, and premises, with all their royalties, freely, fully, entirely, and absolutely. He also covenants and grants, that the quiet and peaceable possession of the same shall, with all convenient speed, be freely and effectually delivered to the King of Great Britain, or to the persons thereto appointed by the said King of Great Britain, for his use, in pursuance of this cession; the inhabitants of the said island (as subjects of the King of Great Britain, and under his sovereignty, crown, jurisdiction, and government) being permitted to remain there, and to enjoy the free exercise of the Roman Catholic religion, in the same manner as they do at present; it being always understood, as it is now declared, once for all, that the same Regulations shall be observed for the exercise and preservation of the Roman Catholic Religion in Tangier, and all other places which shall be ceded and delivered by the King of Portugal into the possession of the King of Great Britain, as were stipulated and agreed to on the surrender of Dunkirk into the hands of the English; and when the King of Great Britain shall send his fleet to take possession of the said port and island of Bombay, the English shall have instructions to treat the subjects of the King of Portugal, throughout the East Indies, in the most friendly manner, to help and assist them, and to protect them in their trade and navigation there.

Article XII.

In order that the subjects of the King of Great Britain may enjoy more ample benefits from their trade and commerce throughout the King of Portugal's dominions, it is covenanted, that the merchants and factors (over and above the grants made to them by former Treaties) shall, in virtue of this Treaty,* have the liberty of residing in all places where they shall judge proper; and particularly that they shall dwell and enjoy the same privileges and immunities, so far as they relate to trade, as the Portuguese themselves, in the cities and towns of Goa, Cochin, and Diu; provided, however, that the subjects of the King of Great Britain, resident in any of the aforesaid places, shall not exceed the number of four families in any one of them.

Royal Charter, granted on the 27th March 1668, *by His Majesty King* Charles II., *transferring the Port and Island of Bombay to the Honorable* East India Company.

LETTERS PATENT,

Granted to the Governor and Company of Merchants of London trading into the East Indies, relating to the Island of Bombay; bearing date the Twenty-seventh of March, in the Twentieth year of the Reign of Charles II., *Anno Domini One thousand Six hundred and Sixty-eight.*

Charles II., by the grace of God, King of England, Scotland, France, and Ireland, Defender of the Faith, &c. To all to whom these presents shall come, greeting: Whereas at the humble suit of our well-beloved subjects, the Governor and Company of Merchants of London trading into the East Indies, and for the honour and profit of this nation, and the encouragement of trade into those remote parts of the world, we have, by our Royal Charter, or Letters Patent, bearing date at Westminster, the third day of April, in the thirteenth year of our Reign, granted unto the said Governor and Company of Merchants of London trading into the East Indies, and their successors, that they and their successors, and their factors, servants, and assigns, in the trade of merchandize, for them and on their behalf, and not otherwise, shall for ever have, use, and enjoy, the whole entire and only trade and traffic, and the whole entire and only liberty, use, and privilege of trading and trafficking, and using the Feat and Trade of Merchandize to and from the said East Indies, and to and from all the islands, ports, havens, cities, towns, and places within their

* Dated the 23rd June 1661.

said Charter; that is to say, to and from the said East Indies, in the countries and parts of Asia and Africa, and to and from the islands, ports, havens, cities, creeks, towns, and places of Asia, Africa, and America, or any of them, beyond the Cape of Bona Esperanza, to the Straits of Magellan, where any trade or traffic of merchandize may be used or had.

And whereas also, by our said Royal Charter or Letters Patent, we have ordained, that there shall be a Governor, and twenty-four Committees of the said Company, to be elected and appointed, in such form as therein is expressed, who shall have, from time to time, the direction of the voyages, of and for the said Company, and the provision of the shipping and merchandizes thereunto belonging, and also the sale of all merchandizes, goods, and other things, returned in all or any of the voyages or ships, of or for the said Company, and the managing and handling of all other business, affairs, and things, belonging to the said Company; and likewise that it shall and may be lawful, to and for the said Governor and Company, for the time being, or the more part of them present at any public assembly, commonly called the Court General, holden for the said Company, the Governor of the said Company being always one, from time to time to elect, nominate, and appoint one of the said Company to be the Deputy to the said Governor, who, from time to time, in the absence of the said Governor, shall exercise and execute the Office of Governor of the said Company, in such sort as the said Governor ought to do, as by our said Charter, reference being thereunto had among divers other grants, liberties, immunities, privileges, and pre-eminences, may more fully appear.

And whereas, by the late Treaty between us and our good brother, the King of Portugal, concluded at Westminster, the three-and-twentieth day of June, Anno Domini one thousand six hundred sixty-and-one, the said King of Portugal did, by the XI. Article thereof, by and with the advice and consent of his Council, freely, fully, absolutely, and entirely give, grant, transfer, and confirm unto us, our heirs and successors, for ever, the port and island of Bombay, in the East Indies, together with all the rights, profits, territories, and appurtenances thereof whatsoever, and as well the property as the direct, full, and absolute dominion and sovereignty of the said port and island, and premises, with all the royalties thereof; the inhabitants of the said island, as our liege people, and subject to our imperial crown and dignity, jurisdiction and government, being permitted to remain there, and enjoy the free exercise of the Roman Catholic religion, in the same manner as they then did, it being then declared, and always to be understood, that the same order should be observed for the exercise and conservation of the Roman Catholic religion, in the city of Tangier, and in all other places which were granted and delivered by the said King of Portugal into our power, which was provided and agreed upon the surrender of Dunkirk into the hands of the English, in pursuance of which said Treaty our said good brother, the King of Portugal, did afterwards cause the said port and island, and premises, to be delivered up into our full, quiet, and peaceable possession, which said port and island of Bombay, and the territories then and there lying and being within the limits of our said Charter, granted unto the said Governor and Company of Merchants trading into the East Indies.

Now know ye: That forasmuch as we have found, by much experience, that the said trade into the said East Indies hath been managed by the said Governor and Company to the honour and profit of this realm, to the end, and out of our earnest desire that the said Governor and Company may, by all good and lawful ways and means, be encouraged in their difficult and hazardous trade and traffic, in those remote parts of the world, we therefore, by the advice of our Privy Council, in all the grants, matters, and things herein contained, of our especial grace, certain knowledge, and mere motion, have given, granted, transferred, and confirmed, and by these presents, for us, our heirs and successors, do give, grant, transfer, and confirm, unto the said Governor and Company of Merchants of London trading into the East Indies, their successors and assigns, all that the said port and island of Bombay, in the East Indies, with all the rights, profits, territories, and appurtenances thereof, whatsoever, and all and singular the royalties, revenues, rents, customs, castles, forts, buildings and fortifications, privileges, franchises, pre-eminences, and hereditaments whatsoever within the said premises, or to them, or any of them belonging, or in any wise appertaining, in as large and ample manner, to all intents, constructions, and purposes, as we ourselves now have and enjoy, or may or ought to have and enjoy the same, by virtue and force of the said grant of our said brother, the King of Portugal, and not further or otherwise; and them, the said Governor and Company of Merchants of London trading into the East Indies, their successors and assigns, we do, by these presents, for us, our heirs and successors, make, create, and constitute, the true and absolute lords and proprietors of the port and island, and premises aforesaid, and of every part and parcel thereof, which to us appertaineth, by force of the said grant from our said brother, the King of Portugal, and not further or otherwise: saving, and always reserving to us, our heirs and successors, the faith and allegiance to us due and belonging, and our Royal power and sovereignty of and over our subjects and inhabitants there, to have, hold, possess, and enjoy the said port and island, and all and singular other the premises hereinbefore granted, or mentioned to be granted unto them, the said Governor and Company of Merchants of London trading into the East Indies, their successors and assigns, for ever, to the only use of them, the said Governor and Company, their successors and assigns, for evermore; to be holden of us, our heirs and successors, as of the Manor of East Greenwich, in the county of Kent, in free and common soccage, and not in capite, nor by Knights' service, yielding and paying therefore to us, our heirs and successors, at the Custom House, London, the rent or sum of Ten Pounds, of lawful money of England, in gold, on the thirtieth day of September yearly, for ever.

MEMORANDUM.—*In the remaining Clauses of this Deed of Grant, provision was made for the Roman Catholic inhabitants being continued in the quiet enjoyment of their religious and other privileges, and the Company was empowered to make and publish, under their own Seal, Laws and Constitutions for the use of the Port, and for the good government of the Island of Bombay, and its inhabitants, and to visit offences with suitable punishments and penalties.*

Treaty between Great Britain and Portugal, for the abolition of the SLAVE TRADE, *dated the 22nd January* 1815.

IN THE NAME OF THE MOST HOLY AND UNDIVIDED TRINITY !

His Royal Highness the Prince Regent of Portugal, having by the X. Article of the Treaty of Alliance concluded at Rio de Janeiro, on the 19*th February* 1810, *declared his determination to co-operate with His Britannic Majesty in the cause of humanity and justice, by adopting the most efficacious means for bringing about a gradual abolition of the Slave Trade, and His Royal Highness, in pursuance of His said declaration, and with the desire to effectuate, in concert with His Britannic Majesty and the other Powers of Europe who have been induced to assist in this benevolent object, an immediate abolition of the said traffic upon the parts of the Coast of Africa which are situated to the Northward of the Line, His Royal Highness the Prince Regent of Portugal and His Britannic Majesty, equally animated by a sincere desire to accelerate the moment when the blessing of peaceful industry and an innocent commerce may be encouraged throughout this extensive portion of the Continent of Africa, by its being delivered from the evils of the Slave Trade, have agreed to enter into a Treaty for the said purpose, and have accordingly named, as their Plenipotentiaries, viz. His Royal Highness the Prince Regent of Portugal, the Most Illustrious and Most Excellent* DOM PEDRO DE SOUZA HOLSTEIN, *Count of Palmella, a Member of His Royal Highness' Council, Commander of the Order of Christ, Captain of a Company of the Royal German Life Gaurd; the Illustrious and the Most Excellent* ANTHONY DE SALDANHA DA GAMA, *a Member of His Royal Highness' Council, and of His Council of Finance, Commander of the Military Order of Saint Benedict of Aviz; and the Most Illustrious and the Most Excellent* DOM JOACHIM LOBO DA SILVEIRA, *a Member of His Royal Highness' Council, and Commander of the Order of Christ, His Royal Highness' Plenipotentiaries at the Congress of Vienna; and His Majesty the King of the United Kingdom of Great Britain and Ireland, the Right Honorable* ROBERT STEWART, VISCOUNT CASTLEREAGH, *Knight of the Most Noble Order of the Garter, a Member of His said Majesty's Most Honor-*

able Privy Council, a Member of Parliament, Colonel of the Regiment of Militia of Londonderry, His said Majesty's Principal Secretary of State for Foreign Affairs, and His Plenipotentiary at the Congress of Vienna, who, having mutually exchanged their full powers, found in good and due form, have agreed upon the following Articles:—

ARTICLE I.

That from and after the ratification of the present Treaty, and the publication thereof, it shall not be lawful for any of the subjects of the Crown of Portugal to purchase slaves, or to carry on the slave trade on any part of the Coast of Africa to the northward of the Equator, upon any pretext, or in any manner whatsoever; provided, nevertheless, that the said provision shall not extend to any ship or ships having cleared out from the ports of Brazil previous to the publication of such ratification; and provided the voyage, in which such ship or ships are engaged, shall not be protracted beyond six months after such publication, as aforesaid.

ARTICLE II.

His Royal Highness the Principe Regente of Portugal hereby agrees, and binds himself to adopt, in concert with His Britannic Majesty, such measures as may best conduce to the effectual execution of the preceding Engagement according to its true intent and meaning; and His Britannic Majesty engages, in concert with His Royal Highness, to give such orders as may effectually prevent any interruption being given to the Portuguese ships resorting to the actual dominions of the Crown of Portugal, or to the territories which are claimed in the said Treaty of Alliance as belonging to the said Crown of Portugal, to the southward of the Line, for the purpose of trading in slaves, as aforesaid, during such period as the same may be permitted to be carried on by the laws of Portugal, and under the Treaties subsisting between the two Crowns.

ARTICLE III.

The Treaty of Alliance concluded at Rio de Janeiro on the 19th February 1810, being founded on circumstances of a temporary nature, which have happily ceased to exist, the said Treaty is hereby declared to be void in all its parts, and of no effect, without prejudice, however, to the ancient Treaties of alliance, friendship, and guarantee, which have so long and so happily subsisted between the two Crowns, and which are hereby renewed by the high contracting parties, and acknowledged to be of full force and effect.

ARTICLE IV.

The high contracting parties reserve to themselves, and engage to determine by a separate Treaty, the period at which the trade in slaves shall universally cease and be prohibited throughout the entire dominions of Portugal; the

Prince Regent of Portugal hereby renewing his former declaration and engagement, that during the interval which is to elapse before such general and final abolition shall take effect, it shall not be lawful for the subjects of Portugal to purchase or trade in slaves upon any parts of the Coast of Africa, except to the southward of the Line, as specified in the II. Article of this Treaty, nor to engage in the same, or to permit their flag to be used, except for the purpose of supplying the transatlantic possessions belonging to the Crown of Portugal.

Article V.

His Britannic Majesty hereby agrees to remit, from the date at which the ratification, as mentioned in the I. Article, shall be promulgated, such further payments as may then remain due, and payable upon the loan of lib. 600,000, made in London for the service of Portugal in the year 1809, in consequence of a Convention signed on the 21st of April of the same year, which Convention, under the conditions specified as aforesaid, is hereby declared to be void and of no effect.

Article VI.

The present Treaty shall be ratified, and the ratification shall be exchanged Rio de Janeiro in the space of five months, or sooner, if possible.

In witness whereof, the respective Plenipotentiaries have signed it, and have thereunto affixed the seals of their arms.

Done at Vienna, this twenty-second day of January, in the year of our Lord one thousand eight hundred and fifteen.

(Signed) Le Conde de Palmella.

(Signed) Castlereagh.

Antonio de Saldanha da Gama.

D. Joachim Lobo da Silveira.

Additional Article.

It is agreed, that in the event of any of the Portuguese settlers being desirous of retiring from the settlements of the Crown of Portugal on the coast of Africa to the northward of the Equator, with the Negroes *bonâ fide* their domestics, to some other of the possessions of the Crown of Portugal, the same shall not be deemed unlawful, provided it does not take place on board a slave-trading vessel, and provided they be furnished with proper passports and certificates, according to a form to be agreed on between the two Governments.

The present additional Article shall have the same force and effect as if it were inserted word for word in the Treaty signed this day, and shall be ratified, and the ratification exchanged at the same time.

In witness whereof the respective Plenipotentiaries have signed it, and have thereunto affixed the seals of their arms.

Done at Vienna, this twenty-second day of January, in the year of our Lord one thousand eight hundred and fifteen.

(Signed) LE CONDE DE PALMELLA.

(Signed) CASTLEREAGH.

ANTONIO DE SALDANHA DA GAMA.

D. JOACHIM LOBO DA SILVEIRA.

Treaty of Commerce and Navigation between Great Britain and Portugal, dated the 3rd July 1842.

Her Majesty the QUEEN OF PORTUGAL AND THE ALGARVES, *and Her Majesty the* QUEEN OF THE UNITED KINGDOM OF GREAT BRITAIN AND IRELAND, *being desirous to maintain and draw still closer the ties of amity which have so happily subsisted between the Crowns of Portugal and Great Britain, and also to encourage and extend the commercial intercourse between their respective subjects, by means of a Treaty of Commerce and Navigation, have for this purpose named as their Plenipotentiaries, that is to say: Her Majesty the Queen of Portugal and Algarves,* DOM PEDRO DE SOUZA HOLSTEIN, *Duke of Palmella, President for life of the Chamber of Peers, Councillor of State, Grand Cross of the Order of Christ, and of the Tower and Sword, Captain of the Royal Guard of Archers, Knight of the Distinguished Order of the Golden Fleece, and Grand Cross of the Orders of Charles III. in Spain, of the Legion of Honour in France, of Saint Alexander Newsky in Russia, Knight of the Order of Saint John of Jerusalem, Count of Sanfré, in Piedmont, Honorary Minister and Secretary of State, &c. &c. &c.; and Her Majesty the Queen of the United Kingdom of Great Britain and Ireland,* CHARLES AUGUSTUS LORD HOWARD DE WALDEN, *Peer of the United Kingdom of Great Britain and*

Ireland, Knight Grand Cross of the Most Illustrious Order of the Bath, Envoy Extraordinary and Minister Plenipotentiary of Her Britannic Majesty at the Court of Her Most Faithful Majesty, &c. &c. &c., who, after having communicated to each other their respective full powers, found in good and due form, have agreed upon and concluded the following Articles:—

ARTICLE I.

The subjects of each of the high contracting parties shall, in the dominions of the other, enjoy all the privileges, immunities, and protection enjoyed by the subjects of the most favoured nation. They shall be entitled to travel, to reside, to occupy dwellings and warehouses, and to dispose of their personal, leasehold, and all other property lawfully held by them, by sale, gift, exchange, or will, or in any other way whatever, without the smallest let, and without any hindrance whatever. They shall be exempt from forced loans, or any other extraordinary contributions not general, or not by law established, and from all military service, by sea or by land. Their dwellings, warehouses, and everything belonging thereto, shall be respected, and shall not be subjected to any arbitrary visits, or search. No examination or inspection shall be made of ir books, papers, or accounts, without the legal sentence of a competent Court, or Judge.

The assessment of the amount to be paid by the British subjects in Portugal and its dominions, for *maneio* or *decima industrial*, and from which they have hitherto enjoyed special exemption, shall in all cases, in future, be made, if so claimed by them, according to the rate to be given by *informadores*, of whom two shall be Portuguese and two British merchants, to be named by the *Conselho de Districto*; and in case any objection should be made by the parties assessed to the amount of the said assessment (which shall in all cases bear a just proportion to the rate at which the native subjects of Portugal are assessed), they shall have a right to appeal to the Tribunal of the Treasury, and to appear in person, or to be heard by Counsel before the said tribunal, and in the mean time no execution shall be made on their property, until an ultimate decision shall have been pronounced by the said tribunal.

It is, however, understood, that British subjects resident in Portugal and its dominions not carrying on trade, or exercising any branch of industry therein, but deriving their incomes from other sources, shall, in like manner with Portuguese subjects, be wholly exempt from the operation of the said *maneio* or *decima industrial* tax.

The subjects of each of the high contracting parties shall also, within the dominions of the other, be allowed the free use and exercise of their religion, without being in any manner disturbed on account of their religious opinions; they shall be allowed to assemble together for the purposes of public worship, and to celebrate the rites of their religion in their own dwelling-houses, or in the chapels or places of worship appointed for that purpose, without any the

58

smallest hindrance or interruption whatever, either now, or hereafter; and Her Most Faithful Majesty does now, and for ever, graciously grant to the subjects of Her Britannic Majesty, permission to build and maintain such chapels and places of worship within Her dominions, it being always understood that the said chapels and places of worship are not to have steeples and bells.

Her Britannic Majesty's subjects shall likewise have full liberty to bury their dead, after the manner and with the ceremonies usual in their respective countries, and in the grounds and cemeteries which they shall have purchased and prepared for that purpose; and the sepulchres of the dead, in conformity to ancient and existing practice, shall in no way, or on any account, be disturbed.

Article II.

The subjects of either of the contracting parties may freely dispose, by will, of the personal effects which they shall possess in the territories of the other, and their heirs, although subjects of the other contracting party, may succeed to their personal effects, either by will or *ab intestato*, and may obtain possession of the same in due course of law, either in person, or by other persons appointed by them to act on their behalf. In the event of the absence of heirs, or of persons duly appointed to act for them, the Consul may be authorised to take charge, in due course of law, of the said effects, until the owner shall have made the necessary arrangements for obtaining possession of the property. If disputes shall arise between several claimants with respect to the title which each may have to the property, such disputes shall be decided by the Courts of the country in which the property is situated; and if hereafter any favour, as regards the possession or inheritance of landed or funded property *(bien fondo)*, shall be granted in the dominions of either of the high contracting parties to the subjects of any other nation, the same favour shall extend reciprocally to their respective subjects, as the case may be, either in Portugal or Great Britain.

Article III.

The subjects of either contracting party, residing within the dominions of the other, shall be free to manage their own affairs themselves, or to commit those affairs to the management of any persons whom they may appoint as their broker, factor, agent, or interpreter; nor shall any such British subjects be restrained in their choice of persons to act in such capacities, nor shall they be called upon to pay any salary or remuneration to any person whom they shall not choose to employ. Absolute freedom shall be given in all cases to the buyer and seller to bargain together, and to fix the price of any goods, wares, or merchandize, imported into, or to be exported from the dominions of either contracting party, the laws and established customs of the country being duly observed.

The subjects of either of the high contracting parties, residing within the dominions of the other, shall be at liberty to open retail stores and shops, under the same Municipal and Police Regulations as native subjects, and they shall not, in this respect, be liable to any other or higher taxes or imposts than those which are, or may be, paid by native subjects.

Article IV.

There shall be reciprocal liberty of commerce and navigation between the subjects of the two high contracting parties; and the subjects of the two Sovereigns respectively shall not pay, in the ports, harbours, roads, cities, towns, or places whatsoever in either kingdom, any other or higher duties, taxes, rates, or imposts, under whatsoever names designated or included, than those which are there paid by the subjects or citizens of the most favoured nation.

No duty of customs, or other impost, shall be charged upon any goods, the produce of the one country, upon importation by sea or by land from that country into the other, higher than the duty or impost charged upon goods of the same kind, the produce of, and imported from any other country; and no duty, restriction, or prohibition shall be imposed upon the importation and exportation, from one country to the other, of the goods and produce of each, which shall not be imposed upon goods of the same kind when imported from, or exported to any other country; and Her Majesty the Queen of Portugal, and Her Majesty the Queen of the United Kingdom of Great Britain and Ireland, do hereby bind and engage themselves, their heirs and successors, not to grant any favour, privilege, or immunity, in matters of commerce and navigation, to the subjects or citizens of any other State, which shall not also and at the same time be extended to the subjects of the other high contracting party, gratuitously, if the concession in favour of that other State shall have been gratuitous, and on giving, as nearly as possible, the same compensation or equivalent, if the concession shall have been conditional.

Article V.

No duties of tonnage, and no harbour, lighthouse, pilotage, quarantine, or other similar or corresponding duties, of whatever nature, or under whatever denomination, shall be imposed in either country upon the vessels of the other, in respect to voyages between the two countries, if laden; or in respect of any voyage, if in ballast, which shall not be equally imposed, in the like cases, on national vessels.

Article VI.

All goods, the growth, produce, or manufacture of their respective possessions, which can legally be imported into either country from the other, in ships of that other country, shall, when so imported, be subject to the same duties, whether they be imported in ships of the one country, or in ships of the other; and in like manner, all goods which can legally be exported from either country to the other in ships of that other country, shall, when so exported, be subject to the same duties, and be entitled to the same drawbacks, bounties, and allowances, whether they be exported in ships of the one country, or in ships of the other.

ARTICLE VII.

In order to promote and encourage the commercial intercourse between the dominions of the high contracting parties, for the mutual benefit of their respective subjects, Her Most Faithful Majesty, and Her Britannic Majesty, agree to take into consideration the duties now levied upon articles, the produce or manufacture of either country, with a view to make such reductions in those duties as may be consistent with the interests of the high contracting parties respectively.

This matter shall without delay be made the subject of a special negociation between the two Governments.

ARTICLE VIII.

Portuguese ships shall be allowed to proceed direct from any port of Her Most Faithful Majesty's dominions to any colony of Her Britannic Majesty, and to import into such colony any goods, the growth, produce, or manufacture of Portugal, or of any of the Portuguese dominions, except such goods as are prohibited to be imported into such colony; or which are admitted into it only from the dominions of Her Britannic Majesty; and such Portuguese ships and such goods so imported in them shall be liable, in such colony of Her Britannic Majesty, to no higher or other duties and charges than would be there payable on British ships importing the like sorts of goods; or on the like goods, the growth, produce, or manufacture of any foreign country, and allowed to be imported into the said colony in British ships. In like manner British ships shall be allowed to proceed direct from any port of Her Britannic Majesty's dominions to any colony of Her Most Faithful Majesty, and to import into such colony any goods, the growth, produce, or manufacture of the United Kingdom, or of any of the British dominions, except such goods as are prohibited to be imported into such colony, or which are admitted into it only from the dominions of Her Most Faithful Majesty; and such British ships, and such goods so imported in them, shall be liable, in such colony of Her Most Faithful Majesty, to no higher or other duties and charges than would be there payable on Portuguese ships importing the like sorts of goods, or on the like goods, the growth, produce, or manufacture of any foreign country, and allowed to be imported into the said colony in Portuguese ships.

ARTICLE IX.

Portuguese ships shall be allowed to export from any colony of Her Britannic Majesty, to any place not under the dominion of Her said Majesty, any goods not generally prohibited to be exported from such colony; and such Portuguese ships, and such goods so exported in them, shall be liable in such colony to no other or higher charges than would be payable by, and shall be entitled to the same drawbacks or bounties as would be there allowed on, British ships exporting such goods, or on such goods exported in British ships.

In like manner, British ships shall be allowed to export, from any colony of Her Most Faithful Majesty, to any place not under the dominion of Her said Majesty, any goods not generally prohibited to be exported from such colony; and such British ships, and such goods so exported in them, shall be liable, in such colony, to no other or higher charges than would be payable by, and shall be entitled to the same drawbacks or bounties as would be there allowable on Portuguese ships exporting such goods, or on such goods exported in Portuguese ships.

Article X.

It is hereby declared, that the stipulations of the present Treaty are not to be understood as applying to the navigation and carrying trade between one port and another situated in the dominions of either contracting party, if such navigation and trade should, in those dominions, be reserved by law exclusively to national vessels.

Vessels of either country shall, however, be permitted to discharge part of their cargoes at one port, in the dominions of either of the high contracting parties, and then to proceed with the remainder of their cargo to any other port or ports, in the same dominions, without paying any higher or other duties in such cases than national vessels would pay in like circumstances; and they shall be permitted to lade in like manner at different ports in the same voyage outwards.

Article XI.

The reciprocal liberty of commerce and navigation, declared and stipulated for by the present Treaty, shall not extend to contraband of war, or to articles the property of the enemies of either party.

The power granted by former Treaties to carry in the ships of either country goods and merchandize of any description whatever, the property of the enemies of the other country, is now mutually renounced.

Article XII.

In all cases in which, in either kingdom, the duty to be levied upon any goods imported from the other kingdom shall be not a fixed rate, but a proportion of the value of the goods, such *ad valorem* duty shall be ascertained and secured in the following manner—that is to say, the importer shall, on making his entry for the payment of duty at the custom house, sign a declaration, stating the description and the value of the goods at such amount as he shall deem proper; and in case the officer or officers of the custom house shall be of opinion that such valuation is insufficient, he or they shall be at liberty to take the goods on paying to the importer the value thereof, according to the declaration of the importer, together with an addition of ten per cent.; and the custom house officer shall, at the same time, return to the importer any duty which the importer may have paid upon such goods; and the amount of these sums shall be paid to the importer on the delivery of the goods to the said officer or officers, which must not be later than fifteen days from the first detention of the goods.

Article XIII.

Inasmuch as all merchandize, of whatever origin, whether admissible for home consumption or not, may be received and warehoused in all those ports of the United Kingdom of Great Britain and Ireland which are, by law, appointed to be warehousing ports for such articles, pending the entry of the same, either for home consumption, or for re-exportation, as the case may be, under the regulations appointed for this purpose, and without such articles being liable in the mean time to the payment of any of the duties with which they would be charged, if, upon arrival, they were entered for consumption within the United Kingdom; in like manner the Queen of Portugal consents and agrees that the ports of Her Most Faithful Majesty's dominions which now are, or which shall hereafter become, by law, warehousing ports, shall be free ports for receiving and warehousing, either for home consumption, or for re-exportation, as the case may be, all merchandize imported in British ships, and all articles whatever, the produce or manufacture of the British dominions, imported by Portuguese ships; and the articles thus received and warehoused, subject to due regulations, shall not be liable, in the mean time, to any of the duties with which they would be charged if they were entered for consumption on their arrival in the dominions of Her Most Faithful Majesty.

Article XIV.

All goods or merchandize found on board of, or which shall have formed the cargo, or part of the cargo of, a vessel of the one country, which shall be wrecked, or left derelict, on or near the coast of the other country, unless the importation of such goods or merchandize shall be absolutely prohibited by law, shall be admitted for home consumption in the country, on or near the coast of which such vessel shall be wrecked or left derelict, or such goods or merchandize may be found, on payment of the same duty, as if the said goods or merchandize had been imported in a national vessel, even though such goods or merchandize could not, by law, be imported into the said country in any other than national vessels; and in fixing the amount of duty to be paid on such goods or merchandize, regard shall be had to any damage which the said goods or merchandize may have sustained.

To prevent frauds, the Board of Customs of each nation shall exercise their judgment, as to the causes of wrecks; and when they are satisfied that the said wrecks were the result of accident or misfortune, and free from suspicion of collusion, they shall authorise, at the option of the proprietor or agent, if present, or otherwise of the Consul, the transhipment, or the sale for home consumption, of the goods or merchandize; provided that such goods and merchandize could have been legally imported by the ships of the one country into the ports of the other country.

If any ships of war or merchant vessels should be wrecked on the coasts of either of the high contracting parties, such ships or vessels, or any parts thereof, and all furniture and appurtenances belonging thereunto, and all goods or merchandize which shall be saved therefrom, or the produce thereof, if sold, shall be faithfully restored to the proprietors, upon being duly claimed by them, or by their agents duly authorised; or, if there are no such proprietors or agents on the spot, by the respective Consuls of the nation to which the proprietors of the said ships, vessels, or goods may belong, and in whose districts such wreck may have taken place, provided such claim be preferred within a year and a day from the time of such wreck; and such Consul, proprietor, or agent shall pay only the expenses incurred in the preservation of the property, together with the rate of salvage which would have been payable in the like case of a wreck of a national vessel; and the goods and merchandize saved from the wreck shall not be subject to duties, unless cleared for local consumption.

If any merchant vessel of either country should be driven into the ports of the other, by stress of weather, for the purpose of effecting necessary repairs, every facility shall be afforded to such vessel for obtaining the assistance it may be in need of. The strictest reciprocity shall be observed, in the most favourable sense, as to the relief to be afforded to such vessel from the duties, charges, and expenses in the ports of either nation, to which vessels entering solely for the purpose of trade are subjected. Sufficient time shall be allowed for the completion of repairs, and while the vessel shall be undergoing repair, its cargo shall not unnecessarily be required to be landed, either in whole or in part; and any difference of opinion which may arise between the custom house authorities and the masters of the said vessels, as to the necessity of landing all, or any part of the cargo, shall be referred to two sworn or public surveyors, one to be named by the chief custom house authority of the port, and the other by the Consul of the nation to which the vessel belongs.

Article XV.

Her Majesty the Queen of Portugal engages that the commerce of British subjects, within the Portuguese dominions, shall not be restrained, interrupted, or otherwise affected by the operation of any monopoly, contract, or exclusive privilege of sale or purchase whatsoever; but that the subjects of the United Kingdom shall have free and unrestrained permission to buy from, and sell to, whomsoever they please, and in whatever form and manner may be agreed upon between the purchaser and seller, without being obliged to give any preference or favour, in consequence of any such monopoly, contract, or exclusive privilege of sale and purchase; and Her Britannic Majesty engages that a like exemption from restraint, in respect to purchases or sales, shall be enjoyed by the subjects of Her Most Faithful Majesty trading to or residing in the United Kingdom. But it is distinctly to be understood that the present Article shall not be interpreted as affecting the special regulations now in force, or which may hereafter be enacted, with a view solely to the encouragement and amelioration of the Douro wine trade (it being always understood that British subjects shall, in respect of the said trade, be placed on the same footing as Portuguese subjects), or with regard to the exportation of the salt of Saint Ubes.

This Article does not invalidate the exclusive right possessed by the Crown of Portugal within its own dominions, to the farm for the sale of ivory, urzella, gold-dust, soap, gunpowder, and tobacco for home consumption; provided, however, that should the above-mentioned articles, generally or separately, ever become articles of free commerce within the dominions of Her Most Faithful Majesty, the subjects of Her Britannic Majesty shall be permitted to traffic in them as freely, and on the same footing, as the subjects or citizens of the most favoured nation.

Article XVI.

It is agreed and covenanted, that neither of the high contracting parties shall knowingly receive into, or retain in, its service, any subjects of the other party, who have deserted from the naval or military service of that other party; but that, on the contrary, each of the contracting parties shall respectively discharge from its service any such deserters, upon being required by the other party to do so.

It is further agreed and declared, that if either of the high contracting parties shall grant to any State any new favour or facility with respect to the recovery of deserters, such favour or facility shall be considered as granted also to the other contracting party, in the same manner as if the said favour or facility had been expressly stipulated by the present Treaty.

And it is further agreed, that if any apprentices or sailors shall desert from vessels belonging to the subjects of either of the high contracting parties, while such vessels are within any port in the territory of the other party, the Magistrates of such port and territory shall be bound to give every assistance in their power for the apprehension of such deserters, on application to that effect being made by the Consul of the party concerned, or by the deputy or representative of the Consul; and no public body, civil or religious, shall protect or harbour such deserters.

Article XVII.

Her Britannic Majesty, on the representation of Her Most Faithful Majesty, and in contemplation of the improving system of law and justice in Portugal, hereby consents to give up the exercise of the rights connected with the Conservatorial Court, so soon, and so long, as British subjects are admitted in Portugal to the benefit of securities similar or equivalent to those enjoyed by the subjects of Her Most Faithful Majesty in Great Britain, as regards trial by jury, protection from arrest without a warrant from a Magistrate, and examination within twenty-four hours after apprehension in *flagrante delicto*, and admission to bail; it being always understood that in other respects the subjects of Her Britannic Majesty in Portugal shall be placed on the same footing as Portuguese subjects, in all causes, whether civil or criminal; that they shall not, except in cases *flagrantes delicti*, be liable to imprisonment without formal commitment *(culpa formada)* under a warrant signed by a legal authority.

Article XVIII.

It is hereby declared, that Her Britannic Majesty, relying upon the guarantees which are or may be afforded to British subjects by the law of Portugal under the present constitutional system, henceforward claims for British subjects in Portugal no privileges which are not enjoyed by Portuguese subjects in the Portuguese or British dominions; it being, however, understood, that Her Britannic Majesty will be entitled, in the event (which God forbid!) of political troubles affecting the operation of the above-mentioned guarantees, to claim the re-establishment and observance of the privileges surrendered by the present and preceding Article.

Article XIX.

The present Treaty shall be in force for the term of ten years from the date hereof; and further, until the end of twelve months after either of the high contracting parties shall have given notice to the other of its intention to terminate the same; each of the high contracting parties reserving to itself the right of giving such notice to the other at the end of the said term of ten years, or at any subsequent time. And it is hereby agreed between them, that at the expiration of twelve months after such notice shall have been received by either party from the other, this Treaty, and all the provisions thereof, shall altogether cease and determine.

It is agreed, nevertheless, that either of the two high contracting parties shall have the right, at the end of five years, to require a revision of any Articles not affecting the principle of the Treaty, on giving six months' notice of a desire to make such revision; provided, however, that it be distinctly understood, that the power of giving such notice shall not extend beyond, nor be recognized after, the termination of the fifth year.

Article XX.

The present Treaty shall be ratified, and the ratifications shall be exchanged at Lisbon, at the expiration of two months from the date of its signature, or sooner, if possible.

In witness whereof the respective Plenipotentiaries have signed the same, and have affixed thereto the Seal of their Arms.

Done at Lisbon, the third day of July, in the year of our Lord one thousand eight hundred and forty-two.

(Signed) DUQUE DE PALMELLA.

(Signed) HOWARD DE WALDEN.

Ratification to the foregoing Treaty, by Her Most Faithful Majesty DONNA MARIA, *Queen of Portugal, dated the 29th July* 1842.

DONNA MARIA, *by the grace of God, Queen of Portugal and the Algarves, on this side of the Sea; in Africa, Sovereign of Guinea; and of Conquest, Navigation, and Commerce, of Ethiopia, Arabia, Persia, and of India, &c. I do hereby make it known to all, who this present Letter of Confirmation and Ratification should see, that on the 3rd day of the month of July, of the current year* (1842), *was concluded and signed, in the City of Lisbon, between myself and Her Majesty the Queen of the United Kingdom of Great Britain and Ireland, through the respective Plenipotentiaries invested with competent authority, a Treaty of Commerce and Navigation, with the view to give all possible plenitude to mutual Commerce between the two States.*

And the present being the same Treaty, the tenor of which is above specified, and as the same has been approved, considered, and examined by me, as regards all its contents, after consulting the Council of State, I do hereby ratify and confirm it, in all its parts; and, by these presents, do make it firm and valid, so that it may produce its due effect; promising in Faith, and under the Royal Word, to observe and fulfil it by all means possible. In witness whereof I have caused this to be passed by me, signed and stamped with the Great Seal of my Arms, and registered by my Councillor, Minister, and Secretary of State.

Given at the Palace of Cintra, the 29th of the month of July, A. D. 1842.

"THE QUEEN." (In the hand-writing of Her Most Faithful Majesty.)

Translation of Regulations in regard to Commerce, passed by the Court of Lisbon, in connection with the foregoing Treaty, under date the 5th June 1844.

Whereas it is necessary to declare which are the ports of the Ultra-Marine Provinces, wherein admission should be granted to vessels belonging to the nations with whom Agreement has been entered into, for the purpose of trading with those Provinces; and whereas such a declaration is every day becoming more urgently required, not only because the faith of the Treaties calls for it, but also because, in the absence of such a declaration, serious inconvenience and evil may result to commerce, at the same time that it is absolutely necessary to organize Rules for the various Customs Officers, according to the exigencies and the nature af the trade of each port; Whereas it is equally necessary to make the said declaration to avoid disputes, which may easily arise from no specification existing of the ports where, in conformity with the Treaties, admission should be granted to foreign vessels; And whereas the security of the said provinces, and the preservation and increase of commercial interests between the various parts of the national territory, as well as the interests of the Portuguese manufacturers, render it requisite that specification should be made of such goods and merchandize, the importation of which into Ultra-Marine Provinces should be totally prohibited, or of such others whose importation should be limited only to cases where they may be of Portuguese manufacture, and imported in Portuguese vessels; And whereas, for these reasons, my Government has presented to the Chamber of the Deputies the necessary legal proposal, which, however, has not come under their discussion, owing to various other matters and circumstances which have prevented it, and I have weighed these reasons, and given my attention to the necessity for the provisions now specially called for, for the good of the Ultra-Marine Provinces, the state of which requires that immediate measures be taken to raise them to wealth and prosperity, at which they can only arrive by means of legal commerce; Availing myself of the authority held out by Article I. of the Regulations of the Second of May, One thousand Eight hundred and Forty-three, having consulted the Council of the Ministers and of the State, I do hereby direct as follows:—

Article I.

British vessels shall be admitted (in conformity with the stipulations of the Treaty of the third of July, one thousand eight hundred and forty-two, entered into between the Portuguese and British Governments) in the ports of the Portuguese possessions named in Table No. 1. The trade of other ports of the Portuguese possessions, not mentioned in that table, shall be considered as coasting navigation, and, as such, can only be made in Portuguese vessels.

Article II.

The importation of the articles mentioned in Table No. 2 into Portuguese possessions is totally prohibited; and equal prohibition exists against the importation, into those possessions, of articles which are likewise produced in those possessions, and exported therefrom.

Exception, however, is made of articles produced in neighbouring countries, when imported by land.

Article III.

The goods and merchandize contained in Table No. 3 shall only be admitted into Portuguese possessions when they are constructed, produced, or manufactured in Portuguese dominions, and conveyed in Portuguese vessels.

Article IV.

The ships and goods from the British East India Company's possessions will be liable, at the Portuguese possessions, to increased duties, equal to the duties which the Portuguese ships and goods pay at the possessions of the said British Company.

Article V.

It is permitted to ship on British vessels, for any foreign port whatever, all kinds of produce from Portuguese possessions, excepting the orchel-weed, and such other articles of produce as are, or may come to be, under the administration of the State, or are contracted for; and these can only be exported in national ships.

Upon all the above, however, duty is to be paid, at the existing rates, or at such other rates as may be established hereafter.

Article VI.

At the ports named in Table No. 1, admission should in like manner be granted to vessels of the different nations with whom it may have been agreed to trade in the Portuguese ports or possessions.

Article VII.

Any legislation to the contrary is cancelled.

The Minister and Secretary of State for the Affairs of Marine and Colonies will have the above published, and given effect to.

Palace of Necessidades, 5th June 1844.

(Signed) "THE QUEEN."

(Signed by) Joaquim Jose Falcao.

TABLE No. 1.

PORTS OF THE PORTUGUESE POSSESSIONS WHEREIN FOREIGN VESSELS MAY BE ADMITTED.

Cape de Verde Islands.

In San Thiago Island (St. Jago), the port of Da Villa de Praia (Porto Praya); in Mayo Island, Port Inglez; in the island of Boavista (Bona Vista), the port of Salrei; in the island of Sal, the port of Madama, or Port Martins.

Coast of Guinea.

The ports of Bissau and Cacheu.

Islands of St. Thomé and Prince.

In Prince Island, the port also called Agulas Bay, or any other place to which the custom house should be transferred; in the island of St. Thomé the port of the fort.

Angola and Benguella.

The port of Loanda, and the port of Benguella.

Coast of Mozambique.

The port of Mozambique.

Portuguese States in the East Indies.

The ports of Goa, Damaun, and Diu.

Archipelago of Solor and Timor.

On the island of Timor, the port of Delly.

Secretariate of State for the Marine and Colonial Affairs, 5th June 1844.

(Signed) JOAQUIM JOSE FALCAO.

TABLE No. 2.

Articles, the importation of which into Portuguese Possessions is totally prohibited.

Artillery guns.
Projectiles.
Fire-lights.

Secretariate of State for the Affairs of the Marine and Colonies, 5th June 1844.

(Signed) JOAQUIM JOSE FALCAO.

TABLE No. 3.

Articles which can only be imported into the Portuguese Possessions when they are of Portuguese Manufacture, and are conveyed in Portuguese Vessels.

Gunpowder.
Fire-arms.
Salt.
Soap.
Snuff, and all kinds of tobacco powder.
Wines of all kinds, except champagne.
Liqueurs.
Spirits.
Vinegar.
Olive, cocoanut, and palm oil.
Zuartes blue cotton cloth.
Scythes.
Small ditto.
Axes.
Chisels.
Nails, of all sorts.
Hats, of all sorts.
Linen cloth.
Pork (smoked and preserved).
Household furniture, of wood.
Wearing apparel, and made shoes.

All kinds of goods and merchandize, whose importation into Portugal is prohibited by the general regulations of the custom houses.

N. B.—In this table the " spirit of sugar-cane" is not included, and it may therefore continue to be admitted, until measures are adopted respecting it.

Secretariate of State for the Marine and Colonial Affairs, 5th June 1844.

(Signed) JOAQUIM JOSE FALCAO.

Treaty between HER BRITANNIC MAJESTY *and the* QUEEN OF PORTUGAL, *for the* SUPPRESSION *of the* TRAFFIC IN SLAVES. *Signed at Lisbon, July 3rd,* 1842.

Their Majesties the Queen of the United Kingdom of Great Britain and Ireland, and the Queen of Portugal and the Algarves, being earnestly desirous of putting an immediate end to the barbarous and piratical practice of transporting the Natives of Africa across the sea, for the purpose of consigning them to Slavery; and Their said Majesties, considering that this infamous practice was declared to be a highly Penal Crime by the Law of Great Britain, in the year One thousand Eight hundred and Seven, and has likewise been prohibited, under severe penalties, by the Law of Portugal, in December One thousand Eight hundred and Thirty-six; and their said Majesties being of opinion, that in order the more completely to prevent for the future the perpetration of this crime, and to render more effectual the operation of the Laws enacted in each country for its punishment, it will be expedient to establish Regulations of Maritime Police, and to constitute Colonial Commissions, to which Regulations and Commissions Vessels navigating under the flag of either party, and not belonging to one or the other of the Royal Navies, shall be amenable ; Their said Majesties have resolved to conclude a Treaty for this purpose, and have accordingly named as their Plenipotentiaries, that is to say, Her Majesty the Queen of the United Kingdom of Great Britain and Ireland, CHARLES AUGUSTUS, LORD HOWARD DE WALDEN, *a Peer of the United Kingdom of Great Britain and Ireland, Knight Grand Cross of the Most Illustrious Order of the Bath, Envoy Extraordinary and Minister Plenipotentiary of Her Britannic Majesty at the Court of Her Most Faithful Majesty, &c. &c. &c. ; and Her Majesty the Queen of Portugal and Algarves,* DON PEDRO DE SOUZA HOLSTEIN, *Duke of Palmella, President for Life of the Chamber of Peers, Councillor of State, Grand Cross of the Order of Christ, and of the Tower and Sword, Captain of the Royal Guard of Archers, Knight of the Distinguished Order of the Golden Fleece, and Grand Cross of the Orders of Charles III. in Spain, of the Legion of Honour in France, of Saint Alexander Newsky in Russia, Knight of the Order of St. John of Jerusalem, Count of Sanfré in Piedmont, Minister and Honorary Secretary of State, &c. &c. &c. ; who, having communicated to each other their respective full powers, found to be in due and proper form, have agreed upon the following Articles :—*

ARTICLE I.

The two high contracting parties mutually declare to each other, that the infamous and piratical practice of transporting the natives of Africa by sea, for the purpose of consigning them to slavery, is, and shall for ever continue to be, a strictly prohibited aud highly penal crime, in every part of their respective dominions, and for all the subjects of their respective Crowns.

ARTICLE II.

The two high contracting parties mutually consent that those ships of their royal navies respectively, which shall be provided with special instructions as hereinafter mentioned, may visit and search such vessels of the two nations as may, upon reasonable grounds, be suspected of being engaged in transporting Negroes for the purpose of consigning them to slavery, or of having been fitted out for that purpose, or of having been so employed during the voyage in which they are met by the said cruizers; and the said high contracting parties also consent, that such cruizers may detain, and send or carry away such vessels, in order that they may be brought to trial in the manner hereinafter agreed upon; and in order to fix the reciprocal right of search, in such a manner as shall be adapted to the attainment of the objects of this Treaty, and shall at the same time prevent doubts, disputes, and complaints, it is agreed, that the said right of search shall be exercised in the manner and according to the Rules following :—

First.—It shall never be exercised except by vessels of war, authorised expressly for that purpose, according to the stipulations of this Treaty.

Second.—In no case shall the right of search be exercised with respect to a vessel of the royal navy of either of the two powers.

Third.—Whenever a vessel is searched by a ship of war, the commander of such ship of war shall, immediately upon coming on board the vessel which is to be so searched, and before he begins the search, exhibit to the commander of the vessel which is to be searched the document by which he is duly authorised to make the search; and he shall deliver to the said commander of the vessel which is to be searched, a certificate signed by himself, stating his rank in the naval service of his country, and the name of the ship of war which he commands; and this certificate shall also declare, that the only object of the search is to ascertain whether the vessel to be searched is employed in transporting Negroes or others in order to consign them to slavery, or is fitted up for such purpose. When the search is made by an officer of the cruizer who is not the commander thereof, such officer shall proceed strictly in the same manner as if he were the commander, after having exhibited to the captain of the vessel to be searched a copy of the above-mentioned document, signed by the commander of the cruizer; and he shall, in like manner, deliver a certificate, signed by himself, stating his rank in the royal navy, the name of the commander by whose orders he proceeds to make the search, that of the cruizer in which he sails, and the object of the search, as has been already laid down. If it appears from the search that the papers of the vessel are in regular order, and that the vessel is employed for lawful purposes, the officer shall enter in the log-book of the vessel, that the search has been made in pursuance of the aforesaid special orders; and the vessel shall be left at liberty to pursue her voyage.

Fourth.—The rank of the officer who makes the search must not be lower than that of lieutenant of the royal navy, unless he be the officer who shall at the time be second in command of the searching vessel; or unless the command shall, by reason of death or otherwise, be held by an officer of inferior rank.

Fifth.—The reciprocal right of search and detention shall not be exercised within the Mediterranean Sea, nor within the seas in Europe which lie without the Straits of Gibraltar, and to the northward of the thirty-seventh parallel of north latitude, and within and to the eastward of the meridian of longitude twenty degrees west of Greenwich.

Article III.

In order to regulate the mode of carrying the provisions of the preceding Article into execution, it is agreed—

First.—That all ships of the royal navies of the two nations, which shall be hereafter employed to prevent the transport of Negroes or others for the purpose of consigning them to slavery, shall be furnished by their respective

Governments with a copy, in the English and Portuguese languages, of the present Treaty; of the Instructions A, for cruizers, annexed thereto; and of the Regulations B, for the Mixed Commissions, annexed thereto; which Annexes, respectively, shall be considered as an integral part of the Treaty.*

Second.—That each of the high contracting parties shall, from time to time, and as often as any changes are made in the ships of war employed in this service, communicate to the other the names of the several ships furnished with such instructions; the force of each, and the names of their several commanders, and of the officers second in command.

Third.—That if at any time there shall be just cause to suspect that any vessel sailing under the flag of either nation, and proceeding under the convoy of any ship or ships of war of either of the contracting parties, is engaged, or is intended to be engaged, in the transport of Negroes or others, for the purpose of consigning them to slavery; or is fitted out for that purpose; or has, during the voyage in which she has been met with, been so employed; it shall be the duty of any commander of any ship of the royal navy of either of the two high contracting parties, furnished with such instructions as aforesaid, to communicate in writing his suspicions to the commander of the convoy; and the said commander of the convoy shall give an acknowledgment in writing of the said communication; and the said commander of the convoy, accompanied by the commander of the cruizer, shall proceed to search the suspected vessel. If the suspicions shall prove to be well founded, according to the tenor of this Treaty, then the said vessel shall be conducted or sent by the commander of the convoy to one of the points where the Mixed Commissions are stationed, in order that the vessel may undergo the sentence applicable to her case.

Fourth.—It shall not be lawful to visit or detain, under any pretext or motive whatever, any merchant vessel when at anchor in any port or roadstead belonging to either of the two high contracting parties, or within cannon-shot of the batteries on shore, unless on a written demand for co-operation on the part of the authorities of such country; but should any suspected vessel be met with in such port or roadstead, due representation of the same is to be made to the authorities of the country, requesting them to take the necessary measures to prevent the violation of the stipulations of this Treaty; and the said authorities shall proceed to take effectual measures accordingly.

Article IV.

As the two preceding Articles are entirely reciprocal, the two high contracting parties engage mutually to make good any losses which their respective subjects may incur by any arbitrary and illegal detention of their vessels; it being understood, that this compensation shall be made by the Government whose cruizer shall have been guilty of such arbitrary and illegal detention. The compensation for damages, of which this Article treats, shall be made within the term of one year, reckoned from the day on which the Mixed

60

Commission pronounces sentence on the vessel, for the detention of which such compensation is claimed.

ARTICLE V.

It is, however, distinctly understood between the two high contracting parties, that no stipulation of the present Treaty shall be interpreted as interfering with the right of Portuguese subjects to be accompanied, in voyages to and from the Portuguese possessions off the coast of Africa, by slaves who are *bonâ fide* household servants, and who may be duly named and described as such in passports, wherewith the vessel must be furnished, from the highest civil authority at the place where such slaves shall have embarked : Provided—

First,—That in such voyages, no Portuguese subject, except he be a Portuguese settler, removing definitively from his residence in a Portuguese possession on the coast of Africa, shall be accompanied by more than two slaves, being *bonâ fide* household servants.

Secondly,—That such a settler removing definitively, with his family, from his residence in a Portuguese possession on the coast of Africa, shall not be accompanied by more than ten slaves, and that all these slaves shall be *bonâ fide* his household servants.

Thirdly,—That such household slaves shall be found at large, and unconfined in the vessel; and clothed like Europeans in similar circumstances.

Fourthly,—That no other slaves shall be embarked on board of the vessel in which the said household servants shall be found; and that the voyage, on which such settler and his family shall be so accompanied by such household slaves, shall be a direct voyage to the Portuguese islands of Cape Verd, Princes, or St. Thomas, from some place in the Portuguese possessions on the coast of Africa, where the said settler shall have been permanently residing.

Fifthly,—That the passports above-mentioned shall enumerate each of the persons on board the vessel, and shall state their names, sex, ages, and occupation, their last place of residence, and the place to which they are going.

Sixthly,—That there be nothing in the equipment or character of the vessel in which such household slaves may be found, which shall justify its detention under the provisions of this Treaty.

But if the equipment or character of the vessel shall justify the detention of the vessel under the stipulations of the present Treaty ; or if any of the regulations specified in this Article shall be unobserved or violated in respect to such vessel, then her master, and her crew, and the owner or owners of the vessel, of the cargo, or of the slaves, shall be liable to be proceeded against as accomplices in an infraction of the present Treaty, and to be punished accordingly ; and the vessel and cargo shall be adjudged and condemned, and the slaves shall be liberated.

ARTICLE VI.

In order to bring to adjudication, with as little delay and inconvenience as possible, the vessels which may be detained according to the tenor of Article II.

of this Treaty, there shall be established, as soon as may be practicable, two or more Mixed Commissions, formed of an equal number of individuals of the two nations, and named for this purpose by their respective Sovereigns.

Of these Commissions, one half shall reside in possessions belonging to Her Britannic Majesty, the other half within the territories of Her Most Faithful Majesty; and the two Governments, at the period of exchanging the ratifications of the present Treaty, shall declare, each for its own dominions, in what places the Commissions shall respectively reside. Each of the two high contracting parties reserves to itself the right of changing, at its pleasure, the place of residence of the Commissions held within its own dominions; provided always, that two at least of the said Commissions shall always be held either on the coast of Africa, or in one of the islands off that coast.

These Commissions shall judge the causes submitted to them according to the provisions of the present Treaty, without appeal, and according to the regulations and instructions which are annexed to the present Treaty, and which are considered as forming an integral part thereof.

Article VII.

The Mixed Commission at present established and sitting under the Convention between Great Britain and Portugal of the 28th of July 1817, shall continue to exercise its functions, and shall, from and after the end of six months after the exchange of the ratifications of this Treaty, and until the appointment and definitive establishment of the Mixed Commissions under the present Treaty, adjudge without appeal, according to the principles and stipulations of the present Treaty, and of the Annexes thereof, the cases of such vessels as may be sent or brought before it; and any vacancies which may occur in such Mixed Commission shall be filled up in the same manner in which vacancies in the Mixed Commissions to be established under the provisions of this Treaty are to be supplied.

Article VIII.

If the commanding officer of any of the ships of the royal navies of Great Britain and Portugal respectively, duly commissioned according to the provisions of Article II. of this Treaty, shall deviate in any respect from the stipulations of the said Treaty, or from the instructions annexed to it, the Government which shall conceive itself to be wronged thereby shall be entitled to demand reparation; and in such case, the Government to which such commanding officer may belong, binds itself to cause inquiry to be made into the subject of the complaint, and to inflict upon the said officer a punishment proportioned to any wilful transgression which he may have committed.

Article IX.

Any vessel, British or Portuguese, which shall be visited by virtue of the present Treaty, may lawfully be detained, and may be sent or brought before one of the Mixed Commissions established in pursuance of the provisions thereof, if any of the things hereinafter mentioned shall be found in her outfit or equipment, or shall be proved to have been on board during the voyage in which the vessel was proceeding when captured, viz :—

First.—Hatches with open gratings, instead of the close hatches which are usual in merchant vessels.

Secondly.—Divisions or bulk-heads, in the hold or on deck, in greater number than are necessary for vessels engaged in lawful trade.

Thirdly.—Spare plank fitted for being laid down as a second or slave deck.

Fourthly.—Shackles, bolts, or handcuffs.

Fifthly.—A larger quantity of water, in casks or in tanks, than is requisite for the consumption of the crew of the vessel, as a merchant vessel.

Sixthly.—An extraordinary number of water-casks, or of other vessels for holding liquid, unless the master shall produce a certificate from the custom house at the place from which he cleared outwards, stating that sufficient security had been given by the owners of such vessel, that such extra quantity of casks, or of other vessels, should only be used for the reception of palm oil, or for other purposes of lawful commerce.

Seventhly.—A greater quantity of mess tubs or kids than are requisite for the use of the crew of the vessel, as a merchant vessel.

Eighthly.—A boiler, or other cooking apparatus, of an unusual size, and larger, or fitted for being made larger, than requisite for the use of the crew of the vessel, as a merchant vessel; or more than one boiler, or other cooking apparatus, of the ordinary size.

Ninthly.—An extraordinary quantity of rice, of the flour of Brazil manioc, or cassada, commonly called farinha, of maize, or of Indian corn, or of any other article of food whatever, beyond what might probably be requisite for the use of the crew; such rice, flour, maize, Indian corn, or other article of food, not being entered on the manifest, as part of the cargo for trade.

Tenthly.—A quantity of mats or matting, larger than is necessary for the use of the crew of the vessel, as a merchant vessel.

Any one or more of these several things, if proved to have been found on board, or to have been on board during the voyage on which the vessel was proceeding when captured, shall be considered as *primâ facie* evidence of the actual employment of the vessel in the transport of Negroes or others, for the purpose of consigning them to slavery; and the vessel shall thereupon be condemned, and shall be declared lawful prize, unless clear and incontestably satisfactory evidence, on the part of the master or owners, shall establish, to the satisfaction of the Court, that such vessel was, at the time of her detention or capture, employed on some legal pursuit, and that such of the several things above enumerated, as were found on board of her at the time of her detention, or had been on board of her on the voyage on which she was proceeding when captured, were needed for legal purposes on that particular voyage.

Article X.

If any of the things specified in the preceding Article shall be found in any vessel which is detained under the stipulations of this Treaty, or shall be proved to have been on board the vessel during the voyage on which the vessel was proceeding when captured, no compensation for losses, damages, or expenses, consequent upon the detention of such vessel, shall in any case be granted, either to her master or to her owner, or to any other person interested in her equipment or lading, even though the Mixed Commission should not pronounce any sentence of condemnation in consequence of her detention.

Article XI.

In all cases in which a vessel shall be detained, under this Treaty, by the respective cruizers of the contracting parties, as having been engaged in transporting Negroes or others for the purpose of consigning them to slavery, or as having been fitted out for that purpose, and shall consequently be adjudged and condemned by the Mixed Commissions to be established as aforesaid, either of the two Governments may purchase the condemned vessel for the use of its royal navy, at a price to be fixed upon by a competent person, to be chosen by the Court of Mixed Commission for that purpose; but the Government whose cruizer shall have detained the condemned vessel shall have the first choice of purchasing her. But if the condemned vessel shall not be so purchased, the said vessel shall, immediately after condemnation, be broken up entirely, and shall be sold in separate parts, after having been so broken up.

Article XII.

When any vessel shall have been declared good prize by one of the Mixed Commissions, the captain, pilot, crew, and passengers found on board the said vessel shall be immediately placed at the disposal of the Government of the country under whose flag the said vessel was navigating at the time of her capture, to be tried and punished according to the laws of that country. In the like manner, the owner of the vessel, the persons interested in the equipment and cargo, and their several Agents, shall be tried and punished, unless they can prove that they took no part in that infraction of the present Treaty on account of which the vessel was condemned.

Article XIII.

Each of the two high contracting parties most solemnly binds itself to guarantee the liberty of the Negroes who may be emancipated under the present Treaty, by the Mixed Commissions sitting within the colonies or possessions of such Government; and to afford from time to time, and whenever demanded by the other party, or by the members of the Mixed Commissions by whose sentence the slaves shall have been liberated, the fullest information as to the state and condition of such Negroes, with a view of ensuring the due execution of the Treaty in this respect.

For this purpose, the Regulations C, annexed to this Treaty, as to the treatment of Negroes liberated by sentence of the Mixed Commissions, have been drawn up, and are declared to form an integral part of this Treaty; the two high contracting parties reserving to themselves the right to alter, by common consent and by mutual agreement, but not otherwise, the terms and tenor of such Regulations.

ARTICLE XIV.

The Acts or Instruments annexed to this Treaty, and which, it is mutually agreed, shall form an integral part thereof, are as follows:—

A. Instructions for the ships of the royal navies of both nations, employed to prevent the transport of Negroes or others, for the purpose of consigning them to slavery.

B. Regulations for the Mixed Commissions.

C. Regulations as to the treatment of liberated Negroes.

ARTICLE XV.

Her Majesty the Queen of Portugal and Algarves hereby declares the Slave Trade to be Piracy, and that those of her subjects who shall, under any pretext whatever, take any part in the traffic in slaves, shall be subjected to the most severe secondary punishment.

ARTICLE XVI.

The present Treaty shall be ratified, and the ratifications shall be exchanged at Lisbon, at the expiration of two months from the date of its signature, or sooner, if possible.

In witness whereof, the respective Plenipotentiaries have signed, in duplicate originals, English and Portuguese, the present Treaty, and have thereunto affixed the Seal of their Arms.

Done at Lisbon, the third day of July, in the year of our Lord one thousand eight hundred and forty-two.

(Signed) HOWARD DE WALDEN. (Signed) DUQUE DE PALMELLA.

Additional Article to the Treaty concluded between Great Britain and Portugal, for the Abolition of Slave Trade, on the third Day of July, in the Year of our Lord One thousand Eight hundred and Forty-two.

As the object of this Treaty, and of the three Annexes which form part of it, is no other than that of preventing the traffic in slaves, without any annoyance to the respective merchant shipping of the two nations; and as this fraudulent traffic is carried on from the coast of Africa, where the Crown of Portugal has also extensive colonial possessions, where legitimate commerce exists, and which it is important in the spirit of this Treaty to promote and protect: the high contracting parties, animated by the same sentiments, agree, that if in future it should appear necessary to either of them to adopt new measures, or alter any of the executive regulations for attaining the said beneficent object, or for obviating any unforeseen inconvenience to the aforesaid shipping or lawful commerce which experience shall have made known, in consequence of those established in this Treaty and its Annexes proving inefficacious or injurious, the said high contracting parties engage to consult together for the more complete attainment of the object proposed.

The present additional Article shall have the same force and effect as if it were inserted, word for word, in the Treaty signed on this day; and it shall be ratified, and the ratifications shall be exchanged within the term of two months from the date of its signature, or sooner, if possible.

In witness whereof the respective Plenipotentiaries have signed it, and have affixed thereto the Seal of their Arms.

Done at Lisbon, the third of July, one thousand eight hundred and forty-two.

(Signed) HOWARD DE WALDEN. (Signed) DUQUE DE PALMELLA.

ANNEX A

To the Treaty between Great Britain and Portugal, upon Slave Trade, of the 3rd *day of July*, 1842.

Instructions for the Ships of the British and Portuguese Royal Navies employed to prevent the Traffic in Slaves.

ARTICLE I.

The commander of any ship belonging to the royal British or Portuguese navy, who shall be furnished with these instructions, shall have a right to visit, search, and detain, except within the limits excepted in Article II. of the Treaty, any British or Portuguese vessel which shall be actually engaged, or shall be suspected to be engaged, in transporting Negroes or others, for the purpose of consigning them to slavery, or to be fitted out with such view, or to have been so employed during the voyage on which she may be met with by such ship of the British or Portuguese navy; and such commander shall thereupon bring or send such vessel, as soon as possible, for judgment before that one of the Mixed Commissions established in virtue of Article VI. of the said Treaty which shall be the nearest to the place of detention, or which such commander shall, upon his own responsibility, judge can be soonest reached from such place.

Article II.

Whenever a ship of either of the royal navies, duly authorised as aforesaid, shall meet a vessel liable to be visited under the provisions of the said Treaty, the search shall be conducted in the mildest manner, and with every attention which ought to be observed between allied and friendly nations; and the search shall, in all cases, be made by an officer holding a rank not lower than that of lieutenant in the navies of Great Britain and Portugal, respectively, unless the command shall, by reason of death or otherwise, be held by an officer of inferior rank, or unless the officer who makes the search shall at the time be second in command of the ship by which such search is made.

Article III.

The commander of any ship of the two royal navies, duly authorised as aforesaid, who may detain any vessel in pursuance of the tenor of the present instructions, shall, at the time of detention, draw up in writing an authentic declaration, which shall exhibit the state in which he found the detained vessel; which declaration shall be signed by himself, and shall be given in or sent, together with the captured vessel, to the Mixed Commission before which such vessel shall be carried or sent for adjudication. He shall deliver to the master of the detained vessel a signed certificate of the papers seized on board the same, as well as of the number of slaves found on board at the moment of detention.

In the authenticated declaration which the captor is hereby required to make, as well as in the certificate of the papers seized, he shall insert his own name, the name of the capturing ship, the latitude and longitude of the place where the detention shall have been made, and the number of slaves found on board the vessel at the time of the detention.

When the commander of the cruizer shall not think proper to take upon himself to carry in and deliver up the detained vessel, he shall not entrust that duty to an officer below the rank of lieutenant in the navy, unless it be to the officer who at the time shall not be lower than third in command of the detaining ship.

The officer in charge of the vessel detained shall, at the time of bringing the vessel's papers before the Mixed Commission, deliver into the Court a paper, signed by himself, and verified on oath, stating any changes which may have taken place in respect to the vessel, her crew, the slaves, if any, and her cargo, between the period of her detention and the time of delivering in such papers.

Article IV.

No part of the crew or passengers, or of the cargo, or of the slaves found on board the vessel seized, shall be withdrawn from it, until the said vessel shall have been delivered over to one of the Mixed Commissions; unless the transfer of the whole or part of the crew or passengers, or of the whole or part of the slaves found on board, should be considered necessary, either to preserve their lives, or for any other humane consideration, or for the safety of the persons charged with the conduct of the vessel after its seizure; in which case the commander of the cruizer, or the officer charged with the said seized vessel, shall draw out a certificate, in which he shall declare the reasons of the said transfer; and the commanders, sailors, or passengers thus transferred shall be conducted to the same port as the vessel and its cargo.

The undersigned Plenipotentiaries have agreed, in conformity with Article XIV. of the Treaty signed by them on this day, the third of July 1842, that the preceding Instructions, consisting of four Articles, shall be annexed to the said Treaty, and shall be considered an integral part thereof.

The third day of July, one thousand eight hundred and forty-two.

HOWARD DE WALDEN. DUQUE DE PALMELLA.

ANNEX B

To the Treaty between Great Britain and Portugal, upon Slave Trade, of the 3rd day of July 1842.

Regulations for the Mixed Commissions which are to adjudge the cases of vessels under the Treaty between Great Britain and Portugal, upon Slave Trade, of the Third day of July, One thousand Eight hundred and Forty-two.

ARTICLE I.

The Mixed Commissions to be established under the provisions of the Treaty, of which these Regulations are declared to be an integral part, shall be composed in the following manner:—

Each of the two high contracting parties shall name a Commisssioner and an Arbitrator, who shall be authorised to hear and to decide, without appeal, all cases of the capture or detention of vessels which, in pursuance of the stipulations of the aforesaid Treaty, shall be brought before them. The Commissioners and the Arbitrators shall, before entering upon the duties of their office, respectively make oath before the principal Magistrate of the places in which such Commissions respectively shall reside, that they will judge fairly and faithfully; that they will have no preference, either for the claimants or the captors; and that they will act, in all their decisions, in pursuance of the stipulations of the aforesaid Treaty.

61

There shall be attached to each of such Commissions a Secretary or Registrar, who shall be appointed by the Sovereign in whose territories such Commission shall reside. Such Secretary or Registrar shall register all the acts of such Commission, and shall, previously to entering upon his office, make oath before the Commission to which he is appointed, that he will conduct himself with due respect for its authority, and will act with fidelity and impartiality in all matters relating to his said office.

The salary of the Secretary or Registrar of the Commissions which are to be established in the dominions of Her Britannic Majesty, shall be paid by Her said Majesty; and that of the Secretary or Registrar of the Commissions which are to be established in the colonial possessions of Portugal, shall be paid by Her Most Faithful Majesty.

Each of the Governments shall defray half of the aggregate amount of the incidental expenses of such Commissions.

Article II.

The expenses incurred by the officer charged with the reception, maintenance, and care of the detained vessel, slaves, and cargo, and with the execution of the sentence; and all disbursements occasioned by bringing a vessel to adjudication; shall, in case of condemnation, be defrayed from the funds arising from the sale of the materials of the vessel, after the same shall have been broken up, of the vessel's stores, and of such part of the cargo as shall consist of merchandize; and in case the proceeds arising from this sale should not prove sufficient to defray such expenses, the deficiency shall be made good by the Government of the country within whose territories the adjudication shall have taken place.

If the detained vessel shall be released, the expenses occasioned by bringing her to adjudication shall be defrayed by the captor; excepting in the cases specified and otherwise provided for under Article X. of the Treaty to which these Regulations form an Annex, and under Article VII. of these Regulations.

Article III.

The Mixed Commissions are to decide upon the legality of the detention of such vessels as the cruizers of either nation shall, in pursuance of the said Treaty, detain.

These Commissions shall judge definitively, and without appeal, all questions which shall arise out of the capture and detention of such vessels.

The proceedings of these Commissions shall take place with as little delay as possible; and, for this purpose, the Commissions are required to decide each case, as far as may be practicable, within the space of twenty days, to be counted from the day on which the detained vessel shall be brought into the port where the deciding Commission shall reside.

The final sentence shall not, in any case, be delayed beyond the period of two months, either on account of the absence of witnesses, or for any other cause; except upon the application of any of the parties interested; in which case, upon such party or parties giving satisfactory security, that they will take upon themselves the expensè and risk of the delay, the Commission may, at their discretion, grant an additional delay not exceeding four months.

Either party shall be allowed to employ such Counsel as he may think fit, to assist him in the conduct of his cause. The proceedings of the said Mixed Commissions shall be open to the public; and all the essential parts of the proceedings of the said Commissions shall be written down in the language of the country in which the Commissions shall respectively reside.

Article IV.

The form of the process shall be as follows:—

The Commissioners appointed by the two Governments, respectively, shall, in the first place, examine the papers of the detained vessel, and take the depositions of the master or commander, and two or three, at least, of the principal individuals on board of such vessel; as well as the declaration, on oath, of the captor, should such declaration appear necessary, in order to enable them to judge and pronounce whether the said vessel has been justly detained or not, according to the stipulations of the aforesaid Treaty; and in order that the vessel may be condemned or released accordingly.

In the event of the two Commissioners not agreeing as to the sentence which they ought to pronounce in any case brought before them, either with respect to the legality of the detention, the liability of the vessel to condemnation, or the indemnification to be allowed, or as to any other question which may arise out of the said capture; or if any difference of opinion should arise between them, as to the mode of proceeding in the said Commission,—they shall draw, by lot, the name of one of the two Arbitrators so appointed as aforesaid; which Arbitrator, after having considered the proceedings which have taken place, shall consult with the two above-mentioned Commissioners; and the final sentence or decision shall be pronounced conformably to the opinion of the majority of the three.

Article V.

If the detained vessel shall be restored by the sentence of the Commission, the vessel and her cargo, in the state in which they shall then be found, shall forthwith be given up to the master, or to the person who represents him; and such master or other person may, before the same Commission, claim to have a valuation made of the amount of the damages which he may have a right to demand. The captor himself, and in his default his Government, shall remain responsible for the damages to which the master of such vessel, or the owners of the vessel or of her cargo, may be pronounced to be entitled.

The two high contracting parties bind themselves to pay, within the term of a year from the date of the sentence, the costs and damages which may be awarded by the above-mentioned Commission; it being mutually understood and agreed, that such costs and damages shall be made good by the Government of the country of which the captor shall be a subject.

ARTICLE VI.

If the detained vessel shall be condemned, she shall be declared lawful prize, together with her cargo, of whatever description it may be, with the exception of the Negroes or others who shall have been brought on board for the purpose of being consigned to slavery; and the said vessel, in conformity with the Regulations in Article XI. of the Treaty of this date, shall, as well as her cargo, be sold by public sale, for the profit of the two Governments, subject to the payment of the expenses hereinbefore mentioned.

The slaves shall receive from the Commission a certificate of emancipation; and shall be delivered over to the Government to whom belongs the cruizer which made the capture, to be dealt with according to the regulations and conditions contained in the Annex to this Treaty, marked C.

The charges incurred for the support and for the return voyage of the commanders and crews of condemned vessels shall be defrayed by the Government of which such commanders and crews are the subjects.

ARTICLE VII.

The Mixed Commissions shall also take cognizance of, and shall decide definitively and without appeal, all claims for compensation on account of losses occasioned to vessels and cargoes which shall have been detained under the provisions of this Treaty, but which shall not have been condemned as legal prize by the said Commissions; and in all cases wherein restitution of such vessels and cargoes shall be decreed, save as mentioned in Article X. of the Treaty to which these Regulations form an Annex, and in a subsequent part of these Regulations, the Commissions shall award to the claimant or claimants, or to his or their lawful attorney or attorneys, for his or their use, a just and complete indemnification for all costs of suit, and for all losses and damages which the owner or owners may have actually sustained by such capture and detention, that is to say:—

First,—In case of total loss, the claimant or claimants shall be indemnified,—

a, For the ship, her tackle, equipment, and stores.

b, For all freights due and payable.

c, For the value of the cargo of merchandize, if any, deducting all charges and expenses payable upon the sale of such cargo, including commission of sale.

d, For all other regular charges in such case of total loss.

Secondly,—In all other cases, save as hereinafter mentioned, not of total loss, the claimant or claimants shall be indemnified,—

a, For all special damages and expenses occasioned to the ship by the detention, and for loss of freight when due or payable.

b, For demurrage, when due, according to the Schedule annexed to the present Article.

c, For any deterioration of the cargo.

d, For all premium of insurance on additional risks.

The claimant or claimants shall be entitled to interest, at the rate of five per cent. per annum on the sum awarded, until such sum is paid by the Government to which the capturing ship belongs. The whole amount of such indemnification shall be calculated in the money of the country to which the detained vessel belongs, and shall be liquidated at the exchange current at the time of the award.

The two high contracting parties, however, have agreed, that if it shall be proved to the satisfaction of the Commissioners of the two nations, and without having recourse to the decision of an Arbitrator, that the captor has been led into error by the fault of the master or commander of the detained vessel, the detained vessel in that case shall not have the right of receiving, for the time of her detention, the demurrage stipulated by the present Article; nor any other compensation for losses, damages, or expenses, consequent upon such detention.

Schedule of Demurrage or Daily Allowance for a Vessel of

Tons					
100	to	120	inclusive,	£5	per diem.
121	„	150	„	6	„
151	„	170	„	8	„
171	„	200	„	10	„
201	„	220	„	11	„
221	„	250	„	12	„
251	„	270	„	14	„
271	„	300	„	15	„

And so on in proportion.

Article VIII.

Neither the Commissioners, nor the Arbitrators, nor the Secretaries of the Commissions, shall demand or receive from any of the parties concerned in the cases which shall be brought before the Commissions, any emolument or gift, under any pretext whatsoever, for the performance of the duties which such Commissioners, Arbitrators, or Secretaries have to perform.

Article IX.

When the parties interested shall imagine they have cause to complain of any evident injustice on the part of the Mixed Commissions, they may represent it to their respective Governments, who reserve to themselves the right of mutual correspondence for the prevention of such injustice for the future.

Article X.

The two high contracting parties have agreed that, in the event of the death, sickness, absence on leave, or any other legal impediment, of one or more of the Commissioners or Arbitrators composing the above-mentioned Commissions respectively, the post of such Commissioners or of such Arbitrators shall be supplied, *ad interim*, in the following manner :—

Firstly.—On the part of Her Britannic Majesty, and in those Commissions which shall sit within the possessions of Her said Majesty, if the vacancy be that of the British Commissioner, his place shall be filled by the British Arbitrator; and either in that case, or if the vacancy be originally that of the British Arbitrator, the place of such Arbitrator shall be filled, successively, by the Governor or Lieutenant Governor resident in such possessions; by the principal Magistrate of the same; and by the Secretary of the Government: and the said Commissions, so constituted as above, shall sit, and in all cases brought before them for adjudication shall proceed to adjudge the same, and to pass sentence accordingly.

Secondly.—On the part of Great Britain, and in those Commissions which shall sit within the possessions of Her Most Faithful Majesty,—if the vacancy be that of the British Commissioner, his place shall be filled by the British Arbitrator; and either in that case, or if the vacancy be originally that of the British Arbitrator, his place shall be filled, successively, by the British Consul and British Vice-Consul, if there be a British Consul or British Vice-Consul appointed to, and resident in, such possessions: and if the vacancy be both of the British Commissioner and of the British Arbitrator, then the vacancy of the British Commissioner shall be filled by the British Consul, and that of the British Arbitrator by the British Vice-Consul, if there be a British Consul and British Vice-Consul appointed to, and resident in, such possessions; and if there shall be no British Consul or Vice-Consul to fill the place of British Arbitrator, then the Portuguese Arbitrator shall be called in, in those cases in which a British Arbitrator, if there were any, would be called in; and if the vacancy be both of the British Commissioner and the British Arbitrator, and there be neither British Consul nor British Vice-Consul to fill, *ad interim*, the vacancies,—then the Portuguese Commissioner and Portuguese Arbitrator shall sit, and in all cases brought before them for adjudication shall proceed to adjudge the same, and to pass sentence accordingly.

Thirdly.—On the part of Portugal, and in those Commissions which shall sit within the possessions of Her Most Faithful Majesty,—if the vacancy be that of the Portuguese Commissioner, his place shall be filled by the Portuguese Arbitrator; and either in that case, or if the vacancy be originally that of the Portuguese Arbitrator, the place of such Arbitrator shall be filled, successively, by the highest civil authority resident in such possessions; by the principal Magistrate of the same; and by the Secretary of the Government: and the said Commission, so constituted as above, shall sit, and in all cases brought before them for adjudication shall proceed to adjudge the same, and pass sentence accordingly.

Fourthly.—On the part of Portugal, and in those Commissions which shall sit within the possessions of Her Britannic Majesty,—if the vacancy be that of the Portuguese Commissioner, his place shall be filled by the Portuguese Arbitrator; and either in that case, or if the vacancy be originally that of the Portuguese Arbitrator, his place shall be filled, successively, by the Portuguese Consul and Portuguese Vice-Consul, if there be a Portuguese Consul and Portuguese Vice-Consul appointed to, and resident in, such possessions: and if the vacancy be both of the Portuguese Commissioner and of the Portuguese Arbitrator, then the vacancy of the Commissioner shall be filled by the Portuguese Consul, and that of the Portuguese Arbitrator by the Portuguese Vice-Consul, if there be a Portuguese Consul and a Portuguese Vice-Consul appointed to, and resident in, such possessions; and in the case in which there be no Portuguese Consul or Portuguese Vice-Consul to fill the place of Portuguese Arbitrator, then the British Arbitrator shall be called in, in those cases in which a Portuguese Arbitrator, were there any, would be called in; and in case the vacancy be both of the Portuguese Commissioner and Portuguese Arbitrator, and there be neither Portuguese Consul nor Portuguese Vice-Consul to fill, *ad interim*, the vacancies,—then the British Commissioner and Arbitrator shall sit, and in all cases brought before them for adjudication shall proceed to adjudge the same, and pass sentence accordingly.

The highest civil authority of the settlement wherein either of the Mixed Commissions shall sit, in the event of a vacancy arising either of the Commissioner or the Arbitrator of the other high contracting party, shall forthwith give notice of the same to the highest civil authority of the nearest settlement of such other high contracting party, in order that such vacancy may be supplied at the earliest possible period: and each of the high contracting parties agrees to supply definitively, as soon as possible, the vacancies which may arise in the above-mentioned Commissions from death, or from any other cause whatever.

Article XI.

The Mixed Commissions shall transmit annually to each Government, a report, relating,—

1, To the cases which have been brought before them for adjudication.

2, To the state of the liberated Negroes.

3, To every information which they may be able to obtain respecting the treatment and progress made in the religious and mechanical education of the liberated Negroes; and such report shall, under the authority of the Government, be annually published in each country.

The undersigned Plenipotentiaries have agreed, in conformity with the XIV. Article of the Treaty signed by them on this day, the third of July, one thousand eight hundred and forty-two, that the preceding Regulations, consisting of XI. Articles, shall be annexed to the said Treaty, and considered as an integral part thereof.

The third day of July, one thousand eight hundred and forty-two.

HOWARD DE WALDEN. DUQUE DE PALMELLA.

ANNEX C

To the Treaty between Great Britain and Portugal, upon Slave Trade, of the 3rd day of July, 1842.

Regulations in respect to the Treatment of Liberated Negroes.

ARTICLE I.

The object and purpose of the letter and spirit of these Regulations is to secure to Negroes and others, liberated in virtue of the stipulations of the Treaty to which these Regulations form an Annex (marked C), permanent good treatment, and full and complete emancipation, in conformity with the humane intentions of the high contracting parties.

ARTICLE II.

Immediately after sentence of condemnation upon a vessel charged with being concerned in illegal slave trade shall have been passed by the Mixed Commissions established under the Treaty to which these Regulations form an Annex, all Negroes or others who were on board of such vessel, and who were brought on board for the purpose of being consigned to slavery, shall be delivered over to the Government to whom belongs the cruizer which made the capture.

ARTICLE III.

The Negroes so liberated and delivered over to such Government shall be placed under the care and superintendence of a Board, consisting of two Members or Commissioners, with power to call in a third Member under the circumstances hereinafter stated.

In those colonies or possessions of Her Britannic Majesty in which, under the Treaty to which these Regulations form an Annex, Mixed Commissions are to sit, the Boards of Superintendence of the liberated Negroes shall consist of the Governors of the said colonies or possessions, and of the Portuguese Commissioners in the said Mixed Commissions; and when the Portuguese Commissioners are absent, then the Portuguese Arbitrators of the said Mixed Commissions shall sit, in the place of the Commissioners, in the Boards of Superintendence of liberated Negroes.

In those colonies or possessions of Her Most Faithful Majesty in which, under the present Treaty, Mixed Commissions are to sit, the Boards of Superintendence of the liberated Negroes shall consist of the Governors of those colonies or possessions, and of the British Commissioners in the said Mixed Commissions; and when the British Commissioners are absent, then the British Arbitrators of the said Mixed Commissions shall sit, in the place of the Commissioners, in the Boards of Superintendence of liberated Negroes.

The several Members of the Boards of Superintendence shall, before entering upon their offices, respectively take an oath, in presence of the principal Magistrate of the place, that they will faithfully execute their office without favour or partiality, according to the true intent and meaning of these Regulations.

Article IV.

In order the better to carry into effect the purposes intended by the present Regulations, a person of known probity and humanity shall be selected and appointed by the Board of Superintendence, to act under its directions, with the title of Curator of liberated Negroes; and such Curator may, under the sanction of the Board, employ such persons as may be necessary to assist him in the execution of his duties.

The Curator so appointed shall, previously to his entering on the duties of his office, take before the Board of Superintendence an oath, in the following words:—

I, A. B., do solemnly swear that I will act, to the best of my skill and knowledge, faithfully and impartially in the execution of my office; and that I will conduct myself with due respect to the authority of the Board of Superintendence of liberated Negroes to which I am attached.

So help me God!

Article V.

The Curator of the liberated Negroes shall be personally present at the delivery of the Negroes to the person charged by the Government to receive them, after the sentence of emancipation is passed, as specified in Article II. of these Regulations.

Duplicate original receipts for the Negroes delivered over to the Government, specifying the number of each sex, shall, at the time when they are delivered as aforesaid, be made out and signed by the officer receiving them.

One original of such receipts shall be given to the person previously in charge of the Negroes, the other shall be given to the Curator, who shall deposit the same in the registry of the Mixed Commission which adjudicated the case of the vessel in which the Negroes were captured.

At the time of the delivery of such Negroes to the Government, in the manner hereinbefore mentioned, they shall be minutely inspected by the Curator:

62

who shall give to each Negro a name, which name shall then be entered by the Curator, in a book to be called "Register of Emancipated Negroes," and to be kept for that purpose in the Office of the Board of Superintendence; and opposite to the name shall be entered a description of the person, with the probable age, with the bodily marks, and with any particulars which can be ascertained regarding the family and nation of such Negro, together with the name of the vessel in which he was captured.

Each Negro shall then be marked on the upper part of the right arm with a small silver instrument, bearing for its device a symbol of freedom.

Article VI.

The Board of Superintendence shall then make known by the public papers its intention to apprentice out the liberated Negroes; and after seven days have elapsed from the announcement of such intention, the hiring or apprenticing of the Negroes shall take place, either by public auction or by tender, as may be thought best; and the Negroes shall then be distributed to their hirers, upon the conditions and stipulations hereinafter mentioned; which conditions and stipulations shall be published at the time of auction or tender, and shall also be embodied in a Contract or Indenture, to be entered into formally between the hirer and the aforesaid Board. The contract or indenture shall be made out in duplicate; it shall be in print, and not in writing; one copy of it shall remain with the hirer, and the other with the Board, under the care of the Curator.

When the sums offered by two or more different persons for the hiring of a Negro are equal, preference shall be giving to the person who will undertake to employ such Negro as a mechanic, or as a domestic servant.

Article VII.

The period of service for which apprentices shall be bound shall be seven years for all Negroes who, at the time of hiring, are above thirteen years of age; but three of the seven years may be afterwards remitted, at the discretion of the Board, upon the recommendation of the master, and upon proof that the apprentice is capable of earning an honest livelihood, and is worthy of such indulgence.

The apprenticeship of Negroes who, at the time of hiring, are under thirteen years of age, shall continue till the age of twenty, subject to a diminution of that term, at the discretion of the Board, upon due proof being given that the apprentice is worthy of such indulgence, and is capable of maintaining himself.

Article VIII.

When more apprentices than one are confided to the same master, care shall be taken to select for that purpose such as are of the same African nation, and, if possible, of the same family; and in no case shall a child under fourteen years of age be separated from its mother; but such child shall always be apprenticed to the same master with its mother.

Article IX.

The name and address of the master, together with the name and position of the estate or house where the liberated Negro is to be resident, shall be inserted opposite to the name of the Negro in his contract or indenture.

Article X.

No Negro shall be apprenticed to any master who resides more than twenty English miles from the town where the Mixed Commission, by which he was liberated, is established; and if any master, to whom such Negro shall have been so apprenticed, shall afterwards change his residence, he shall be required to give immediate notice thereof to the Curator.

The apprentices must always reside at that particular estate or house of the master, which is registered as being within the above-mentioned distance from the place of sitting of the Mixed Commission.

Article XI.

No person shall be entrusted with one or more liberated Negroes, unless he shall prove to the Board that he posseses ample means for the employment, maintenance, and support, of such Negro or Negroes, and unless he shall make himself answerable, under the penalty of eighty dollars for each Negro, that the conditions under which such Negro is received shall be duly observed.

Article XII.

The master shall engage to pay a stipulated sum for the hire of each apprentice.

The Curator may, if the amount is to be paid down in one sum, demand it previously to the hire; and if the sum is to be periodically paid, the Curator may demand the same quarterly in advance.

Article XIII.

The Master shall undertake—

1. That the apprentice shall be maintained with wholesome and abundant food; and shall be provided with such clothes as are usual, according to the custom of the country.

2. That he shall be instructed in the truths of the Christian religion, in order that he may be baptized before the expiration of the second year of his apprenticeship.

3. That he shall be vaccinated as soon as possible after having been delivered into the charge of the master; that in sickness he shall have proper medical advice, and shall be treated with due care and attention; and that in case of death he shall be decently buried, at the master's expense.

4. That the apprentice shall be taught some useful business, or be instructed in some trade or mechanical art, whereby he may be enabled to maintain himself when the period of his service shall have expired.

5. That whenever an infant is born of any female apprentice, immediate information thereof shall be given by the master to the Board of Superintendence, in order that the fact may be duly registered.

6. That baptism of an infant, so born, shall take place within three months after its birth, and that the freedom of the child shall be recorded in the Register of Baptism; but that such child shall remain with its mother, and shall be maintained and treated by the master of the mother, in the same manner as an apprentice, until the apprenticeship of the mother ceases.

Article XIV.

No master shall, in any case, be authorised to transfer to another master his apprenticed Negro, without the special and written sanction of the Board; and if the master shall leave the country, or shall change his residence to a part of the country beyond the limits hereinbefore fixed for persons having apprentices, or if he shall become so reduced in his circumstances as to be obliged to give up his establishment, then, and in any of these cases, he shall report the same to the Board, and shall bring his apprentices, and deliver them up to the said Board, by whom they shall be received, and shall afterwards be apprenticed to another master for the remainder of the period which such apprentices may have to serve, and under the same conditions as those imposed upon the first master. But in no case shall the master be allowed to deliver up his apprentice to any other authority than to the said Board, or to the Curator under the orders of the Board.

If any apprentice shall be guilty of crimes which render him obnoxious to the laws of the country, or shall be guilty of habitual drunkenness, insubordination, wilful carelessness, or destruction of his master's property, the master may in such case bring him before the Board of Superintendence, and upon proof of the facts, the said Board shall have power to cancel the indentures.

Article XV.

If an apprentice should run away, his master shall give immediate information thereof to the Curator, who shall instantly proceed to a summary investigation of the fact, for the information of the Board of Superintendence

Any master who shall be proved to have improperly disposed of an apprentice, whom he has reported as dead or absconded, shall pay as a fine the sum of three hundred dollars.

The half of this fine shall be paid to the informer, and the remainder to the Curator, to be placed at the disposal of the Board, for the purposes hereinafter mentioned.

Article XVI.

If an apprentice should fall sick, the master shall give immediate notice thereof to the Curator, in order that he, or one of his assistants, may visit such apprentice, and report to the Board the nature of his disorder, and the manner in which such sick Negro is taken care of.

If an apprentice should die, notice thereof shall immediately be given to the Curator, in order that he, or one of his assistants, may attend, for the purpose of ascertaining that the deceased Negro was really and truly the apprentice described as such in the Register.

For this purpose the Curator or his assistant shall make such inquiries as he may judge necessary, interrogating the inhabitants of the house in which the Negro has died, the neighbours, or any other persons; and shall take such other means as he may judge necessary to enable him to ascertain the truth, in order that the burial of the Negro, which is to be at the expense of the master, may take place without further delay.

A summary report of the result of this inquiry shall then be drawn up officially by the Curator, and shall be delivered without delay to the Board.

The Curator, after having identified the body of an apprentice who may have died, shall investigate the cause of the death; and if the death shall appear to have been natural, he shall note that fact in the Register.

If the cause of death be doubtful, or shall appear to be otherwise than natural, he shall interrogate the other Negroes, and other inhabitants of the house, and shall take such other means as may appear necessary to ascertain the facts of the case; and if there shall appear reason to suspect that the death of such Negro has been occasioned by violence, improper usage, or culpable neglect, he shall take the proper course for bringing the offender to trial before the courts of the country.

Article XVII.

If the master of any apprentice shall commit any breach of these conditions, a fine shall be imposed upon him of not less than fifty, and not exceeding one hundred dollars; one half of which shall go to the informer, and the other half shall be placed at the disposal of the Board of Superintendence, for the purposes hereinafter mentioned. And in case of any gross misconduct of the said master towards his apprentice, such master shall, if the Board of Superintendence shall think fit, besides paying the above-mentioned fine, forfeit all further right to the services of the apprentice; and the said apprentice shall be taken from such master, and shall be apprenticed to another master for the remainder of his term of apprenticeship.

Article XVIII.

If the master of an apprentice shall die, his heir, or the person to whom the possession of such apprentice shall devolve, shall, within four days after the death of such master, report the same to the Board of Superintendence.

The Board shall thereupon issue their order to the Curator, to bring the apprentice before them; and when the apprentice is so brought, the Board shall apprentice him to another master, under the established conditions.

If the heir, or the person in possession of such apprentice, shall neglect to report the death of the master within four days, he shall pay one dollar a day for each apprenticed Negro belonging to such deceased master, until he shall have delivered them all up to the said Board; and he shall, moreover, be subject to the other penalties which attach to the non-performance of the conditions established by these Regulations.

Article XIX.

If any liberated Negro be apprenticed to, or hired by, the Government, the contract shall contain the same conditions and stipulations, in regard to the Negro, as are hereinbefore prescribed for cases in which the Negro is apprenticed to a private individual.

Article XX.

Liberated Negroes shall, at the discretion of the Board of Superintendence, and when it shall be ascertained that their own free will has been previously obtained, be permitted to become soldiers or sailors in the regular land or sea forces of the State in whose territories they shall have been emancipated.

The Board shall take care in such case to ascertain that the Negroes fully understand, and are aware of the nature of the engagement which they enter into by so enlisting.

The Government into whose service the Negroes enlist shall sign a receipt for them, which receipt shall be delivered to the Curator at the time of the enlistment; and the Board shall take means to ensure that the full and permanent emancipation of such Negroes shall be secured to them, according to the true spirit of these Regulations.

Article XXI.

Those liberated Negroes who may not be apprenticed, or who may not have enlisted into the sea or land forces of the State to which the colony or possession in which they may be belongs, or whose indentures shall have become void, or shall have been cancelled, shall be provided for by the Government of such colony or possession. They shall be kept within twenty miles of the place where the Mixed Commissions are sitting.

The expense of maintaining and supporting such Negroes shall be borne by the Government of the colony, but they shall be under the care and superintendence of the Board and Curator; and the present Regulations shall be applicable to them in every respect, excepting as regards apprenticeship.

Article XXII.

The Curator shall endeavour, by means of an interpreter, to explain to each Negro the nature of any contract by which he may become bound; and shall inform him, that if he should at any time be ill-treated by his master, he must make his complaint to the Curator, or to the Board of Superintendence of liberated Negroes.

Article XXIII.

It shall be the duty of the Curator, or of his assistant, to visit once, at least, in every three months, all places where there are any liberated Negroes under the superintendence of the Board; he shall examine and inspect all such Negroes, receive their complaints, inquire into those complaints, and search out the truth, and investigate any abuses that may affect the said Negroes; and he shall also inquire into the general conduct of the Negroes themselves.

The Curator shall then bring to the notice of the Board every complaint on the part of the said Negroes, and every breach of the conditions and stipulations of the contract under which the Negroes serve; and, in all cases of well-founded complaint, the Board shall take proper means for affording redress.

The inspections above described are not to be made at stated periods, but at uncertain times, and unexpectedly.

The Curator shall also report to the Board, every three months, the state in which he finds the liberated Negroes; and his report shall be entered in a book to be kept for that purpose, to be called "Curator's Reports," and to be deposited in the Office of the Board, so that, on reference thereto, the condition and behaviour of every liberated Negro may be easily known.

Article XXIV.

All proceedings of the Curator, together with a statement of all facts which may from time to time come to his knowledge, respecting the liberated Negroes, shall be immediately communicated by him to the Board of Superintendence; and he is not to institute any proceedings, nor to take any steps in respect to such Negroes, without the knowledge and sanction of the Board.

Article XXV.

The Curator shall receive all the sums which are to be paid for the hire of apprentices, and all the monies arising from penalties incurred by Masters; and shall render an account thereof to the Board of Superintendence.

The amount is to be applied to the purposes hereinafter mentioned.

Article XXVI.

When the prescribed term of service of any apprentice shall have expired, the Curator shall, under the direction of the Board of Superintendence, summon such apprentice, together with his master, to appear before the said Board. The master shall then give up to the Board the indenture of the Negro, and the Negro shall receive from the Board a certificate, specifying that such Negro has completed the term of his apprenticeship, and is entitled to all the rights and privileges of a free person.

The Curator shall see that this certificate be authenticated and registered, according to the custom of the country.

Article XXVII.

The Board of Superintendence shall have the power to admonish the Curator, and any other officer serving under the Board, if such Curator or other officer should fail to execute his duty faithfully; and if the Board shall see necessary, they may dismiss such Curator or other officer, and appoint successors.

Article XXVIII.

The necessary proceedings for recovering such sums as may be due from masters on account of the hire of apprentices, and for enforcing the payment of the several fines and penalties hereinbefore imposed, shall be instituted in the proper Courts of law of the country where the Boards of Superintendence shall respectively reside, and shall be carried on at the instance of the Board.

The expenses of such proceedings shall be defrayed as hereinafter mentioned; and the high contracting parties hereby engage, that within six months from the exchange of the ratifications of the Treaty to which these Regulations are annexed, they will grant the requisite authority and powers to the courts of law of the country where the Boards of Superintendence are respectively held, to take cognizance of the actions which, for the due execution of these Regulations, may be brought in such courts of law at the instance of the Boards, so that the penalties hereinbefore mentioned may be recovered, and the levy of the monies hereinbefore mentioned may be enforced; and the payment of the amount thereof may be made to the person appointed by these Regulations to receive such penalties and monies.

Article XXIX.

The money arising from the hire of liberated Negroes, and also from the penalties incurred by the masters, shall be deposited by the Curator in a chest with three keys, one of which shall be kept by each Commissioner of the Board of Superintendence, and one by the Curator.

The Curator shall so deposit the several sums as soon as he receives them, making previously a regular entry of the receipt, in a book to be kept for that purpose.

This money shall be applied in the following manner, that is to say: a portion thereof, at the discretion of the Board of Superintendence, shall be paid to the Curator, and to the other officers employed under the said Board, for their salaries; so much of the remaining portion as shall be needful, shall be applied towards defraying the expense of prosecuting masters for breach of the conditions and stipulations of their contracts, and also towards defraying the other expenses incurred for carrying these Regulations into effect; and the remaining balance, if any, shall be laid out, at the discretion of the said Board, in the promotion of the comfort and welfare of the liberated Negroes, either during their term of service, or at its expiration, and especially in rewards to liberated Negroes for good conduct.

The accounts of these monies, and of the manner in which they have been applied, shall, at the expiration of every year, be made up in duplicate by the Curator; and after these accounts have been examined and approved by the Board, one of such duplicates shall be transmitted by each Commissioner to the Government on whose part he is acting.

If the fund shall not prove sufficient to liquidate the just and necessary demands made for the purposes required, the deficiency shall be made good in equal moieties by the two Governments.

Article XXX.

In the event of a difference arising between the two aforesaid Commissioners of the Board, regarding the appointment of any officer under them, or regarding any other matter in the execution of these Regulations,—if such difference shall occur in a British colony or possession, the Board shall call in the person who officiates in that colony or possession as Portuguese Arbitrator to the Mixed Commission under the Treaty; and if the case shall occur in a Portuguese colony or possession, the Board of Superintendence shall call in the person who officiates in that colony or possession as British Arbitrator to the Mixed Commission under the Treaty; and the Board of Superintendence of liberated Negroes, thus formed, and being composed of the two Commissioners and of one Arbitrator, shall, by the majority of voices, decide all such points of difference.

It shall not be permitted to the Members of the Board of Superintendence, nor to any officer acting under them, to demand or receive from any one, excepting as herein specified, any emolument, under any pretext whatsoever, for the performance of the duties which are imposed upon them by the present Regulations.

Article XXXI.

Nothing that is contained in these Regulations shall be construed to exempt any liberated Negro from his liability, as a free man, to be proceeded against for any offence committed by him (except as herein provided for) against the laws of the country in which he is located. But in all cases where any offence against such laws is imputed to a Negro under the care of the aforesaid Board of Superintendence, the laws shall be administered to him as to a free man; and the Curator shall, either personally, or by a responsible individual deputed by him for the purpose, attend the courts of justice of the country, to see that justice is done to the Negro.

Article XXXII.

It is further stipulated, with a view to avoid the unnecessary multiplication of words, that everything contained in the foregoing Regulations which applies to masters, shall be construed as applying equally to mistresses; and that everything in the said Regulations with respect to Negroes and apprentices, which applies to the masculine gender and singular number, shall be construed as

63

applying equally to the female sex and to the plural number, unless such construction shall be in express opposition to any other enactment of these Regulations.

ARTICLE XXXIII.

These Regulations shall be inserted in the official Gazette or journal of the countries whose Sovereigns are contracting parties to the Treaty ; and also in the official journal or Gazette of the place where the Mixed Commissions are respectively held ; and the Governments of the said countries shall convey to the said Boards of Superintendence of liberated Negroes, to the Curators, and to their assistants under those Boards, such authority as may be requisite, to enable the said Boards of Superintendence, Curators, and officers acting under them, respectively, to perform the duties, and to exercise the powers entrusted to them by these Regulations.

ARTICLE XXXIV.

The high contracting parties agree, that if in future it should appear necessary to adopt new measures, in consequence of those which are laid down in this Annex turning out inefficacious, the said high contracting parties will consult together, and agree upon other means better adapted for the complete attainment of the objects they have in view.

The undersigned Plenipotentiaries have agreed, in conformity with the XIV. Article of the Treaty signed by them on this day, the third of July, 1842, that the preceding Regulations, consisting of thirty-four Articles, shall be annexed to the said Treaty, and be considered an integral part thereof.

The third day of July, one thousand eight hundred and forty-two.

HOWARD DE WALDEN. DUQUE DE PALMELLA.

Protocol of a Conference held at the Foreign Office, August 12th, 1847, between the Plenipotentiaries of Great Britain and Portugal.

The Plenipotentiaries of Great Britain and of Portugal having met to take into consideration certain matters connected with the execution of the Treaty between Their Majesties the Queen of the United Kingdom of Great

Britain and Ireland, and the Queen of Portugal and the Algarves, signed at Lisbon on the 3rd July, 1842, for the suppression of the slave trade;

The Plenipotentiary of Great Britain stated, that it had been found that great facilities exist for carrying on the slave trade within the dominions of the Crown of Portugal on the East Coast of Africa, owing to the present inability of the Portuguese Government to employ a sufficient naval force effectually to prevent the export of slaves from that coast; and that in order to supply this defect, Her Britannic Majesty's Government had requested of the Government of Her Most Faithful Majesty, that permission may be granted for Her Britannic Majesty's ships employed in suppressing the slave trade, to enter the bays, ports, creeks, rivers, and other places within the dominions of the Crown of Portugal on the East Coast of Africa, where no Portuguese authorities are established, in order that those ships may prevent the slave trade from being carried on in such places.

The Plenipotentiary of Great Britain further explained, that by the permission thus requested, it is intended that the vessels of Her Britannic Majesty shall be authorised to pursue and capture slave vessels which may be found in any such places as before mentioned, and also to destroy any barracoons or other arrangements which may be made on shore for purposes of slave trade.

The Plenipotentiary of Portugal hereupon declared, that the Government of Her Most Faithful Majesty, desirous to fulfil and carry out by all means in its power the obligations contracted by the Treaty of 1842, above mentioned, consents to grant the permission requested on the part of the British Government.

In recording this decision in the present Protocol, the Plenipotentiaries of Great Britain and of Portugal declare that the permission so given is granted and accepted, upon the following conditions :—

1*st.*—The permission is limited to a period of three years, commencing from this date.

2*ndly.*—It is limited to places where no Portuguese authorities are established.

3*rdly.*—The Lords Commissioners of the Admiralty shall give the most positive orders to those Commanders of Her Britannic Majesty's ships of war who shall have occasion to make use of this permission, to avail themselves of every opportunity to communicate to the nearest Portuguese authorities the circumstances which may take place in the exercise thereof; or, in default of such opportunities, to cause those circumstances to be made known in some other way to the Portuguese Government.

4*thly.*—The permission shall never be made a plea for attacking, disputing, or weakening the rights which the Crown of Portugal has, or may have maintained or claimed, with regard to any point, upon the said East Coast of Africa, nor for injuring or interrupting legal commerce.

(Signed) PALMERSTON.

TORRE DE MONCORVO.

Protocol of a Conference relating to Slave Trade on the East Coast of Africa, held at the Foreign Office, on the 19th of November 1850.

Protocol of a Conference held at the Foreign Office, on the 19th November 1850, between the Plenipotentiaries of Great Britain and of Portugal.

Whereas by the Protocol of a Conference between the Plenipotentiaries of Great Britain and of Portugal, held at the Foreign Office on the 12th of August, 1847, the Government of Her Most Faithful Majesty consented to grant, for the period of three years from that date, permission for Her Britannic Majesty's ships employed in suppressing the slave trade, to enter the bays, ports, creeks, rivers, and other places within the dominions of the Crown of Portugal on the East Coast of Africa, where no Portuguese authorities are established, and to prevent the slave trade from being carried on in such places;

And whereas the period for which such permission was granted as aforesaid has expired:

The Plenipotentiary of Great Britain requested that such permission may be renewed; and the Plenipotentiary of Portugal declared that the Government of Her Most Faithful Majesty, with the desire to fulfil and carry out to the utmost of its power the obligations contracted by the Treaty signed at Lisbon on the 3rd of July 1842, between Great Britain and Portugal, for the suppression of the slave trade, consents to grant the permission requested on the part of the British Government for a fresh period of three years, commencing from this date, under the conditions laid down in the Protocol of the 12th of August 1847, above referred to;

And as this permission is for Her Britannic Majesty's ships employed in suppressing the slave trade to enter the bays, ports, creeks, rivers, and other places within the dominions of the Crown of Portugal on the East Coast of Africa, where no Portuguese authorities are yet established, and to prevent the slave trade from being carried on in such places: it is understood and agreed by Her Britannic Majesty's Government, that the said permission shall cease in all its effects, with respect to any of the said bays, ports, creeks, rivers, and other places, and to every one of them, as soon as, and in proportion as, Portuguese authorities shall be established, either in any or in every one of those bays, ports, creeks, rivers, and other places.

(Signed) PALMERSTON.
THE CHEVALIER DE RIBEIRO.